Michelle Morgan was the president of the Marilyn Lives Society, a UK fan club, from 1991 to 2007. She is the author of *Marilyn's Addresses* and is the co-producer of the upcoming documentary *Gable: The Ties that Bind*, with Tegan Summer Productions. She lives in Northamptonshire.

MARILYN MONROE

Michelle Morgan

ROBINSON

Constable & Robinson Ltd
55–56 Russell Square
London WC1B 4HP
www.constablerobinson.com

First published in the UK by Robinson,
an imprint of Constable & Robinson, 2012

The original illustrated *Marilyn Monroe Private and
Undisclosed* was published by Constable, 2007

A copy of the British Library Cataloguing in
Publication data is available from the British Library

ISBN 978-1-78033-128-7 (paperback)
ISBN 978-0-78033-129-4 (ebook)

Printed and bound by CPI Group (UK) Ltd, Croydon, CR0 4YY

3 5 7 9 10 8 6 4 2

This book is dedicated to my dear friends Bill and Mac Pursel, whose support and friendship over the years has meant more than they'll ever know.

Acknowledgements

I would like to once again thank the hundreds of people who helped with the first edition of this book. Without their help and support, I would have never written one biography, never mind a follow-up.

In addition to that, I would like to thank the following people who have made this book into what you are holding in your hands today:

Firstly to Eric Woodard, who not only sent me heaps of information on Marilyn's doomed 'Rain' project, but spent hours finding the contact details of various Marilyn-related people for me. I am greatly indebted to him for this alone, as well as the countless other things he has helped me with during the writing of this book. Eric, you are truly one-in-a-million and I will always value our friendship.

To Bill Pursel, for not only agreeing to be re-interviewed by me, but also for providing a letter Norma Jeane wrote to him in 1946. The letter shed much light on her feelings for Bill and her time in Las Vegas, and proved to be invaluable for this book. Bill and his wife Mac also spent hours researching the Willett family for me in Las Vegas and have patiently put up with my questions and emails over the course of the past five years. I am forever grateful for their friendship.

To the members of the Knebelkamp family who trusted me with their memories, despite never publicly speaking about Marilyn before. Their generosity and kindness have been breathtaking and I am forever grateful for their trust in sharing their stories.

To Janet Clarke, who helped me with much of the research on the Atkinson family, as well as helping with various aspects of the Willett family history, too. Janet spent hours trawling through family history resources and without her research that part of the book wouldn't be half as memorable as it is now.

To James Glaeg who sowed the seeds for my research into the Knebelkamp family and their friend, Catherine Larson. His insight and generosity have been boundless and have enabled me to finally uncover the truth about Marilyn's early life and family.

To all the people who agreed to be interviewed for my last book, and to the following 'new' people who agreed to share their memories for this edition: Bonnie Roth, Forrest Olmstead, Jo Olmstead, Bob Stotts, Michael Thornton, Alan A, Horace Ward, Darrell Von Driska, Jim Henaghan Jr, Howard Sheehan Jr, Christine Krogull, Mary Sims, Annabelle Stanford, Allison Ittel, Jon Ittel, Steve Hayes, Tony Hand, John Gilmore, John Thorndike, Peggy Heriot, Susan Elliott, Margaret Gibbon, Peter Evans, Alice Wexler, Sue Ellen McCann, Doris Drennen and Tom Tierney.

To Lois Banner for allowing me access to her interview with Pat Traviss at Rockhaven Sanitarium and for many interesting conversations.

To the following people who sent me photographs from their collections, some of which appeared in the first edition of this book, and others that have been exclusive to this one: Eric Woodard, Bill Pursel, Don Obermeyer, Kristen Obermeyer, Gus Zernial, Christine Krogull, Sandy Robinson, Mike Lawler, Doris Drennen, Christine Heas, Tina Garland, William Carroll, George Bailey, Greg Schreiner, Horace Ward, Jim Henaghan Jr, the late Paul Kanteman, Win Rossette, Albert Wimer, Sandy Robinson, Henry Doody, Greg Silva, Robert Siney, Andrea Pryke, Lasse Karlsson, George Finch and Evan Finch.

To the members of the 'Marilyn Monroe Question Group' on Facebook; the members of Everlasting Marilyn; and visitors to my own Michelle Morgan Author Page on Facebook for providing inspiration and help.

To Amy Condit, Stan Taffel, Helen Brown, Greg Schreiner, Mary Sims, David Stenn, Mona Miracle, Jill Adams, Merja Pohjola, Rebecca Staley, Shaney Evans, Sally Cretu, Julia Wilson, Lou Cella, Andrea Pryke, Jeane Trendhill, Dawn Jones, Tara Hanks, Robert

Siney, Ruth Jenkins, Greg Silva, Sue Craft, Karen Hollis, Ian McMaster, Heather Driscoll-Woodford, Vicki Gardner, Lorraine White, Ben Kay, Alison Lowe, Katy Forrester, Elisa Jordan, Christine Heas, Leslie Summey, Jackie Craig, Marijane Gray, Lisa Burks, Ann Chamberlain, Anne Buchanan, Carla Orlandi-Smith, Carla Valderrama, Melissa Gluck, Bob Vieten, Rupert Taylor, Carole Sampek, Carolien Krijnen, Caroline Mitchinson Lawther, Charles Casillo, Lucy Carr, Katie Bleathman, Jill Tivey, Darrell Rooney, David Marshall, Jennifer McLaughlin, Joey Traughber, Johan Grimmius, Lady Doryan, Leland D. Petty, Maureen Brown, Michelle Armstrong, Michelle Justice, Rebecca Swift, Roger G. Taylor, Ross McNaughton, Roy Turner, Sandie Bradley, Savvy Anka, Scott Fortner, Sunny Thompson, Ted James, Susan Rogers, Susan Griffiths, Svea Ross, Ron Steens, Tina Lindholm, Tina Garland, Mark Robinson, Richard Workman, Neva Kanteman, Bill Niles, Nick Homenda, Nancy Hunter, Valerie Hillyard-Samuel, Claire Welling, Suus Marie and Melinda Mason. All of the above have contributed support, information, friendship or a combination of all three.

To Christina Rice from the Los Angeles Public Library, who went above and beyond the call of duty and gave me countless hours of help and ideas. To say I couldn't have done this without her would be an understatement.

The same goes for Stacey Eubank, who helped with articles and research for both this book and the previous one. Her kindness knows no bounds.

To Leo Hollis and everyone at Constable & Robinson for making this book a reality, and to Robert Smith, my agent.

To my friend and business partner Tegan Summer who has provided so much support and friendship over the past two years and has enabled me to truly believe in my abilities as a writer.

To my friend Andrew Hansford for constantly inspiring me and making me laugh.

During the course of a person's lifetime, you meet many friends; some you keep, others you let go. I have been extremely lucky in my life to have known a group of friends since I was a little girl. We all have vastly different personalities but have stuck together through thick and thin; they are my honorary sisters and I love each and every one. So for sharing my hopes and dreams and for keeping my secrets, I'd very much like to thank my dear friends Claire, Helen, Mandy, Sharon, Loraine, Katharine and Jackie. I am so happy to have you all in my life.

To my whole family and particularly: Mum, Dad, Paul, Wendy and Angelina for encouraging me not only with this book but for my whole career as a writer. They must have lost count of the number of times they have heard the word 'Marilyn' over the years, but have continued to listen to my stories and encourage me in my dreams. Not a day goes by when I don't thank God for letting me be born into such a sharing and funny family and I am extremely grateful for everything they do for me.

Though they are no longer with us, I'd like to thank my wonderful grandparents who were all born in Marilyn's era and constantly entertained me with tales of 'the old days'. Through learning about their early lives, I grew to love everything about the 1920s, 1930s, 1940s and 1950s, and their tales will continue to inspire me forever.

To my daughter, Daisy, who was born during the writing of my last book. She is now growing into a bright, artistic, talented young lady and continues to teach me so much every day. She picked out most of the photos for this book; she is the inspiration behind everything I do and I am extremely lucky to have her.

To my husband Richard, who has been my better half for the past twenty-four years. We have been through so much together and I can't even remember what life was like before he came into my world. He is the love of my life and the person who has always encouraged me to live my dreams. I am very grateful to have him in my life.

And to anyone I may have missed . . . I'm sincerely sorry for the oversight but thank you too!

Contents

Preface

I have been a huge fan of Marilyn Monroe since I 'discovered' her whilst on holiday as a teenager in 1985. I was drawn to her beauty – both inside and out – and the fact that, despite her insecure early years, she went on to become the most famous movie star in the world. That was quite an achievement and her determination and strength inspired me.

Over the years I have read many books about Marilyn; many good, some not so good, and a few just plain awful. I got so tired of reading scandal, gossip and made-up tittle-tattle that I decided to write my own biography; the conclusion of which was my 2007 book, *Marilyn Monroe: Private and Undisclosed*.

The book took me four years to write and research, and I was – and still am – hugely proud of it. Miraculously, after writing the book, other people in Marilyn's life could see that I was no scandal-driven author, and began to come forward to share stories that proved once again that Marilyn was not constantly depressed, nor was she a tragic dumb blonde. The information I have obtained over the past four years has now been included in this new edition, and I am positive that it shows Marilyn's story in the truest way yet. I hope that readers will agree with me.

Michelle Morgan
Michelle@MichelleMorgan.co.uk

Chapter 1

The Lady with the Red Hair

Marilyn Monroe's mother – Gladys Pearl Monroe – was not a happy child. She was born on 27 May 1902, to Della and Otis Monroe, and together with her brother, Marion, spent her first few years constantly on the move. When she was seven years old her father died within the confines of the California State Hospital for the mentally ill, and although it was later revealed that the cause was syphilis of the brain, his relatives believed he had died insane, hence beginning a legacy of fear that would haunt the entire family.

By 1910 Gladys was living with her mother, brother and ten lodgers at 1114 East 10th Street, Los Angeles, and by 1912 Della had married Lyle Arthur Graves, a switchman who had once worked with Otis. The marriage was short-lived, and the two eventually divorced in January 1914 when Lyle moved to Ohio, where he later remarried. Della, too, was on the lookout for new adventures and by 1916 had sent her son Marion to live with a cousin in San Diego, while she moved with Gladys to a boarding house at 26 Westminster Avenue, Venice, Los Angeles.

Shortly afterwards Della met and fell for Charles Grainger, a widower who worked in the oil industry. He had been working in Rangoon since April 1915 and had arrived back in the United States on 19 July 1916, just months before he met forty-year-old Della. She wished to live with him at his home at 1410 Carrol Canal Court, but Gladys' disapproval and Grainger's reluctance to take on the judgemental offspring put a spanner in the works, and Della was left wondering how she could rid herself of her fourteen-year-old daughter. She didn't need to wonder long, however, as along came Jasper Newton Baker, who, despite being twelve years her senior, courted Gladys and shortly afterwards made her pregnant. This, of course, gave Della an instant reason to rid herself of the teenager; she insisted that the pair marry on 17 May 1917 and even swore Gladys to be eighteen years old, when actually she was just shy of her fifteenth birthday.

Della was then free to move in with Grainger and Gladys. Her new husband lived at 1595 21st Street, while he worked as a hotel manager at 219 South Spring Street. Eight months after the wedding, Gladys bore Baker a son called Robert Jasper (aka Jackie or Kermitt), and several years later a daughter named Berniece Gladys. The marriage was not a happy one, and by 1920 both Gladys and Baker were broke and living at 343 Fifth Avenue with Baker's eighteen-year-old brother Ardry, a concessionaire at an amusement park.

Jasper believed Gladys to be an unfit mother, especially as their son, Robert, had once almost lost an eye when Gladys left some broken glass in the trash. Then on another occasion the Bakers were arguing in the front seat of their car, whilst Robert managed to open the door in the back, falling from the seat and severely injuring his hip in the process. It would be unfair to blame Gladys directly for Robert's problems, but Jasper never forgot the incidents: 'Your mother was a beautiful woman,' he told Berniece, 'but she was also very young, too young to know how to take care of children.'

Baker was also known to beat his wife, and on one occasion whilst visiting relatives in Kentucky he took offence at her spending time in the company of one of his brothers, beating her across the back with a bridle until she bled. Terrified of her husband, Gladys finally filed for divorce in 1921, and during divorce proceedings (in which she claimed they were married one year earlier in order to cover up the fact that she was pregnant) she disclosed that Baker had called her vile names, had beaten and kicked her, and had caused 'extreme mental pain, anxiety and humiliation, as well as to suffer grievous bodily pain and injury'. The divorce became official in May 1922 but this was not the end of the drama, as during one fateful weekend Baker decided he no longer wanted his children in the care of Gladys, and snatched them out of California to live a new life with his mother in Kentucky.

Gladys was understandably devastated by this turn of events, and spent all her savings trying to get her children back. She went to Kentucky and begged Baker's sister for help. However, instead of gaining assistance, Gladys found herself banned from visiting her daughter and unable to take her son, who had been admitted to hospital to try and fix his ongoing hip problems.

Waiting for Robert to be released from hospital, Gladys gained temporary employment at the home of Harry and Lena Cohen, who lived at 2331 Alta Avenue in Louisville. There she acted as housekeeper and looked after the Cohens' daughters, Dorothy and Norma Jean. The family were used to having staff around the house: according to census reports, in 1920 eighteen-year-old Effie Newton worked as a servant for them, and by 1930 they had grown to employ not only a maid but a chauffeur, too. So the arrival of Gladys in the Cohen home caused not even a stir, and her presence and departure were all pretty uneventful. Later rumours would surface that Gladys caused many 'uncomfortable' moments in the Cohen household, but in fact so unmemorable was Gladys that the family did not even realize she went on to become Marilyn Monroe's mother until many years later, and long after the death of both Harry and his wife Lena.

Norma Jean Cohen's daughter Bonnie confirmed this in 2009: 'There were no letters or stories, and we know that my grandmother, Lena Cohen, had no idea that her ex-employee was Marilyn Monroe's mother. I knew my grandmother for over thirty years so I know this is true. Plus this would have been good "family history" information but it was never discussed; and it would have been if we had known.'

After working with the Cohen family for a short time, Gladys became disillusioned about regaining her children. Baker had remarried and the family seemed settled, so Gladys reluctantly accepted the fact that she'd lost them. She visited the family to say goodbye and then disappeared from their lives.

On her return to Los Angeles, Gladys obtained a job at Consolidated Film Industries, where she became friends with a colleague called Grace McKee. The two spent quite some time together, going out dancing, having fun and gaining something of a reputation among the male employees at Consolidated.

Whilst living at 1211 Hyperion Avenue, Gladys shocked everyone when, on 11 October 1924, she suddenly married Martin Edward Mortensen, a twenty-seven-year-old divorcee who worked as a meter man for the Los Angeles Gas and Electric Company. He was in love with his new wife, but it was not reciprocated; she complained to friends that he was 'dull' and it wasn't long before she had fallen for Charles Stanley Gifford, a twenty-five-year-old divorcee and one of the bosses at Consolidated.

'Gifford was a real likeable guy,' remembered one friend; while another described him as 'well-dressed, and always drove a pretty nice car'. He had a dark side, however, as witnessed by his first wife, Lilian, and detailed in divorce papers submitted by her shortly after they separated in 1923: Gifford 'continuously pursued a course of abuse, threats and intimidation calculated to harass, annoy, hurt and worry the plaintiff'. This was just the tip of the iceberg. Lilian said she also experienced physical injury and accusations that she was being unfaithful to him, when actually she believed that he was undertaking affairs with women where he worked, as well as taking illegal drugs. Things had come to a head during June 1923, when Gifford verbally abused her before striking her so hard on the cheek that she was 'knocked against the bed post', sustaining severe bruising. The divorce papers also claim that a blood clot was formed under her cheek and urgent medical attention was required to remove it.

Whether or not everything cited by Lilian was true will never be known, but certainly the marriage had been turbulent and by the time the divorce was finalized and Gladys Baker arrived in his life, Gifford was enjoying his new-found freedom and had no plans to settle down. Unfortunately for Gladys, she believed she could persuade him to change his mind, and on 26 May 1925, walked out on Martin Edward Mortensen.

During the autumn of 1925, Gladys became pregnant. It has been said that there were various men who could have been the father, including a twenty-eight-year-old colleague called Raymond Guthrie. Friends at the studio claimed that Gladys had dated blue-eyed, brown-haired Guthrie for several months that year and that he could very well be the father. Raised by his aunt and uncle since a baby, Guthrie had also recently divorced and was certainly in a position to date Gladys, though all records indicate that she never considered him to be her baby's father.

The official ruling is that the father was unknown, though evidence suggests it was Gifford, and this was most certainly the belief of Gladys. For instance, family letters and memories show that both Gladys and Norma Jeane named him as the father on several occasions, and in August 1961, an article appeared in *Cavalier* magazine which said: '[Marilyn's] father is very much alive and residing in Southern California. He was once connected with the movie business, although he no longer is today.' This would certainly be a nod in Gifford's direction, since by that time he was living south of Los Angeles, where he was running a dairy farm.

Gladys broke the news of the pregnancy to Gifford during a New Year's party at the family home, presumably that of his father, carpenter Frederick Gifford, who lived at 12024 Venice Boulevard. Later, as the pregnancy became obvious, it created quite a stir in the Gifford family; particularly with his sister Ethel, who lectured him intensely, demanding to know what he intended to do about the situation. The argument culminated with Ethel telling her brother, 'Look, either marry the woman or do something.' According to relatives, Gladys was not seen at their home any more.

Shunned by the Gifford family, Gladys then tried to gain sympathy from her mother, who by this time was living on her own at 418 East Rhode Island Avenue, while Charles Grainger was now working overseas. Della acknowledged disgust that her daughter was once again pregnant with an illegitimate child, and then sailed off to South-East Asia on 20 March 1926 in order to visit her husband.

When Gladys gave birth on 1 June 1926, she had hoped Gifford would accompany her to the hospital. She was greatly disappointed, however, as he purposely stayed away, refusing to have anything to do with her or the child. Gladys perhaps would not have been shocked by this had she known that in 1922, when his wife Lilian gave birth to their son Charles Stanley Jr, Gifford took her to the Lomashire Hospital, excused himself immediately and walked out of the building.

Knowing that Gifford was to play no part in the child's upbringing, Gladys reluctantly decided to get on with her life. She named the child after the little girl she had looked after whilst in Kentucky and, for the sake of respectability, also gave the surname of her former husband, hence naming her Norma Jeane Mortenson (she added an 'e' to Norma Jean and changed Mortensen to Mortenson on the birth certificate). Shortly afterwards she changed her mind and declared that both she and her daughter would be known by the surname of her first husband, Baker.

Shortly after the little girl's birth, perhaps feeling mild curiosity or a pang of guilt for the way he had treated her in the past, Gifford asked Gladys if he could see the child. His plea fell on deaf ears, however, and she refused point-blank to let him have anything to do with her. 'He felt the mother had been unfair,' remembered Gifford's minister, Dr Liden. 'She had cut him off and didn't allow him to see the child.'

On leaving hospital, Gladys took Norma Jeane to her apartment at 5454 Wilshire Boulevard, but it was only a matter of days before she made a trip to East Rhode Island Avenue to deposit her child at number 459, the home of the Bolender family.

Ida and Wayne Bolender lived across the road from Gladys'

mother Della, on a two-acre plot of land in Hawthorne; an agricultural area dominated by lots of space, dairies and farms. A postman for many years, Wayne and his wife had applied to become foster-parents just before the Depression and for the next thirty-five years continued happily opening their home to any child who needed their help.

Contrary to popular belief, Gladys did not immediately abandon her child with the Bolenders; instead, she moved in with the family and left Norma Jeane in their care while she commuted to and from her job in Hollywood. 'Mrs Baker was with me,' Ida later told *Cavalier*. 'She stayed in Hollywood when working nights as a negative cutter and stayed with me while working days.' However, the long journey and the responsibility of single-motherhood soon became too much for Gladys, and she ultimately took the decision to return to her old life.

Leaving her baby behind, Gladys moved in with her friend and colleague, Grace McKee, and the two shared a space at the Rayfield Apartments at 237 Bimini Place. Going from the quiet seclusion of the Bolender home to this colourful apartment block must have been something of a thrill for Gladys. But in spite of now living the life of a single girl once again, she didn't give up on her daughter and always paid $25 a month to the Bolenders for her care. She also often stayed at the weekend, involving herself with family life, and later showed up on the 1930s census as a 'boarder' in the Bolender home. Norma Jeane 'was never neglected and always nicely dressed,' said Mrs Bolender. 'Her mother paid her board all the time.'

On 15 August 1926, Della sailed from Hong Kong and arrived in San Francisco on 8 September. On her return to East Rhode Island Avenue, she was introduced to her granddaughter for the first time, though she never developed much of a bond with the child, seeing her as more of a sin than a joy. Sick with malaria and often delusional, she made her feelings quite clear just months later when she was caught trying to smother the child with a pillow. She was immediately banned from the

Bolender home, but Della still tried to gain access to Norma Jeane, as Ida Bolender later recalled: 'She did come over one day for no reason I know of. She just broke in the glass of our front door and I believe we called the police.'

For Della, this sequence of events was the beginning of the end and she soon found herself admitted to the Norwalk Mental Hospital, suffering from manic depressive psychosis. She was never to leave the hospital, and when she passed away, Della Monroe Grainger contributed to the legacy of mental illness that had begun with the death of her husband.

After the turmoil of recent days, the Bolender family tried their best to continue life in a normal way for their foster-children, Norma Jeane and a baby boy called Lester. Born on 23 August 1926 whilst his parents, Pearl and Carl Flugel, were living in a tent, Lester had come to the Bolender home after the Flugels decided they were too young to care for him. Married for just over a week before the birth of their son, the couple handed the baby to Ida Bolender and returned to their home state of Washington, where they later had four more sons, Milton, Gerald, Robert and William. The couple kept their first son a secret from their family, and it wasn't until Pearl's death in 1988 that they discovered a 1927 letter from Mrs Bolender, describing Lester's life in California. The now elderly Lester travelled to meet his long-lost family but unfortunately, even at this late stage, one of the brothers refused to believe they were related and apparently never accepted Lester as his brother.

But back in 1926, when both Lester and Norma Jeane were just babies, they were nicknamed 'the twins' and raised as brother and sister. 'They have great times together,' wrote Mrs Bolender. 'Lots of people think them twins. I dress them alike at times and they do look cunning . . .'

Eventually the Bolender family made a decision to officially adopt Lester, and asked Gladys if they could adopt Norma Jeane too. Gladys, having already lost two children, was appalled at the Bolenders' plans and turned them down flat. However, they were not the only ones interested in the child as, according to several reports, Charles Stanley Gifford also had plans to raise her. By this time he was living on his own at 832 N. Alta Vista Boulevard, and had learned that Norma Jeane had been placed in a foster home. He contacted Gladys to tell her he intended to raise the little girl himself, but was sent away with nothing more than a scolding from his ex-lover, who had developed a deep loathing for him since her troubled pregnancy.

How Gifford thought he could possibly raise the child on his own is a mystery. He was not listed as her father on the birth certificate, and divorce records from his first wife Lilian show that he had been verbally abusive and distant from his other children, calling them derogatory names on many occasions.

But even if his temper was not an issue, there was no way Gladys was going to let the man she claimed to detest raise her child. Instead, she continued to visit her daughter at the weekends, though as Norma Jeane grew, the stopovers became more and more confusing for the child. One day when she referred to Ida Bolender as 'Mama', she was immediately put in her place. 'The woman with the red hair is your mother,' explained Ida, though this did not end the confusion. 'But [Wayne] is my daddy,' exclaimed Norma Jeane. 'No,' replied Ida. After that, the child became afraid to call anyone mummy or daddy, as not even Gladys referred to her as a daughter.

As for her father, Gladys told Norma Jeane that he had been killed in a car crash either before she was born or when she was a young baby – the story differing according to Gladys' mood at the time. Her story was cruel but contained a kernel of truth, as in 1929 she was told that the man she had named as Norma Jeane's father – Martin Edward Mortensen – had been killed in a car crash. Unknown to Gladys, it later transpired that it was a completely different person who had died, and her ex-husband was actually alive and well and living in California. For his part, Mortensen added to the confusion by years later claiming to friends that he was Norma Jeane's real father, but this is extremely unlikely – and certainly not the belief of Marilyn or her mother.

At irregular intervals, the young child would travel to her mother's home in Hollywood, and stare quietly at a photo of Charles Stanley Gifford, which hung on the wall despite Gladys' claims of hatred towards him. Gifford bore a striking resemblance to Clark Gable and, from that moment on, Norma Jeane always thought of the actor as something of a surrogate father. Unfortunately, looking at the photo was the only thing Norma Jeane enjoyed about her visits to her mother, who was so uptight that she would often chastise her for turning the pages of a book 'too loudly'. As a result the child spent most of her time hiding in the closet, waiting to be taken back to the Bolenders' house.

Gifford, meanwhile, was living just miles away at 3014 Chesapeake Avenue, in a house that he jointly owned with none other than Raymond Guthrie, the laboratory technician whom Gladys had dated in 1925. How the two men ended up buying a home together is a mystery, and we can only imagine the interesting conversations that could have occurred within those four walls. The two shared the house for several years before Guthrie moved on, but Gifford was to stay there throughout Norma Jeane's childhood and well into her first marriage. It is not known if he ever tried once more to gain access to his daughter, but if he did, Gladys kept very quiet about it and never discussed it with Norma Jeane.

There has been a great deal of talk as to the kind of upbringing provided by the Bolender family, with various stories concocted by the film studio and Marilyn herself to present her tale as something of a Cinderella story. These stories may have provided a good deal of public sympathy for the star, but according to her foster-sister, Nancy Bolender, they gave her parents nothing but heartache: 'Mother and Daddy always felt bad about the things written about Marilyn Monroe's young life that said she was brought up in poor homes and not loved or taken care of.'

In later years, Ida Bolender became very upset about the way Norma Jeane's life was misrepresented, and told reporters, 'We treated her like our own child because we loved her.'

Unfortunately, this affection didn't protect them from the constant rumours that have circulated ever since and while Norma Jeane's early years were not exactly the best, life with the Bolender family was not one of hardship and destitution. 'Life was safe, secure and comfortable,' remembered Nancy, 'with plenty of playmates. [The Bolenders] truly loved us and protected us and nurtured us with all of their hearts.'

The family did have strict values and religious beliefs, and certainly no idle time was allowed. 'Idle hands are from the devil,' was something Lester Bolender frequently told his foster-siblings. However, while Ida was very schedule-oriented and was never known to laugh, she did have her reasons. A childhood bout of scarlet fever had left her with hearing loss in one ear, and later she had to use hearing aids and learn to lip-read in order to communicate with friends and family.

Life had been hard for Ida and looking after a team of children in the 1920s was no picnic, but her mother lived next door and she often helped out. The children always had clothes made for them by Ida herself, and most of the food was grown on their land: there was an abundant supply of apples, tomatoes, corn, watermelon, and string beans, and the only items they had to buy from the store were flour, butter, sugar and coffee. On such occasions the family would pile into Wayne Bolender's Model T and travel into town, where Ida would do her shopping and the children stayed in the car with Wayne, playing guessing games, singing songs and telling stories.

On some occasions Norma Jeane even took great joy in sitting on her foster-father's lap, while pretending to drive the car. Wayne loved little Norma Jeane as one of his own, considering her his baby, and the child spent a lot of time with him, sitting on a stool while he shaved and asking questions such as, 'Who is God?', 'Where does he live?' and 'How many people live in the world?'

For Norma Jeane, there were many happy times with the Bolender family, and she would often find herself spending days at nearby Redondo beach, or climbing the apple tree outside her bedroom window, with Lester in tow. The two would drag blankets up to the branches in order to make a fort, while in the yard, the chickens, rabbits and goat would go about their business, oblivious to the antics above.

Norma Jeane was also the proud owner of a small dog called Tippy, which she spent many hours playing with, and there were afternoons spent playing hopscotch on the sidewalk with Nancy. While going to the cinema was frowned upon (although Marilyn later claimed that she snuck into a movie theatre once or twice), Norma Jeane was still allowed to listen to the radio – her favourite shows being *The Green Hornet* and *The Lone Ranger*. 'I used to get terribly excited,' she said about listening to *The Lone Ranger*. 'Not at the horses and the chases and the guns, but the drama. The wondering how it would be for each person in that situation.'

On a creative level, there was always music in the house, as Ida loved listening to symphonies on the radio and the family would often sing when they got home from church. Norma Jeane even learnt to play the piano that sat proudly in the Bolender home, and she carried this passion throughout her life, always having a piano in her own home as an adult.

The religious beliefs of the Bolender family were also passed on to the child and, according to Nancy Bolender, she was taught about God and told that he was utterly trustworthy and bigger than any situation she could face in her lifetime. It is this aspect of her life with the Bolender family that has been blown out of all proportion over the years, with stories emerging of the family being so consumed with religion that they had no time for the children, and continually criticized Norma Jeane for doing what they considered to be sinful acts. However, this is certainly not how Nancy remembers her parents: 'I never heard them criticize or talk badly about anyone. They accepted people for who they were and loved them unconditionally.'

On 14 September 1931 it was time for both Norma Jeane and Lester to start school. Foster-sister Nancy remembered watching 'the twins' skip to the Washington Street School, followed by Tippy, Norma Jeane's beloved dog. The children continued their schooling there until the Los Angeles earthquake struck on 10 March 1933, when they were relocated to the 5th Street School (now the Ramona School). Years later, music teacher Evelyn Gawthrop remembered Norma Jeane as a timid child who nevertheless got on well with the other children.

However, being timid did not prevent Norma Jeane from realizing that making up stories was a good way of gaining sympathy and attention for herself. She began telling tales about the Bolenders to her school teacher and on one occasion even went so far as to fabricate a story that she had seen little Nancy being pushed against an oven by her foster-parents. In later years – in the privacy of her notebooks – she admitted this was done only as a way of gaining attention from the trusting teacher, and that the incidents she described had never happened at all.

Norma Jeane loved singing at school, and her skills were put to good use when she was chosen to perform in the Easter sunrise services at the Hollywood Bowl. The event consisted of a children's chorus standing in the shape of a cross, all wearing black capes. As the sun rose over the Bowl, the children were instructed to take off the black robes and reveal their white clothes underneath, thus changing the cross from black to white. Marilyn later lamented that she became so engrossed in checking out all that was going on around her that she forgot to take off her robe, thus becoming a black spot on an otherwise white cross. However, the mistake must have soon been rectified, since all photos of the children's cross taken around that time have no 'black dots' to be found.

Norma Jeane's time with the Bolenders came to a sudden halt in 1933 when two never-to-be-forgotten events occurred. The first was the death of Norma Jeane's dog, Tippy, who, it is said, was killed by a neighbour after a particularly noisy barking session. Shortly after this, Norma Jeane's mother decided that she'd had enough of living without her daughter, and announced that she wanted to buy a house for them both to live in together. The couple were obviously shocked but could do nothing to prevent the removal of Norma Jeane from their home, even though they surely must have been worried about what her future would bring.

Norma Jeane was not keen on moving away with the 'lady with the red hair' and when the day of her departure finally arrived, the children became so upset that they hid in the closet, hoping they would not be found. No matter what Norma Jeane thought of the family, the idea of living with the mother she hardly knew was even more disturbing, though she was quickly found in the closet and marched to her mother's waiting car.

The family were absolutely devastated to lose her and never forgot the little girl who had touched their lives for so long: 'It was a sad time for Mother and Daddy,' remembered Nancy Bolender, 'because they truly loved her. They had raised her from infancy to eight plus years of age. That's a long time and when so much of yourself is put into training, nurturing and loving a child it is like losing your own flesh and blood.'

Chapter 2

Dreams and Nightmares

Once Gladys had reclaimed her daughter, she moved the child into the home of English couple George and Maude Atkinson, and their twenty-year-old daughter, Nellie.

In 1915 George Atkinson had left his family's fishmonger business in Grimsby, and sailed to the United States in the hope of getting work in Hollywood. Maude and Nellie followed him, arriving on the 27 October 1919, and together they settled in an apartment located at 4716 Santa Monica Boulevard, where George tried to etch out a role for himself in the entertainment industry. He did not have quite the success he had hoped for, however, and finally settled for bit parts in movies, and as a regular stand-in for fellow British actor, George Arliss. By 1930 the family had moved to a small house at 1552 La Baig Avenue, just yards away from all the major film studios in town, before relocating once again to Afton Place, where they became acquainted with Gladys Baker in 1933.

For Norma Jeane, living with Mr and Mrs Atkinson was a completely different experience to living with the Bolenders. The English couple were described by Marilyn as being 'happy, jolly, and carefree'. However, the happy-go-lucky existence of the couple confused the child, particularly because she had spent the first seven years of her life being told that much of what she was now witnessing was wrong. Norma Jeane prayed for them and felt guilty whenever she enjoyed their company and the stories they told of their acting life. 'They liked to drink a little, smoke, dance and sing and play cards – all of the things that I had been taught were sinful. And still they seemed like very nice people to me.'

Norma Jeane lived with the Atkinsons for several months and during this time she would often visit Grauman's Chinese Theatre and fit her own hands in the handprints of the stars. She would spend hours sitting in the movies, watching the actors and actresses on the screen, and then imitating them in her little bedroom at home. She fell in love with the cinema and dreamt of being a famous actress like her new idol, Jean Harlow.

But it wasn't all fun and games. Several days after she had moved into Afton Place, Norma Jeane was enrolled at Selma Avenue School. This was yet another upheaval in the child's life, and when she arrived at the school without her parents to accompany her, it didn't help conquer her fears.

In an interview Marilyn gave to Liza Wilson in 1952, she recalled that all of the other children had parents with them, and when a well-meaning teacher asked if her parents were dead, the confused child replied, 'Yes, Mam, I think so.' Another student who was watching exclaimed to her mother, 'Look Mummy. That girl's an orphan.' Norma Jeane was devastated by this remark and, in her own words, 'leaned against a wall and bawled'.

Eventually Gladys was true to her word and took out a mortgage on a small, three-bedroom house at 6812 Arbol Drive, located near the Hollywood Bowl. Gladys bought the house with the dream that all her children could live together under one roof, and although Grace McKee begged her not to take on the responsibility of a mortgage, all requests for calm went unheard. In September 1933 Gladys and Norma Jeane moved into their first home together, but it was also agreed that the Atkinson family would come too, paying some of the mortgage and looking after Norma Jeane while Gladys was working.

Marilyn later described the Arbol Drive home as 'A pretty little house with quite a few rooms. But there was no furniture in it, except for two cots that we slept on, a small kitchen table, and two kitchen chairs.' However, the lack of material items was more than made up for by the fact that, finally, Norma Jeane had her mother to herself for the first time in her entire life.

Gladys did her best to provide a stable upbringing for the child, taking her to movies and even visiting Catalina Island at one point, where Norma Jeane was able to stay up way past her bedtime and watch her mother dance to the Curt Houck Orchestra in the Catalina Casino. Gladys also taught Norma Jeane about her religion, Christian Science, and tried to involve her in the practice by performing 'healings' on the child from time to time. Materially, things were looking up too when Gladys found a piano, which was said to have belonged to actor Fredric March, and placed it in the unfurnished living room. It became the focal part of the entire house, and Gladys told Norma Jeane that one day she would listen to the child playing beside the window, while she sat beside the fire.

Unfortunately this was not to be, as two shocking events rocked Gladys' world. Shortly before taking Norma Jeane out of the Bolenders' care, Gladys' grandfather, Tilford M. Hogan, had committed suicide. A local newspaper had described how the old man hanged himself in the barn on the afternoon of 29 May 1933, while his wife was out shopping. Shortly after that, on 16 August 1933, Gladys' son, Robert 'Jasper' Baker, died of tuberculosis of the kidneys. The child was only fifteen years old, and the end of his life was the conclusion of the many years he had been plagued by bad luck and unfortunate events.

The news of both these shocking events did not reach Gladys until she had already moved in with Norma Jeane, and it hit her like a thunderbolt. Her first reaction was a tirade of abuse towards her young daughter: 'Why couldn't it have been you? Why couldn't it have been you?' she screamed over and over again at the shocked and confused child. Already emotionally fragile, the news sent Gladys into a spiral of depression and anxiety from which she could not emerge. While the move to the Arbol house was supposed to have been a new start for both her and Norma Jeane, Gladys now found herself more and more unable to cope with the responsibility of working and looking after her child.

Throughout 1934, Gladys' emotional health worsened and she was continually evaluated at Los Angeles General Hospital. Grace McKee tried to look after both Gladys and Norma Jeane, but it was a losing battle. Eventually Gladys was persuaded to put the house up for sale, and an advert ran in the *Los Angeles Times* on 21 October 1934, describing it as a three-bedroom, three-bath English stucco house, on the market for $4500.

Meanwhile, Norma Jeane spent her time playing outside with empty whisky bottles: 'I guess I must have had the finest collection of bottles any girl ever had. I'd line them up on a plank beside the road and when people drove along I'd say "Wouldn't you like some whisky?"' With her mother's descent into mental illness growing more apparent each day, Norma Jeane began to feel increasingly unwanted: 'I was a mistake. My mother didn't want to have me. I guess she never wanted me. I probably got in her way. I wish . . . I still wish . . . she had wanted me.'

But Gladys was unable to show love to anyone, not even herself, and eventually her emotional problems reached a climax, when in January 1935 she had a complete breakdown. Norma Jeane was in the kitchen having breakfast when she suddenly heard a commotion coming from the hallway. Her mother was screaming and shouting, and the Atkinsons were trying desperately to calm her down.

When the child returned from school that day, her mother was gone, and when Norma Jeane asked where she was, she was told, 'Your mother is very sick; you won't be able to see her for a long, long, time.'

'I figured my mother was really dead but they wouldn't tell me because they didn't want me to cry,' she later said. 'I didn't know my mother was alive for many years.' Her mother was not dead, of course, but she was judged insane on 15 January 1935 and committed to the state institution at Norwalk.

Lois Banner and Mark Anderson's book, *MM – Personal: From the Private Archive of Marilyn Monroe* (2010), includes a 1962 letter to Marilyn's sister Berniece from Harry Charles Wilson, who claimed to have been in a relationship with Gladys during this time. 'The tragedy of her sickness was almost more than I could bear,' he wrote. He described how he had courted Gladys during the year before her breakdown; visiting restaurants with her and Norma Jeane; taking the child to see the Christmas Parade on Hollywood Boulevard and spending time together as a family. He was deeply in love with Gladys and told her so at Christmas 1934, but was left devastated when she was admitted to hospital shortly afterwards. 'I almost lost my mind over it,' he said.

According to the letter, Wilson continued to visit and correspond with Gladys for some years afterwards, until they eventually lost touch completely in 1945. 'I have prayed for her many times and cried myself to sleep in lonesomeness for her,' he wrote. His letter has the ring of truth, as he mentions personal information that was not yet widely known to the public.

We know little about Harry Wilson, but research for this book reveals that he was born in 1891; worked as a boat builder; and had been married at least twice before he met Gladys Baker. It is impossible to say whether Gladys reciprocated the love Harry felt for her, but one thing's for sure: he held a torch for his lost love for many years; not marrying again until shortly before his death in 1970.

Back in 1935, and with Wilson having no legal rights to either Gladys or Norma Jeane, Grace McKee decided to take over full responsibility of both mother and daughter. On 25 March 1935 Grace filed a petition to be guardian of the estate, and thereafter began the long task of logging and assessing Gladys' possessions and debts.

It was decided that Norma Jeane would be better off staying in the Arbol house with the Atkinson family, as she had warmed to the couple and it seemed pointless to uproot her again. However, there were many times when she felt completely isolated as a result of her mother's illness. Records show that there were various families living in Arbol Drive at the time, including the Harrell family who were just down the road at number 6816. But while there were often children playing at the Harrell home and various others in the street, Norma Jeane's feelings of inadequacy made her feel nowhere near comfortable playing with them.

One day, when Norma Jeane decided to run round the block just for the fun of it, some neighbourhood boys stopped to ask what she was doing. Before she could answer, another child snapped, 'Don't bother her. She's just like her mother – crazy.' It was comments like that which led Marilyn to deny the existence of her mother, often declaring that she was dead.

An oft-repeated tale about Marilyn's life is that she was molested as a child aged nine or ten. As Marilyn told it, a 'gentleman' by the name of Mr Kimmell lived in the house where she was staying, and one day he called her into his room, locked the door, and indecently assaulted her. The general consensus is that the child was sexually assaulted, rather than raped, and when it was over she ran to her foster-mother who slapped her face for telling lies.

Some authors have dismissed this story as complete fabrication by Marilyn, while others, such as Donald Wolfe, insist that the incident took place while Norma Jeane lived on Arbol Drive, and that her mother was the one who slapped her face. Wolfe also names the molester as Murray Kinnell, a character actor who gave Bette Davis her big break in Hollywood and who had also worked on three of Jean Harlow's films: *The Public Enemy* (1931), *The Secret Six* (1931) and *The Beast of the City* (1932).

It is impossible to know for sure if Murray Kinnell had anything to do with Norma Jeane, but if the assault story is true, and if it was indeed Kinnell who was the perpetrator, when did the assault take place and why was Kinnell living at the Arbol house?

Marilyn never mentioned that she was molested whilst in the care of her mother, which could be because she was covering up for her or because the incident didn't happen while she was living with her at all. The Arbol house only had three bedrooms, so unless the Atkinsons shared a room with their daughter, and Norma Jeane shared with her mother, there would have been no room to take in a boarder. However, there is a possibility that the attack did take place at the Arbol house but after Gladys had been admitted to Norwalk.

As previously explained, George Atkinson worked as a stand-in for movie star George Arliss, and he, by chance, was a friend of Murray Kinnell. They had worked together in a number of movies, including *Voltaire* (1933), *The House of Rothschild* (1934) and *Cardinal Richelieu* (1935); the latter was filmed in March 1935, while Norma Jeane still lived with the Atkinson family. It is possible that the Atkinsons moved Norma Jeane into Nellie's room, hence creating more space in the home, and that George Atkinson invited Murray Kinnell to stay in the empty room, where he had the opportunity to molest young Norma Jeane. We will never know what really happened in that house, but one thing is clear: from that moment on, the child began to stutter when faced with difficult situations, such as reading aloud in class. 'The continual state of being frightened had started me stammering,' she later recalled, 'and people laughed at me when I stammered.'

There has been much talk about why Norma Jeane was removed from the Atkinsons' care. Some say she had to be taken away because Grace McKee felt the couple were mistreating her, but this is inaccurate, as letters show Norma Jeane kept in touch with Nellie Atkinson for years afterwards, and Grace gave permission for the family to visit the child after she had moved out. Other sources state that the entire Atkinson family were moving back to England, and could no longer look after the child, but this is simply not true either.

Travel records for this time show that while Maude and Nellie Atkinson had travelled back to the UK for three months during the summer of 1924, there were no departures or arrivals listed for any of the family during the mid-1930s. However, there is evidence that would suggest the Atkinsons may have thought about travelling back to England shortly after Gladys had her breakdown. On 18 February 1935, George's brother Richard passed away at his home in Grimsby and his death could have caused the family to think about returning home. While the Atkinsons may have flirted with the idea, it is highly unlikely that the trip ever took place, as society pages show that their daughter, Nellie, was maid of honour to her friend Margaret Appleton at the end of May and attended numerous wedding showers, parties and ceremonies throughout the coming year. She also married in Los Angeles on 17 March 1939; the wedding announcement clearly stating that the family were formerly of Grimsby and now living in Hollywood. Added to that, when Maude passed away in March 1944, the obituary reported that she had lived in southern California for twenty-five years, so any trip to England must have surely been a short one.

The reality of Norma Jeane's removal from the Atkinsons' care was actually the fact that, with Gladys gone, Grace had been forced to sell her friend's belongings in order to pay off her debts. Gladys' 1933 Plymouth Sedan (which she was still paying for) was listed in the inventory, along with the Franklin Grand Piano (which Grace's aunt Ana Lower eventually bought) and a small radio. Grace kept detailed records of her expenditure, and court records show that on 22 May 1935 a payment of $25 was made to Mrs Atkinson for the care of Norma Jeane, but no other payments appear after that. Five days later, on 27 May, the Arbol Drive house was re-listed for sale and on 12 June the home was given back to the previous owners, the Whitmans.

Years later, while driving through the area with her sister-in-law Elyda Nelson, Norma Jeane pointed out the home she once shared with her mother. 'I lived there once,' she said, 'before mother was ill. It was beautiful. The most wonderful furniture you can imagine: a baby grand piano and a room of my own. It all seems like a dream.'

Once the child moved out of Arbol Drive, she was transferred into the care of Elsie and Harvey Giffen, who lived at 2062 Highland Avenue. Harvey Giffen had known Gladys while she worked at the laboratory, and as a favour to Grace the family took Norma Jeane into their home. They grew so fond of her that they even hoped at one point to adopt her. From the confines of the hospital Gladys put a stop to the plan, just as she had done with the Bolender family years before. Gladys was determined that no one would ever take her little girl away, but it seems as though nobody ever thought to explain that to Norma Jeane. 'No one ever seemed interested in adopting me permanently,' she later said. 'I've often wondered about this.'

In early summer, Grace and Olive Monroe, Gladys' sister-in-law, travelled to Norwalk and grilled the staff about Gladys' condition. In a letter dated 15 August, Grace told a friend, Myrtle Van Hyning, what she had been told by a doctor: 'He explained to me that Gladys' type of insanity is the hardest case to do anything with. Her brain did not develop like an ordinary person's. They examined her brain with a floroscope [*sic*], and it proved to be about one third the size of a normal human being's.'

The doctor then went on to explain that if Gladys had never had any worries and had someone to take care of her, she could probably have gone on to live a normal life, However, her condition was incurable and, although she might be able to leave the institution for a while, she would have to be taken back with her condition 'worse than ever' if she encountered any worries.

Sadly, Gladys knew nothing of this, and fully thought that she would one day be able to go back to her most recent job at RKO, where she was still well thought of by colleagues. Grace later recalled that she was loved and respected; 'honest, hard-working, thrifty, dependable and kindly to everyone'. Another colleague described her as a 'demure little lady who sat at her splicing machine and communicated with no one during her work day'. This may have been true, but the bosses at the studio decided they simply had no time for Gladys Baker and her illness. They decided enough was enough and Grace was in the unfortunate position of knowing they would never allow her friend to return to work under any circumstances.

Knowing there was no turning back for Gladys or Norma Jeane, plans had to be made for a permanent place for the child to stay. The Bolender family wanted Norma Jeane back, but Grace would not allow this, although the former foster-parents did on occasions take the child to see her mother at Norwalk. Nancy Bolender Jeffrey remembers, 'Many Sunday afternoons were spent picking her up at one of the homes she was at and taking her over to visit her mother at the Norwalk Mental Institute. We would sit on the lawn and eat and visit and watch Norma Jeane and her mother play together. The Bolenders wanted to make sure that their relationship as mother and daughter was not interrupted any more than could be helped. She was always glad to see us and to go with us to see her mother.'

On 10 August 1935, Grace McKee travelled to her aunt and uncle's house in Las Vegas and secretly married a gentleman by the name of Ervin 'Doc' Goddard, a divorcee with three young children: Nona, Eleanor (Bebe) and John. Grace had met Goddard three years before, when she had encouraged his film ambitions and introduced him to B-movie director Al Rogell, who gave him a part in one of his movies. After that, Goddard appeared in several films as an extra, but had failed to make the splash he had dreamed of when he'd first met Grace. Whilst conducting their courtship at Doc's home at 6146 Eleanor Avenue, he proposed to Grace and she accepted, though they decided to keep the wedding secret, most likely to avoid upsetting Norma Jeane. However, after a week's honeymoon, the couple arrived back in Los Angeles, where news travelled around the movie studio like wild fire, and on 19 August 1935 the couple found themselves splashed over the pages of the *Los Angeles Times*.

The secret was out and Grace was eager to convince Norma Jeane that she would still be more than welcome in her new life. To prove it, she moved the child into her home on Barbara Court, but lack of money and the arrival of Goddard's daughter, Nona, meant that within weeks Grace decided that the situation wasn't working out. And so it was that on 13 September Norma Jeane had her first look at the building that was to be her new home for the foreseeable future.

The Los Angeles Orphans Home was a red-brick building based in the heart of Hollywood. The location couldn't have been more painful for Norma Jeane: it was just blocks away from Afton Place where she first lived with her mother. The child had not been told where she was going, but as she was led up the front steps her eyes fell upon the sign, and she immediately realized what was happening. Screaming, 'I'm not an orphan, I'm not an orphan,' the confused child tried desperately to persuade Grace to take her home, but to no avail. Before she knew what was happening, she was placed in the Girl's Cottage, in the south wing of the building, in a room that slept twelve girls.

'It seemed very big,' Marilyn told *Redbook* columnist Jim Henaghan in 1952, 'but maybe it wasn't. Maybe I just remember it as big.' There were two dormitories – one large, and one small; the smaller one being seen as the better room, which the girls would try desperately to work their way up to. 'I don't know why, because, after all, it was still the orphanage,' she said in 1952. In the large room, Norma Jeane's bed was located right next to the window overlooking RKO studios, which caused a lot of heartache for the little girl, 'I used to sit at the window and cry,' she said, 'knowing that my mother had once worked there.'

Norma Jeane bitterly resented the fact that her mother had been taken away, and that she had to live in an orphanage when she was not an orphan. But while Norma Jeane was infuriated with the situation, she wasn't the only non-orphan in the place. During the time she was there, reports show that most of the children were half-orphans, which Norma Jeane actually believed she was, since her mother had long-since insisted her father was dead.

That said, Norma Jeane still felt that the whole situation was unfair and would never speak with any kindness about her time at 'the Home', repeating stories of how unpleasant it was until the very end of her life. 'A child disturbed and unhappy could get that impression,' said Margaret Ingram, Superintendent of the home in the 1960s, but insisted that life in the orphanage was not the nightmare Marilyn painted it to be.

Meanwhile, Grace Goddard continued her life as normal, working in the film laboratory through the day and rehearsing for the Columbian Drama League production of *Up Pops the Devil* at night. The play premiered at the Wilshire Ebell Theater on 29 September 1935, little more than two weeks after she waved goodbye to Norma Jeane, and while it is unlikely the child ever got to see her 'Aunt Grace' in the production, she almost certainly heard about it during her visits to the orphanage.

Grace tried to call in on Norma Jeane every week, bringing presents and clothes and taking her out for visits to the hairdresser or the occasional movie. She took an active interest in the child's welfare, and when she discovered her to be extremely upset after a visit from Mrs Bolender, Grace immediately wrote to the home's superintendent, Sula Dewey. The undated letter asked that nobody be allowed to 'see or talk to little Norma Jean [*sic*] Baker, unless you have my written permission to do so'. She went on to say that she especially did not want her to be visited by Ida Bolender, as 'her visits seem to upset the child'. Grace included a list of people who were allowed to see Norma Jeane: Elsie and Harvey Giffin, Maude, George and Nellie Atkinson, Gladys's sister-in-law, Olive Monroe, and Olive's mother, Mrs Martin.

On 6 December 1935, Mrs Dewey wrote a reply to Grace, on Los Angeles Orphans Home Society letterhead:

Dear Mrs Goddard
When Mrs Bolender was here I told her she should not talk to Norma about her mother.
The physicians have said Mrs Baker would not get well – that means the child must have first consideration.
Will you please give a letter to each person you want Norma to see and go out with? This would be an extra check. If I just tell

the ones who are on duty the names of the ones to see Norma there might be a slip.

Norma is not the same since Mrs B. visited with her. She doesn't look as happy. When she is naughty she says, 'Mrs Dewey, I wouldn't ever want my Aunt Grace to know I was naughty.' She loves you very much.

I'll do as you request. We want to do all we can to make Norma happy, and to please you.

Sincerely yours

(Mrs) S. S. Dewey

Although Marilyn would always insist that life in the orphanage was hellish – often on a par with the story of little orphan 'Annie' – it would seem that the care of the children in the institution was actually very good. Each child received five cents every Saturday as pocket money, along with candy that was kept in large containers in the closet. They also had a barber – Sam David – who would visit the home every six weeks, and hold haircut parties where the children could choose a hairstyle and stay up way past their bedtime.

There were gardens to play in, trips to the home's Manhattan beach house in the summer, and every October the home opened to the public for the annual fruit and jam shower. This event lasted two days and saw visitors from all over, touring the establishment and giving gifts of jams, jellies, chocolate, canned fruit and vegetables for the coming year.

There was also an abundance of activities during the festive season. Indeed, in December 1935, three months after Norma Jeane's arrival, the Los Angeles chapter of the National Association of Cost Accountants took the children to the Army and Navy Club, at 1106 South Broadway, for a mammoth Christmas party. The children were able to meet Santa Claus, who presented them with gifts, and then enjoyed a full dinner, before returning to the orphanage at 7 p.m. Then on 18 December, the children, including Norma Jeane, were entertained by the Federal Theater Project, who put on a show which included clowns, magicians, dancers, acrobats and singers.

On Christmas Eve the children attended services at the Vine Street Methodist-Episcopal church, where some of them were chosen to sing, and then on Christmas Day they sang carols in the auditorium above the dining room, before receiving gifts of clothes – sweaters (made by the home's knitting club), underwear, shirts and trousers or skirts.

Bill Fredenhall arrived at the orphanage in March 1934, eighteen months before Norma Jeane. He has many memories of his time there, and of the festive season in particular: 'At Christmas we had several special trips out to large parties. One year I remember I attended a party where Joe E. Brown was the master of ceremony. You will remember him as Jack Lemmon's "boyfriend" in *Some Like It Hot*. We would receive gifts at these occasions and one Christmas my brother and I were taken out and given complete outfits: suits, shirts, ties, shoes. We wore these clothes when we left the Home for good in 1940.'

There were also Christmas trees in different areas of the orphanage, each one containing toys and gifts for the children. Photographs of the home, taken around the time of Norma Jeane's stay, show children clutching hobby horses, huge dolls, roller skates and teddies, while gifts also came from local people and even the fire brigade. Bill Fredenhall remembers: 'The Fire Department favoured the home at Christmas; they would arrive with the sirens going and a truckload of gifts. That was exciting! That happened each year. Christmas was a big deal at the Home and is another example of how they made it a swell place to be – remember this was in the depths of the depression and in that regard we were quite fortunate.'

Shortly after settling into life at the home, Norma Jeane was asked to look after Bill, as he was younger than she was, and the staff thought it would do her good to look after someone other than herself. The girls at the orphanage all had a younger boy that they 'mothered', and this practice went on until the home finally closed its doors in 2005. 'My time with Norma

Jeane would have been after meals in the yard,' remembers Bill. 'On the swings with other kids of similar ages; I remember very clearly the swings, slide and holding hands, and she would give me a peck goodnight when it was time to go in.'

Whilst at the orphanage, Norma Jeane's day would start with breakfast, and then she would clean her teeth and brush her tongue. The reason for this practice became apparent as she and the other children passed the home's nurse on the way out of the building: she would examine their tongues and if there was the slightest hint of a 'coating', the children would be given a dose of castor oil. Needless to say they made sure they kept their mouths extremely clean.

After the inspection, Norma Jeane made her way to Vine Street School, which she later recalled as the hardest thing she had ever done in her life. According to Marilyn, the girls would all wear different coloured gingham dresses, and she would often hear other pupils pointing towards her and her friends, whispering, 'They're from the home.'

Shortly after beginning her schooling at Vine Street, she became friendly with three boys in her class. This was short-lived, however, when they found out their new friend was from the orphanage. The boys made fun of her status; the friendship turned sour and Norma Jeane went deeper into her shell. 'I was always shy and scared,' she later recalled.

The school was close to orange groves, and on a cold day Norma Jeane and the children would stand out in the yard and look at the smoky skies caused by the burning pots of oil, protecting the groves from frost. After school she would make her way back to the home and play until dinner was ready, then there was time to listen to the radio, or read a book from the extensive collection in the library; much of which had been donated by Oliver Hardy, one half of the famous Laurel and Hardy duo.

At the weekend Norma Jeane was taken to Sunday school at the Vine Street Methodist Church, where each child was given a penny to put into the collection. Some of the children got wise to this, however, and soon started hiding their pennies in their clothes – particularly the boys' neckties, so that they would not be found when required.

But the weekends were not just about going to church. There were also trips to such places as the Ringling Brothers circus, Tom Mix circus, the Ambassador Auditorium, Griffith Park Observatory, the Le Brae Avenue Tar Pits, and various parks. Bill Fredenhall also recalls a studio birthday party for Shirley Temple, along with movies at the nearby RKO studio, held at least once a month. These outings would often result in autographs and presents for the children, along with the odd penny or two from actors on the lot. There were also several movies made at the home, some of which included the children as background players.

When Norma Jeane was old enough, she was given the opportunity of working in the laundry or the kitchen to earn money, and it is here that a large part of the controversy creeps in regarding her memories of the home and her role within it. Marilyn would later complain to interviewers that she often had to wash and dry hundreds of dishes, but Bill Fredenhall remembers it a little differently: 'Marilyn was talking about the job of kitchen help. We were paid, and this was obviously the type of chore that needed doing daily. We had lots of help and we made lunches too . . . I recall the fun of spreading butter, and peanut butter on a huge layout of sliced bread, and then slapping on a leaf of lettuce and putting it into a bag together with apples and oranges.'

So what about Marilyn's tales of hundreds of dishes and chores? 'I am sure her comments about the dishes were coloured by her biographers,' says Bill. 'Part of the poor, unhappy child routine. I would guess there were fewer than twenty staff, including matrons, cooks, hospital and laundry staff, but we were loved, protected, trained and cared for.'

One of the people responsible for caring for the children was Mrs Sula Dewey, whom Grace had written to about Norma Jeane. Out of all Marilyn's recollections of the orphanage, perhaps the only happy one was that of Mrs Dewey allowing her to apply a little make-up to her cheeks and being able to pat her little dog. She was kind and caring, but could also give out discipline when it was called for.

There have been many tales of the unhappy life lived by the children at the home, but very few of these are true. One of the more outlandish stories is that of birthday celebrations: it is said that on a child's birthday, a large cake would be wheeled out so that the children could sing 'Happy Birthday'. However, this was no ordinary sponge; it was made of wood with only a tiny space inside for one piece of real cake. The 'orphan' would eat the real slice, and the wooden cake would be wheeled back into the cupboard until the next birthday came along. However, this is untrue. 'A wooden cake? I doubt it,' says Bill Fredenhall. 'I never saw it. It sure sounds like one of those "tales". I don't remember any birthday celebrations. But almost for sure Mrs Dewey would take the opportunity to give one a few pieces of candy, at least.'

While Bill can't recall any specific birthday parties at the home, there was at least one party each year, given by Lorena Ann Taplin, whose father, Judge Taplin, had spent eight years of his childhood there. On 19 April 1936, Lorena travelled to the orphanage and celebrated with the children, sharing a frosted birthday cake and ice cream, and treating them all to a film screening. The celebrations were intended for all the children, and almost certainly included Norma Jeane.

For the most part, Norma Jeane kept herself out of trouble at the orphanage and tried to settle in as best she could; her grades were good, she was quiet and well-behaved, and participated in all activities, but there were times she found herself getting into trouble, just like any other ten-year-old child. When asked about her escapades years later, Marilyn admitted that after some encouragement by the 'tough' children, she agreed to escape from the orphanage by jumping over the hedge. Of course, the escape did not go to plan, and before they knew it, the disgraced youngsters were hauled back into the building.

Chapter 3

'Norma Jeane, Human Bean'

Much has been said about how long Norma Jeane actually lived at the Los Angeles Orphans Home, with most authors agreeing that her stay was around two years, beginning in 1935 and ending in 1937. However, court records show that the last payment made by Grace Goddard to the orphanage was on 21 June 1936, and she had certainly removed Norma Jeane from the home by October 1936, since this is when she started to be paid for her care.

Norma Jeane moved into the Goddard home at 3107 Barbara Court, and after the time spent in the orphanage she revelled in her new family. Grace loved having the child around and, as they were both fans of Jean Harlow, she began to mould Norma Jeane into her idol. Along with her sister, Enid Knebelkamp, Grace encouraged her young charge to consider acting as a future profession, as later recalled by Enid's friend, Catherine Larson: 'Aunt Enid and Aunt Grace always knew Marilyn would make it in Hollywood; they had a sort of quiet certainty about it because they thought she was such a beautiful girl.'

Spurred on by dreams of stardom, Grace would take Norma Jeane to Columbia Studios, where she was working in the film library, and show her off to her co-workers. One of them, Leila Fields, later told biographer Maurice Zolotow that Grace adored Norma Jeane and took her everywhere with her, convincing the child that she would one day be a famous movie star. Fields gave Grace all the credit for Norma Jeane's success and concluded that 'Grace had an obsession about her.'

Another colleague, Olin Gleason Murphy, later recalled: 'Miss McKee would have someone bring a little girl to the lab an hour or so before noontime closing. We workers were introduced to her, and every introduction was the same over and over ... "Baby I want you to meet Olin. Olin this is Norma Jean, isn't she pretty? Norma Jean shake hands with the nice man, fine, now turn around and show the big bow on the back of your dress."' This routine would repeat over and over again, with Grace having the child tell everyone that when she grew up she was going to be a movie star. Murphy described it as 'brainwashing' that continued for the entire time Norma Jeane was with Grace.

The Goddard house on Barbara Court wasn't exactly a dream home, but at least it wasn't the orphanage. Grace bred cocker spaniels and Norma Jeane spent much of her time playing with the animals. Life was once again beginning to settle down into some kind of normality, but money was extremely tight for the Goddard family, and on more than one occasion both Grace and Norma Jeane found themselves waiting in a long line for stale bread. As Doc's daughter Bebe later remembered, 'Daddy was not a very dependable type of character when it came to breadwinning.'

Added to the financial worries were various other stressful events during 1937. In January, Gladys caused concern by escaping from guards whilst being taken from Norwalk State Hospital to Portland, Oregon. The incident was kept secret from Norma Jeane, but did make the pages of the *Los Angeles Times* on 21 January.

Then later in the year came two pieces of sad news. Firstly, Norma Jeane was devastated when her idol, Jean Harlow, died suddenly at the tender age of twenty-six. Then in September 1937, there was tragic news for Grace from Las Vegas.

Her uncle Kirby Willett was about to retire from his Union Pacific railroad job and move with his wife Minnie to a farm near San Diego. He had worked for many years on the railroad and moving from Las Vegas to the quiet countryside of

California was something to which both he and Minnie were looking forward. Unfortunately, during a trip to California on 16 September, Kirby was involved in an automobile accident and killed instantly. Grace and Doc had married at the Willett home in Las Vegas, and when news of Uncle Kirby's death reached Grace she was both shocked and devastated.

The news only contributed to the other problems being experienced by the Goddard family at that time and it wasn't long before Grace took the decision to move both herself and Norma Jeane out of the family home. They moved in with Grace's sister, Enid Knebelkamp, and Norma Jeane became friends with her young daughter, Diane, who later shared her memories with her own daughter, Jo: 'Norma Jeane was very sweet and always nice to my Mom. My Mom said that she was also very smart and the family didn't like that she was portrayed as being a dumb blonde.'

Over the years it has been said that Grace removed the child from her Barbara Court home because Doc Goddard had made a fumbled pass at Norma Jeane when he was drunk. This seems highly unlikely, especially since she returned to the home several years later and kept in touch until Grace Goddard passed away. Almost sixty years later, his daughter Eleanor 'Bebe' Goddard talked to the 'All About Marilyn' fan club about the stories: 'The fact is that my father never touched Marilyn. He was a real lady's man in that he loved women and they loved him, but that was only a big show and I never encountered a more faithful man than my father was to his wives.'

However, in spite of that, there were certainly problems between Doc and Grace, and for the next few months both she and Norma Jeane shuttled back and forth between the Knebelkamp home and that of Grace's Aunt Ana Lower. Doc meanwhile rented a room from Mrs Cora A. French at 920 Hyperion Avenue and listed himself quite ambitiously as a director on official records. Eventually, however, the couple reunited and moved into a home at 6707 Odessa Avenue. This was a positive step for them, but not so for Norma Jeane, who was moved from the Knebelkamp/Lower homes and placed in that of her aunt, Olive Monroe.

Olive Monroe was born Olive Brunings (aka Olyve Brunnings) and married Gladys Baker's brother, Marion Otis Monroe, in San Diego on 20 September 1924. Together they had three children, Jack, Ida Mae and Olive Elizabeth. On 20 November 1929, just over nine months after the birth of their third child, Marion told his wife he was leaving on routine business, but would be back by 6.30 p.m. in time for dinner. He never returned and all attempts to find him failed. Whether Olive believed he had deserted her, or something more sinister had befallen him, is unclear, but eventually she was forced to declare herself destitute and petitioned to have Marion declared dead, in order that she could receive aid from the state.

Although she kept in touch with Gladys, and even travelled with Grace to visit her in the institution, one has to wonder if Olive was entirely convinced when Grace approached her about looking after Norma Jeane. By 1937, Olive was living with her mother, Christian Science practitioner Ida Martin, along with her three children. Being in a negative financial position, perhaps she was consoled with the idea of the $30 per month that she would be paid for caring for Norma Jeane; it would certainly enable her to loosen the purse strings a little. And so it was that Norma Jeane found herself delivered to the home of the Martin/Monroe family on Oxnard Avenue (now Oxnard Street), in December 1937.

From the start it was a tricky situation, with a house full of women and a boisterous twelve-year-old boy, all vying for space and attention. As well as that, Ida's seventy-eight-year-old mother Olive Henderson was also living with the family at the time, which added more stress and reduced the breathing space. The woman was fairly temperamental and Norma Jeane's memories of her consisted of scary tales of the 'old days' and being unfairly accused of tearing one of the other girl's dresses.

As with many of her childhood memories, Marilyn's stories of the Monroe/Martin family were not altogether positive, and she later lamented always being the last in line for the bath, when the water had already turned putrid and cold. She also had vivid memories of Christmas with the family: 'All the children got presents under the tree. I got a 10-cent manicure set and at that period in my life, believe me I didn't have the least interest in my cuticles.'

But it would seem that it definitely wasn't all hardship. Norma Jeane became friends with her cousin Ida Mae, who later remembered that the two of them would get into all kinds of mischief: once, they planned to run away to San Francisco where it was rumoured Marion Monroe had been spotted; and another time they tried to make wine (complete with grape stomping in bare feet), only to discover that all they'd achieved was an intense stench under the front porch. Norma Jeane also felt comfortable enough in Ida Mae's company to confide that she had been molested before she entered the orphanage, and had bathed for days afterwards.

During the time living with her aunt and cousins, Norma Jeane attended the Lankershim School on Bakman Avenue. It was here that she really started to live an imaginary life and dreamed the day away, before taking a long walk home, engrossed in her pretend world: 'I remember a vacant lot that I used to cross on my way home from the Bakman Avenue school in North Hollywood,' she said. 'It was just a dirty old lot overgrown with weeds, but from the moment I stepped on to it, it became a magic and private place where I could be all of the people I had been thinking about all day in the classroom.'

On 3 March 1938, while Norma Jeane was still living with the Monroe/Martins, Los Angeles was hit by a catastrophic natural disaster, when a great flood struck. The floodwater came from the mountains, swirled around the city and its suburbs in the middle of the night and began to recede shortly after dawn, but the damage created had been astronomical. Newspapers estimated $25,000,000 worth of damage, homes were without power and thousands of people found themselves fleeing for their lives from the swollen rivers.

The Martin/Monroe family was, like thousands of others, affected by the floods and had to relocate from their Oxnard Avenue home. Court records state that Ida Martin was paid for Norma Jeane's expenses until August 1938, but when foster sister Bebe Goddard was interviewed by the 'All About Marilyn' club, she claimed that Norma Jeane moved out of the Martin home after the flood, and was placed temporarily into the home of Grace's brother, Bryan Atchinson, his wife, Lottie, and their daughter, Geraldine. 'Uncle Bryan' lived at 1826 East Palmer Avenue but it is probable that while Norma Jeane lived there, the Monroe/Martin family continued to receive payments so they could pick up the pieces after the disaster.

When Norma Jeane moved in with the Atchinson family, she once again changed schools; this time to Vine Street School, which she had attended during her time at the orphanage. But she had hardly had time to settle at all, when in September 1938 Grace moved the child into the permanent care of the woman who was to become the biggest influence of her entire life: Ana Lower.

Edith Ana Lower (known to everyone as Ana) was Grace's paternal aunt and was fifty-eight years old when Norma Jeane came to live with her. She had been married for a time to a gentleman by the name of Edmund H. 'Will' Lower and together they had bought various rental properties, earning them a modest income. By 1938 Ana was divorced, but still earning money from some of the properties, and supplemented her income by working as a Christian Science practitioner. She lived in a two-storey duplex at 11348 Nebraska Avenue, where she occupied the upstairs apartment, while renting out both the unit below and the house next door, and in the mornings she could be seen on the sidewalk, sweeping up the fruit that had fallen from the abundance of fig trees located outside her property. 'She was nice looking; sort of a grandmother type,' remembered friend

Bill Pursel. 'Very alert and kept a nice clean house with no junk lying around.'

When Norma Jeane first pulled up outside Aunt Ana's home, she feared the worst. She had stayed here before, during Grace's marital problems, and presumed this would be just another in a long line of foster homes and foster-mothers. However, from the moment Norma Jeane entered Ana Lower's home, her mood shifted and she discovered 'a wonderful human being' who changed her whole life and gave her more confidence in herself. Aunt Ana provided Norma Jeane with kindness and love; something she had very rarely experienced in the past, and the child revelled in her devotion.

Ana believed wholeheartedly in Christian Science, and in 1935 had travelled up to San Francisco to nurse her sister, Hattie, while she was fighting a losing battle with cancer. A caring soul, Ana passed what she could on to Norma Jeane, and also took her to Christian Science services. As Gladys Baker had practised the religion too, it wasn't totally unfamiliar to Norma Jeane, but she didn't find the religion totally helpful. 'I've read Mrs Eddy [founder of Christian Science and author of *Science and Health, with Key to the Scriptures*] and tried to put some of her ideas into my life, but it doesn't work for me,' Marilyn was later to say.

Unfortunately, almost as soon as she arrived on Ana's doorstep, she also entered puberty, which brought yet more heartache for the young girl. Her periods were so painful that she would often lie on the floor, sobbing in agony. Aunt Ana, who was well over 'the curse', did her best to help Norma Jeane, but to no avail. Being a Christian Scientist, tablets were not an option, so Ana turned to her beliefs in order to bring comfort to the youngster: 'Aunt Ana used to pray with me, but it seems I had such a strong belief in pain that she couldn't overcome it,' Marilyn later recalled. And thus began a lifetime of painful periods and endometriosis, which ruled Marilyn's life until the day she died.

Menstruation aside, Norma Jeane's life with Ana was fairly settled and calm; she worshipped the middle-aged lady who in turn gave her the love and protection she had so often sought. But once again, schooling presented the child with problems, namely the fact that she stuttered quite badly, and only had a very limited wardrobe, of which the children loved to make fun. Attending the seventh grade at Sawtelle School, Norma Jeane made hardly any friends and felt alienated much of the time: 'In school I was very quiet. I was never the life of the party. Everyone talked so glibly; they all knew the latest slang and the smartest stories, and I'd stand around like an idiot – never knowing what to say.' Adding to her feelings of alienation was the fact that she was tall and skinny, making her a talking point with other students. She was cruelly nicknamed 'Norma Jeane, Human Bean' and was labelled as being dumb with no personality. She was extremely hurt when one boy in her class told her, 'I hope some day your legs fill out.' But at least Ana provided a sympathetic ear when she arrived home at night, which is something she had rarely experienced in the past.

In early 1939, Norma Jeane received a letter from Grace, telling her that she had a half-sister called Berniece. Grace had, of course, known about the existence of both Berniece and her late brother Robert for many years, but had not felt that it was her place to tell Norma Jeane. Finally, Grace had received a letter from Berniece to inform her that Gladys had been in touch from Agnew State Hospital, where she was residing at the time. Gladys had told her all about her half-sister Norma Jeane, and begged her eldest daughter to remove her from the institution. Spurred on by this, Berniece (who previously had no idea she had a half-sister and had believed her mother had probably died) contacted Grace, who in turn passed the letter on to Norma Jeane.

The child, who had searched for family stability her whole life, was thrilled to discover she had a sister and wanted to know all about her. Berniece had been married on 7 October 1938 to Paris Miracle, and having settled into married life in Pineville, Kentucky, was now pregnant with her first child. Grace immediately wrote a long letter to Berniece, passing on news of Norma

Jeane, and revealing that it had always been Gladys' wish to have her children with her. Norma Jeane then wrote herself, enclosing a photograph and thus beginning an important relationship, which would last until her death some twenty-three years later.

Meanwhile, on hearing of Berniece's existence, Grace's mind went into overtime, and she wondered whether Norma Jeane could possibly move in with her new sister. However, there were two problems with this plan: firstly, Gladys had always vetoed any idea of Norma Jeane leaving the state of California, and secondly, Berniece had neither money nor room to accommodate another child. Later Grace saw this for herself when she made a pitstop in Pineville during a trip to West Virginia.

A year after she arrived at Ana's house, Norma Jeane changed schools once again, and although she flunked arithmetic, she did do well in English and literature, once writing a paper on Abraham Lincoln, which was judged the best in the class. This seemingly small achievement was a great boost for Norma Jeane's confidence and suddenly the child didn't feel so dumb any more. Added to that, her once skinny body had begun to fill out, which attracted the attentions of some of her fellow students: 'The boys didn't have cars, they had bikes. They'd come by the house and whistle or they'd honk their little horns. Some had paper routes and I'd always get a free paper.'

While Norma Jeane did enjoy most of the attention, some was certainly unwanted and unnecessary. On the way home from school one day, she noticed an older boy standing on the corner, who started shouting obscene remarks as she passed. Hoping it would be a one-off occurrence she ignored him and made her way home. Unfortunately, the next day he was there again, and before long he was harassing Norma Jeane to such an extent that she told an older friend that she found the whole thing intimidating and rather scary. The problem was eventually solved with the help of a friendly storekeeper and a local policeman. 'The fellow was let go with a stern warning,' recalled her future sister-in-law Elyda Nelson, 'and after that Norma Jeane went her way with no one molesting her in the neighbourhood.'

Soon boys were walking her home from school, and they would often stand and talk outside Aunt Ana's home. Other kids would come along, and soon there would be a large crowd gathered on the pavement, eventually to be ushered into the house by Aunt Ana, joking that they were 'starting to resemble a mob'.

The new attention spurred Norma Jeane on to have her first – albeit inappropriate – crush on a twenty-two-year-old man who lived across the street, who would often say hello and pat her on the head. One day, while Norma Jeane was outside Aunt Ana's home, the man came past on his way to the movies. Asking if she'd like to go with him, Norma Jeane couldn't believe her luck and after gaining permission from Aunt Ana, hopped into the car for what she thought would be a romantic date. She immediately tried (and failed) to act in a sophisticated manner, later commenting, 'I was gawky, I was giggly, I was stupid,' and after laughing at his driving technique, opening her own door and falling over herself on the way into the theatre, the young man drove her home, in no mood to ask her out again. (It is generally believed that this man was actually soon-to-be actor Howard Keel, who she went on to date for a short time in the late 1940s.)

Norma Jeane's confidence took a severe downturn after the failure of her first crush, and wasn't made any better when some of the girls at school made a point of commenting on the fact that her clothes weren't as pretty and up-to-date as theirs. One day she returned home in tears because of a cruel comment from one of the other girls, and Aunt Ana sat her down to console and inspire her: 'It doesn't matter if other children make fun of your clothes or where you live,' she said. 'It's what you are that counts. You just keep being your own self, that's all that matters.'

Aunt Ana's inspirational talks – which mainly consisted of telling the child not to worry about what others thought of her, to take things as they come and to work hard at the things she wanted to accomplish – slowly but surely helped to inspire confidence in Norma Jeane. Before long, she was wearing make-up to school, which helped give her the confidence to say yes when schoolmates asked her on dates. 'And that way I sort of slid painlessly into going out,' she later said.

Norma Jeane became very fond of the actress Ginger Rogers and was given photos of her by a girl who lived across the street. She decided that she wanted to be just like Ginger and, to her amazement, Aunt Ana not only tolerated the notion, but also encouraged her to read lines aloud, while never criticizing her fledgling talent. 'She was most tolerant of my big ambition of being an actress,' Marilyn later said.

Unfortunately for Norma Jeane, Aunt Ana was in failing health, but cared too much to allow her to worry, and tried to carry on as best she could. 'She was a gentle woman in her sixties, very dignified and wise,' recalled Marilyn. 'She had heart trouble but she never told me about it.' Instead, Ana continued her inspirational talks, but began adding theories on how loneliness wasn't the worst thing in the world, and urging Norma Jeane to always be herself and stand on her own two feet. 'I didn't realize that she was preparing me for her death,' Marilyn later said.

Eventually it became clear that no matter how willing Aunt Ana's heart was, her body just wasn't up to the strains of raising a child, and a new home would have to be found for Norma Jeane. The Bolender family had continued to visit the child, but it was not possible for her to go back to them. Instead, in February 1940, it was determined that Norma Jeane would move in once again with guardian and former foster-mother Grace and her husband Doc Goddard.

By the time Norma Jeane arrived at the Goddard home at 14743 Archwood Street, Doc's daughter, Bebe had moved in with the family. Bebe had suffered a distinctly unhappy childhood featuring foster homes and a mentally unstable mother, so the two children immediately had much in common.

She settled into Emerson Junior High. Many years later, archivist Roy Turner interviewed several of her classmates, with most looking back on their time with Norma Jeane in a positive light. There was one comment that kept recurring throughout the interviews, though, and that was the aura of loneliness about her: 'I did not see her too often in school,' remembered Marian Losman, 'but when I did she seemed alone.' Ron Underwood remembered: 'She was somewhat shy and withdrawn, and seemingly had few friends,' while Tom Ishii said, 'She was alone most of the time.'

There were also memories of her 'plain clothes' and the 'powder blue suit that she wore often', but this all changed when Norma Jeane very suddenly started to bloom. She began to take a keen interest in her hair and clothes, and was instructed by Grace in the art of make-up and grooming. Together Norma Jeane and Bebe spent many hours designing clothes and hair-styles; some of the designs she sent to her half-sister, Berniece, while others Bebe kept with her for the rest of her life. Her social life was beginning to hot up, too: she joined the Emerson Girls Glee Club, and also became firm friends with Bob Stotts, Betty Duggen and Bill Heison, who were a year older than her at school.

Stotts met Norma Jeane shortly after she began at Emerson Junior High, when the books and papers she was holding were carried off in a gust of wind. The two kids got talking and it wasn't long before they were hanging out together, going on various excursions, playing Monopoly at the Stotts home, and talking with Bob's mother, Dorothy Muir.

'She was a sweet person,' remembers Bob Stotts, 'well-liked and very thoughtful. No one ever said anything bad about her; she was a happy child and I never saw her cry or be moody at all. I can remember several occasions when our crowd would come over to my house to dance and have a snack after school. Norma Jeane would help my mother with the dishes before she joined the rest of us to dance. She loved to dance and was very good at it.'

Norma Jeane took it upon herself to teach the boys all the latest dance moves – often to tunes such as 'Begin the Beguine' – and would often collapse in a fit of non-offensive giggles when they got it wrong. In fact giggling was something she did often in their presence, as Stotts' mother, Dorothy, remembered in 1973: 'She was never rude, always nice. I would describe her as being quiet and reticent but no matter what you said to her, she would giggle.'

She was also prone to embarrassment: 'Norma Jeane would stub her toes verbally on more things in two minutes than you could think of in a year, and then she would blush like mad,' remembered Dorothy. 'I won't say that she lived at our house during the years we knew her, but she was there every chance she got.'

On 25 February 1940 Norma Jeane, Betty Duggen and Bill Heison travelled to Green Valley Lake with the Stotts/Muir family, where they were all photographed playing in the snow. The trip was not without incident, however, when on the way home a large rock came hurtling down the mountainside and crashed into the middle of the car's bonnet. Norma Jeane was sitting in the 'rumble' seat at the back of the car at the time, and when told by Dorothy Muir how close they had come to being killed by debris, Norma Jeane laughed. 'My head's too hard,' she said. 'That old rock would have bounced right off and wouldn't have left a dent.'

As winter turned to spring, more outings were held, this time out to the desert to see the wild flowers. Dorothy Muir remembered Norma Jeane picking a huge bouquet and holding on to it 'as she might have held an infant'. 'I never saw anything so lovely,' Norma Jeane told Dorothy. Her love of flowers is confirmed by later boyfriend Bill Pursel who remembered she loved watching them blow in the wind, and always commented on how 'free' they looked.

Now that she was settling into her new life, Grace promised Norma Jeane that she would never again have to worry about stability; that there would always be a home for her with the Goddard family. Grace would listen intently as Norma Jeane told her foster-mother anything that was on her mind, and as her trust grew, the teenager became close to the entire family.

She enjoyed many family get-togethers and started spending more time with Grace's sister and brother-in-law, Enid and Sam Knebelkamp. She was later filmed trying on a new fur coat and posing with other family members outside the Knebelkamp home.

'As far as I can see, she was well treated and happy,' remembered Bob Stotts, while his mother added, 'Norma Jeane spent her teen years in a very good neighbourhood environment with an adult who was just as concerned for her welfare as any parent might be.'

The house on Archwood Street, where Norma Jeane had settled with Grace and Doc, backed on to the home of the Dougherty family, who were very close friends with the Goddards. Ethel Dougherty could often be seen chatting over the back fence with Grace, and the two of them enjoyed many a plan and scheme over the years. Ethel's son was a strapping young man called Jim, who was five years older than Norma Jeane, and considered both Bebe and Norma Jeane as just kids who weren't particularly interesting in any way.

At the time, Jim was dating a young woman called Doris Drennen, the 1940 May Queen of Santa Barbara County. She had met him while living with her sister Joan and brother-in-law John Ingram, who also happened to be Jim Dougherty's teacher at Van Nuys High School. She remembers: 'Norma Jeane was a couple of years younger than me. After school she would come over to Jimmy's house and wait for her foster-mother to pick her up after she got off work. I would see her when Jimmy and I would stop by for Jimmy to change clothes or retrieve something. I usually stayed in the car and waited for him to return. She would be playing ball by herself in front of Jimmy's house. She'd bounce the ball then throw it in the air and catch it, peek at me then throw it again.'

Neither girl knew it at the time, but Doris would become quite a sore point for Norma Jeane during the next few years. It all started during 1941, when the Goddards decided to move into a bigger home at 6707 Odessa Street, where they had lived in the late 1930s. Grace and Doc quickly went about doing the place up, and eventually took photos of their work, showing a comfortable home with a large dining table, rocking chair, piano, many books, a china cabinet and floor-length mirror. In September 1941, Norma Jeane and foster-sister Bebe enrolled as students at Van Nuys High School. This proved a bit of a problem regarding transport, so Grace, who was still in contact with Ethel Dougherty, asked her friend if Jim could run the girls home from school in the evening. He reluctantly agreed and it was arranged that Bebe and Norma Jeane would walk from Van Nuys High to the Dougherty house, where they would wait for Jim to take them home.

The first time this happened, Jim was sleeping in preparation for the 'graveyard shift' at Lockheed, where he worked. When Norma Jeane and Bebe arrived, they were so noisy they woke up the exasperated Jim, who immediately told them off. However, Norma Jeane's apologetic reaction to his outburst won him over, and he found it impossible to be angry with the girls any more.

Shortly before this, Jim had proposed to his girlfriend, Doris, who turned him down immediately. Jim later said she had told him he wouldn't be able to keep her in the manner to which she wanted to become accustomed and the relationship came to an end. However, Jim's heartbreak was Norma Jeane's delight, and she decided to try her hand at flirting with the handsome older boy. During their car rides she would make a point of always sitting in the middle; touching Jim's knee as she laughed at his jokes. Indeed, it got so intense that Bebe would often feel completely left out of the proceedings: 'As I recall, there was quite a flirtation when Jimmy was bringing us home from school,' she later told the 'All About Marilyn' fan club.

These flirtations eventually led to a first date for the couple, which was 'encouraged' by Grace Goddard and Ethel Dougherty and took place at the Christmas party of Doc's company, Adel Precision Products. There they danced together and Jim was surprised to discover he was having a good time, while Norma Jeane seemed to enjoy herself too and leaned in close during the

slow dances. They began to date, but although both held each other in high regard and enjoyed going out together, Jim worried about the five-year age gap between them. The relationship was in danger of fizzling out, just as a devastating announcement came from the Goddards: they had plans to leave California and move to West Virginia – and would not be taking Norma Jeane with them.

Chapter 4

Mrs Dougherty

When Grace and Doc decided to move out of California, they approached Sam and Enid Knebelkamp to ask if they would be willing to take Norma Jeane into their home. Understandably, however, they had their hands full with their own daughter and had to turn the proposition down. Several other plans also fell through and eventually – feeling the need for a quick solution – Grace approached her neighbour Ethel Dougherty about the possibility of Jim marrying Norma Jeane.

Knowing how upset Jim had been when his relationship with Doris Drennen had ended, Ethel believed that a marriage to Norma Jeane would be a good alternative and spoke to her son about it. Unfortunately for her, however, he laughed off the suggestion, declaring that their relationship wasn't serious and, besides, he felt that she was far too young to be marriage material.

But when Ethel explained that Grace was worried Norma Jeane would have to return to the orphanage, he showed a glimmer of interest in 'saving her'; so much so that before he could change his mind, Ethel excitedly announced, 'Let's set it up for June.'

Some people have insisted that the entire courtship and marriage were only executed because of the 'arrangement' between Grace and Ethel Dougherty, but others insist that the couple did have a lot of feelings for each other and would have probably married at some point anyway.

'The idea of an arranged marriage almost made him vomit!' remembers Paul Kanteman, Jim's nephew. 'Yes there was an introduction and maybe a little push in that direction, but he would not allow anyone to push him into anything, let alone marriage. Believe me, he would never have gotten married to her if he hadn't had great feelings for her. He wasn't the worst looking guy on the block, and could get just about anybody he wanted or pursued.' Indeed, Jim later admitted enjoying being thought of as Norma Jeane's 'Knight in Shining Armour' and agreed to save her from the orphanage.

When Marilyn spoke of the marriage years later, she never mentioned Jim as a knight in shining armour. Instead, she always spoke without emotion, saying that the Goddards could not afford to take her to Virginia, so, 'Instead of going back into a boarding house or with another set of foster-parents, I got married.' She also declared that 'it brought me neither happiness nor pain. It was like being retired to a zoo.'

It is true that Norma Jeane felt tremendously let down and abandoned by Grace Goddard and despised the idea of going back to the orphanage, so marriage was the better option at the time. However, Jim later insisted that they were genuinely happy with each other, and fell more and more in love every day. If Norma Jeane had any feelings to the contrary, she kept them well hidden but did admit to worrying that her future husband might be marrying her out of duty or obligation.

The couple went out shopping for a ring and, to Jim's amazement, Norma Jeane insisted on a cheaper one than the ring he originally picked out. They returned to the Dougherty home to break the news that they were officially engaged, and Norma Jeane appeared extremely happy to other members of the family. Nevertheless, during a family picnic at Lake Sherwood, she was unusually pensive, despite Jim serenading her with his guitar. 'Her only contribution to the fun was a quiet smile of pride – and six lemon pies,' recalled sister-in-law Elyda Nelson.

Jim and Norma Jeane began dating regularly, and spent time with each other at the beach, hiking in the Hollywood Hills, boating at Pop's Willow Lake and fishing at Lake Sherwood. It was at the lake that she first spent time with Jim's nephew, Paul

Kanteman, who was around eight years old at the time: 'As I remember, I thought she was very pretty and nice. We had a row boat and Norma Jeane rowed while we fished. She did do a good job of rowing, and we caught some nice bass.'

Norma Jeane wanted to finish high school, 'but I discovered that school and marriage don't mix. We were poor, so naturally my job was to keep house on the lowest possible budget.' She made arrangements to leave University High School, but when she told her social studies teacher, he exclaimed that she would ruin her life if she got married, insisting she probably didn't even know what love was. It was this decision, to leave school before graduation, which would plague her for the rest of her life. She lied about it in interviews, claiming she graduated after her marriage, and forever tried to 'catch up' with her education by attended courses and paying for private tuition. But in the summer of 1942, the decision was made and she left full-time education, shortly before her marriage, to concentrate on becoming Mrs Dougherty.

The wedding preparations were hastily but lavishly prepared and the couple received various items from friends and family, including a coffee set, gold-coloured vases, bath towels, wash cloths, embroidered dish towels and: 'The most beautiful cocktail set I have ever seen in my life . . . It is really beautiful.' The ceremony was to take place at 432 South Bentley, the home of Chester and Doris Howell, which had been picked out because Norma Jeane loved the idea of a ceremony based around the large, winding staircase. Aunt Ana busied herself with the dress, while Norma Jeane picked out the wedding rings, and notices appeared in the local paper. Even one of the younger members of the family, Paul Kanteman, had lots to do on the run-up to the big day: 'A couple of weeks before the event my Mother and I went to Shulman's Men's store in Van Nuys to buy me some clothes that would be fitting for a ring bearer: a new pair of black pants, white shirt and black, shiny shoes. I remember going to school and telling all the kids that my Uncle was going to marry the most beautiful girl in the world and that I was to be their ring bearer. We had a rehearsal and I was taught how to do the hesitation step and how to hold the pillow that would have the ring pinned to it. I practiced that step all the time so that it would be just right and my Uncle Jim would be proud of me. If my mother asked me to do something, it was always to the hesitation beat – I'm sure everyone was glad when it was all over and my productivity level returned to full-time!'

Norma Jeane had been keen to live with her in-laws once the marriage had taken place, but on 8 June 1942 the couple found and leased a furnished apartment at 4524 Vista Del Monte and, according to Paul Kanteman, they were the first to live there. 'It was small but nice,' he remembered. 'It had a small bedroom, living room, bathroom and a tiny kitchen; so tiny that if you were to turn around too quickly, you might stick your own finger in your eye!'

Tiny or not, it would be home for Mr and Mrs Dougherty, and Norma Jeane was so proud of it that she later drew a detailed floor plan and mailed it to Aunt Grace. 'We sure have a cute little house,' she wrote. 'I'm going to take a picture of it and send it to you.' Watching Norma Jeane take such pleasure in preparing her new home made Jim realize just how much he loved her. 'I sometimes thought my heart would burst. She was everything to me,' he wrote.

On 19 June 1942 at precisely 8.30 p.m., Norma Jeane glided down the winding staircase to be given in marriage by Aunt Ana. She looked every bit the blushing bride, shaking with nerves and dressed in an embroidered lace gown with long sleeves, full skirt and sweetheart neckline; her veil was white lace and she carried a bouquet of white gardenias.

Neither Gladys nor the Goddards were in attendance, but Mrs Bolender was there, at the insistence of the bride. Jim's sister Elyda remembered her as 'a docile and subdued little person, her pride and devotion cast a glow of warmth over the whole event'. Aunt Ana played the music whilst Jim's brother Marion was best man and Lorraine Allen, a friend from University High, was Norma Jeane's Maid of Honour. Also present were

Joan and John Ingram, sister and brother-in-law of Jim's ex-girl-friend Doris Drennen. Doris later recalled: 'My sister Joan knew Norma Jeane better than I did. One time she told me that Norma Jeane was clever in using the two assets she had, her figure and her pretty face. Both would get her ahead in life.'

In all the wedding ceremony went without a hitch, and immediately afterwards there was a small celebration at the home of the Howells. This arrangement had caused some tension just days before the big day, as Elyda Nelson recalled: 'Someone brought up the question of who would give the reception after the wedding. Norma Jeane spoke up promptly and said, "The bride's parents are supposed to take care of that." "I know dear," one of the catty feminine neighbours said, "but you have no parents." The look of sadness Norma Jeane gave me I'll never forget, and to this day I detest the thought of that offending woman.'

After the reception, Jim's brother Marion thought it would be funny to 'kidnap' Norma Jeane and force both her and Jim to go to the Florentine Gardens, a nightclub on Hollywood Boulevard. This too caused tension, however, when a waiter accidentally spilled soup all over Jim, and then he was persuaded to dance on stage with a chorus girl, much to Norma Jeane's chagrin.

Years later, Jim reflected on the evening and decided that possibly Norma Jeane was looking for a reason to argue with him, as she was not looking forward to their wedding night. Plagued with insecurities, she had asked Grace Goddard if it were possible to 'just be friends' with her husband, and had ploughed through a sex education book given to her by Aunt Ana. Neither the talk nor the book made her feel any more confident, however, and on the wedding night itself, she spent a long time locked in the bathroom.

Although Norma Jeane tried her hand at cooking – baking bread every other day and experimenting on her new relatives – her lack of skills soon became very apparent: she put salt in Jim's coffee by mistake, and famously cooked carrots and peas just because she liked the colour. Things were made worse by the fact that Jim's brothers, Tom and Marion, had thought it a good idea to stock the newlywed's cupboards with food. Unfortunately, the kindly gesture wasn't all it was cracked up to be, as Paul Kantcman remembered some sixty years later: 'They decided stocking the cupboards would be a great wedding present, as Uncle Jim and Aunt Norma would surely appreciate this. These guys were practical jokers and took all the labels off every item on the shelf. A lot of cans look alike as far as size is concerned, especially when they are undressed. Aunt Norma asked me to have lunch with her at the new house, and it was like a treasure hunt, shaking this can and that can until we found one that sounded right. We were going to have tuna salad sandwiches that day, but the can of tuna turned out to be water-chestnuts, and the peas turned out to be fruit cocktail! So when I say the lunch was different it really was, but Aunt Norma kept a stiff upper lip and laughed about it.'

At age sixteen, Norma Jeane had gone from a footloose young girl to a married woman in just a few short months. She quickly learned how to keep a clean, tidy house, and often spent time gossiping over the back fence with the other neighbours on the street. 'It really keeps me busy cleaning the house and fixing meals,' she wrote to Grace Goddard on 14 September 1942. 'Everybody told me that it is quite a responsibility being a house-wife and boy, I'm finding it out. But it really is a lot of fun.'

Fun it may have been, but the emotional upheaval of being married at such a young age was huge. Neither Jim nor Norma Jeane knew how to react in an argument, and she once went tearing out of the house in her nightclothes after a fight, only to be followed by a stranger in the street. On another occasion Norma Jeane furiously hit Jim over the head with a trashcan, after he'd criticized the fact that she'd mistakenly fed him raw fish. Jim tried to cool her off in the shower, only to find that this made her even more irate and he was forced to walk the streets until she had calmed down.

She also struggled with a lack of life-skills: she divided a bottle of scotch between four people; threw a cup of coffee over a sparking electrical socket; and she didn't like nor understand the jokes told by Dougherty's friends. Although he didn't mean to hurt Norma Jeane's feelings, Jim made the mistake of mocking her naivety and later reflected that he perhaps teased her too much. 'I think my teasing was the one thing that made her unhappy during our marriage,' he said. 'I was young myself and didn't know very much about how to treat a woman.'

Of course, Norma Jeane wasn't Jim's first serious partner, as he had been in a relationship with Doris Drennen for a long time before that. Since Norma Jeane had not had a serious boyfriend before, this 'other woman' bothered her considerably, as she later wrote to Grace Goddard: 'Doris Drenen [*sic*] is Jim's ex – remember? I remember only too well.'

Doris was unaware of the jealousy, however, as she recalled seventy years later: 'The few times I saw her I would describe her as insecure and lonely, but truthfully I didn't give her much thought. At that time her hair was more or less like mine, brown with blonde highlights from the Southern California sun, like a dishwater blonde. I was nineteen at the time and I was old enough to be rather sure of myself when it came to boys. I had no idea that she was jealous of me, if she really was.'

Norma Jeane held the grudge towards Jim's ex-girlfriend for quite some time, though she really needn't have worried, as by December 1942 Doris was married to Lieutenant George Grandstaff McCann Jr and would stay with him until his death in 1984. However, Norma Jeane wasn't the only one prone to jealousy, as witnessed by Bob Stotts, who hadn't seen his friend since she'd started dating Jim Dougherty: 'I ran into Norma Jeane on the street for the first time in several years. She invited me home to meet her aunt, but when we got there the aunt wasn't there. I stayed and we sat in the room – her on one side and me on the other – when suddenly the front door almost came off its hinges and there was Jim Dougherty, obviously expecting to see something not right. I met with him very briefly but then said I had to go, and quickly left.'

But in spite of the couple's petty jealousies, the marriage did provide Norma Jeane with a stable and secure relationship. She clung to that idea ferociously, calling her new husband 'Daddy' and dramatically threatening to jump from the Santa Monica Pier if things ever went wrong between them. Her insecurities ran high and when Jim worked the graveyard shift at Lockheed, he never told her how dangerous the job was, for fear of how it would affect her. As it was, if he forgot to kiss her goodbye she would think she had done something wrong, and if she forgot to hide a small note in his lunchbox, she would apologize profusely when he returned.

'Jimmy is so swell to me,' she wrote at the time. 'In fact I know that if I had waited five or ten years I couldn't have found anyone who would have treated me better.'

Norma Jeane saw to it that she placed her husband's interests above her own, and although she never liked to fish or hunt, she went along with Jim on hunting expeditions, learning to shoot a rifle that he had given to her as a present. Interestingly, his ex-girlfriend Doris Drennen had done the same: 'Jimmy was always gentle and kind to me, but I would describe him as the "rugged type"; a man's man. In high school he played football and was a star. He loved to hunt and shoot guns; he taught me how to shoot and [brother-in-law and sister] John and Joan would go hunting with us. I never really cared for that type of life style and somehow I can't think of Norma Jeane as a hunting- shooting type either but she probably went along with it in order to fit in. I know I did.'

James Dougherty later remembered the interests he and Norma Jeane enjoyed together: 'On a weekend we might go to a ranch in Lancaster called "Marcotti's"; they grew alfalfa for cattle and we would hunt rabbits until we became sleepy and then curl up in the front seat of our Ford and sleep. Then sometimes we would pack a lunch and go to Lake Sherwood; rent a boat and row out on to the lake and fish. We always caught enough fish for a meal – we enjoyed the fresh air and the sunshine. For a night out it would be the movies or once in a great while the

Coconut Grove where we dined and danced. Then there was Gobel's Lion Farm in Thousand Oaks; that's where a lion peed on Norma and she was mortified. We would visit the farm when they fed the lions and boy did they roar!'

Norma Jeane bonded well with Jim's family and although Marion Dougherty was too much of a tease for her to form a real bond with him, Paul Kanteman remembered that they 'got along just fine and she thought he was pretty funny'. She loved Jim's brother Tom, and Jim later remarked that she thought his father was 'the greatest guy in the world'. Paul Kanteman agrees with this prognosis: 'When Grandpa met Norma Jeane he thought she was a treasure and the feelings were mutual. From their first meeting there was an attraction for each other that made a bond that was as if they had been together since birth. Maybe she was like a granddaughter to him and her feelings seemed to be the same towards him. She looked up to him and respected all that he said. They were great friends from the first meeting.'

In Autumn 1942 Norma Jeane attended a baby shower for Nellie Atkinson, daughter of former foster-parents George and Maude. 'She got so many lovely things and I had such a nice time,' Norma Jeane later wrote.

She also spent time with Jim's sister: 'She was the most beautiful little creature I had ever seen,' Elyda later said. 'Not only did she have beauty, but everything else it takes to make a lady. I loved her from the beginning.' Jim would always take Norma Jeane to visit on Sundays, and as time went on, Jim's young wife and Elyda spent more and more time together: 'During the first year, Norma Jeane came to my home many times, to play with my son, Larry. "My first baby has to be a boy," she told me. She was wonderfully kind and patient with me while I was carrying my little Denny, who was two weeks overdue. At the time I was staying with my mother in Van Nuys, so Norma Jeane stayed with me during the day, and Jim picked her up at night.'

When the baby was eventually born, Norma Jeane helped look after him, and as a result she became extremely fond of all Elyda's children, as Paul Kanteman remembered: 'Aunt Ana was a Christian Scientist and Norma Jeane went along with their teachings and practices. I remember one incident that related to my brother who at the time was a baby about ten or eleven months and had become very ill with Scarletina and bronchial pneumonia. He was in very bad condition and Aunt Norma and Aunt Ana both went to work on him in prayer and whatever else they do, and he recovered. He is now retired and is about 6 foot 3 so I guess something worked.'

The first Christmas spent as a married couple was almost certainly spent at the home of Jim's parents, which was the biggest of all the Dougherty homes. It was always the gathering spot for family get-togethers and holidays, and was a haven of fun and music. Paul Kanteman remembered: 'My grandfather played the fiddle, guitar, banjo and chorded piano, while my mother played the fiddle and a little violin and sang. Aunt Norma would just sit there with her eyes glued on Uncle Jim when he would sing a love song to her or some cute holiday song that was directed to her. She would occasionally join in and sing a little but as I recall would rather just watch.'

In January 1943 the lease on the Vista Del Monte apartment ran out at the same time as Jim's parents were out of town. As a result, the couple moved into the Dougherty family home at 14747 Archwood Street, which they shared with Jim's brother Tom. It was during this time that Norma Jeane received news that was to change the course of her life forever. Gladys decided it was time for Norma Jeane to discover who her father was, and sometime between September 1942 and February 1943, she was informed. Jim Dougherty later remembered: 'Her mother told Grace that Stanley Gifford was her father, and Grace told my mother, who told Norma Jeane.' The young woman was bowled over by this news, and on 16 February 1943, she wrote excitedly to Grace, sharing her plans to visit Mr Gifford as soon as possible, and declaring that the discovery of her father had made her a new person. 'It's something I have to look forward to,' she told her former foster-mother.

Norma Jeane was determined that Gifford would be pleased to see her, so when a friend read her fortune and predicted that they would successfully meet, she became even more excited. But when she finally found the confidence to contact him by telephone, it was all in vain. Jim Dougherty remembered: 'She called him and he hung up on her. It took a lot of tender loving care to bring her out of the disappointment.'

Shortly after this incident, in spring 1943, the couple moved into a new home, this time located at 14223 Bessemer Street. During Norma Jeane's stay at this house, she was particularly distressed one day to notice a cow standing out in the rain. As Dougherty arrived home, he was shocked to see his wife trying desperately to pull the creature into the house and even more surprised when she asked him to help. Jim's nephew Wes Kanteman remembers: 'The cow was a young Jersey Heffer that had beautiful eyes and Norma Jeane used to stand by her pen and just stare at her, remarking at how pretty she was. Then the torrential rain came one night and the cow was standing by the fence and Norma Jeane apparently thought she wanted in so she opened the gate and was going to bring her into the house. After much conversation about the matter, Uncle Jim convinced her that she really belonged in her pen and Norma Jeane finally gave in and it was over, but she still thought that the cow would have been better off in the living room!'

Wet cows aside, the couple settled nicely into their home, until the Second World War prompted Jim to leave his employment at Lockheed to do something for his country. He decided to join the merchant marines and was sent to San Diego for basic training, before moving to Catalina Island to take up the post of physical instructor at the Maritime Service Training Base. It was just a short time later that Norma Jeane joined her husband in a $35-a-month hillside apartment (possibly 323 Metropole Avenue, Avalon), which boasted a living room, bathroom and kitchen.

Life on the island was idyllic in many ways: 'We had a very normal life,' Jim later recalled. 'Norma cooked and cleaned and

I was the breadwinner.' She also spent time shopping at local stores, and wrote to her sister, Berniece, urging her to move to the island too. She would spend hours washing her hair and face, and gave just as much attention to her dog, Muggsie, whom she adored: 'She spent hours bathing him, grooming him, teaching him tricks,' remembered Elyda Nelson. 'They were inseparable when Jim was not home.'

In the evenings, the couple would sit on the porch and make plans for the future, or Jim would play guitar and sing; sometimes they invited friends around to dance to tunes on their new record player. 'We would visit the beach and swim or skin dive for abalone and bosters or just lay in the sun,' Dougherty later remembered. His nephew, Paul Kanteman, confirms this: 'Norma Jeane thought it was really something that her guy could disappear into the Pacific Ocean and come up with something on his spear for dinner that evening.' Unfortunately, watching Jim dive wasn't the only thing that interested Norma Jeane, who revelled in the attention given to her by the other men on the beach. Understandably Jim didn't appreciate this half as much, especially when one of the lifeguards took an overly keen interest in his wife.

The attention Norma Jeane received whilst at the beach – any beach – was recalled by Grace Goddard's great niece, Jo Olmstead: 'I do remember that my Mom [Diane Knebelkamp] said Norma Jeane took her to the beach a few times and that she was so beautiful the boys just stared at her.'

At Christmas 1943, a dance was held at the Catalina Casino, which Norma Jeane had visited ten years before during a rare trip with her mother. The evening was not a success, however, as Jim became upset with the comments and dance requests from male admirers aimed at his young wife. Eventually he'd had enough and told Norma Jeane that they were going to leave. 'Well I will come back as soon as you're asleep,' she threatened, but Jim stood firm; she could come home with him now or not at all. They returned home together.

Although Jim was keen to start a family, Norma Jeane did not share his enthusiasm. She questioned her sister-in-law about child-rearing, and despite telling her that she certainly wanted to have a baby one day, the idea of becoming a parent terrified her. This fear of childbirth was sparked during her upbringing with Grace Goddard. The women in her family had a long history of problems, miscarriages and still births, and Grace's sister, Allis Atchinson, was the only one who'd had any living children. Unfortunately, she was to die herself in 1931 whilst giving birth to her daughter, Diane.

'Allis already had one child,' remembered Diane's daughter, Jo Olmstead, 'but was warned by her doctor that it would be dangerous for her to become pregnant again. She desperately wanted a child though, and it resulted in her death.' The child's father gave permission for Allis' elder sister, Enid Knebelkamp, to adopt the child and forever more the death of Allis would add to the sorrow and fear that had haunted the Atchinson women for many years.

According to Catherine Larson, friend and neighbour of Enid Knebelkamp, the entire family – including Norma Jeane – talked endlessly about the subject of death in childbirth. 'That whole family positively had a terror of – an obsession with – death in childbirth. I've never seen any other family like it!' Catherine later said. Catherine's friend, James Glaeg, recalled: 'Enid Knebelkamp lived in constant fear of death in childbirth, and Catherine told me it was discussed on innumerable occasions with Marilyn/Norma Jeane.'

'I don't remember that fear was specifically discussed but rather sorrow,' recalled Jo Olmstead. 'I have no doubt that these things were discussed with Norma Jeane; my mother and grandma Enid discussed them with me when I was a young child. I can certainly understand why Norma Jeane would fear childbirth.'

This is reinforced by Jim Dougherty, who remembered that Norma Jeane was always lukewarm to the idea of having a baby, and at one point became hysterical when her period was late and she mistakenly thought she might be pregnant. However, when Jim was told he would have to leave Catalina in order to fight for his country, Norma Jeane suddenly became scared of being alone, and uncharacteristically begged him to make her pregnant. This time, however, it was Jim who was against the idea, worried that if he didn't return from war, she would be left with a child to raise on her own.

Concerned about leaving his young wife, Jim arranged for her to stay with his parents while he was away. On the day he left, Norma Jeane presented him with an expensive watch (which she had used their entire savings to buy), before going to visit her sister-in-law Elyda. As she walked up the path, an admirer in a convertible wolf-whistled, causing her to explode with fury: 'Move on old man,' she yelled. 'Go pick on somebody nearer your own age.'

That night there was a family meeting between the Dougherty parents and siblings, and Norma Jeane asked if mother-in-law Ethel could get her a job at Radioplane, a company which made target planes for Air Corps gunnery practice. Ethel worked as a nurse there and agreed to try her best for her daughter-in-law, who couldn't bear the idea of endless hours of inactivity.

True to her word, on 18 April 1944, Ethel got her a job at the factory, as a typist. It didn't go quite to plan though, as Marilyn later recalled: 'I only did 35 words a minute and didn't do them very well, so they gave me a job inspecting parachutes.' Unfortunately, that didn't last long either: 'They quit letting us girls do that and they had the parachutes inspected on the outside but I don't think it was because of my inspecting.'

They moved her over to spraying parachutes, which her mother-in law objected to immediately, as Elyda later recalled: 'I remember Mom bawling her out for working in the paint shop. "Honey," she said, "you'll ruin your beautiful hair – and all those fumes – it's just not good for your health." But Norma Jeane persisted, even though she came home looking a wreck.'

Regardless of any health concerns she may have had, Norma Jeane worked ten hours a day and was on her feet the entire time. Still, she became a popular and trusted member of the team; she was rated above average by her managers, admired by her male co-workers and, in July 1944, she was even crowned Queen of the Radioplane picnic, winning a $50 war bond and a mention in the 15 July edition of the *Radioplane Static*. Then on 31 August she was mentioned once again after winning a gold button for making a useful suggestion with respect to plant operations.

But despite her popularity with male colleagues, she remained faithful to her husband, as Elyda Nelson later wrote: 'Naturally Norma Jeane was aware that other wives and sweethearts dated while their men were away, but she never did. Furthermore, she never gossiped about these situations nor would she listen to gossip.'

Although living with her in-laws couldn't have been the easiest of situations, she seemed to accept life at the Hermitage Street house, and would often have morning coffee with her mother-in-law, before going shopping together later in the day. Still close to her new nephews, Norma Jeane was pleased when she heard that Paul Kanteman was coming for an extended visit, and over sixty years later he remembered the week with great affection: 'We hadn't seen each other for a while and I really did miss her. Grandma asked me if I would like to spend a week or so with them and Aunt Norma. Well my response obviously was "Yes", and it was good to see her again as she was my buddy and I wanted to spend some time with her.

'She asked me a few days later if I would like to have lunch with her and I replied, "Yes, as long as you aren't cooking." She said, "There is a great hamburger place on the west end of the Valley called The Hangmans Tree." I thought that sounded great as I certainly loved hamburgers, so off we went.' When there was a mix up over the drinks order, 'She stood her ground and they made the right coke, and it was a good lunch. Aunt Norma could be one tough lady if provoked.'

She could be extremely late too, which caused problems with her in-laws; as Paul witnessed during his holiday: 'A couple of days after the coke incident, Grandma asked if we would like to go out for dinner and a movie that evening. We all thought it would be a great idea and all we had to do was pick the movie. Well evening came and it was time for dinner but Aunt Norma wasn't quite ready. We waited a little while and then decided to go to dinner without her. When we came back to pick her up for the movies, Grandma went in to see if she was ready yet and came back out of the house alone, telling Grandpa that Norma Jeane was still wandering around without a stitch on! Grandma sounded a little perturbed and we went to the movies without her.'

'I just love that girl,' Ethel later lamented, 'I never knew anyone more unselfish, but she is so lost in her own world that she frightens me.'

In Autumn 1944, Norma Jeane decided she wanted to visit her sister, Berniece, in Detroit, along with Grace Goddard in Chicago. (Two postcards dated 28 October 1944 place the trip at least two months later than sometimes thought.) She cleared out her savings account, and despite suffering from travel sickness, she made the trip alone to reconnect with her foster family, and connect to her real family for the very first time.

When Norma Jeane arrived in Detroit, Berniece, her husband Paris Miracle, his sister Niobe and Berniece's daughter Mona Rae met her at the station. They were immediately bowled over by the eighteen-year-old in cobalt blue suit and a heart-shaped brimmed hat, and drove her to Canada for a visit to a bird sanctuary, before taking her to the Miracles' apartment, where she was to stay for most of her holiday.

The trip was a real confidence-booster for Norma Jeane, who had never spent any time with her blood family – the last time being the disastrous year or so she lived with her mother. Both girls only vaguely knew Gladys, and the trip enabled them to discuss their mother and their late brother, Robert.

The trip was cut short when Jim unexpectedly announced that he would be returning to California very soon on leave. Norma Jeane bid farewell to her sister, and travelled to Illinois to visit with the Goddards. During the short visit to Chicago and Huntington, she saw Grace's new workplace and reacquainted herself with Doc Goddard's daughter, Bebe, spending time with her friends at the Goddard home, 322 Wilson Court, and Maully's South Side Confectionary at 915 8th Street.

'She didn't look like Marilyn Monroe at the time,' recalled Nelson Cohen, who married Bebe in 1950. 'I only met her briefly but she was pleasant enough, perfectly normal.'

Another friend, Diane DePree Miller, describes Norma Jeane as, 'An ordinary looking girl, with light brown hair. She was very shy and kept to herself.'

The visit was brief, but enjoyable, and in a letter to Grace dated 3 December 1944, Norma Jeane described just how much the trip meant to her and how much she missed her foster-mother. As well as yearning for Grace, however, the letter seems to indicate that Norma Jeane was helping her out financially too: 'I shall send you more money a little later,' she wrote. This generosity towards friends and loved ones was something that stayed with Norma Jeane throughout her life, and would often get her into financial trouble herself.

Chapter 5

Model Girl

Once home it was back to work at Radioplane, and on the very day of her return, she was spotted by some photographers working in the plant. They liked the look of the fresh-faced brunette, and before she knew it, Norma Jeane had been whisked away from her duties in order to pose for photographer David Conover. Wearing her uniform of grey slacks and green blouse and with her Radioplane identity card clearly visible, the look on the young girl's face says it all – this was far more exciting than inspecting or spraying parachutes.

The pictures taken that day at Radioplane changed Norma Jeane from a semi-content bride into an excited young woman, full of possibilities and ambition. Conover told her he would like to take more photos, and later returned to Radioplane, snapping her in a variety of different outfits. He told her that she could become a model; that he had a lot of contacts he wanted her to look into, but at first she believed he was only flirting with her.

However, after studying the photos he had taken, and discovering that she could earn $5 an hour modelling as opposed to working ten hours a day at the factory, she began to realize there might be a future there after all. She tried her hand at a few photo sessions and by 10 February 1945 had made enough money in order to buy back her mother's Franklin grand piano from Aunt Ana. Unfortunately, the timing coincided with Jim returning home to California, so she decided to wait until his shore leave was over before taking on any more modelling jobs.

When Norma Jeane briefly discussed the idea of modelling with her husband, he seemed to like the idea: 'I thought it was easier than working at Radioplane,' he later said, but he did make it clear that when the war was over, he wanted to start a family and settle down. The pair went to Big Bear Lake for a week's holiday, but although she later described it as 'a grand time', there were a variety of problems: Jim hated the discovery that his wife had started drinking alcohol; she became jealous when he played blackjack with some college girls; and they had an argument about Jim's plans to have children.

Shortly after their return home, Jim rejoined his ship and Norma Jeane put her plans for modelling into action. When she wrote to Grace on 4 June 1945, she revealed that she hadn't worked at Radioplane since January. What she forgot to say, however, was that she was still actually employed until 15 March, when the management finally grew tired of her phoning in sick and terminated her employment. She was relieved; life at the factory had exhausted her, she said; 'I just don't care about anything when I'm that tired.'

Thanks to David Conover, she was introduced to Potter Heuth, who agreed to take some photos of her on the condition that she worked 'on spec' – she would be paid if and when he found a buyer for the prints. Norma Jeane eagerly agreed and she discovered just how easy modelling came to her: it was fun, the photographers seemed to like her and she thoroughly enjoyed herself.

Unfortunately her new-found career did not have the same affect on Ethel Dougherty, who was worried about Norma Jeane's marriage to Jim. She felt threatened by her daughter-in-law spending so much time working with other men; a feeling that wasn't helped when she witnessed frequent arguments between the couple during Jim's trips home.

Another thing causing friction was that Norma Jeane no longer had time to look after her dog, Muggsie. Before she had begun modelling, she had loved bathing, walking and brushing the dog, but when time grew short, Muggsie became somewhat neglected. 'The last time I saw Muggsie she was tied to a tree and very dirty. She died soon after,' remembered Jim Dougherty.

Finally, Norma Jeane couldn't stand the frictions at the Dougherty home any longer, and decided to move back to the warmth of Aunt Ana's home in West Los Angeles. This did not prevent problems, however, and Paul Kanteman remembered a particularly stressful episode: 'Uncle Jim was on leave and called to see if I could go fishing in a couple of days' time. He picked me up the next day, but Aunt Norma couldn't be with us as she was modelling for a magazine cover that day. We had to get our fishing tackle together anyway, and we could kill most of the day doing that without any problem. The next morning Aunt Norma announced she couldn't go with us that day either as they hadn't finished shooting yet. Uncle Jim didn't seem too thrilled as he really wanted to spend more time with her. Up the coast we went, to just south of the Malibu pier. She dropped us off with our tackle and a lunch with the promise to be back no later than mid-afternoon. Well afternoon came and went, evening came and went and no Aunt Norma . . . It was about eleven that night when we saw the little Ford Coupe pull up and stop. We scrambled into the car and off we went. Not a lot was said on our way back to Aunt Ana's home in West Los Angeles. I do remember going upstairs to my room and passing by Aunt Norma's room and hearing her crying. I went downstairs and told Uncle Jim what was going on. He immediately went to see what the problem was, as not much had been discussed about the day at that point. She told him she was shooting a cover for a magazine depicting the Thanksgiving Turkey, the set was an actual barn in the country with a large pile of hay, which is where they worked. Before they could begin, she had to remove her wedding rings as they certainly didn't want a married woman posing for this cover shot, but in removing or putting the rings away, they became lost in about ten tonnes of hay. The afternoon had been spent trying to find them, but they were, however, found the next day – to everyone's relief.'

Norma Jeane's relationship with Jim became worse and worse, to the point that every time Jim saw her he could almost guarantee an argument. When Lee Bush from the Schwarz Studio photographed her on 18 May 1945, she posed in a bikini, although Jim had previously begged her not to wear such a revealing outfit. Her response was typical: she had to do the shoot as the money would come in useful to fix their car. Jim let that slide, but made it clear that he intended to start a family very soon; an idea that still didn't interest Norma Jeane in the least.

When Jim was away (and often when he was there), her mind was frequently on her career, and how to further it. She heard about a photographer called Paul Parry, and one day walked into his office wearing a pink sweater. There were two other men in the room, and when she asked Parry if he thought she could make it as a model, their reaction was plain to see. As it turned out, when Parry used her for a fashion layout, an advertising manager told him she'd never amount to anything as a fashion model, but this did not prevent Norma Jeane from wanting to pursue other avenues and other photographers. Shortly after an extended photo shoot with Conover, Norma Jeane got her chance to do just that.

William Carroll from the Ansco Color film processing and printing service in Los Angeles was looking for a model to use in an advertising counter display. As luck would have it, David Conover and Potter Heuth came into the shop regularly, and on one particular day Heuth was armed with some slides of Conover's shots of Norma Jeane. 'Those Conover pictures displayed a girl of outstanding charm,' remembered Carroll in his book, *Norma Jean: Marilyn Monroe 1945.* 'Not totally beautiful but fresh in a most delightful girl-next-door manner. And that was the exact type I wanted to decorate our point-of-purchase counter display for my laboratory services.'

Heuth gave Carroll Norma Jeane's number, and he rang her that day. He remembered: 'Norma Jeane was very calm and sounded serious as she questioned me as to the source of her number and my contacts with Potter and David. At this point in time I'd say she was concerned about my level of professionalism, to eliminate the potential trouble of working with an amateur photographer who is just trying to meet a pretty girl.'

And so it was that Carroll made the journey to Aunt Ana's house early one summer morning, and was pleasantly surprised to discover that Norma Jeane was not only ready on time, but she also lived up to his expectations. She came with a supply of clothes, and also her make-up case, which she placed on to the seat next to her, before the couple headed off towards the sea and, in particular, Malibu: 'Norma Jeane brought with her a good selection of personal clothing, all of which had been ironed and was ready to use. Note that this was not "model" clothing as I have no reason to believe she had any. Just a good clothes-closet selection from which we used almost everything.'

As they drove, Carroll explained his intentions for the photos, and Norma Jeane threw in her suggestions of informal shots and no bathing suits, so as to not offend the clients in his shop. They stopped at Castle Rock and Norma Jeane set about putting on her make-up, while Carroll took informal shots. The results from this photo session are quite beautiful; her hair was lighter than usual as a result of the summer sun, although the natural beauty is everywhere apparent.

'She had no professional manner,' remembered Carroll. 'This is a point I must emphasize by comparing her conduct with the many other models photographed during that period. Norma Jeane was naturally a competent person who constantly demonstrated a strong desire to help me make the best possible use of our time on the beach. We had many laughs and shared ideas easily because her model-based reactions were simply that of a young woman seeking to give the best possible assistance to producing excellent pictures. Keep in mind that at this point she had little professional experience except for a two-week trip with David [Conover], whose pictures preceded mine by just a few months.'

Although still wearing her wedding ring, Norma Jeane shared some of her marriage woes with Carroll, who even now refuses to discuss what was said: 'We did talk at length, during our lunch break, about personal problems and pleasures. I had recently ploughed through a difficult divorce and (probably) felt that talking with a non-involved neutral person, as Norma Jeane was, could ease my bad memories. Norma Jeane responded rather completely but her very personal comments were hers and should not be made a source of public concern.'

At the end of the session, Carroll drove his model home, paid her $20 for the day's work, and then rang her about a month later: 'She told me she had signed with the Blue Book Agency. Her daily rate (set by Blue Book) had jumped to $50 a day; a figure I decided I would not pay so never used Norma Jeane again.'

The Blue Book Agency was run by a woman called Emmeline Snively and based in the grounds of the Ambassador Hotel. Through her contact with Potter Heuth, Norma Jeane walked into Snively's offices on 2 August 1945, in the hope of being signed. Studying the photos on the wall, she was anxious to know if she too could one day become a cover girl. Snively noted that: 'She was cute-looking, but she knew nothing about carriage, posture, walking, sitting or posing. She was a California blonde – dark in winter, light in summer.'

She also saw that Norma Jeane's curly hair was completely unmanageable and knew that if she was going to be in the least bit successful, it would have to be bleached and straightened. 'When she bent over, nothing happened,' remembered Snively. 'Not a hair moved. We wished she could get her hair straightened but she couldn't afford it.'

That said, she did see potential in the 'round-faced girl with an astonishing bust which made her size 12 dress look too small'. She asked for a photo, and was presented with one of David Conover's shots, which impressed Snively enough to recommend Norma Jeane attend a $100, three-month long modelling course, which she could pay off with her modelling jobs. Norma Jeane was thrilled, and filled out the application form immediately, lying about her age (claiming to be twenty instead of nineteen), and noting that her hair was blonde and curly, and her height 5 foot 6. She mentioned no ambitions to act, but did say she danced a little, and sang too.

When she was successfully enrolled, Norma Jeane walked into her first modelling class and was friendly to everyone, despite the fact that the other girls all had their mothers with them, while she had arrived alone. Snively gave her lots of attention because of that and the young model soaked it up; mastering hand positions, posture and make-up techniques, as taught by Maria Smith and Mrs Gavin Beardsley. She began studying photos of herself given to her by photographer Potter Heuth and Bob Farr, and learned how to improve her photographic technique, asking the photographers to tell her where she was going wrong. She never repeated a mistake, nor did she ever miss a modelling class, which led Snively to declare that with her gumption, she would become a big star.

However, although she was extremely determined and gifted in front of a camera, Snively did note that clothes were a problem for Norma Jeane. She only seemed to own two different outfits: a white dress with green yoke and teal blue tailored suit 'that didn't do a thing for her'. Later, much to Snively's chagrin, she wore the blue outfit for one of the first photographic jobs she had with the agency: a photo shoot with Larry Kronquist for an American Airlines booklet which was shot at the Douglas Aircraft Company.

On 2 September 1945, a test was shot of Norma Jeane and eight other girls in the grounds of the Ambassador Hotel, then on 5 September 1945 Snively got her a job as a hostess in the Holga Steel Files booth at an industrial show. Her job was to showcase the files and give out leaflets, and she was a hit – the report coming back from the company that she was excellent. Being paid $90 for ten days work, Norma Jeane immediately turned all of it over to Snively in order to pay for her studies. From that moment on, Snively knew she was working with 'a fair, honest and very fine girl,' and made a point of getting her as much work as she possibly could.

Norma Jeane attended audition after audition, and built up a good relationship with every photographer she worked with, including Lazlo Willinger, John Randolph, and Larry Kronquist, who had shot the American Airlines photos. Snively recalled: 'She was sincerely eager. She made everyone she talked to feel as if he were the only guy in the world. She did this naturally without design or premeditation.'

After a failed audition for a Montgomery Ward catalogue, Snively decided that maybe Norma Jeane should specialize in pin-ups because of the way her body looked in a bikini. This did not stop the young model being criticized, however, and her photos were surprisingly difficult to sell, as art directors complained that her nose was too long and her smile cast shadows. Snively later remarked that, 'She smiled too high, that's what was wrong, and it made deep lines around her nose. We taught her how to bring her smile down and show her lower teeth.'

During this time she was still having problems within her marriage, and although Snively was aware of this, Norma Jeane never discussed her personal problems with her. Instead, Snively believed that she was still faithful to her husband and refused to date other men: 'Many of my other girls whose husbands were overseas dated several nights of the week. But not Norma Jeane.'

Marilyn spoke about this herself in 1953 when she said, 'I used to meet a lot of wolves among the buyers . . . I didn't have much trouble brushing them off. I found if I just looked sort of stupid or pretended I didn't know what they were talking about, they soon gave up in disgust.'

She would also drive herself home after photo sessions to avoid any embarrassing episodes with photographers, but her driving almost got her killed when she had an accident in the little Ford that she and Jim owned at the time. When she telephoned Elyda Nelson that night, she was laughing but on the verge of tears: 'I guess I must have been dreaming again,' she said, 'because I drove head-on into a street car. You should see our poor car, it's completely demolished.' Luckily, Norma Jeane survived with just a bump to the head;

'I guess it's a miracle that I'm alive,' she told her shocked sister-in-law.

Snively had many photographer friends who were interested in 'discovering' a new model, and both she and Norma Jeane jumped on this opportunity, often arriving at studios for 'test shots', even though she was already becoming quite established. As a result she was 'discovered' by an assortment of photographers, but Snively never considered this to be dishonest, since Norma Jeane's style was forever changing, making her 'new' all the time.

Shortly before Christmas 1945, Jim came home on shore leave, only to be told that Norma Jeane would be leaving to go on an extended modelling trip along the coast with photographer Andre de Dienes. He was understandably perturbed and urged her to cancel, but she refused, stating that if she refused to go, she'd lose that job and anything that came along in the future. They argued once again, and Norma Jeane left the house to spend the next few weeks in the company of another man, much to the dismay of her husband.

Norma Jeane first met de Dienes after he had asked the Blue Book Agency for a girl who might be willing to pose nude. She had arrived at his hotel room wearing a pink sweater with her hair tied in a bow, and although she was wearing a wedding ring, de Dienes claims she told him she was in the process of getting a divorce. 'Do you love your husband?' he asked. 'No,' she replied.

After posing in a bikini at a nearby beach, de Dienes asked if she would be willing to go on location with him, and after a meeting with Aunt Ana, it was agreed that Norma Jeane could, indeed, go on the trip. Alongside de Dienes, Norma Jeane travelled by car to the Mojave Desert, Darwin Falls, Las Vegas, Cathedral Gorge, Yosemite, Portland and Death Valley, where on 15 December, Norma Jeane sent a postcard to Jim, telling him how much she missed him.

The card (addressed 'My Dearest Daddy' and signed 'All My love, Your Baby') shows no sign of any problems in the marriage, but it is interesting to note that she mentions nothing about the trip at all. Perhaps she didn't want to rock the boat by talking about it, or maybe it just wasn't turning out the way she had originally hoped. Certainly by the end of the journey, Norma Jeane and de Dienes had lurched from one disaster to another: they were accosted by strange men at Cathedral Gorge; they suffered various flat tyres; he discovered he'd left his wallet in one hotel room; and in another their belongings were stolen when Norma Jeane left to go shopping. She was so upset by the latter event that she decided to telephone Jim and return home, but was persuaded not to by de Dienes, who by this point had fallen in love with the girl and begged her to marry him. 'I wanted to marry this nice young girl. What was wrong with that? I was a nice young boy myself,' he said in 1962.

Since Norma Jeane was already married, and they had only known each other for a short time, it is hard to know what possessed de Dienes to ask her to be his wife, and it would certainly seem that marrying someone else was the last thing on Norma Jeane's mind. But her lack of interest did not discourage him, and after a disastrous trip to visit her mother (in which Gladys barely noticed that they were even in the room), de Dienes claims that he and Norma Jeane slept together.

By this time de Dienes was completely besotted and after making love again the next day, he drove her back to Aunt Ana's house, promising that he would marry her soon. It would take a variety of unanswered letters and tense phone calls before de Dienes realized that marriage to another man was the last thing on Norma Jeane's mind: 'I phoned from New Mexico and she said, 'Andre please don't come [to Hollywood]. I can't marry you. Forgive me.'

1946 brought a variety of changes both professionally and privately, and started with Norma Jeane finally agreeing to have her hair straightened and bleached. Emmeline Snively had tried unsuccessfully for months to get the model to do something with the 'unruly, shapeless, mop,' telling her that not only did frizzy hair prevent her from wearing hats properly, it also stopped her fulfilling her potential, since blondes were definitely more in demand. But Norma Jeane had always resisted the temptation, declaring that if she had her hair bleached, she would have to continue doing so and just couldn't afford it.

Finally, in February 1946 she was persuaded to visit Frank and Joseph's salon, where they gave her hair a straight permanent to make it more manageable; a regular permanent at the ends after shaping; and an all-over bleach. The result was phenomenal and resulted in a successful job for a shampoo advert.

Once her hair had been fixed, Snively decided that it was time for Norma Jeane to be 'discovered' again and on 6 March she sent her along to photographer Joseph Jasgur for some more 'test shots'. Jasgur didn't think much of her to start with, deciding that her hips were too broad, her clothes too tight and her figure imperfect, but he did like her eyes; he took test shots of her on a street behind Beverly Boulevard and then took her for something to eat afterwards. Snively later revealed that he believed she was too thin and unsexy, and would always feed her hamburgers when he thought she looked hungry.

And so began a quick succession of modelling jobs for the newly transformed model. On 10 March she had another session with Jasgur, this time at the Don Lee Towers, above the Hollywood sign, and then on 11 March, she posed for photographer Earl Moran, who painted her portrait for potential advertising customers. On 12 March 1946, she was snapped by a young photographer called Richard Miller (who was to use her throughout March and April), and on 18 and 23 March she went with Jasgur to Zuma beach, where she was photographed alone in the sand, and also with the cast of a local production called *The Drunkard*. (Many years later, Jasgur published a book entitled *The Birth of Marilyn*, which included a photo of Norma Jeane apparently showing six toes. These photos caused huge media interest and are still talked about today, but the extra 'toe' in the Jasgur photos is merely a bump in the sand.)

Amongst the abundance of modelling jobs coming her way, Norma Jeane was also being told she should get into the movies. This got her thinking about the next stage in her career, and she mentioned briefly to Emmeline Snively that she might be interested in doing bit parts. She didn't immediately share this with her husband, however, who was later shocked when he found a screen test script when he came home on leave.

Declaring that she just had the script out of curiosity, Jim tried to persuade his wife that thousands of young women wanted to be a star, but it fell on deaf ears. 'I used to confide in my husband sometimes, my childish dreams of becoming an actress. He'd laugh and assure me I'd never make it,' she remembered. Shortly after, Jim reluctantly drove his wife to a screen test, only for her to discover that it wasn't a real test at all; the 'producer' had borrowed the office from a friend. Once in the room, he told Norma Jeane to recite her lines while performing a variety of reclining poses. 'He was getting sillier by the minute and I maneuvered over toward the door and made a hasty exit,' she recalled in 1953. As she got back into Jim's car, she slumped in the seat and looked at her husband. 'You're right,' she said, 'They're just a bunch of fresh guys.'

Old flame Bob Stotts was to bump into Norma Jeane that year, after his discharge from the Army. He saw immediately that she had turned into a beautiful woman but noticed a subtle change in her personality – as if she was acting a part in front of him. Norma Jeane told Bob that she was modelling and interested in getting into the acting business. 'She seemed all starry-eyed about the whole thing, but she didn't see it as the ultimate goal in her life. I had seen a news stand with half a dozen magazines, all with her image on them and she told me that modelling was more fun than acting tryouts. Screen tests were hard, difficult she said and certainly not as easy as modelling.'

In the entire time Stotts knew her, Norma Jeane had never mentioned a career in the movies: 'If she had any theatrical aspirations, we never knew about it. Her main ambition seemed to be to eventually become a good housewife.'

'The last thing in the world that I would have picked was a movie star,' wrote Stotts' mother Dorothy. 'She was a good dancer, but a movie star, well . . .'

Norma Jeane asked Bob to dinner that night, but knowing that her husband was overseas he decided against it. This was the last time any of the Stotts family saw Norma Jeane. 'We often wished we'd kept in touch somehow,' wrote Dorothy. 'Possibly doing so would not have altered the course of events, but friends – real friends – might have made a difference.'

Meanwhile, Norma Jeane was receiving far too much attention from men desperate to 'make her a star', and this led Snively to introduce Norma Jeane to Helen Ainsworth, a theatrical agent at the National Concert Artists Corporation. She walked into the office, and immediately the string on her hatbox snapped, leaving a trail of hairpins, lipstick, curlers and make-up strewn all over the floor. Ainsworth's colleague, Harry Lipton, looked up from the magazine he was reading and saw a young girl who was flushed, confused and looked like 'a freshly cut piece of strawberry shortcake'. Picking up the entire contents of the box, he made a joke, and was happy when Norma Jeane smiled and seemed to relax.

The interview went well but she didn't speak much and changed the subject immediately when asked about her personal life; the only thing she did divulge was that she had always dreamed of being an actress. At the end of the interview, both Ainsworth and Lipton agreed that she had possibilities and signed her to the agency, assigning her to Lipton to handle personally. This was the start of Norma Jeane's venture into the movies, and she couldn't have been happier – professionally at least.

At home, things couldn't have been worse. She and Jim were still arguing and on 9 March, when he shipped out again, he left a note for his wife, saying, 'I've gone. After I've finished sailing and can settle on the beach we can give it another try if you like. Don't think there's someone else, there isn't, but well I've told you how I feel.' Determined not to give up on the relationship,

Jim left on his trip hoping that things could be patched up, but it was not to be.

On 26 April 1946, Norma Jeane appeared on the cover of *Family Circle* for the very first time, and shortly after started jotting down reasons why she wanted to divorce Jim Dougherty. 'My husband didn't support me,' she wrote. 'He embarrassed me; he ridiculed me, and treated me like a child'. Finally, she made plans to travel to Las Vegas, where she would have to stay from May to July, in order to legally divorce Jim, who was at this time blissfully unaware that their problems had come this far.

In the months prior to the trip, Norma Jeane become close to her agent, Harry Lipton, often calling him at odd hours of the night, just to be able to talk to someone. She told him that she believed Jim had married her because otherwise she would have had nowhere else to go, but described him as 'a very nice man'. As a result of her opening up to Lipton, he helped arrange the trip to Vegas, but as he put her on the train, he noted that she showed, 'neither relief nor joy nor distaste at getting a divorce. Her reaction was that of someone leaving a fairly close acquaintance – not a husband.'

Once in Las Vegas, Norma Jeane settled into 406 South Third Street, home of Grace Goddard's aunt, Minnie Willett, the widow of Uncle Kirby who had died in a traffic accident almost ten years before. Minnie, aged sixty-nine, was a very well-respected member of the Las Vegas community who was active in civic affairs and establishments such as the Rebekah Lodge, the Old Timers club auxiliary and various other organizations. She was friends with a number of high-profile Las Vegas families, and after her husband's death had continued her hobbies with great abandon.

While Minnie's days were a great rush of activities and goals, she hadn't had the easiest of lives. Before she had married Grace's Uncle Kirby, she had given birth to a boy named Frank, who was later raised as one of the Willett family. Frank was a sporty boy who took part in basketball and boxing, but he also had his problems; going missing for weeks at a time and forcing his family to advertise in newspapers to trace his whereabouts.

In 1923 he married Annie Beadle, but the marriage was unhappy and ended in 1928 when she shot herself with Frank's shotgun, moments after he had stormed out after a huge argument. All this news was reported back to Grace in Los Angeles and it is safe to say that Norma Jeane would have been privy to this family scandal during the course of growing up.

By the summer of 1946, Frank had long since moved away and Minnie was quietly living alone, continuing her civic affairs and organizing various get-togethers. As a result, when Norma Jeane moved into the house she was immediately invited to days out with prosperous Las Vegas families, but even so, she was not at all happy at the thought of staying in Nevada for the entire summer. She didn't want to leave her Los Angeles modelling career; there were rumours of movies in the pipeline; and to make things worse her health was not excellent. In a letter to an unknown friend, she lamented: 'I was in the hospital twice – first with an acute mouth infection (I had four wisdom teeth pulled). I was out of the hospital for just one day and they put me back with the measles. Oh what an awful time.'

However, her luck changed one day when she walked on to Aunt Minnie's porch, wearing white shorts and a halter top, with her hair pulled back and tied with a ribbon.

At that moment, a young man by the name of Bill Pursel was talking to a former high-school friend who was raking the yard. 'My friend introduced her to me, and she came off the porch so we could shake hands. There was a picket fence between us but our eyes were locked. Her first words were, "Pleased to meet you" and I said "Same here." We then just stood there staring at one another for a few seconds. Finally I said, "Would you like to go for a walk?" She said "Sure" and we took off.'

The new friends ended up in a Las Vegas restaurant called Corey's. There Norma Jeane told Bill that she was in the city to obtain a divorce from her husband, James Dougherty. 'She left the impression that she just wanted to be free,' says Bill. 'She was not bitter.' That night the couple went to see a movie, and from that moment they became firm friends and spent almost every day together.

Bill remembers: 'She was a beautiful gal. We were just two young adults going out; we'd go to the movies, the lake, and all over the place: we went to Mount Charleston, west of Las Vegas, Hoover Dam, and to Lake Mead, which was a great place to go for a swim as well as fishing or boating. We would find a café or somewhere out of the way and sit opposite each other. She would stare right into my face and it would make me nervous because she was so beautiful. We would often write notes to each other on napkins and pass them to each other while we were dining.

'One Sunday we drove to Southern Utah to visit a National Park. It was crowded that day and I noticed there was quite a bit of attention from a gathering of girls. A female park ranger approached and recognized Norma Jeane from a magazine cover she had done, which explained the attention we were drawing.

'We also visited Bryce Canyon, where many western movies have been filmed. It was along there where Norma Jeane told me she would like to become a movie actress, and I think also it was the first time we kissed.'

As well as spending time with Bill, Norma Jeane also took time to get to know his family, and was a dinner guest on at least two occasions at the family home at 925 South 3rd Street.

'She was a lovely, lovely girl; a very sweet girl,' remembered Bill's sister, Jeanne Chretien. 'She could have been the girl-next-door – my mom liked her a lot and Mom was very particular about people! In fact Norma Jeane later wrote to Mom, who was very approving of her going out with Bill. She would also speak with her on the phone – she wouldn't speak to just anyone, but she loved Norma Jeane.' Jeanne was married and both she and her husband Henry would tease Bill about the relationship: 'What a beauty – how are you getting such a gorgeous doll?' was one of their light-hearted comments. Around the dinner table, however, their talk was that of a more serious nature: 'She was a very down-to-earth person,' said Chretien. 'She was very intelligent, smart, sweet and wholesome. She liked poetry and talked a lot about the poet Carl Sandburg.'

'She dearly loved his writing,' recalled Bill Pursel. 'She loved to read and Sandburg was at the top of her list.'

Bill remembers the relationship Norma Jeane developed with his mother. 'Mom was very inquisitive about the girls my brother and I dated. There seemed to be an immediate close relationship between Mom and Norma Jeane, and Mom was very impressed by the way Norma Jeane pitched right in to help get supper on the table and to clean up afterwards. The connection they had impressed me because they took to each other so naturally.' However, while Mrs Pursel may have liked her young visitor, that still didn't stop her demanding to know if Norma Jeane had washed her hands before allowing her to help with dinner, much to the amusement of the other house guests.

While Norma Jeane left a good impression on the Pursel family, she seems to have been just as fond of them. 'You're really swell and I enjoyed your company very much,' she later wrote to Bill.

There have been countless rumours that Norma Jeane travelled back and forth to Los Angeles when she was supposed to be resident in Las Vegas, but Bill Pursel doubts this: 'I don't know if she went back and forth to LA during her time here, but I doubt it because after we met we saw one another nearly every day. She also would call me at the service station where I worked, and, she brought her little Ford in for me to service. I think she stayed the whole six weeks, and I think she stayed at this same home on South 3rd Street.'

She was certainly a resident in Las Vegas when Jim Dougherty telephoned her. He had received a letter and divorce papers from her lawyer while he was at sea, and was gutted. He didn't return the papers, nor did he write to his estranged wife; instead, he cancelled her allotment (the portion of military pay set aside for dependents). The moment he reached dry land, he tracked

her to Las Vegas and dialled the number. In shock and not wanting to believe what he had read in the letter, he was dismayed
when she answered the phone with a bright, 'Hi Bill.' When
she realized that she was speaking to Jim and not Bill Pursel, she
proceeded to scold him for cutting off her allotment, which
she said she found out about when she was in the hospital. Still
in denial, Jim decided to visit his wife when he arrived in Los
Angeles shortly afterwards.

Norma Jeane was supposed to stay in Las Vegas until 10 July
1946, but actually she stayed a week longer than that, leaving
on 18 July. Bill Pursel offered to drive with her, and together
they set off in her Ford Coupe: 'We got about 90 miles south
of Vegas to a town called Baker. We were driving down Baker
Grade when the car started missing . . . we just made it to a
service station. I realized we had lost the fuel pump and told
the mechanic . . . then we walked about a mile up the road to a
place called "Failings". We returned, only to find the mechanic
had stripped the car and had parts everywhere. We then walked
all the way back to "Failings". Norma Jeane complained that
her feet were getting hot and she could feel the heat through
her sandals. I carried her for about forty yards before we finally
reached the restaurant.'

While the couple were back in the café, Bill wrote a light-
hearted poem about their dilemma, after which Norma Jeane
thanked him for helping with her car problems; folded up the
poem and popped it into her shirt. The couple stayed a few
hours before heading back to the service station and resum-
ing their journey. 'As we drove on we reached a checkpoint at
Yermo where we were asked whether we had any fruit or veg
in the car. Norma Jeane was wearing a white halter and shorts
and her hair was pulled back with a ribbon. The male officers at the checkpoint ordered her to get all her suitcases out of
the trunk and she became angry because they made her open
all of her luggage, which entailed three cases and an overnight
bag. Norma Jeane was furious and crying as they searched her
clothes and cosmetics, but they eventually put everything back,

closed the trunk and told us we could leave. When we continued our drive she was still crying so I pulled over. She scolded me for not interfering with the search, and after explaining that there was nothing I could have done, she eventually calmed down. I told her that she was most beautiful when she was angry and it was true!'

To cool off the couple found a park in San Bernardino and soaked their feet in a pond. Norma Jeane was happy, recalls Pursel, laughing like a child while splashing her feet in the pond. She was finally free and looking forward to the future.

'I had no money to get a motel or buy supper, so told Norma Jeane that I would be boarding a Greyhound bus back to Vegas while she continued her drive to Los Angeles. She interrupted saying I could stay at her Aunt Ana's house, but I did not feel comfortable with that and besides, I had to be at work for 6 a.m. I asked her if she knew the way back from where we were; she said she did and started to cry. I told her I would come to see her soon, put her in the car, kissed her goodbye and sent her on her way. Twenty minutes later I was on a bus back to Vegas and it suddenly dawned on me that I missed her. I missed her very much.'

While driving back to Los Angeles, Norma Jeane became even more upset when she found herself being followed by a male admirer. In a letter to Bill, she complained: 'After I left you yesterday and got back on the highway some wolf followed me all the way home. He drove like a crazy person, he would drive his car real close to mine and kept saying "When are we going to get together?" Something new – a highway wolf!' She also thanked Bill for his company and asked him to keep in touch: 'I would like very much to hear from you Bill; how you got home, how you are, what you're doing etc. So please drop me a line. Don't forget when you're ever in LA to stop by to see me.'

But while Norma Jeane may have looked forward to Bill's visit, one visitor she wasn't so sure about came in the shape of her mother, Gladys, who had moved into Aunt Ana's Nebraska Avenue home. In July 1945, she had been released from the mental institution, on the condition that she would move in with her Aunt Dora Graham, in Oregon. The idea was that she would be able to adjust to her new life away from the hospital, and that after a year she would be allowed to look after herself.

Gladys embraced this new freedom with both hands, and spent her time 'healing' sick people with her Christian Science practices. However, she became bored of living within the confines of Aunt Dora's home, and before her adjustment year was finished she decided to travel to Los Angeles, where she was met at the bus station by Norma Jeane and her then husband Jim. She then proceeded to move in with Aunt Ana while her daughter was in Vegas, eventually sharing a room with Norma Jeane on her return from Nevada.

For both Norma Jeane and her sister, Berniece, this period would be a time of great optimism and change but, ultimately, disappointment.

Chapter 6

'This is the end of Norma Jeane'

Coming home from Las Vegas, closer than ever to being a free woman, Norma Jeane must have had mixed feelings about living with her mother. 'It seems rather nice to be home again,' she wrote to Bill Pursel, 'but I do miss Vegas a little – I think the place sort of grows on one.'

Although still in the safety of Aunt Ana's home, this was the first time she had had any prolonged contact with Gladys since she was a small child, and the relationship was strained, so when Bill Pursel came to visit it must have come as a welcome relief. He installed himself at the home of his Aunt Louise at 11611 Blix Street, North Hollywood, and remembered seeing Norma Jeane's mother when he arrived at Nebraska Avenue to visit: 'Norma Jeane and I were leaving Aunt Ana's one day around noon when an attractive lady was emerging from an apartment basement below Aunt Ana's home. Norma Jeane introduced me to this lady as her mother; the lady acknowledged the introduction with a smile and then promptly turned and retreated back down the few steps to the basement apartment. I wondered what I said to cause this rather hasty exit. Norma Jeane just stood there for a few seconds, then said, "Let's go." I didn't ask any questions but I knew something wasn't right. This lady was neatly dressed; I would guess she was in her forties, rather slim, quite attractive, but noticeably shy and when she walked away I thought she had maybe forgotten something. Little did I know that Norma Jeane's mother had mental problems – such a thing never dawned on me and I had thought that perhaps as the divorce wasn't final yet, that maybe Norma Jeane's mother resented her daughter dating so soon. There was no voluntary explanation from Norma Jeane which also puzzled me. But it was none of my business so I asked no questions and just let the whole thing drop.'

Although Jim Dougherty never mentioned it in either of his later memoirs, he also encountered Bill Pursel during this trip. Bill remembered: 'I did meet Jim Dougherty when he came to Aunt Ana's home to get some keys from Norma Jeane. She was expecting him because she had the keys ready to hand to him when he came through the door. Aunt Ana let him in, and Norma Jeane introduced me to Jim in a polite way – she didn't identify me as anyone special. He acknowledged the meeting with a friendly handshake; he was very polite and I think he said, "Glad to meet you" to me and "thanks" to her . . . I noticed no animosity or jealousy on his part, nothing seemed awkward or confrontational and he left immediately without any conversation with Norma Jeane.

'One thing I did notice (which is important because I saw it directed towards me in August 1950) was that Norma Jeane was standing – looking right into the eyes of Jim Dougherty – smiling politely but no talking except a short friendly acknowledgement. There was no bitterness, just very matter of fact and almost cold . . . We did not discuss the meeting afterwards – I felt it was not my business to ask her anything; in fact Norma Jeane never talked about Jim or her family, and I never questioned her or pressed her for answers. She was a very fragile gal mentally but strong physically; she loved to laugh and to just be happy without any pressure. I stayed away from prying into her past; we only talked about the present and the future and I liked that.'

Her need to keep her private life to herself is testified by many others in her life. For instance, aside from Jim, the Dougherty family had no idea Norma Jeane had a sister; while friend Dorothy Muir later told the *National Tattler*: 'All we ever learned was that she was an orphan – father dead, mother hospitalized. Questions regarding her mother's health she managed to evade.

She would laugh and talk without apparent reservation, at the same time carefully avoiding anything personal.'

Aside from tying up loose ends from her past, July and August were full of hope and new starts for Norma Jeane, not least of which was the possibility of a movie career. During the summer she'd been in Vegas, she had appeared on a variety of magazine covers, one of which was a publication called *Laff*. Entrepreneur Howard Hughes saw the young model and asked his office to call Emmeline Snively and express an interest. Snively was thrilled, and made sure that the newspapers knew all about it. This resulted in Norma Jeane's first gossip column mention, but did not lead to any further notice from Hughes, or his company. However, the talk generated by the newspapers led several studios to pay attention to the young model, and before she knew it, Norma Jeane was invited to Twentieth Century Fox for a meeting with Ben Lyon, Head of Talent.

Although widely believed that the meeting between Lyon and Norma Jeane took place on 17 July (followed by a screen test on the 19th), in reality she did not leave Vegas until 18 July. Instead, the meeting took place a week later, and on 25 July 1946 Ben Lyon sent a memo to a colleague, instructing him to draw up an optional contract for Norma Jeane. As well as that, a screen test was arranged for 14th August, as Bill Pursel remembers: 'Norma Jeane came up with a short script which we practised at my Aunt Louise's home in North Hollywood. I don't know if the skit she had was the same one used at the studio or if there was more than one skit, but the script we practised had two parts, one female and one male.'

The couple practised for four or five hours, with Bill urging her to get into the part, but even at that early stage of her career, Norma Jeane made hard work of learning the lines, as Bill's sister Jeanne remembered: 'Bill said that he knew Norma Jeane's lines long before she did – she didn't learn them very quickly.' Bill confirms this: 'She froze; wouldn't read her part of the script. This was a shock to me and I asked what was wrong. She was afraid I think, so we just wrapped it up right then.'

On 14 August she arrived at Twentieth Century Fox for the screen test, while Bill waited impatiently at Nebraska Avenue with Aunt Ana. 'Norma Jeane came home,' remembered Bill, 'and came running up the walk, flying into the house all bubbly and excited. She was smiling and happy because after the black and white test they had taken a second test in Technicolor, which, she told us, was supposed to be important.'

The test was indeed an important break for Norma Jeane, and it led to her first contract, which she signed on 24th August 1946. However, the name Norma Jeane wasn't in the least bit 'star like', so it was decided that it would need to be changed. Ben Lyon told her that she reminded him of the actress Marilyn Miller, and decided he'd like her to be called Marilyn. Monroe was her personal choice, since it was her mother's maiden name.

Bill Pursel remembered speaking with Norma Jeane about the name change: 'She didn't make a big deal about it to me, but she wasn't happy about it. She didn't like Marilyn (and told me she couldn't even spell it) but the Monroe part she liked OK because it was a family name, or something. The part she was irked about was that she wasn't consulted before it was a done deal – I think she wanted the name Jeane kept because she was fond of Jean Harlow. I congratulated her on the spunk she showed with the studio and I continued to call her Norma Jeane because this is who she really was – calling her Marilyn seemed distant then, and it does now.'

That night, the couple went out to celebrate her new career. 'I think we had three drinks apiece, which brings up an important point: Norma Jeane did not smoke or drink or mess with drugs when I knew her. She had a pure soul and she guarded it well.'

Later that evening, Norma Jeane said good night to Bill and returned home. Standing before a mirror she picked up a lipstick and scribbled, 'This is the end of Norma Jeane.' Marilyn Monroe was born.

Things moved quickly for Marilyn after being signed to Twentieth Century Fox. A studio biography was prepared, describing her as an orphan who was discovered whilst babysitting for a studio executive. It was pure fantasy but she went along with it, not overly concerned to admit that both her mother and father were alive. Each day she would report to Twentieth Century Fox at 8 a.m. and take part in all kinds of lessons there: pantomime and dance three times a week, as well as acting, music and speech. She also spent a lot of time at the studio 'gallery' where she would pose for publicity photos, and sometimes she would ride in parades and take part in banquets, but for the most part she would 'hang around' the studio and try to soak up as much information as she could.

After spending all day at the studio, Marilyn travelled back to Aunt Ana's home and practised what she'd learned, all the time being criticized by her mother, who was showing every sign of not approving of her daughter's acting aspirations. Her sister, Berniece (who visited in late summer 1946), tried to get their mother to encourage Marilyn in her new career, but it was not to be: 'I don't like her business,' was all the woman had to say.

Shortly after signing to Fox, actor Alan Young was organizing a float in the Hollywood Christmas parade. He was new in California at that time and didn't know much about the event, so phoned Ben Lyon who told him he'd organize four or five girls to sit on the float. Young liked this idea and, as luck would have it, one of the girls selected for the event was Marilyn (who was still calling herself Norma Jeane), who sat with the others, waving and cheering on the float. Young remembers: 'After the parade, we went to the Brown Derby but I didn't drink, and neither did Norma Jeane, so we decided instead to go and get some cocoa together. I asked if she would like to go to a party with me, which was taking place several weeks later, and she said yes. She seemed like a frightened rabbit at first, and I didn't realize she had been raised without parents. I really liked her.'

The couple only went on a couple of dates; the first being to a friend's party: 'I went to pick her up from Aunt Ana's house and Ana looked at me with great suspicion, as I was taking out her "daughter", and was a little older than Norma Jeane, but she let her go anyway. I had seen a photo of a church in Ana's house, and Norma Jeane told me it was the Christian Science church and that she used to go to Sunday School there and loved it. We spoke a lot about it in the car.

'On the way to the party we got lost and I realized that I'd have to go home and get directions. Norma Jeane looked at me very suspiciously, and when we pulled up outside the house, she refused to go in with me. I assured her that my parents would be there, so she did come in, and it was all very friendly. Of course my parents thought it was a serious thing because I'd brought a girl home! My mother was a Christian Scientist too, so they both had lots to talk about.'

That date was a success, and Marilyn appeared in several publicity photos with Young, showing them both attempting to play the bagpipes. However, the last date they went on wasn't so successful: 'Well I thought I'd better kiss her goodnight,' remembered Young, 'because I didn't want her to think I was square. I went to kiss her cheek, and she turned her head so I got her ear instead. I was so embarrassed about it that I never phoned her again.'

That was the end of their short 'relationship', but the couple were to meet again several years later, when Marilyn had become successful: 'I was working at the studio and was sitting in make-up, when a blonde girl rushed up and yelled "Alan!" She kissed me and asked about my parents and asked me to give her a call. After she had gone, the make-up man asked how long I'd known Marilyn Monroe and I answered, "About two minutes!" That was the last time I ever saw her.'

On 13 September, Marilyn went back to Las Vegas briefly in order to complete her divorce from Dougherty. In the presence of her 'Aunt' Minnie she was questioned briefly by her lawyer, C. Norman Cornwall, and claimed falsely that she was still resident in Las Vegas, and fully intended to make her home there. When asked to explain why she had charged James Dougherty with mental cruelty, she answered, 'Well, in the first place my husband didn't support me and he objected to my working, criticized me for it and he also had a bad temper and would fly into rages and he left me on three different occasions and he criticized me and embarrassed me in front of my friends and he didn't try to make a home for me.'

After listening to her plea, and questioning Minnie Willett, the divorce was granted, and Marilyn returned to Los Angeles a free woman.

Not long after the divorce was granted, Berniece left Los Angeles, and shortly after, Gladys decided she no longer wished to stay in California and moved back to Oregon. Around the same time, Marilyn determined it was time to gain some independence of her own, and left Aunt Ana's in search of her own place.

She found a small apartment at 3539 Kelton Avenue, and fully embraced the chance to live by herself for the first time in her life. She started to frequent Schwabs drug store, which aside from selling the obvious, also acted as a café and hangout for budding actors. She became friendly with newspaper reporter Sidney Skolsky, who had offices at Schwabs, and with Steve Hayes, who later managed Googies, the coffee shop next door.

Hayes remembers being introduced to Marilyn by Sydney Chaplin, whose brother, Charlie Jr, dated her briefly. In his 2008 book, *Googies: Coffeeshop to the Stars*, Hayes recalled: '[Sydney and I had] been talking at the bar in the Garden of Allah, and when it became crowded we walked across Sunset to Frascati's to grab some dinner. Marilyn hung out there and at The Garden in her early years and when she saw Sydney she quickly joined us for a drink.'

Sharing the same favourite joints, the pair would often run into each other around town, and soon became friendly. 'Marilyn was anything but dumb,' remembers Hayes. 'Her only problem was she was incapable of concentrating on more than one thing at a time – and anything for a long time. To combat that she skipped from one subject to another, hoping no one would catch on.'

Marilyn continued her studies at the studio, but became disheartened when her trips to the casting department always resulted in the same outcome – no call. Darryl F. Zanuck, the head of the studio, seemed to barely notice her presence and was certainly in no hurry to use her in any productions. However, he could hardly fail to notice her increasing popularity, evident in events such as a trip to Castroville and Salinas in order to take part in various publicity events.

After travelling for hours on a bus packed with Italian fishermen, Marilyn eventually arrived at her destination, where she was shocked to find hoards of fans and admirers. Stanley Seedman, the owner of the Carlyle's store where she was due to make an appearance, had ordered 200 photos, but soon found it was not enough to satisfy even a minority of the followers who had turned out to greet her. More photos were ordered and he later told reporter Ken Schultz, 'We didn't know how big this was going to go. Before the week was over we had given out either 1000 or 1200 of them.'

The trip was a huge success and Marilyn was bestowed with various titles including the rather curious 'Artichoke Queen'. Finally, Zanuck could ignore her growing popularity no more and in February 1947 her contract was extended, and she won parts in two films: *Scudda Hoo, Scudda Hay* and *Dangerous Years*.

In the first, *Scudda Hoo, Scudda Hay*, Marilyn had an uncredited role and played in two scenes, although one later ended up on the cutting-room floor, and the other went so fast that it would take a trained eye to spot her. In the second film, Marilyn spent a week on the set starting on 30 July 1947. For her efforts she received a speaking part as a waitress, although as she later wrote to her sister, 'I'm in it but for heaven's sake don't blink your eyes, you might miss me.'

During this time, both Marilyn and Shelley Winters started to attend lessons at the Actors Lab, an establishment led by Morris Carnovsky and his wife Phoebe Brand, and located at 14355 Laurel Ave. Marilyn truly believed in the work that was being done there, so much so that several years later she tried to convince Bill Pursel to attend too. Bill remembered: 'She tried to enrol me in Actors Lab; she wanted me to become an actor, I guess, as I had done some acting at high school. Without my knowledge she set up an appointment and I know she was disappointed when I didn't go, but I had no intention to forfeit my last year at Woodbury College where I was an honor student and tops in my major.'

Inspired by her work at the Actors Lab, Marilyn jumped at the chance of attending classes being taught by actor Charles Laughton at his home on Curson Avenue. It was, however, an unfortunate experience; just starting out and not classically trained, Marilyn felt intimidated by her other classmates and the intensity of the classes, and left after only a few sessions. She did, however, continue her studies at the Actors Lab, and started to take an interest in books – buying them from Pickwick Books, Martindales Book Store and Marian Hunter's Book Shop.

But attending the Actors Lab wasn't the only training Marilyn was interested in pursuing, and she began lessons at the Beverly Hills home of Twentieth Century Fox's acting teacher Helena Sorell. Over fifty years later film fan Christine Krogull visited Helena at the home where she had taught Marilyn all those years before. 'The apartment had undergone no major changes,' recalled Christine. 'You could feel and smell the history there. Marilyn had once been photographed in front of a painting in Helena's living room and it was still there, in exactly the same place!'

Christine spent a few hours talking with Helena, who shared her memories of Marilyn with her. 'She told me that Marilyn was an extremely talented student. She always followed her advice, rehearsed and practised a lot, and was very friendly. During one training scene she was to eat a slice of bread with meat. Helena played in the scene with Marilyn and when they came to the point of eating, Marilyn stopped – began to search for some-thing – took imaginary salt and pepper shakers and pretended to sprinkle them over the meat because in her opinion that was what was missing from the scene. Helena was surprised because

Marilyn had done it so naturally and was more surprised the next day when she came with a present of a real salt and pepper shaker – in the shape of a cat and dog.'

On 15 April 1947, Marilyn attended the Annual Ceremony and Presentation of Honorary Colonels at the Hollywood Legion Stadium, where she received a badge of honour along with seventeen other 'Studio Starlings'. Then during the summer of 1947, Marilyn and Bill Pursel were able to get together once again, when she and some other starlets were required to travel to Las Vegas for a publicity event at the Flamingo Hotel. Bill remembered: 'Norma Jeane asked me to meet her there, but when I arrived I wasn't allowed in. The curtains were pulled across the door and when I told the security man that there was a girl in there I was meeting, he said, 'Oh sure there is', however, he parted the curtains and I could see some dance girls on stage. Norma Jeane's group was seated right in the centre of the room, flanking a long table just below the stage, and she spotted me and yelled and waved. I was very embarrassed, especially when I entered the showroom and the spotlights went right on me! She had saved me a seat and when I made my way to her, we hugged one another and everyone cheered.'

The couple went out to the pool to catch up, but after just ten minutes one of Marilyn's group came out and sternly demanded she go back inside. 'The man was very aggressive and I confronted him by threatening to throw him in the pool,' remembered Bill. 'He backed off and left, but then Norma Jeane told me she was supposed to be inside with the rest of the girls, shilling at the gaming tables. [A shill is a person who works for the gambling house and is supplied money with which to gamble.] I was so angry I snapped at her and took her back inside.' For a time, Bill sat at the bar with the actors David Niven and Sonny Tufts, before excusing himself and heading to the door to leave. 'I spotted Norma Jeane and waved bye to her as I left.'

When Pursel told his sister, Jeanne Chretien, what had happened, she was shocked. 'Bill told me they were trying to boss Norma Jeane around and I was appalled,' remembered

Chretien. 'I said, "That's awful, she's such a sweet girl," to which Bill replied "No one's going to treat her like a tramp while I'm around."'

On 11 June Marilyn signed an agreement with Twentieth Century Fox to reconfirm her contract, and a month later, on 20 July, she appeared at the Brentwood Country Club for Fox's Annual Golf Tournament. This event did not further her career, but another golf tournament on 17 August proved to be highly influential, when she was assigned the job of caddy to actor John Carroll and his wife, MGM talent scout Lucille Ryman. The Carrolls were interested in and took pity on the young, determined actress, and quickly befriended her.

This support couldn't have come at a better time, as just when she was starting to feel slightly confident about her career, Marilyn was unceremoniously dropped from Twentieth Century Fox. Her agent, Harry Lipton, had the unenviable task of telling her the news, and she was, of course, absolutely devastated. Lipton remembered: 'Her immediate reaction was the world had crashed around her ears – unhappiness and tears. And then typical of Marilyn she shook her head, set her jaw and said "It really doesn't matter. After all, it's a case of supply and demand."'

What did matter, however, was that before her contract ended, Marilyn had been rehearsing for the Twentieth Century Fox annual show, held on the Fox lot. With a staunch determination and a commitment to her cause, she was determined that even though she had been dropped, she would still go through with the event. Kathleen Hughes Rubin remembered: 'The show was made up ninety per cent from secretaries, mailroom people etc, but there were always a few contract players too. My cousin was in the show and had told me all about Marilyn, saying that she was incredibly talented but had just been dropped. She was sure that if the executives saw the show, they would re-sign her.

'Marilyn sang a song called "I never took a lesson in my life" and wore a sexy dress. I can still remember what it looked like! She sang and danced a little – the song was a double entendre song and she did it wonderfully ... but although Marilyn was wonderful, the executives didn't re-sign her.'

After being dropped from the studio, Marilyn's income plummeted and before long she found herself in financial dire straits, often not having enough money for food or rent. One of the reasons for this was the purchase of a record player, which Marilyn had bought on instalment when she first signed to Fox. She later remembered that this 'splendiferous' player did everything but fry an egg; it cost $1,500 and was custom-made. Her agent, Harry Lipton had remarked that she 'was out of her mind' to buy it, and in the end, according to him, he had to make several payments on it himself.

However, when her option was not picked up at Fox, she returned home one day to find a man waiting to take away her record player. 'I was almost heartbroken as I watched him carry it away, and to this day I have yet to see a more beautiful cabinet or player,' she remembered. Although she later claimed to have learnt from the experience, this wasn't the last time she would find herself tied up in financial difficulties, and friends began to worry that she had no idea about money at all.

Her days of unemployment were long and filled with insecurities. Sometimes the young actress would mope around her small apartment, wondering why she was such a failure and had been unable to make things work. Other times she would read and keep herself busy, studying at the Actors Lab, taking singing lessons, involving herself with occasional modelling work and neglecting her social life in favour of trying to ignite her career. Her friendships started to suffer as a result, and Bill Pursel remembers at least one occasion when their plans had to be cancelled: 'While I was at the University of Nevada, Norma Jeane was going to come up to the University for a dance, but she called it off just a few days before the event because of a photo shoot she couldn't cancel. I was disappointed and she was very unhappy, but it just wasn't possible with all that she was doing with her career at the time.'

But sometimes work took a back seat and Marilyn would go 'people-watching' at Union Station, or stargazing in Hollywood. Johnny Grant, Hollywood's honorary Mayor and friend of Marilyn in the early days, remembered, 'She used to like to sit in the Roosevelt Hotel Lobby, observing people, and would occasionally make new friends. She had a mad crush on Clark Gable and would stand in front of his house, hoping to see him come or go. She would also often place her hands and feet in the moulds of other stars at Grauman's Chinese Theatre.' Unfortunately, at this point in time it must have seemed that her dream of stardom was just as far away as it had been when she had done the same thing as a little girl.

It was during this time of aloneness and very little work that some authors have claimed she became a call girl. However, Marilyn effectively responded to such stories in 1953 when she spoke about being broke and receiving a phone call from a man who wanted to 'help' her: 'He gave details of what I would be expected to do. He was brutally frank and all I could think of to say was that he shouldn't talk that way over a public telephone. I didn't realize how silly that sounded until I hung up and then I started to laugh.'

It seems highly unlikely that the girl who constantly complained of being pestered by 'wolves' would ever sell herself for money. But while that story is ridiculous, it is nothing compared to another rumour that, at this point in her life, Marilyn became pregnant and gave the baby up for adoption. Bill Pursel laughs at both theories: 'Wow! I don't believe this for one moment. As far as I know this is a bunch of poppycock. I do know there were several women jealous of her after she became Marilyn Monroe and besides, call girls earn big money – I saw no evidence of this with her. I would put no credence at all in these rumours. It's nothing but bilge . . . blather . . . hogwash . . . someone's cheap imagination. It sorta makes me angry, or can't you tell? She wasn't pregnant when I knew her; she probably had several boyfriends over the years, but when these stories exaggerate the involvement into pregnancy or even intimacy they are way out of bounds. She had too much class to be so careless about who she dated. At least this is where I come from.'

This is backed up by agent Harry Lipton, in an article for *Motion Picture* in May 1956. He described a party in which a high-powered man offered Marilyn gifts in exchange for certain favours: she refused, turned to her agent, demanded they leave and cried all the way home in the car. 'What can I say to men like that, Harry?' she asked her agent, to which he replied, 'You'll learn.' This hardly seems the behaviour of a seasoned call girl, and a hungry one at that.

Marilyn moved around a lot at this time and sometimes found herself staying at the home of Aunt Enid and Uncle Stan Knebelkamp, in order to save money while commuting to and from Hollywood. She also lived in her fair share of cheap apartments, including one on Avon Street, where she later claimed to have experienced a trauma that left her extremely shaken and distressed. Although there are several versions of what actually happened, the general gist of the story is that Marilyn had received her last pay cheque from Twentieth Century Fox and, as the bank was closed, was seeking another way of cashing it. She was in the process of asking a restaurant manager, when she was approached by a policeman, who offered to accompany her to a clothes shop across the street. Once there, Marilyn wrote her name and address on the cheque; cashed it; thanked the policeman and left.

That night, while asleep, Marilyn was alarmed to discover the policeman cutting the screen on her door, to gain entrance to her home. 'I was scared silly,' she said in 1953. 'I ran out of the front door and over to the neighbours.' Unfortunately, several residents refused to let her in for fear of 'becoming involved', but she eventually found one who was willing to call the police, who later arrested the intruder and identified him as a fellow police officer. The incident had a lasting effect on Marilyn and she spoke of it often in interviews, along with her agent Harry Lipton, who later told how he was so concerned he'd also phoned the police himself.

The morning after the intruder incident, Marilyn phoned Lucille Ryman and John Carroll, the couple who had befriended her at the charity golf match, and who had been loaning her various sums of money since September 1947. When she relayed the intruder story to the couple, they were appalled and moved her into their home at 8497 Fountain Avenue, while they moved to their ranch in the San Fernando Valley.

'It was just wonderful,' remembered Marilyn in 1952. 'It was the first nice place I'd ever had, and I felt really independent and sure that something good was going to happen to me.' Unfortunately, although she enjoyed her new home, she still had trouble forgetting the intruder incident and Harry Lipton later recalled that she was rather afraid to live alone and was forever looking over her shoulder. As a result, she would often spend nights at the Ryman-Carroll ranch in the Valley, but was still haunted by the fact that several neighbours had refused to get involved during the intruder incident. According to Lipton, this brought back disturbing memories of her insecure childhood, and she became very upset as a result.

In spite of any memories of childhood traumas, Marilyn was still very much in touch with Grace Goddard's family and began taking afternoon coffee with Grace's sister, Enid Knebelkamp and her friend Catherine Larson. Catherine had first been introduced whilst Marilyn was walking barefoot around a flowerbed in the side yard. Now the three women met regularly at Enid's house, where Catherine quickly developed an opinion on the actress. According to friend James Glaeg, Catherine felt Marilyn to be 'worthy of admiration' but not brilliant, or beautiful. 'She was the kind you want to cuddle,' she told James, before adding that she had always wanted to take Marilyn aside and advise her to get out of the acting business, feeling that she would never make it in Hollywood. 'The surprise was on me,' she later admitted.

Marilyn's acting aspirations took a positive turn when she landed a part in the play, *Glamour Preferred* at the Bliss-Hayden Theater. Running from 12 October to 2 November, she was cast in the role of Lady Bonnie Towyn, a young actress who tries to steal the main character's husband. The play, which was written by Florence Ryerson and Colin Clements, wasn't particularly thrilling, but it did give Marilyn a chance to work in the theatre, and she shone in the part, prompting one of her co-stars to comment that when she walked onstage, no one noticed any of the other actors.

The play also gave her the opportunity to be properly intro-duced to Annabelle Stanford, a model and actress who had been on a photo shoot with Norma Jeane in Las Vegas, and had also dated Bill Pursel's brother Dick. She recalls: 'Dick had told me that I looked just like Bill's girlfriend, Norma Jeane and even photographers would often say the same thing. When I even-tually met Marilyn, she was sat in an observation seat at Bliss-Hayden, and was introduced as a new cast member. I looked over and we both shouted, "It's you!" because we'd both been hearing how much we looked alike from the Pursel broth-ers. She was a charming, delightful woman with a wonderful sense of humour, and was well liked by people. I never heard anyone talking about her in a coarse way; there was nothing slutty about her; nothing trash. In fact no one I knew ever saw any trash in her. Any image of her being trashy was purely in a guy's dreams.'

Chapter 7

Starlet

By December 1947, Marilyn had moved from the home of the Carrolls – John Carroll and Lucille Ryman – into a house at 4215 Rowland Street, Burbank. However, they were still very much involved in Marilyn's life, and agreed to manage her career from 1 December 1947 to 29 February 1948. The agreement gave Marilyn a $100 a week income, in exchange for the Carrolls receiving any money from her acting career, minus 10 per cent to be paid to agent Harry Lipton.

According to Lucille Ryman, Marilyn became something of a problem, and would repeatedly ring her and John at work, even though she was requested not to do this. 'Under Marilyn's baby-doll, kitten exterior, she is tough and shrewd and calculating,' said Ryman, when interviewed in the mid-1950s. When the friendship later soured, it left bad feelings particularly with Lucille, who later claimed that Marilyn had attempted to seduce John Carroll on their first meeting, and asked Ryman to divorce him, so she could attempt a relationship with him herself.

But while still contracted to represent her, the Carrolls introduced Marilyn to Pat De Cicco, the ex-husband of slain 1930s film actress Thelma Todd. It was through De Cicco that she was introduced to sixty-nine-year-old Joseph Schenck, one of the 'big fish' at Fox. Schenck was immediately taken with the starlet, and she began spending many hours at his home at 141 South Carolwood Drive.

Much has been written about this relationship, with some implying that she was little more than a sexual plaything for the ageing mogul. However, Marilyn always publicly denied this, insisting that the two were just friends and that she spent so much time at his home because his cook served good food. She later told director Elia Kazan that the ageing mogul had asked her to marry him, knowing that she would be well taken care of if something ever happened to him. She refused the proposal, but enjoyed their friendship and the trips to his home.

Schenck himself denied any romantic involvement when interviewed by Ezra Goodman in the mid-1950s: 'She used to come here quite often for dinner. I think she liked to eat. We have good food here. No, I never had any romantic thoughts about Marilyn and she never had any such thoughts about me.'

Although she never asked him for favours related to her career, shortly after Marilyn and Schenck became friends, he persuaded Columbia Pictures boss Harry Cohn to take a look at her screen test. Unfortunately, the married Cohn was interested in Marilyn for more than her acting ability, and tried to persuade her to take a trip to Catalina Island on his yacht. Marilyn assured him that she'd only be interested in going if his wife came too, sending Cohn into a fury.

Shortly after the incident with Cohn, Marilyn met up with Aunt Enid and friend Catherine, during one of their regular coffee afternoons. There she shared the story of the executive trying to entice her on to his yacht. Catherine's friend James Glaeg recalled: 'Catherine told that story before I read it anywhere. "There's one thing I can say for Marilyn," Catherine said – as though there were a lot of things she couldn't say for her – "She was a good girl."'

Most authors claim that it was Schenk's introduction to Harry Cohn that got Marilyn a contract at Columbia Pictures, but in an article entitled 'The private life of Marilyn Monroe', drama coach Natasha Lytess tells a rather different story.

Lytess was a failed actress who had once been contracted to RKO. According to her, she had been asked by Max Arnow from the Columbia talent department to take a look at a starlet called Marilyn Monroe. He didn't think much of her possibilities and wanted a second opinion, but when Lytess first saw her, she wasn't sure either: 'The first time I met Marilyn Monroe, I thought to myself, "That voice!" My ears couldn't take it. Her manner was also almost apologetic and plainly revealed an "I know I'm not good enough, but I'll try" attitude.'

However, something about the girl impressed Lytess enough to know she wanted to help her, but had no idea what she could do, given the short time she had to work with her. According to Natasha, Marilyn was not under contract to Columbia at that time, and she paid for her own lessons. However, they had only worked together for a couple of weeks when Max Arnow called to complain: 'I've just looked at the report card of Marilyn Monroe,' he said. 'You are spending a lot of time with her. Too much. I suggest you drop her.' Natasha refused and instead the two of them worked together on an audition piece from a long-forgotten film called *They Knew What They Wanted*, which impressed the studio bosses enough to sign her.

An ecstatic Marilyn signed the six-month, $125-a-week contract on 9 March 1948, and told Natasha that this was the first time in her life she would have the security to work at her studies and not have to worry about rent or food. She saw the contract as a new beginning; a chance to make her dreams come true at last: 'The Columbia contract was different,' she later wrote, 'I was sure that my big opportunity had come.'

Before her 'big opportunity' was able to develop, however, Marilyn was devastated to learn that her beloved Aunt Ana had passed away. The old lady had been ill for some time, but this did not prevent Marilyn's heart from breaking with grief. 'I was left without anyone to take my hopes and my troubles to. I was miserable,' she remembered. She returned to the apartment she had once shared with her favourite 'Aunt', and going through her belongings she discovered that Ana had left a book for her, *The Potter*, along with a note on the title page that read: 'Marilyn dear, read this book. I don't leave you much except my love. But not even death can diminish that, nor will death ever take me far away from you.' The young actress was devastated and never forgot the lady who had encouraged her through thick and thin, right from day one.

Marilyn's grief was relieved somewhat when she was cast in a low-budget musical called *Ladies of the Chorus*, which began shooting on 22 April and finished on 3 May 1948. The film cast Marilyn as Peggy Martin opposite Adele Jergens, who was only nine years older than Marilyn, yet bizarrely found herself playing her mother. Marilyn looked young and beautiful in the role, although the plot was hardly exciting – Peggy and her mother, Mae, are working together in a burlesque show, when Peggy gets her big break and steals the heart of a wealthy young bachelor (Rand Brooks). The romance falters when her mother disapproves and his family finds out what Peggy does for a living, but like all fairy tales, romance wins out in the end and they all live happily ever after. Marilyn herself later admitted to hating the film, but could not deny that it had given her a great chance to sing and dance in a movie.

Her two songs, 'Every Baby Needs a Da Da Daddy' and 'Anyone Can See I Love You', were done under the guidance of musical supervisor Fred Karger, who worked for Columbia at the time. Karger was thirty-two years old when he met the twenty-one-year-old starlet, and had recently divorced. He was living with his mother, sister and child, and was in no mood for a serious relationship, but this did not stop him being attracted to Marilyn. She herself fell in love with the musician: 'I fell in love with an ordinary man who played the piano,' she said. 'I had always been attracted to men who wore glasses and when he put his on the first time to read some music, I was overwhelmed. He stopped playing, came over and kissed me and a new life began.'

Unfortunately, the relationship was ultimately not a happy one for Marilyn. Fred Karger was feeling bitter after his divorce, and she often felt as though he was putting her down and belittling her intelligence and dreams. He did not inspire confidence, and in actual fact it would seem that she actually got along much better with his mother and sister than she did with him. But that said, she did fall heavily for Karger, declaring that, 'when he came into my room and took me in his arms, all my troubles were forgotten. I even forgot Norma Jeane.'

Marilyn later told author Ben Hecht that Karger refused to marry her because he didn't want his child to be raised by a woman like her. Then to add insult to injury, Karger happily helped her move into her next home; a room at an establishment especially designed for single women.

Built in 1926 to help women who worked in the industry, the Hollywood Studio Club was an attractive, three-storey building located at 1215 Lodi Place, in the heart of Hollywood. By the time Marilyn became aware of its existence, it had been home to some 7,000 girls, and on 3 June 1948, the young actress left her small apartment and moved into a double room at the club, where she paid $12 for room and board.

When Fred Karger dropped her off, she looked around the room she would share with opera student Clarice Evans, and was not overly impressed. It reminded her of the orphanage, and there were various rules and regulations to stick to – primarily no smoking in the lobby, no shorts in the dining room, and absolutely no men allowed on the upper floors. She decided to keep herself to herself, and soon gained a reputation of being curiously quiet, never taking part in any small talk about boyfriends or gossiping in any way. Still, Evans later told biographer Maurice Zolotow that she went on more dates than any of the other girls, and received more phone calls than anyone else, even though she was still dating not just Fred Karger but old flame Bill Pursel, too.

During this time, Marilyn's career was still very much on her mind, and on 15 August she opened in a play entitled *Stage Door* at the Bliss-Hayden Theater. The three-act play was written by Edna Ferber and George S. Kaufman and centres on sixteen young actresses who all share rooms in a boarding house run by an elderly woman called Mrs Orcutt. The main character is a young woman called Terry, who is trying to make it big in the theatre. By the end of the play, she has won her dream role and is fully intent on never having to share a bedroom ever again. The story of the main character's life and dreams in the boarding house reminded Marilyn of her own life at the Hollywood Studio Club, and it is no coincidence that around the time of being in the play she moved out of her shared room and into a private one at the club for $16.50 rent a week.

In September 1948 Bill Pursel found himself in Los Angeles again, when he enrolled at the Woodbury College, a business school where he planned to study advertising. Despite still being involved with Fred Karger, Norma Jeane began spending a lot of time with Pursel, and the two would often hang out together, lunching in the Columbia commissary, and enjoying each other's company. As Pursel remembered: 'We didn't have a favourite place to go; we would just stop on the spur of the moment at a place that looked quiet and secluded. She was rather close-mouthed about her personal life, though she did talk about what happened in her modelling career or where she had been on certain shoots. But, most of our conversation was quiet and private like, and then there were the notes on restaurant and bar napkins – I sure wish I had those – we wrote back and forth about the kind of house she (we) wanted; the number of children, the type of dog, and all sorts of other stuff including little games back and forth.'

They also attended a dance at the popular and crowded Palladium dance hall in Hollywood, where clarinet player Woody Herman was playing with his band. Norma Jeane made quite an impression that night, as remembered by Pursel: 'As the two of us danced close to the stage, Woody Herman was looking at Norma Jeane and almost walked straight off the edge of the stage! He just caught himself, but the clarinet came out of his mouth. She didn't see this because her back was to the stage, but the oohs of the packed crowd got her attention. I jokingly told her it was all her fault and we laughed about it later.'

Perhaps one of the most interesting things about Marilyn's friendship with Bill Pursel was her relaxed and interested attitude towards him, and as a result, their time together was both enjoyable and carefree: 'She would always ask me about my studies at college and about my baseball playing and stuff like that. She never dressed up for me, this is one of the things I liked about her. She was very beautiful with little make-up and her hair pulled back with a ribbon.

'I remember a date we had one night to go grunion hunting on the beach. When the grunion are running, loads of people flock to the beach with buckets and nets to catch these little fish. I remember Norma Jeane and I, pants rolled up to our knees, with a couple of buckets, frolicking in the surf with dozens of other people, scooping up these little swarming fish. Norma Jeane and I would look for some small children and give our catch away; it was a fun adventure and I enjoyed watching her gleefully bouncing about and yelling "I've got some, I've got some." She was so much fun to be with; so childlike and free. Here she was, wet and sandy from falling in the surf, bubbling with laughter and scooping up these little wiggly fish to give to some child who was too small to compete in the splashing surf.'

But it wasn't always children who were interested in Norma Jeane, such as on one occasion during another beach excursion with Bill when an overenthusiastic vendor gave her a whole armful of hot dogs, instead of just the one she ordered: 'She was well aware of her attractiveness, but she didn't flirt, and her appearance was always one of class. When we were together she was with me and when she talked to me (sometimes it was just a whisper) she looked me squarely in the eyes. She once asked me if the remarks and whistles bothered me. I joked, "Why would the whistles bother me – they are whistling at me, not you!"'

But while Norma Jeane may have joked about Bill's envy, she did possess rather a lot of jealousy of her own. On one occasion she knew she couldn't make a dance date with Bill, but left it to the very last minute to cancel, to make sure he couldn't take anyone else. Then on another occasion, the two were sat in the Columbia cafeteria: 'Norma Jeane asked if she could see my glasses so I took them off and handed them to her. She immediately smeared butter on the lenses to stop me looking at the many good-looking girls who were dining there.'

Bill also remembers a Spanish girl who worked in the office where he had a part-time job during his college days in Los Angeles. 'She was kinda stuck on me; she was older than me but a very attractive gal.' When Norma Jeane found out about his admirer, she became quite keen on moving in together. 'I told her not to get the cart ahead of the horse as I wanted to finish college before starting to play house. She said, "But I'm not getting any younger Bill, and I've noticed those Spanish eyes where you work".' Bill had to convince Norma Jeane that he wasn't interested in his admirer and the subject was eventually dropped.

Encouraged by Bill's interest in opera, Marilyn was happy to learn that *Madam Butterfly* was to be performed at the Hollywood Bowl on 3–4 September 1948, with Eleanor Steber in the title role and Eugene Ormandy conducting. Bill picked her up in his car, and the two headed up to the Bowl to see the performance. Pursel remembered: 'She sat very close to me, listening intently to the opera. She was very quiet and moody all evening, but I asked if she was okay and she said she was. When we went to eat after the performance, she was melancholy throughout our dinner, so we just sat quietly, with very little talk. It wasn't until years later that I read Norma Jeane had been in some kind of pageant at the Hollywood Bowl when she was a little child, and she had missed a cue or something. As fragile and fearful of rejection as she was, I thought maybe this little goof may have stayed with her and being in the bowl had turned her thoughts back to that early time in her life, but I didn't push it. She sure had a right to be blue without me or anyone else tugging at her to explain why.'

While it is very possible that the trip had stirred up unhappy memories for Marilyn, it is also likely that she was thinking about Fred Karger, who was growing ever colder towards their relationship. She was still in love with the musician but his lack of concern for her feelings and his often hurtful and tactless remarks were hard for her to bear. The relationship was failing fast, and Marilyn knew it.

For the rest of September, it seemed as though nothing went right for Marilyn. The first stroke of bad luck happened when she was called into the office at Columbia. She had been told by friends at the studio that the rushes of *Ladies of the Chorus* had gone well, and that she was up for an important role, so it was with happiness and hope that she went into the meeting. Unfortunately, she had not been brought in to arrange a part in a big production, and instead was told that although the studio felt she would go far in her career, there was simply no work for her at Columbia. On 8 September, the shocked actress was dropped from her contract, and was absolutely devastated. Later in her life, she was able to look back on her experience and admit that she hadn't been ready for a career when she first had the opportunity, but at the time the news came as a crushing blow.

'Things were tough,' she said. 'I limited myself to two meals a day – breakfast and dinner – and went back to modelling. I went without new clothes, everything, earning just enough to pay the rent and take my lessons.' But doing the odd 'cheesecake' shot was not enough to keep the wolves from the door, as she was soon to find out. When she had signed to Columbia, a dress shop sent a representative to her home to ask if she would like to buy clothes on credit. Marilyn thought the deal was acceptable, and picked out two suits, a black dress, some shoes and hosiery, coming to $200 in total. However, as soon as the contract expired, the shop demanded she pay for the clothes and as a result, she almost lost her car. 'Once again I had to scratch enough together to bail it out,' she said.

On 12 September she finished her work on *Stage Door*, and on 21 September she was involved in a minor car crash on Sunset Boulevard, on the way to an audition. By pure chance, a photographer by the name of Tom Kelley was driving down Sunset at the time, and stopped to help. A tearful Marilyn explained that she was late for her appointment and had no money for a cab, so the photographer gave her $5 and his business card. It was an important introduction and one she would utilize in the near future.

In the autumn of 1948 Marilyn went on a few dates with an editor called Dan Cahn. He was a friend of Stanley Rubin, a producer who was developing a television series. Rubin had made a thirty-minute pilot programme that was a success, and now the American Tobacco Company had commissioned twenty-six episodes, which he was to adapt, cast and produce.

Rubin had shared his news with Dan Cahn, who in turn told him he was dating a young actress who was beautiful, talented and in need of a job. Rubin remembers: 'Dan asked if she could be used in the show, and I told him to get Marilyn or her agent to call and make an appointment to come in and read. Her agent called and he brought her into the office. She looked at the script for twenty or thirty minutes then said she was ready to read. She was pleasant and beautiful; she read for me, I thanked her and she left.'

Rubin liked the actress, but was worried that she was so inexperienced and nervous that she might hold up shooting. When Cahn rang to ask about Marilyn's fate, Rubin told him that he would not be able to hire her for that particular series, but would possibly use her in the next. For Marilyn this was yet another disappointment on her road to stardom, but when the two finally did work together some six years later, on *River of No Return*, she never held it against him: 'She was gracious enough never to mention the failed audition for the TV series,' laughed Rubin, 'and the fact that I was now eager to have her in 'River of No Return'!'

Several months after being dropped by Columbia, *Ladies of the Chorus*, the only film she had made there, was released. It received little attention from audiences or critics but there was one person who did take an interest: her ex-husband, James Dougherty. As his nephew, Paul 'Wes' Kanteman remembered: 'Uncle Jim had just come out of the police academy when her first picture came out and he was walking the night-time beat on Van Nuys Blvd. Just about every time he passed the movie theatre he would go in and watch a bit of the movie and continued to do this for a while. I would imagine he saw most of her pictures even though he would never tell anyone. We used to talk about these times when travelling to a place where we were going to hunt. He would open up to me but not to anyone else that I am aware of.'

Although James had moved on and claimed he was 'too cotton-pickin' busy to go to the movies', Norma Jeane was never far from his thoughts, and as it turned out, his telephone. His nephew, Wes Kanteman remembered: 'She had become rather disenchanted with the whole Hollywood thing and called Uncle and asked if she could come home. He was or could be pretty stubborn and told her no; that she had already made her bed and would have to sleep in it. She was pretty upset and hung up.'

For Jim, having Marilyn attempt a reunion – albeit a misguided one – must have been an extremely difficult time for him, but his heart had been broken once, and he was unwilling to let it happen again. Paul Kanteman knows just how much this must have hurt his uncle: 'He really loved that woman and in my mind did till the day he passed away. I watched him many times and saw the tears come to his eyes. Yes, there was a great love there and I still believe it was mutual. It was a love that had gotten past both of them and they had gone in other directions and could do nothing about it. Of course he had married again which I'm sure was on the rebound but they had children together and that was important to him.'

By the end of 1948 any serious romance that she had shared with Fred Karger had fizzled out, and as Marilyn looked towards the New Year, a new gentleman entered her life, in the form of Johnny Hyde, an agent who was Vice-President at the William Morris Agency. Marilyn met Hyde one evening at a friend's house, and they got along so well together that he called her the next day, inviting her to lunch. After that they became very close and it's fair to say that the fifty-three-year-old Hyde was more than a little smitten with the twenty-two-year-old starlet.

The already married Hyde was a small, slightly built man with a heart condition, but he was nonetheless one of the most influential agents at William Morris. At first he didn't know where she lived, but that didn't stop Hyde bombarding Marilyn with letters, gifts and cards, asking her to write to him at the Arizona Biltmore in Phoenix, where he was staying for a time. 'What is your street address?' he wrote in one early letter, 'All is forgiven because you say you miss me,' he wrote in another. He called her 'My Precious Girl' in one card, and 'My Dear Marilyn' in another, while in public he would refer to her as 'Baby'. Simply put, Johnny Hyde had fallen heavily for Marilyn, and he very much hoped that she felt the same way.

When he saw her in person, he began to encourage her to continue her acting career and made plans for her to leave her agent, Harry Lipton, and sign with William Morris. Marilyn later remembered: 'When I first mentioned my acting hopes to Johnny Hyde, he didn't smile. He listened raptly and said, "Of course you can become an actress!" He was the first person who ever took my ambitions seriously and my gratitude for this alone is endless.'

Actually he wasn't the first person who had taken her seriously, but Marilyn was so grateful to him that she was willing to give him full credit. In return Hyde introduced Marilyn to a great deal of literature and classical music, and taught her how to manage her time. Usually when out of work, Marilyn would sleep late, have a long breakfast and while away the hours on the telephone, but Hyde encouraged her to stop that; to study and use every spare moment to better herself. As a result, she became more confident, started speaking up for herself and even improved her punctuality. Introducing her to a dramatic script entitled *The Brothers Karamazov*, Hyde encouraged Marilyn to aim for dramatic parts and take herself seriously, and as a result, he soon became an inspiration, a father figure, protector and, soon, her lover. Johnny Grant remembered: 'He was a short little fellow and he really broke his ass on her behalf.

I used to see them together at Ciros quite a bit – she was truly fond of him.'

Although Hyde was an obvious mentor to Marilyn, she was still experiencing the occasional let-down, as witnessed by model and contracted actress Annabelle Stanford. 'I remember one day I was at Columbia studios when I came across Marilyn standing with a small, beautifully dressed man [Hyde]. She was wearing a black satin cocktail dress and I remember thinking that she shouldn't be wearing such a dress at that time of day. Marilyn was crying because she had been turned down for a part; turned out that it was a part that had just been given to me.'

On 29 February 1949 Marilyn's contract with the Carrolls came to an end, and on 2 March 1949, thanks to Johnny Hyde, Marilyn signed with the William Morris Agency. Later that month, on 13 March, she left the Hollywood Studio Club and moved into a one-bedroom suite at the Beverly Carlton Hotel, complete with kitchenette and plenty of room for her books. By this time Hyde had left his family and moved into a large house at 718 North Palm Drive, installing booths and a dance floor in the dining room, to emulate Romanoffs, Marilyn's favourite restaurant in Hollywood. She spent many nights in the house – probably far more than she spent at the Beverly Carlton – but by keeping her room at the hotel, she was assured not only independence, but also respectability.

But just living part-time with Marilyn was not enough for Hyde. He had fallen deeply in love with the actress and on more than one occasion, begged her to marry him, emphasizing that if he were to die she would inherit everything if she was his wife. 'A producer I discussed it with said, "What have you got to lose?" I said "Myself – I'll only marry for one reason: Love."' Unfortunately for Hyde, Marilyn would never be in a position to marry him, and she was most certainly still seeing other men at the time.

Still, even though Hyde adored Marilyn, he didn't consider her completely perfect, and made an appointment for her to see plastic surgeon Dr Michael Gurdin. Gurdin decided that she needed her chin reshaped (but not her nose as some have claimed) and inserted a prosthesis into her jaw to soften her profile. The scars from this procedure are revealed in James Haspiel's book, *Marilyn: The Ultimate Look at the Legend.*

When Fred Karger discovered that Marilyn was dating Johnny Hyde he became extremely jealous and went to her house to ask for her hand in marriage. Despite any feelings she may have had in the past, she turned Karger down flat, but this didn't stop his new-found infatuation, and eventually his mother paid a visit, asking Marilyn to reconsider. She refused, but the two women remained friends until the end of Marilyn's life.

In April 1949, photographer Philippe Halsman was assigned to write a story for *Life* magazine, to find out how good eight Hollywood starlets were at acting. The starlets were found by editor Gene Cook, and Halsman photographed them in his room at the Beverly Hills Hotel, asking each girl to act out four basic situations: listening to a good joke, enjoying an invisible, delicious drink, being frightened by a monster and kissing a fabulous lover.

When Marilyn walked into the room Halsman discovered a painfully shy girl who was wooden in her actions, and he was not impressed. But when she embarked on the kissing part of the exercise, his opinion changed and he discovered that she was an intense and hard-working starlet. He wanted to encourage her and told her that while most models couldn't act, she showed great promise and thought she should move to New York to continue her acting career. 'I didn't go,' she later said, 'but I was thrilled by his encouragement.'

Chapter 8

Highs and Lows

In spring 1949, Marilyn's finances were becoming a great concern once again, and she fell behind not only with her rent, but also with the payments on the car she relied on to get to auditions. Tom Kelley, the photographer who had helped when she crashed on Sunset Boulevard, had asked her to pose nude for him several months before, but she had turned him down. However, when she was threatened with the repossession of her car, she decided enough was enough, and called his number.

On 27 May 1949, Marilyn arrived at Kelley's studio at 736 North Seward Avenue. Kelley was known as a perfect gentleman, but to add a touch of respectability to the proceedings, Marilyn requested that his partner Natalie Grasko be in attendance. And so it was that with 'Begin the Beguine' playing on the record player, Marilyn removed her clothes, reclined on a red velvet blanket, and afterwards was paid $50 for her efforts. When asked years later what it felt like, Marilyn replied, 'Very simple . . . And draughty!' and although the photos are considerably tame compared to modern standards, she was so anxious not to be recognized that she signed the release 'Mona Monroe'.

Initially Marilyn had felt OK about posing nude, since she certainly needed the money and was somewhat naively convinced that no one would actually see the photographs. However, as time wore on she became increasingly worried, especially when it became clear to her that Kelley intended to sell them to a calendar company. She admitted her concern to Bill Pursel, who remembers: 'She told me she had done something she was ashamed of, and she wanted to tell me about it before I found out elsewhere.

'She said she wanted to apologize and started to cry, before finally telling me she had posed nude and had done it because her rent was way past due. She then asked if I would look at the pictures and when I said yes she produced them. My first reaction was that these photos were not pornographic at all and they were actually very good. She said the photographer had promised not to sell them but I told her that he probably would, since selling photographs was what he did for a living. I told her that I thought the pictures were in good taste and she asked if I was ashamed of her, to which I said no, but that neither she nor I could undo something that was already done and I was in no position to object to them anyway.'

Early in 1949, Marilyn was stopped by agent Louis Shurr who told her: 'Lester Cowan, producer of "Love Happy" was looking for someone "just your type" for added scenes. I rushed over and was hired on the spot. I not only got on the screen but stayed there for one full minute. I could hardly believe it.' The film was a Marx Brothers comedy acting alongside Groucho in a small but memorable role, playing a woman who requires detective Groucho's help, because 'Men keep following me.' The detective rolls his eyes, shrugs and exclaims, 'Really? I can't understand why.'

This was the extent of Marilyn's cameo appearance, but it was an important role, and took her on a publicity tour in the summer of 1949, taking in New York, Chicago, Detroit, Cleveland, Milwaukee, New Jersey, Rockford and Oak Park, Illinois. The tour was an important step for the actress, but she was confused as to why they had asked her to appear at all: 'I was on screen less than sixty seconds but I got five weeks work out of the part by going on the PA tour, which promoted the film in eight major cities. I felt guilty about appearing on the stage when I had such an insignificant role in the film, but the people in the audiences didn't seem to care.'

On the morning of 21 June, she travelled to Warrensburg,

New York, to present the *Photoplay Magazine* dream house to Mrs Virginia MacAllister and her son, Rusty. Mrs MacAllister had lost her husband to polio in 1945 and had been forced to move in with her parents in order to get her life back together. Marilyn and actors Don DeFore, Donald Buka and Lon McCallister were watched by a crowd of 500 local people, as they visited the house on James Street and presented Mrs MacAllister with the keys. The actors also gave interviews to the media; met local people; and posed for dozens of photos both inside and outside the house. It was good exposure for Marilyn, and the results were eventually published in the November 1949 issue of *Photoplay*, which was quite an achievement for the budding actress.

By sheer chance, Andre de Dienes was in New York at the time of the *Love Happy* tour, and he took Marilyn to Long Island in order to take some photos on the beach, wearing bathing costumes. She also did an interview with columnist Earl Wilson, who later wrote about the encounter in his 27 July 1949 column. He was not overly impressed with the twenty-three-year-old-actress, and regarded some of what she told him as being the work of her publicists. She had been nicknamed the 'Mmmm Girl' by cinemagoers who had seen *Love Happy*, and most of the interview was taken up with discussing this tag, along with some other minor details about her early life and the film. In all, Wilson was very dismissive of Marilyn in the interview – something that he was to apologize for later in her career.

The tour proved to be tiring work – appearing on stage at film screenings, publicity appearances, signing autographs and having her photo taken constantly. Needless to say, by the time the tour had hit Chicago, Marilyn was exhausted, physically and mentally. She took to wearing a slave bracelet on her ankle and later said, 'I wore it because I didn't belong to anyone although I longed to.' She'd had enough of the loneliness on the road, and wanted desperately to go home. Bill Pursel remembered receiving a disturbing phone call from her, whilst she was in the

Windy City: 'She was crying and she was threatening to throw acid into her face to put a stop to the constant picture-taking of her. She had no privacy, and some of the photographers were rude and demanding, as though she owed them something. I tried to console her, and even though she owed them nothing, I told her it was part of the game. I asked her to immediately contact her agent to intercede and call off the wolves or she was going to fire him immediately.

'I told her to tell her agent she was not a piece of meat and even though she understood the photo shoots were important to her career, and she tried to be congenial and cooperative, there comes a time when she deserves some space, and this was the time. I offered to fly to Chicago, but she said it wasn't necessary 'cause she would be home in a few days. She finally stopped crying and settled down.'

When Marilyn arrived in Los Angeles a few days later, she called Bill again. He remembered: 'We spent a very quiet evening together and all was normal. She was starting to have some second thoughts about following a movie career – she wanted to be an actress, not a sex object. We discussed schooling and training, and the difficulty involved and how only a few beautiful girls become stars.'

He later reflected on why she would be so upset with the constant attention: 'Allow me to say, Norma Jeane was a very attractive female who could draw men like flies. She was constantly being pursued, and she had an engaging personality – she was kind and gentle. So, when beauty and kindness are wrapped in a glamorous package like her, things can be explosive on the outside, but underneath this sparkle there was a profound softness and glow.'

Although she thought briefly about giving up her career, Marilyn soon picked herself up and auditioned for a part in the Twentieth Century Fox film, *Ticket to Tomahawk*, staring Dan Dailey and Anne Baxter. Marilyn was to play the small part of Clara, a showgirl in a troop who join Dan Dailey in a rendition of 'Oh, What a Forward Young Man You Are.' Actress Kathleen

Rubin had been up for the part herself, and remembered: 'I couldn't dance and even after spending all day with a dance instructor, I couldn't remember a simple time step. Eventually, when it got to 6 p.m. the dance instructor told me to forget it! The studio then called for Marilyn because they knew she could dance. Although the film was mostly shot on location, one scene was a dance scene on the Fox lot. I went to see the shoot and thought Marilyn was terrific in it. Between takes Marilyn, Dan Dailey and the others would come and sit in a circle to chat; she was very nice during that time, and I really liked her a lot.'

The part Marilyn played wasn't an important role, but it did give her a taste of location filming when the company travelled to Silverton, Colorado. The local newspapers were buzzing with the news that a film crew would be visiting the town, and on 29 July 1949, it was reported that the director, Richard Sale, had arrived. By 19 August, Empire Street had been remodelled and revamped to look like 1900s America, with saloons, business establishments, general stores and a jail; along with various extras, actors and actresses in attendance. The filming went on until mid-September, though it is likely that Marilyn did not stay on location the entire time, as her part was very small.

Around this time, Marilyn met and befriended a gentleman by the name of A.C. Lyles, who worked at Paramount Studios. Almost sixty years later, he remembered how they first met: 'I was in St Louis opening a picture for Paramount when I read Erskine Johnson's column in which he listed some young actors and actresses who he thought had a chance to make good. One was Marilyn Monroe. At that time, I didn't know Marilyn. I sent the column to her care of the Screen Actors Guild. When I returned, there was a message at the studio for me to call her. She came to the studio to have lunch with me and that was the start of our friendship. My first impressions were the same as Erskine's. She was most attractive, a saucy personality, and had all the qualities to be successful given opportunities. After that, we had lunches in the Paramount commissary, went to see movies at Grauman's Chinese Theatre, and sometimes dinners at the Brown Derby.'

Shortly after the shooting of *Ticket to Tomahawk*, Marilyn took the decision to cut her hair into a shoulder-length bob. This new cut gave her a whole new image and sophistication that was missing from the 'girl-next-door' look of long, wavy hair. Meanwhile, Johnny Hyde continued to squire Marilyn around town, showing her off and making sure influential people saw her. A.C. Lyles remembered: 'It was very obvious he was extremely fond of Marilyn and wanted to do everything in his capacity as a highly respected agent to advise Marilyn's career. She was extremely fond of Johnny. Her friends also liked him and were grateful for his friendship with Marilyn. I don't know if he ever asked Marilyn to marry him. We all loved Johnny and I'm sure that included Marilyn.'

The first acting part she obtained after changing her image came towards the end of 1949, and was that of Angela, Louis Calhern's mistress in the John Huston movie, *The Asphalt Jungle*. Lucille Ryman and Johnny Hyde had put Marilyn forward for the part, but it was her audition that secured her the role. She had rehearsed for three days with Natasha Lytess, and although extremely nervous, she was determined to do a good job. Marilyn performed the audition whilst sitting on the floor, and afterwards begged the director to let her do it again. It was unnecessary, however, as Huston was impressed enough to hire her for the part – the most important of her career so far.

By now Marilyn was extremely reliant on the support of Natasha Lytess, and as a result, the coach was a constant presence on the *Asphalt Jungle* set, even giving up her job at Columbia in order to give 100 per cent of her time. This was the beginning of what would become a director's nightmare, where Marilyn would look to her coach for guidance instead of the director himself. In fact, in one particular scene, Marilyn can be seen quickly glancing off set in the direction of her coach, to see if her performance was OK. Still, in spite of that, Marilyn did a tremendous job with the four scenes she had, and when the film was released on 23 May 1950, it gained favourable reviews not only for the main cast, but for her too.

On 28 October 1949, Louella Parsons reported in her syndicated column that Marilyn had called her with great excitement, to tell her about her part in *The Asphalt Jungle*. During the call she lavished her thanks on Joseph Schenck, 'who gave me my first job in the movies,' Johnny Hyde for signing her, and John Huston for accepting her. 'I am just grateful to everyone,' sighed the woman described by Parsons as 'One of the sweetest girls I know'. This was a far cry from the desperately unhappy girl who had phoned Bill Pursel just a few months before; for once she was enjoying her success and making the most of her new-found popularity.

By the beginning of 1950, Marilyn was auditioning for parts at the newly formed Players Ring Theater at 8351 Santa Monica Boulevard. She never won a part but by this time Twentieth Century Fox were becoming keen on her once again, and on 5 January 1950, she began shooting *The Fireball*, followed in April 1950 by the small but important role of Miss Caswell in *All about Eve*. The film was a vehicle for film legend Bette Davis, with co-stars Anne Baxter, George Sanders and Celeste Holm, making it the first film Marilyn had appeared in with such a hugely talented cast. 'It was only a small part,' she said, 'but I was thrilled to be working with Sanders, Bette Davis and Anne Baxter.' The experience was daunting, but she really held her own, and although only hired initially for one week's work, she ended up spending a month on the set.

However, she made relatively few friends, particularly because every time she had a scene to play, shooting would be held up by her continual lateness. Celeste Holm later remembered that the actor Gregory Ratoff once declared, 'That girl will be a big star!' to which Holm retorted, 'Why, because she keeps everyone waiting?' The actor replied, 'No, she has a quality.' But someone who did not feel the same way was George Sander's wife, Zsa Zsa Gabor, after rumours surfaced on the set that Marilyn had had an affair with the actor. True or not, the episode was to come back to haunt her several months later, when she was invited to a party given by photographer Anthony Beauchamp. On realizing that Marilyn was not only at the party, but also speaking to her husband, Zsa Zsa is said to have stormed into a bedroom with her mother, staying there until her husband was ready to leave.

But Marilyn probably didn't spend much time worrying about Zsa Zsa, as she was much too busy with her career. She was still in great demand from photographers, and on 17 May 1950, Earl Leaf travelled to Hyde's North Palm Drive home and photographed her in the garden, playing with her new chihuahua Josefa, and posing among the trees and shrubbery. Shortly after, she took part in a screen test for a new gangster film called *Cold Shoulder*, which was to be produced by George Jessel. The screen test went well enough to draw the attention of the media, and on 18 July 1950 Louella Parsons announced that Marilyn had won the part and would be acting opposite Richard Conte and Victor Mature. The part was still being talked about in August, but it was all an illusion; under instructions from studio boss Darryl F. Zanuck, *Cold Shoulder* was shelved.

But it wasn't all bad news. Because of her new 'bobbed' hair and the small parts in *The Asphalt Jungle* and *All about Eve* Marilyn started to draw attention from syndicated journalists such as Sheilah Graham, and the aforementioned Louella Parsons, who started to compare the starlet to Lana Turner. This comparison was flattering but she was eager to dispel any similarities: 'I don't think I'm another Lana Turner,' she said. 'I think I have a personality all of my own.'

Interestingly, during the summer of 1950, it was reported that Twentieth Century Fox had bought the rights to Anita Loo's screenplay, *Gentlemen Prefer Blondes*. On hearing about this, Louella Parsons wrote in her 2 September column that they should consider using Marilyn for the part of Lorelei Lee. Her wish came true some two years later, when Fox did choose her to play Lorelei in the film. But for now she had to content herself with playing small roles, and for most of 1950 Marilyn worked hard and won parts in films such as *Right Cross* and *Hometown Story*, along with making a television commercial for Royal Triton Gasoline.

Determined to make it as a star in Hollywood, Marilyn spent a lot of time studying the actresses at Twentieth Century Fox, and in particular, Betty Grable. During an interview with film and theatre critic Michael Thornton eight years after Marilyn's death, Celeste Holm recalled that the starlet had been obsessed with Betty Grable and would follow her around, sit through her films many times and try to emulate her position and success. 'She wanted to be Betty Grable,' Holm told Thornton.

Several years later Betty Grable told Thornton herself that it was true Marilyn used to follow her around, 'to the point that it got a little bit scary'. However, she eventually understood her fascination and told Thornton that she thought Marilyn was a person with no clear identity of her own, and that everything she did was a desperate search for identity.

Her search and perseverance were beginning to pay off, however, as she continued to win small mentions in the many gossip columns that crowded the Los Angeles newspapers. Her love life was also winning publicity when Sheila Graham reported on 12 October that Marilyn had been spotted at the beach with none other than Peter Lawford, the man who would be pivotal in introducing her to the Kennedy family some eleven years later. Marilyn denied the involvement, however, saying 'as a matter of fact I've never had a date with Peter. We were at the same table at a night club and I may have danced with him, but that hardly constitutes a date and certainly not a romance.'

Lawford had apparently been pursuing Marilyn for several years. Bill Pursel remembers driving over to see Marilyn several years before, while she was still living with her late Aunt Ana: 'When I drove up to Aunt Ana's house, there she was standing alongside a convertible with Peter Lawford inside; his arm hanging out, talking to Norma Jeane. She saw me, and came dashing across the street and jumped into my car with a smiling. "Hi, Bill." We took off leaving Lawford sitting in his convertible.

I asked Norma Jeane if I was interrupting something and she said, "No you aren't . . . You just rescued me from a beach wolf." She laughed, and said he'd been after her before.'

But while Bill may have 'rescued' her from Peter Lawford back in 1947, by the summer of 1950 their relationship was about to end. One of their last dates was at a drive-in movie, as Pursel remembered: 'It was a double feature and Norma Jeane had been on a photo shoot at Catalina Island all day. We were as close to being in love that night as we ever were; she laid her head in my lap and went to sleep, and I could feel the warmth and closeness. Later, while we dined I looked into her eyes and told her I might be falling in love. She smiled and said, "That's my line, even though you said it first." We kissed across the table; the waiter appeared and asked us if we would like to order some dessert and we laughed.'

But while love may have been on the table just a few months before, by the time Bill graduated from college Marilyn had decided the relationship was over. It came as a shock to Bill, particularly as they had briefly talked about marriage and had recently looked around show houses during a day out in San Diego.

The last time he saw Norma Jeane was on the evening before he was due to travel to Las Vegas. He remembered: 'I was packed to go home early the next morning; it was around 7.30 p.m. and I called her to say bye. She said she had a couple of pictures for me and could I come by in the morning; I said we are leaving at dawn, could I come by now? She said OK, so, I drove to her apartment, and she answered the door with a smiling "Hi." She was in a white terrycloth bathrobe, did not invite me in and before I could say anything she said, "I'll be with you in a minute," then disappeared to her right, leaving me standing in the hall. She left the door wide open and just inside there stood two large suitcases; each of them had silver initials near the handles: the initials were RR.

'Norma Jeane came back to the door and asked me if I had a pen; I didn't; she said hers was about out of ink, but she would try to make it write and she again disappeared for a few moments leaving me standing in the hall. When she reappeared she handed me two large photos; I said thank you, she smiled and said, "I hope you like them." I told her they were very nice. She then moved behind the two suitcases and said, "I really do hope you like them Bill." I said I liked them very much and we just stood there looking at each other. I was stunned by her look; it was the same look she had given Jim Dougherty when he came for the car keys back in 1946. Finally I said, "Good bye," and she responded with "Bye" and sort of gave me a little wave. I turned and slowly walked away; so angry that I nearly tore the photos up. As I reached the stairs down I heard her door slowly close and this was the last time we ever saw each other. I walked away feeling like an intruder, which I guess I was.'

The friendship had been important to both of them, and had seen them through some exciting and difficult times, but now it was over and the two were destined never to see each other again. Still, it did not stop Pursel caring for the girl he always knew as Norma Jeane, and sixty years later, he still remembers their friendship with great fondness: 'It was an exciting time of my life – I was settling down after twenty-two months of war in Europe, I was getting good grades in college, I was maturing, and I had a gorgeous blonde to squire around, but ... I knew early on that this interlude in our lives wasn't going to last: Norma Jeane was hell bent to make it in Hollywood, and I just kept encouraging her. I had a long way to go in college, and even though she wanted me to go to Actors Lab and pursue an acting career I had other ideas. I knew I had to let her go, but it was a great (and personal) ride while it lasted. I was saddened, but not surprised, when she crashed a few years after we lost contact with one another. There wouldn't be anything to gain to embellish this connection between Norma Jeane and me – it's best to just say we were close and had fun together.'

By now Marilyn was living in an apartment on North Harper Drive, which she shared with Natasha Lytess, her daughter,

Barbara, and their cook, Clara. It was an arrangement that suited Marilyn down to the ground, as it gave her a chance to work with her coach at all times of the day and night. However, it didn't always suit Natasha and she became fed up with having to clear up after Marilyn's chihuahua Josefa, even going to far as to threaten her with the Society for the Prevention of Cruelty to Animals if she didn't take better care of it.

In August Marilyn took a vacation with Natasha Lytess to Palm Springs, and at the beginning of September, Lytess began working at Twentieth Century Fox. The end of September brought a flurry of activities for Marilyn: on 28 September, she signed a release form for a LeGalion perfume campaign; and on 1 October she placed some of her personal effects into storage at the Janis Van and Storage Company, while also writing a cheque for $10 to Grace Goddard, who had moved back to California and had taken on the unofficial role of Marilyn's assistant.

Things were moving along nicely, but it wasn't long before she was dealt a massive blow when Johnny Hyde was admitted to hospital in early November. Louella Parsons reported on 7 November that he had a bout of flu, but in reality his heart problems were getting worse and he did not have much longer to live. Newspapers at the time told how Marilyn was 'devotion itself to her agent and best beau', and that she was an everyday visitor to his bedside. Natasha Lytess was later to deny this, however, stating that Marilyn was forever late in visiting Hyde, and he once even phoned Lytess to ask where Marilyn was, and complained of her selfishness at keeping him waiting.

'I loved him dearly, but I was not in love with him,' Marilyn said in 1952. She knew that Hyde longed to marry her, but she just couldn't do it – they both knew that, and yet Hyde refused to let the subject go. Perhaps by being late to the hospital, by fussing with her hair and make-up for hours on end, Marilyn was putting off the inevitable conversation of him asking for her hand in marriage, and her having to turn him down, yet again.

Friend and lover, Elia Kazan summed it up when he wrote in a letter to Marilyn, '[Johnny] made you his when you really didn't love him – which is a terrible thing to do to anyone. You took shelter under his roof like a hurt animal.' In turn, she was to confide to Kazan that the more Hyde begged her to be his wife, the less she loved him and indeed began avoiding him because of his anxiety over their relationship.

Hyde couldn't stop his infatuation, however, and continued to beg her to become his wife. When she turned him down on one particular occasion, he finally felt he'd had enough and told her the relationship was over. Marilyn did not wish to cause her lover any hurt, and telephoned him the next day, when he was particularly abrupt on the phone. Later that day she went to visit Hyde and was shocked when he asked if she would consider pretending to be his fiancée instead, an offer which she immediately turned down.

In December, thanks to Hyde, Marilyn shot another screen test at Twentieth Century Fox, and later that month she started shooting a small role in *As Young as You Feel*. All this became insignificant, however, when Johnny Hyde suffered a major heart attack and died on 18 December 1950. Marilyn later told reporter Jim Henaghan that Johnny had once said that if he died, she was to hold him in her arms, and life would come back again. When she was told of his death whilst standing in the hospital corridor, she later claimed to have run into his room and held Hyde's body for half an hour before finally giving up. This seems quite unlikely, however, as his family were at the hospital and had already refused her entry into the room, disliking her immensely: 'They thought I was awful,' she later said. So much so, it would seem, that as soon as Hyde passed away, they issued orders that Marilyn was to stay away not only from his North Palm Drive home, but also his funeral, which was to take place on 20 December. 'They were spitting tacks,' remembered actress Annabelle Stanford.

Ignoring his family's wishes, on 19 December Marilyn went shopping for a funeral outfit at I. Magnin, and that night claimed to have sneaked into the North Palm Drive house, where Johnny's body was lying. According to Elia Kazan, she spent the entire night with the body, and then slipped out of the house in the morning to prepare herself for the funeral at Forest Lawn Memorial Park.

Rumour has it that she became hysterical during the funeral and one of Hyde's children later remembered hearing Marilyn shouting his father's name over and over again. Marilyn herself later told reporters that she 'felt such a sadness for him, I threw myself on the coffin and wished I was dead with him'.

The actress was absolutely devastated to lose her protector and it took his death for her to realize the true extent of her feelings towards him. She later expressed her feelings to Jim Henaghan: 'Once I was in love with a man. He was old enough to be my father and people called me a dumb blonde because they didn't understand and I knew they didn't understand and I was afraid to talk about it. And then he died.'

Despite being seen as something of a gold-digger, Marilyn received nothing from Hyde's will, and ended up with a few pieces of bed linen and several towels as reminders of their relationship. She sank into a deep depression over the loss of her mentor, and just a day or two after the funeral, Natasha Lytess claims Marilyn made an attempt to take her own life. According to the drama coach, she found a note pinned to her pillow which read: 'I leave my car and my fur stole to Natasha,' and another on her bedroom door, saying 'Don't let Barbara [Lytess' daughter] come in.' Natasha then claimed that Marilyn was lying in bed with her cheeks 'puffed out like an adder'. When she didn't answer Lytess' call, the drama coach said she forced open her mouth and scooped out a handful of dissolving pills.

This story came to light when Natasha Lytess wrote an embittered account of her relationship with Marilyn after they had parted ways, and could very well be exaggerated. What is more interesting, however, is that while Natasha Lytess quite happily reported Marilyn's 'attempted suicide', she failed to mention her own apparent overdose on Tuesday, 23 February 1943.

Astonishingly, her story is almost word for word the same as the one she attributed to Marilyn nearly eight years later:

allegedly Lytess overdosed on tablets at her home on North Harper Drive, and was discovered unconscious on a bed by some friends. She was then rushed to West Hollywood Hospital, where she was treated for an overdose of sleeping pills and later discharged. According to police reports, Natasha disclosed that she had been 'upset due to personal reasons' and had 'mistakenly taken too many tablets in order to get some rest'. The whole story was then reported in the *Los Angeles Times* on 25 February 1943 but has remained long buried until now.

Chapter 9

Miss Cheesecake

In early January 1951, film director Elia Kazan arrived in Los Angeles with his friend, the playwright Arthur Miller. The two were in California to drum up interest in Miller's screenplay, *The Hook*, which Kazan planned to direct. Kazan moved into the home of producer Charles Feldman, and immediately realized that Feldman and his friends Pat De Cicco and Raoul Hakim had a variety of girls they would squire around town, show off at important parties and generally treat in a discourteous manner. One of these girls was Marilyn Monroe.

Kazan later wrote to Marilyn and begged her to stop 'hanging out' with De Cicco, though he never gave a reason for it. However, since he was once rumoured to be a possible suspect in actress Thelma Todd's death, it can be understood why Kazan would have his concerns. More insight on De Cicco can be given from Marilyn's friend, John Gilmore: 'Pat De Cicco was a sharpie, would-be actor come low-rung gangster/wannabe producer, but firmly a supplier of available girls for Hollywood "big wigs" that catered to a mixed pallet of stars, high-roller producers and entrepreneurs like Joe Schenck. Marilyn's connection with him stems from a few girls recruited from modelling jobs, like "gimme three blondes, a redhead and a brunette for Saturday". I don't think he gave a rat's ass about the girls, other than making him look good in the eyes of the big boys. In short, De Cicco was a thug who could turn on the charm. He wasn't personally interested in bedding the cutie-pie

(above left) A stylish Gladys Pearl Baker, nee Monroe – Norma Jeane's mother. She was a troubled woman and spent most of her life in institutions. *(from the collection of Greg Schreiner)*

(above right) C. Stanley Gifford was the man most believed to be Norma Jeane's father. Marilyn tried on various occasions to visit him at his dairy farm in Hemet, but was turned away every time. *(from the collection of Eric Woodard)*

(below) A rare beach outing for Norma Jeane *(left)* with her mother, Gladys *(behind)*. Despite being raised in foster homes, she did occasionally see and live with her mother, though a close bond was never formed. *(unknown photographer)*

(above) Life at the Los Angeles Orphans Home was firm but fair. Here the children watch a flag being raised outside the building, during the time that Norma Jeane lived there.
(from the collection of George and Evan Finch)

(right) Norma Jeane, photographed just after she left the orphanage, aged about ten, during the time she lived in Barbara Court with her foster mother Grace Goddard.
(unknown photographer)

In September 1938, Norma Jeane moved into 'Aunt' Ana's home at 11348 Nebraska Avenue, where this photo was taken. She began to make friends, among them Ana's nephew, Max Ritchie, who took this photograph. *(from the collection of April and Jim Dakis)*

(right) When she hit her teens, Norma Jeane's figure started to fill out and she was noticed by boys and girls alike. *(unknown photographer)*

(below) Mr and Mrs Dougherty, circa 1943, posing happily on the Island of Catalina, shortly before Jim left to fight for his country.
(from the collection of Paul Kanteman)

In 1945, photographer William Carroll was looking for a model to use in an advertising counter display. He hired Norma Jeane, seen here with a huge smile on her face. *(William Carroll)*

(right) Bill Pursel in the late 1940s, around the time he and Norma Jeane were dating. The two met in 1946, while Norma Jeane was in Las Vegas obtaining her divorce from Jim Dougherty, and they were to remain close for the next four years.
(from the collection of Bill Pursel)

(below) Norma Jeane leans against a car, perched jauntily on one leg. This photo was given as a gift to Bill Pursel from Norma Jeane, and he pinned it to the wall of his college dormitory.
(from the collection of Bill Pursel)

This snapshot was given to Bill Pursel by Norma Jeane early in their relationship. She was living at 4215 Rowland Street at the time, which was where this rare shot was taken. *(from the collection of Bill Pursel)*

(above) Marilyn *(centre)* is photographed in a boat alongside an unknown model *(left)* and Annabelle Stanford *(right)*. Annabelle modelled with Marilyn on several occasions and dated Dick Pursel, the brother of Marilyn's boyfriend Bill. *(unknown photographer)*

(below) Although her star was rising, Marilyn continued to live with Aunt Ana Lower. She is seen here outside what is believed to be Ana's house on Nebraska Avenue. *(unknown photographer)*

blondes or the nameless brunettes and redheads; he chased bigger fish for notoriety – he wanted fame.'

But while De Cicco and his ilk were interested in Marilyn, she couldn't have cared less about them, as she was still mourning the loss of Hyde. On the set of her new film, *As Young as You Feel*, director Harmon Jones complained that she spent most of the day crying and hiding out on the next set. When Kazan met Marilyn, he immediately felt a sense of sorrow for the mourning actress, and asked if she would like to have dinner with him. Marilyn initially refused his offer, though she finally agreed and the two became close; the already married Kazan provided a willing ear for her grief over the loss of Hyde and her tales of past romantic disappointments. It wasn't long before they became not just friends, but lovers too.

One evening Charles Feldman was hosting a party in honour of Arthur Miller, but because Kazan had already made a date with another woman, he asked Miller to take Marilyn to the party instead. They had briefly met on the set of *As Young as You Feel*, and when Miller suggested he pick Marilyn up in his car, she was taken aback. When Hyde wanted to escort her somewhere, she had always taken a cab, and when she mentioned this to Kazan, he was amazed: 'Why should you be "used" to going to parties in a taxi?' he wrote. 'For Christ's sake you're so much better than the people who throw the parties!'

The Feldman party was both a success and a wake-up call: for Marilyn, it enabled her to spend time with someone who was interested in her opinions; but for Miller it spelt doom, as despite being married with two children, he could feel himself being drawn to his companion. They spent a lot of time together following the party, with Kazan and Miller using Marilyn as their 'mascot', and enjoying various escapades, including one where Marilyn dressed up as a secretary for a meeting with MGM boss Harry Cohn. Cohn had held a grudge against Marilyn since the time he'd unsuccessfully asked her to travel to Catalina Island with him, but had no idea she would later turn up as a secretary in his own office. The incident was a joke, a little revenge, and although it is unclear as to whether or not Cohn actually recognized the starlet, the group of three must surely have enjoyed the challenge.

But it wasn't all fun and games for Kazan, Miller and Marilyn. She had fallen hard for the playwright and made no effort to hide her feelings from Kazan – even when they were making love. Miller, on the other hand, was terrified by his feelings towards her, and abruptly cut short his trip to California, returning to his wife before he could have any regrets. The two would innocently keep in touch by sending letters and book lists, but it would be four years before they were to meet again.

Kazan left California shortly after Miller, and Marilyn saw him off at the station, sad that once again she would be on her own and wondering if she would see him again. Before he left, she revealed to Kazan that she was pregnant, but later wrote and told him she'd had a miscarriage. Many authors have wondered if Marilyn was ever pregnant at all, claiming that she had made up her condition in order to back Kazan into a corner. The incident is seen as nothing more than a stunt to gain attention and pity after his decision to return to his wife, but this seems a little too harsh. After all, the couple were sexually active, as confirmed by Kazan in his autobiography, so the chance of her falling pregnant most certainly wasn't impossible.

Nevertheless, the two remained friends and shortly after his return to New York, Kazan wrote to tell her that he would do everything in his power to stay close to her, given the circumstances. He then went on to write a deeply thought-provoking letter, urging her to learn everything she could about acting; spend more time on her own; go to college; speak up for herself; 'don't take any shit from anyone'; and cease living with Natasha Lytess.

Marilyn took his ideas on board, and shortly after receiving the letter, she moved away from Natasha, into 8573 Holloway Drive, with friend Shelley Winters. The two young women were ideally suited, and spent many hours playing classical music, listening to Sinatra and talking about men. They also went to the theatre together, and on one occasion even took Natasha Lytess to the Circle Theater to see Sydney Chaplin rehearse a play that was being directed by his father, Charlie. Unfortunately, the three women had to make an early exit when Lytess was overheard criticizing the elder Chaplin, much to his annoyance.

Another friend at this time was actor Dale Robertson, who got to know Marilyn well when they were both at the beginning of their careers. Robertson remembered: 'We would go to ball games together and she was very pleasant company, but we were never boyfriend and girlfriend because we just weren't attracted to each other.'

The two enjoyed each other's company, but even so, Robertson could sense sadness in Marilyn: 'She had a rough time for a while, and her biggest enemy was herself,' he remembered, more than fifty years later.

While her career was beginning to work out for her, it is true to say that, personally, she was still having a hard time, and none more so than when she asked Natasha Lytess to accompany her on a trip to visit her father. Since the time she had phoned him whilst married to Dougherty, Marilyn had begun to make a name for herself in movies, and felt that Gifford would now want to make contact with her. She was to be proved wrong, however, when she and Lytess travelled to Hemet where Gifford was now living. Several miles away from his home, Marilyn attempted to call him from a payphone, but without luck; when she eventually got through, Gifford did not want anything to do with his daughter, citing the fact that he already had a family and a wife.

The incident once again caused a great deal of trauma in Marilyn's already fragile personal life, and it was around this time she was introduced to a $25-an-hour psychiatrist, Dr Judd Marmor. This was to be the beginning of a long and often painful journey into psychoanalysis, which was to last until the very end of her life.

On 8 February 1951, reports surfaced in the newspapers that although Marilyn had been in virtual retirement since the death of Hyde, she was now due to appear in a Fox movie entitled *A WAC in his Life* (later retitled *Love Nest*). Shortly before shooting began, however, Marilyn took Kazan's advice once again, and enrolled at university.

She found one course that interested her – 'Backgrounds of Literature', which was described by UCLA as 'Historical, social and cultural aspects of various periods with an introduction to the literature itself'. According to Marilyn's school record, the course began on 5 April 1951 and was conducted by Ms Claire Soule in room 616 at the UCLA Extension's Hill Street building, in downtown Los Angeles. Every Thursday she would travel to the building in time for the 7 p.m. start, and would engross herself in her studies until the class ended at 9 p.m., making it home in time to ready herself for her work the next day.

There was only one problem with this situation: while Marilyn deeply enjoyed Ms Soule's insights into literature and gained much from the course, her star was well and truly on the rise, and she began to be recognized by her fellow classmates. She had, by now, appeared in several high-profile films; she was renegotiating her contract with Fox due to her increasing popularity; and on 29 March she had even presented an Academy Award at the Pantages Theater. Her fellow students started to stare at her, and when Ms Soule asked why, Marilyn told her she acted in films.

This answer shocked the teacher, who replied 'Why I thought you were a young girl straight out of the convent.' 'She was very sincere when she said it,' laughed Marilyn, many years later. For several weeks after being recognized, she still made the journey to the Extension building, but eventually she decided the recognition was causing too much trouble, and dropped out before the class finished on 31 May.

On 5 May 1951, Marilyn's relationship with her coach was put under strain when Lytess wrote to her, c/o William Morris, to ask if she would pay $1,000 Lytess owed to her dentist. Marilyn was shocked but agreed to pay the dentist in instalments of $200 per week, which Lytess promised to repay to Marilyn at a rate of $25 per week. Thankfully for both actress and coach, Marilyn signed a new, renegotiated contract with Fox on 11 May 1951, and began filming a small part in *Let's Make It Legal*, starring Claudette Colbert and Macdonald Carey.

Marilyn was cast as Joyce Mannering, yet another sexy blonde with little to do or say, but, despite that, she certainly made her presence felt when she was continually late on set and cheekily told director Richard Sale to call Joe Schenck if he had a problem with her behaviour. Sale was not fazed and threatened to call the head of Fox, Zanuck, instead, a move which prompted Marilyn to storm off set, only to return shortly after to apologize for her behaviour.

While Twentieth Century Fox was still wondering how exactly to use Marilyn, she was loaned out to RKO for a part in *Clash by Night*, starring Barbara Stanwyck, Paul Douglas and Robert Ryan. Her friend Sidney Skolsky helped her obtain the part in the film, which revolved around Stanwyck's character Mae, who marries dependable Jerry (Douglas) and has an affair with his best friend Earl (Ryan). Marilyn played Peggy, the girlfriend of Mae's brother, and it was by far the best role she had ever played. Although the part was still relatively small, she really made it her own and the performance was nothing less than superb, but still, there were problems on the set – most of which were not of Marilyn's making.

Firstly, director Fritz Lang seemed to dislike her, and did not appreciate Natasha Lytess being on the set. Also, although the cast was made up of brilliant actors, many of them did not know how to deal with the attention Marilyn was beginning to receive both in the media and from the public. Of particular concern was Paul Douglas, who seemed to cause more than his share of bad feeling on the set: one of the extras thought he seemed intoxicated on several occasions; he objected to Marilyn's name being above the film titles; and even exploded at her when she called him by his first name.

Still, Marilyn was determined to do her best in the part, and she worked exceptionally hard, as writer Richard Baer remembered: 'Marilyn was always on set on time, she wasn't yet a big star and was very anxious to please. I didn't think she was at all difficult or demanding and she was concerned about what people thought of her. Sometimes other actors gathered around to watch her scenes because they knew she wasn't classically trained and they would laugh and smirk. I thought that was unkind, but she wasn't terribly accomplished and had no real training, which made her easy to ridicule. She was ambitious and determined with her eyes on the goal, and Jerry Wald knew there was something special about her. I have nothing bad to say about this woman at all.'

As mentioned by Baer, some of the actors were less than helpful to Marilyn, and a rather sad example of this was when she was filming a scene in which she had to run down some stairs. She ended up falling down the steps and instead of being concerned for her welfare, various members of the crew found the whole thing highly amusing and actually laughed out loud. Marilyn emerged from the staircase uninjured, and continued shooting her scene, which required a great deal of guts and emotional backbone.

Baer and Marilyn became good friends whilst on the set, and she relied on him to tell her how she looked in the rushes, but he became exasperated when she refused to trust him enough to give out her telephone number or address. She would call him many times and the two would discuss everything from Johnny Hyde to her work on the film, but still she would not cave in to his requests for her address. 'I would often say, "My hand is aching and my ear is sore from being on the phone, can't we just do this face to face?" But she would always say, "No."'

Much of the film was made in the seaside resort of Monterey, California. One eyewitness was Nanciele Finnegan, who was seventeen at the time, and had a front-row seat when the film crew set up camp in her parent's front yard. Several members of her family were involved in the production: her sister was filmed sitting on the front porch, petting a rabbit; her brother was shown rolling a large tyre down the driveway; and even the family car, a Model T Ford, was filmed for the huge sum of $50 per day. However, the most amusing contractual obligation was for Nanciele herself, who was paid NOT to appear on camera: 'What a disappointment to have a contract to not appear in the film,' she remembered. 'Still, the money did help to ease the awkwardness involved in having to avoid using the doors or walking by the windows whenever the director yelled, "Action."

For most of the filming, Marilyn's trailer was parked outside the Finnegan home, and this gave Nanciele an almost direct line to the actress, who enjoyed speaking with her: 'I found her very sweet and approachable. Sometimes when waiting for filming to start she'd catch my eye and wink, other times we'd drink Coca-Colas and laugh.' She also remembers being asked by the cast to join them for a catered meal, but whilst most of the cast were friendly and professional, she wasn't so impressed with Barbara Stanwyck: 'She was aloof and avoided the others – including other cast members as well as her fans. She definitely refused autographs. Marilyn made a point of being available to chat with fans and to sign autographs; I wondered at the time if Barbara was going through some personal crisis to appear so cold to both fans and co-workers.'

Once *Clash by Night* was in the can, Marilyn returned to Fox and unsuccessfully auditioned for a part in a film called *Wait Till the Sun Shines, Nellie*, opposite David Wayne. More successful was a test she made for *Night without Sleep*, which she filmed after working on the part with Lytess for days on end. The test was so successful, in fact, that not even Darryl Zanuck could deny that she was good for the part of Nell, a psychotic babysitter, and he offered her the part.

She was thrilled by the chance to do something different, and even decided to move back in with Lytess in order to work on her part at any time of the day or night. She also took to jogging around the back alleys in the early morning to keep herself fit, and began receiving fan mail – mostly from men proposing marriage. She started receiving titles such as 'Miss Cheesecake', 'Miss Pin-up 1951' and her personal favourite,

'Miss Flamethrower', while *Stars and Stripes* magazine voted her the GI's favourite pin-up, confirmed by the huge amount of mail she was receiving from GIs every day. In order to answer them all, she employed the services of foster-mother Grace Goddard, and even took to sending photos at her own expense, as she felt the studio ones were too small. Fame was at last knocking on her door, and she was determined that her new fans would know how much they meant to her.

When she won a Henrietta Award for best newcomer, Marilyn bought her first expensive evening gown – a red, low-cut, velvet gown which fitted tightly to her knees, before flaring out. It was designed by Oleg Cassini and Marilyn loved it, but when she attended the awards it caused a sensation, with many women declaring it offensive and too extreme. It was the first time her taste in clothes had been subjected to such harsh criticism, but it would not be the last. When she wore a strapless red silk taffeta gown to a party shortly afterwards, the press declared that it was proof she was utterly lacking in taste. Marilyn, however, was defiant. 'I'm truly sorry, but I love the dress,' she declared, whilst saying of the Henrietta Awards dress, 'Frankly I love the gown and wish I had more occasions to wear it.'

One day at the studio an executive stopped and berated her for wearing jeans and a T-shirt to work: 'An actress should always look her best,' he declared to the shocked actress. She was to get her own back on the many people who knocked her dress sense, however, when photographer Earl Theisen dressed her in a potato sack, proving once and for all that it didn't matter what she wore, she would always look terrific. The fans loved it.

While Marilyn's admirers were learning more and more about the public aspect of her life, the very private details of her health were being well hidden and are still shrouded in mystery today. She continued to suffer badly with endometriosis and Natasha Lytess remembered occasions where Marilyn would literally stop dead and bend over in agony. Her heavy periods interfered with her modelling work, too, as former model and actress Annabelle Stanford remembers: 'We were doing a shoot for Bernard of Hollywood in Palm Springs, and Marilyn was lying on her stomach next to the pool. I got my hair wet so the shoot was over for me, and as I walked towards the changing room, I noticed that Marilyn's period had started all over her pale pink bathing costume. I casually dropped my towel over her bottom, then accompanied her to the bathroom where I helped her to rinse out her costume.'

Although her medical records are sealed, the cheques she wrote in 1950 and 1951 hint at the level of her medical problems at the time: on 5 November 1950 and again on 15 November, cheques were written to a Dr Seligman for the amount of $40 each; then on 26 October 1951, a cheque was made out for the large sum of $200 to a Dr A. Gottsman. Finally, a cheque was written on 9 November 1951 to an unknown doctor, for the sum of $50. It is not possible to confirm what these treatments were for, but it is clear to say that her health was certainly an issue at the time.

Meanwhile, on the advice of Lytess and actor Jack Palance, Marilyn began taking classes with renowned teacher, Michael Chekhov. It was her first introduction to the 'Method' acting technique, and it was this early influence that inspired her to look deeper at the process when she moved to New York in 1955.'

In public she was still stating that she didn't mind people thinking of her as a dumb blonde – 'It has never bothered me because I've always known I wasn't' – but in private it was driving her to distraction, and she confided to Chekhov that she was tired of fluffy parts with nothing to do or say. She also became upset when the teacher told her she kept getting those parts because of the sexual vibrations she gave off. 'But I want to be an artist, not an erotic freak,' she told him.

Chekhov liked his young pupil but couldn't help becoming more and more frustrated with her lateness and absenteeism in class. Finally, he suggested they stop meeting, after one late arrival too many, and Marilyn was devastated. She wrote him a note to ask him not to give up on her, explaining that she was only too aware of how much she tested his patience. Of course, the plea worked and Chekhov allowed her to come back to class, on the understanding that she would take her lessons more seriously, which she did, so much so in fact, that she once arrived at his home a day earlier than expected.

By the time *Night without Sleep* began shooting in December 1951, it had been retitled *Don't Bother to Knock*, and it was to give Marilyn her first starring role. It was completely removed from anything she had ever done before, with the story revolving around one night in a hotel where Marilyn's character, Nell, is in charge of looking after a little girl. Over the course of the evening, the emotionally disturbed Nell becomes more and more fragile until finally she is completely derailed. Although it was very much Marilyn's film, the studio were still intent on keeping the actress in her place. Asked later if she got on with her co-star, Richard Widmark, Marilyn retorted, 'Dick Widmark? They never let me get anywhere near him.'

Marilyn requested once again that Natasha Lytess be on the set, and bombarded Zanuck with letters, begging him to allow the coach to be with her, even going so far as to say that there was no way she could work without her there. Zanuck relented, but it was not a good call, as Lytess felt she had been put on the spot by Marilyn, and even worried that her job at the studio would be put at risk. She was proved right one day when Marilyn told director, Roy Ward Baker, that Lytess was the only person who could help her with a particular scene. The moment it was finished, he headed for the telephone and the coach found herself fired the very next day.

According to Lytess, Marilyn ignored her calls for the next few weeks, and she was left completely distraught. Finally, she took the dramatic decision to inform her student that if no help was given, she would do something to herself so that it would hit the headlines. Faced with this emotional blackmail, Marilyn finally helped her teacher, and Zanuck reinstated her.

When *Don't Bother to Knock* was finally released, it received mixed reviews. People were confused to see Marilyn in such a dramatic role, and fan Nanciele Finnegan remembered, 'the intense shock I felt when I went to see it. I expected to see the chum I'd come to know, but recognized in the fragile psychotic portrayed there, that Marilyn was an Actress'. Nanciele is astute in her observation; even though the film was shocking at the time and Marilyn's character not in the least bit likeable, there was no doubt that she could act.

In late 1951, Marilyn began a friendship with business manager David March that was to affect her entire life. March initially got in touch with the actress when he was interested in signing her to his company Leslie and Tyson, but eventually a deep friendship was formed. The two began to talk regularly on the telephone, then started visiting each other, sitting beside the fire, sharing problems and putting the world to rights. Unfortunately, March could be quite outspoken at times, and during one particular chat he made the mistake of telling his new friend that she procrastinated too much. She did not appreciate this and her anger was explosive but thankfully brief; the two carried on with their friendship relatively unscathed, which is just as well, as 1952 would be a year of great challenge, both professionally and privately.

Chapter 10

The Past versus the Future

In early 1952 Marilyn moved once again, this time into a home at 1121 Hilldale Avenue in West Hollywood. She had been moving around frequently since she left Aunt Ana's home in 1947, and was beginning to tire of it: 'I have a horror of signing leases,' she said, although the waif inside her seemed unable to ever settle in one place. Sometimes she would relish the time she had on her own, filling her home with white flowers, lounging on the sofa reading books, and listening to records while grabbing a quick bite to eat. At other times the solitude of living alone got her down, and she would get in her car and drive to the beach or spend her evenings walking around the streets near her home, enjoying the anonymity of night, when all around her was still and quiet. It was also during times of loneliness that she would try her hand at poetry, a hobby she continued throughout her life. 'My poems are kind of sad,' she said, 'but then so is life.'

During 1952, she had small appearances in *We're Not Married*, *O. Henry's Full House*, and *Monkey Business*. The latter starred Cary Grant and Ginger Rogers, with Grant playing Doctor Fulton, a man who finds the elixir of youth. One of the other cast members was Bob Cornthwaite, who played Fulton's assistant, Dr Zoldeck. He had worked with director Howard Hawks previously, and when Hawks specifically asked for him to be in the film, he was happy to oblige. Arriving several days after the start of production, Cornthwaite's first encounter with Marilyn happened during a break in production when John Wayne and Gary Cooper were visiting the set: 'Marilyn walked past and everyone was looking. Hawks turned to me and said, "I think that the overdeveloped quality in the little blonde girl is going to be funny." I thought, "My God" because she was becoming quite a star and everyone was jumping around for her. But Hawks had hired her because he had to, not because he wanted to. He didn't like her abilities and didn't conceal it.'

Meanwhile, Bob began to feel sorry for Marilyn, as it was obvious that some people on the set just didn't understand her: 'She was very likeable and also stubborn, which is what saw her through. Lots of people didn't cotton on to her. She had the strength of a puppy dog that hadn't been indulged and had been abused but would not give up. She was persistent and that stood her in good stead, but people just had to go along with what she was because she was not going to change – she was stubborn which was both her strength and her weakness. Working with Marilyn – there was a "blankness" – she was both aware and divorced from things, and sometimes I would wonder where her mind was at. I had grown a beard for my last role and Hawks had asked me to keep it on; one day Marilyn and I were waiting for our cue to do a scene and she stared at me, before finally saying, "It's real isn't it?" I didn't know what to say to that!'

Beards aside, Marilyn's behaviour on set was starting to cause worry and concern. She was continually late, which Cornthwaite believes was a defence mechanism as there was just so much she didn't know: 'She was determined to hold on to her position but was afraid to be there,' he remembered. 'Marilyn was ambitious and didn't want to spoil her chances of success but knew if she stuck to her guns and made demands, she might get away with it.'

Even though she was regularly late on set, the cast and crew enjoyed watching the play between her, the actors and producer, Howard Hawks. There were also several humorous moments on set, not least of which was when the monkeys hired to appear in the film took a keen interest in the leading actor. Cornthwaite remembered: 'The monkeys fell in love with Cary Grant and would leap across the set to give him cuddles. They hated

Marilyn and would pinch her and pull her clothes, and she was flummoxed by it – she had had that behaviour from men, but not from monkeys!'

Marilyn didn't make many friends on set, and gave off the aura of a lost child who just couldn't quite fit in. As Cornthwaite remembered: 'Ginger Rogers and Cary Grant were both professionals and there was no overt behaviour towards Marilyn, but they didn't particularly welcome her – she had a different level of professionalism. But what held it all together was Howard Hawks because he had such power. He was the producer and although there was meant to be another director, he was never there – it was always Hawks who directed as well as produced.'

But not even Hawks could completely control Marilyn's behaviour on set. She was extremely stubborn, which was her greatest strength but could also be her supreme weakness. 'Perhaps she couldn't help her behaviour,' wonders Bob Cornthwaite. 'She was so disturbed emotionally and psychologically and just couldn't help it.'

She was also feeling physically unwell, and suffered from persistent stomach aches, which led her to book an appointment to see a doctor at Cedars of Lebanon hospital on 1 March 1952. Cornthwaite recalled: 'She kept saying she had appendicitis and couldn't work and she had to shoot a scene with Cary Grant in the car, which was set for a particular day. Hawks called Zanuck in advance and said, "I don't care if she has appendicitis. She can go to the hospital and I want her back on the set on that day and every day." He had the prestige to do it.'

The operation was delayed until the end of production, and Marilyn returned to the set in poor health and with something else on her mind – a blind date with baseball legend Joe DiMaggio.

In 1951, Marilyn did a series of photos with the Chicago White Sox during spring training at Brookside Park in Pasadena, California. One of the players to pose with the starlet was Gus Zernial, who remembers Marilyn with great affection: 'I was

really attracted to her beauty but more than that. She was attractive both inside and out – a beautiful person to talk to and I also
believe she had a lot more to offer than the way she was shown
by Hollywood.'

The result of these photos was that New York Yankee player
Joe DiMaggio took an interest in the blonde in the shots, and
when he found out that mutual friend David March could set
up a blind date between them, he was more than happy to go
along with it.

On 8 March 1952, DiMaggio's dream came true when
March managed to persuade a reluctant Marilyn to go to the
Villa Nova restaurant to meet the baseball star. She had no idea
who he was, and had seriously thought about calling the whole
thing off, worried that he would be a big-headed sports star with
a huge ego and no personality. March accompanied DiMaggio
and actress Peggy Rabe to the restaurant, in time for the 6.30
p.m. dinner, but Marilyn did not show.

Almost two hours later, at 8.15 p.m., DiMaggio sat nervously drinking vermouth and tearing a menu into tiny pieces,
when she finally made her appearance, wearing a blue suit and a
white, low-cut blouse. She was extremely happy to discover that
DiMaggio was not the ego-driven sports star she had expected,
and was actually a quiet individual, who seemed a little shy: 'He
came alone, and I came alone to an Italian restaurant, to meet a
group of friends. But we left together – and ahead of everybody
else,' she later told reporter Aline Mosby.

Marilyn drove DiMaggio back to the Knickerbocker Hotel,
but politely refused his request for another date. However,
shortly afterwards they enjoyed an evening at the beach, and on
17 March Marilyn watched Joe play baseball – the one and only
time she saw him play.

In order to decide whether or not to go out with DiMaggio,
Marilyn started questioning her friends. One of the people she
chose to contact was Bill Pursel, tracking him down thanks
to his mother, who had happily given Marilyn his new phone
number. By this time Bill was a married man living in Las Vegas

and Marilyn was a fond but distant memory. 'This was the first call I had had since we had parted in 1950,' recalled Bill.

'She said she was ringing to tell me about a guy she had just met who I would probably have heard of. She was having some fun with me, giving me clues such as he's a retired baseball player; he played for my favourite team the Yankees etc. We went back and forth until finally I guessed she was talking about DiMaggio and she told me she'd met him at a party a few nights before. "Do you want to date him?" I asked, and she replied, "I don't know – that's why I called you." She then asked me questions about DiMaggio including whether or not I knew him. I told her I didn't, but that he was an idol of mine, and she then changed the subject, asking me if I ever visited Los Angeles and saying she knew that I'd got married. "Is she pretty?" she asked. "Yes, she's very pretty," I said, and she immediately changed the subject back to Joe. I told her he was a quiet type who would probably be very good for her. Looking back I guess I didn't give her the right info; I hadn't known at that time that he had a jealous nature.'

The relationship with DiMaggio wasn't smooth sailing even from the beginning, as he not only came with an ex-wife, actress Dorothy Arnold, but also a son, Joe DiMaggio Jr, who was ten years old. Marilyn did her best to befriend the child, even taking him to the pool at the Bel Air Hotel, remaining by his side, and buying him cake and ice cream. It didn't take long for them to become friends, but when Joe Jr started calling Marilyn 'The Doll' in front of his mother, and then the pool outing hit the headlines, Dorothy was furious.

'Joe is taking the boy to places not suitable for his age,' Dorothy was reported as saying, while years later, a relative gave her opinion on the 'feud' between Marilyn and Joe's ex-wife and the adoration of Joe Junior: Dorothy 'was not one to talk about anyone – she was a very caring, down-to-earth person. I only remember her great dislike for Joe and Marilyn as they were taking Joe Junior to bars, which upset Dorothy to no end. She fought constantly about child support. Joe Junior liked Marilyn a lot, but he did not like his father. Joe Senior wanted Joe Junior to play ball as well as he did – the son was always pressured to do better, but he couldn't live up to his father's standards.'

Added to that, DiMaggio was now in retirement from baseball and had no interest in fame or the acting business. He was attracted to Marilyn as a human being, not an actress, and as a result, she was forced to attend parties and award shows not with DiMaggio, but with friends such as Sidney Skolsky. She spoke about this to reporter Sheila Graham: 'It wouldn't matter what I won or whether I'd want him to come with me or not, he never would. At least he's very consistent.' Despite that, he was anxious to make a success of things with Marilyn, and even visited the set of *Monkey Business*, where he allowed photographs to be taken of the two of them together. Actor Bob Cornthwaite remembered that, 'Joe DiMaggio would pick her up every night after work and I would run into him coming into the studio while I was leaving, but we never got to speak to each other.'

Within days of meeting DiMaggio, rumours began to surface that Marilyn once posed nude, and the photos were now showing up on calendars all over the country. She had already been warned that their discovery was close, when a man clutching the calendar approached her in the street in early 1952. 'This ought to be worth quite a bit of money to you. Suppose I showed it around town?' asked the stranger. Marilyn refused to be blackmailed by the assailant and gritted her teeth: 'Mister,' she said, 'I'd just adore for you to show it around Hollywood – would you like me to also autograph it for you?'

When the studio asked their new star if she had posed nude, she felt no reason to deny it, much to her bosses' chagrin. There was a huge frenzy, with executives demanding that she lie about it, then changing their minds and deciding she should say nothing at all. But Marilyn felt no reason to deny it and finally an understanding was reached and statement prepared, which allowed Marilyn to put forward her version of events – that she was broke and needed money for her rent. She played the sympathy card and won, with the public not only forgiving the nude scandal, but also loving her more for her honesty and candour. Marilyn was immediately relieved, and once it became apparent that the photos would not negatively affect her career, she actually became quite proud of them. Mayor Johnny Grant, who delivered a copy of the calendar to her, confirms this: 'She expressed the fact that she had never seen it before and was happy to receive it. She had just gotten out of the shower and the only thing she was wearing was a towel – on her head! When she opened the door, she halfway hid behind it, exposing almost the same scene I had just seen on the calendar.' Tom Kelley later said that Marilyn was personally responsible for the notoriety of the photos, since she had autographed a great many of the calendars and gave them away as gifts for her friends. However, although she was proud of the photos, in December 1952 Marilyn took action to stop the nude pictures being sold on ashtrays, glasses and cocktail trays, stating, 'I don't know exactly what rights I have, but it seems to me I should have some say in the way my own picture is used.'

Almost as soon as *Monkey Business* had wrapped, Marilyn booked herself into the Cedars of Lebanon hospital in order to have her appendix removed. She arrived at night, and was disheartened to discover she would have to give the name of her next of kin, in case of emergency. As she later told reporter Isabel Moore: 'It was so strange and awful to realize I just didn't have anyone to call on. But of course, I've always been alone and I guess I always will be alone.'

Technically, Marilyn was not alone. She still had a foster family who loved her deeply and was very much in touch with Aunt Grace, as well as Enid and Sam Knebelkamp. However, at that point in time the relationship with both families had become a little strained, with the discovery of the calendar photos. 'The family did not approve,' remembered the Knebelkamps' son-in-law Forrest Olmstead. With that in mind, Marilyn decided not to name any of her foster family as next of kin, and eventually gave the name of her friend David March instead.

She retired to her hospital bedroom, but as she lay in bed that night, Marilyn's thoughts turned to children, and she reached for a pen and notepad. In the note she scribbled to Dr Rabwin, she asked him not to remove any ovaries, to prevent large scars and to ensure she could still have children. When the doctor found the note stuck to her stomach he was concerned enough to have a gynaecologist on hand to deal with any possible problems. He needn't have worried, however, as the operation went without a hitch and Marilyn was returned to her room – minus one appendix – shortly after.

As if appendicitis and the nude calendar scandal wasn't enough, Marilyn's world came crashing down once again when an executive arrived at the hospital to tell her that reporter Erskine Johnson was about to announce that she was not the orphan she claimed to be. Gladys Baker was well and truly alive, and the enterprising journalist had discovered her existence, much to the dismay of both the studio and their star. Still recovering from her operation, Marilyn couldn't have been at a lower point, but she kept a brave face and explained to the executive (and the media) that she had never lived with her mother and wanted to keep her existence a secret due to her ill health. When her reasons were published, she once again won the sympathy of the public, but not so much the media, who wondered how many other skeletons were hidden in her bulging closet.

One person who was extremely concerned by the discovery of Gladys Baker was journalist Jim Henaghan, who had interviewed Marilyn both at the Beverly Hills Hotel and at his Malibu home. During their conversations she had opened up about her childhood, describing how her father had died in an automobile accident, and her mother had passed away shortly after. The two became friends, and he gave her a B-B gun as a present, while she returned the favour by presenting him with a statuette she had won for the New Star Award for her Rapid Rise to Stardom in 1952.

Henaghan's son, also called Jim, remembers that his father thought a lot about Marilyn: 'He had very good relationship with many stars because he never did hatchet jobs on them. Ms Monroe and Ms [Elizabeth] Taylor were among many who were his friends. He liked Marilyn and was in a position to see the way she was ground down and marginalized by some of the many who made a living off her.'

The friendship between star and columnist was warm and when he came to write his latest feature, Henaghan dedicated a large amount of space to the story Marilyn told him about being an orphan. He was therefore shocked and humiliated to discover that she had not only lied to him as a journalist, but also as a friend, and his first reaction was to telephone a studio employee. In the phone call, he described Marilyn as a lying blonde who had made a jerk out of him to his editor, and asked the employee to give Marilyn the message that she could 'take her hearts and flowers and peddle them someplace else in future'.

The employee rang Marilyn at the hospital and within ten minutes she had telephoned Henaghan and apologized, citing a sense of shame for the reason why she had lied, and explaining that her mother was sick for many years and she had never got to know her. The friendship between Marilyn and Henaghan cooled for a while, though not for long according to his son, who remembers: 'I lived with him in Hollywood from 1958 to 1961 and came home to find Ms Monroe at the house more than once.' However, for now the relationship became strained and it was too late to stop the article, which eventually ran in *Redbook* in June 1952, under the title of 'So Far to Go Alone'. This forced Marilyn to send an angry letter of explanation to the editor, which read: 'I frankly did not feel wrong in withholding from you the fact that my mother is still alive . . . since we have never known each other intimately and have never enjoyed the normal relationship of mother and daughter.' She later softened her opinion, and told another reporter: 'I realize that I never should have withheld the fact from the press. But my motive was one of consideration for a person who has suffered much, and for whom I feel a great obligation.'

Another reporter who spoke with Marilyn during her time in hospital was Isabel Moore, who arrived with mutual friend David March. Still in pain from the operation, and obviously thinking about her mother, Marilyn opened her heart about having children of her own: 'I know how I'd feel if I had children. I'd never want them to feel I didn't love them more than anything else in the world. If I ever have a little girl, I think I'll be a wonderful mother to her, and if I can help it, I'll never be away from her for a minute.'

At the time Marilyn was defending her family history, Stanley Gifford, the man she believed to be her father, was still living in Hemet with his wife, Mary. It had been in July 1950 – less than a year before Marilyn tried to contact him – that Gifford had left the bright lights of Hollywood far behind. He worked hard with his wife to establish the Red Rock Dairy, named after the 1,000 Rhode Island Red and Plymouth Rock chickens that occupied their five-acre ranch. Twenty cows eventually grew to 115 and they were soon in a position to open a retail dairy: 'Five people promised to try the milk,' remembered Mary Gifford. 'After many hours of hard work and much advertising, the business grew to three routes.' The couple also opened a small cash and carry store on the premises, and sold freshly baked goods and ice cream to locals who would come to taste their wares and admire the resident monkey at the front of the store.

It seemed an odd job for someone who had once enjoyed the life of a motion pictures salesman, but Stanley Gifford settled into it with great enthusiasm. But while he was somewhat mellower than he had been in Los Angeles, Gifford still had a severe manner, as recalled by Darrell Von Driska, who remembers him as 'a stern man who wore bib overalls; rubber dairy boots; had a moustache and occasionally a cigar in his mouth. I'm sure to his adult friends he was more accommodating.'

It is not known if Marilyn had tried to visit Gifford since the ill-fated trip with Natasha Lytess, but by 1952, after her recent family problems, she was ready to try again. Driving with Joe DiMaggio, the pair arrived in Hemet late one evening, and proceeded to dine at nearby Von's Midway Drive-In, owned by the Von Driska family. Son Darrell recalls: 'When Joe and Marilyn visited Von's Midway Drive-In I had just left to go home and finish my homework. My dad called to tell me that Joe DiMaggio, one of my boyhood heroes, had just left and I missed him. Needless to say I was bummed. Two years later, after seeing "Niagara" I also wished I had seen Marilyn.'

After dining at the restaurant, Marilyn apprehensively went to the Red Rock Dairy in an attempt to see Mr Gifford, only to be turned away once again. He denied he was her father, recalls Darrell Von Driska. 'I feel, as others do, that he was protecting his wife.'

At the time of Marilyn's visit, very few people in the town knew of her possible relation to Stanley Gifford, but as the years went on, rumours started to circulate. Hemet local Bill Jennings remembered that if anyone asked Gifford about Marilyn, he 'would wink and deny it'. This attitude led many residents to believe that he was indeed the father of a famous movie star, though even after Gifford's death in 1965, they were careful not to disclose any details to outsiders for fear that his well-respected widow would be inundated with unwanted visitors.

But while most of the residents had simply come to the conclusion that Gifford was Marilyn's father, some felt they knew for sure, as Darrell Von Driska remember: 'Mr Gifford told his close friend, Charles Benson, that the rumours were true; he was the father of Marilyn. It was further confirmed when, on his deathbed, he confessed to Don Linden, the late Pastor at Hemet First Presbyterian Church, that he had a romantic relationship with Marilyn's mother. He never openly admitted to being Marilyn's father in an effort to save his wife's reputation and possible embarrassment because she was a school teacher.'

Marilyn was hurt very deeply, and she never attempted to contact her father again. However, there are still some who believe that while en route to Palm Springs, she would sometimes take a slight detour to Hemet to buy milk from her father's dairy.

Chapter 11

'I'm trying to find myself'

Although Marilyn was now earning $750 a week at Fox, in May 1952 her finances were once again causing concern and Fox wanted to put Marilyn on a budget. The studio came up with an idea to arrange for her salary to be pro-rated for fifty weeks, and a loan to be drawn up for $1,700. However, in early June when Fox representative Tom Pryer approached Marilyn with the relevant papers, she refused to sign and demanded they be returned to the studio, citing the fact that she had never requested her salary to be pro-rated in the first place. This was the first but certainly not the last time that Marilyn would stand up for her rights as an artist. At a time when no one dared rock the boat where the major studios were concerned, this small incident was a significant step for Marilyn, and one that shows that she was a push-over for no one.

On 1 June 1952, Marilyn's twenty-sixth birthday, she was thrilled to receive word that she'd won the role of Lorelei Lee in the forthcoming Fox production of *Gentlemen Prefer Blondes*. Shooting was due to begin in January 1953, but first she was to star in *Niagara*, playing the role of Rose Loomis, a cunning wife who schemes to have her husband (Joseph Cotton) murdered by her young lover. Unfortunately for the murderous Rose, the plan backfires and she finds herself on the wrong end of the dangerous plot.

Filming began but was interrupted briefly on 26 June when Marilyn was called to testify against two men charged with using her name to sell photos. Jerry Karpman and Morrie Kapland had nine misdemeanour counts brought against them, one of which was 'unlawfully using the name of Marilyn Monroe for the purpose of selling nude and indecent pictures falsely represented to have been posed by Marilyn Monroe'.

The enterprising pair had mailed hundreds of letters 'signed' by Marilyn Monroe, promising 'un-retouched photographs in almost every pose imaginable', and declaring that she was selling them as she was out of a job and needed to raise money. Marilyn arrived at the court, dressed in a blue skirt and jacket, and open-toed white shoes, along with two publicity men. She immediately took to the witness chair, gave her name as Norma Jeane Dougherty and examined the handwritten letters; she denied she knew the accused and rejected the claim she had ever posed for the pictures. Defence Attorney William J.F. Brown then questioned her, and quite bizarrely demanded to know if she had ever heard of President James Monroe.

'This is completely immaterial,' said Deputy City Attorney William E. Still, before Marilyn was excused after ten minutes on the stand. Her presence was brief but effective, for Judge Kenneth L. Holaday found the defendants guilty of five of the nine charges and declared that they would be sentenced on 17 July.

Court appearance over, Marilyn travelled to Niagara for location shots on the film. Checking into a local hotel, she met a woman called Blanch Maj who was working as a chambermaid. Ms Maj later shared her memories of the encounter with her niece, Pat Brennan: 'One morning my aunt was cleaning the suite, when Marilyn returned to the hotel. My aunt was admiring her shoes and the fact that her shoe size was so petite, like her own. When Marilyn checked out, she left a very generous gratuity and two pairs of her own new shoes!!!! We were all so excited and most impressed with the fact that we had Marilyn's very own shoes in our family.'

The filming went well, and Marilyn became friendly with the local people employed as extras. One of them, Patricia Henderson, was around Marilyn's age at the time of the filming, and the two women 'hit it off like sisters', according to Mrs Henderson's son, Timothy: 'My mother said that she was like a schoolgirl chum at lunch breaks and liked "getting away from Marilyn" even for an hour. She remembered her complexion as being perfect and that she ate a lot.'

Mrs Henderson was also used as something of a stand-in for Marilyn, in the scene where Rose finally meets her demise: 'She was paid $50 for doing two of Marilyn's screams in the final bell tower scene, which was about what my dad made a week teaching. Mom was used for the screams in order to save Marilyn's voice for the speaking parts.'

Despite having an aversion to the movie business, Joe DiMaggio travelled occasionally to Niagara in order to be with his girlfriend, and together they would travel seven miles or so to a secluded restaurant called Shimshacks, where they dined quietly and even agreed to be photographed together on at least one occasion. When Joe could not be with her, she spent some of her free time eating out with her fellow cast members, in restaurants including the Red Coach Inn, where local man Joseph Jacob worked. He remembered: 'We gave the screen stars some privacy and kept an area of the restaurant closed so they could enjoy some quiet time without interruption. As you might guess, people followed Marilyn Monroe everywhere she went, wanting to sit in the seat she was in, wanting the napkin she used, asking what did she order, etc. I had the privilege of serving Marilyn that afternoon, and it was a day I'll not soon forget. I say this because that day I didn't meet Marilyn Monroe, I felt that I met a beautiful, statuesque vision of what God intended a woman to look like. She could have been wearing a potato sack and had curlers in her hair and it would not dull her beauty, which I found to be both inside and out.

'I had the fortune of speaking to Miss Monroe directly that day while the others walked in the lobby and the outdoor patio taking in the view. I found her to be nothing of the glamour queen we portrayed her as, but more the down-to-earth girl we all wish superstars to be. She drank a vodka martini, and although we spoke casual conversation she did ask if I could imagine knowing a thousand people and not having any friends. This chance meeting with Marilyn Monroe showed me that under all of the glitz and glamour beats the heart of one person, one single person, that gets happy, sad, frustrated and lonely. Just like the rest us.'

On other days, Marilyn was shown around the local sights by a number of tour guides, one of whom was local politician Arthur E.C. Jolley, who also owned Jolley Construction, the company which built some of the movie sets. His daughter, Lisa Truax, remembered that her father showed round not just Marilyn, but also Jean Peters, and he later described it as one of the greatest highlights of his career.

Another person to meet Marilyn (and be photographed with her), during her time in Niagara, was a young man by the name of Robert Slatzer, who later became a notorious figure in the life and legend of Marilyn Monroe.

On 29 August columnist Dorothy Kilgallen commented on the meeting between the couple, declaring that Slatzer was 'a dark horse in the Marilyn Monroe romance derby'. Then on 18 September (on the same day that Marilyn tossed out the first ball at the Sixth Annual 'Out of this world series' at Gilmore Field), Slatzer stood in for Kilgallen, and wrote a short article about his friendship with Marilyn. In it he revealed that they had met in 1947, while Twentieth Century Fox employed them both, and they lost their jobs at the same time. 'I didn't see her again until last June in Niagara Falls,' he said. 'I didn't know that Norma Jeane was now Marilyn.' He then went on to describe how he had sent Marilyn a number of books to read, including several by Thomas Wolfe entitled *You Can't Go Home Again* and *Look Homeward Angel*.

This story would have been perfectly harmless enough had it not been for the fact that years after Marilyn died, Slatzer changed his story to include a long romance spanning many years, and a secret marriage, which he claimed was annulled on the instructions of Twentieth Century Fox. According to

Slatzer, the couple were married in Mexico on 4 October 1952, and returned there a short while later in order to bribe the judge to burn the wedding certificate. One of the problems with this story is that cheques show Marilyn was shopping with Natasha Lytess that day, and nowhere near Mexico.

While there is no doubt that Slatzer met Marilyn, the general consensus is that the couple did not have a deep relationship and certainly never married. Added to that, Marilyn's views on the studio's reaction to marriage were later expressed when rumours began to surface that she was secretly married to Joe DiMaggio. On 21 October she said, 'If I wanted to get married now, I would. And if I already were, the studio's wishes would not be important enough to make me keep it secret.'

August saw a party held in Marilyn's honour at the home of Ray Anthony; on the 24th she recorded a radio play entitled *Statement in Full*, and then on 2 September she was asked to travel to Atlantic City for the world premiere of *Monkey Business*.

Unfortunately, a mixture of Marilyn's lateness and traffic problems forced the star and her entourage to miss the 9.00 a.m. train, much to the dismay of the studio, who had to charter a plane to get to Atlantic City on time. The plane apparently cost Fox $800, although when questioned, she later retorted, 'It didn't set the studio back as much as they let on. They could afford it.' Taking the plane meant that Marilyn arrived just three minutes later than originally planned, with the Mayor and members of the public there to meet her before she was whisked off to several publicity appearances, including riding in an open-topped car and attending the premiere itself at the Stanley Theater, where she said a few words about the film in the intermission.

Another event planned for that day was a photo session with four ladies from the armed forces. Seeing that Marilyn was wearing a low-cut dress, an enterprising photographer stood on a chair and aimed his camera right down the front of it. Nobody thought anything about the incident at the time, until an Army

Public Information Officer saw the image and demanded that it should not be used due to its revealing nature. This was enough to drum up a huge amount of interest in the photo, which forced Marilyn to release a statement saying, 'I am surprised and hurt. People looked at me all day – I thought they were admiring my Grand Marshall's badge.'

After that, Marilyn was bombarded by letters from women, sending her bras and underwear with notes saying, 'You need these more than I do.' Marilyn thought this was funny and encouraged the comments by declaring, 'Girdles and bras are unnatural. They distort a girl so. So I never wear them!' However, years later she admitted that this wasn't quite accurate: 'I was once credited with having made such a remark in an interview. If I did say that and it was true then it was probably just a very hot day.'

Women also started writing to accuse Marilyn of putting the country into a worse state than it already was. 'They accuse me of starting the rapes. Rapes went on long before I came,' she was to say, before reflecting, 'It's a little dull when [women] don't make remarks isn't it?'

A little time later, Marilyn wrote an article entitled 'Am I too daring', in which she thought hard about the comments attributed to her by other women: 'All of my adult life I have preferred to dress for men rather than for women. For this reason, I suppose, I cannot expect other women to appreciate or even like my clothes. But I do and I was hurt by the accusation that I have no taste in my manner of dress.' And slightly later: 'I'm beginning to feel like a piece of statuary that people are inspecting with a magnifying glass; looking for imperfections – taking apart my dress, my voice, my figure, my acting – everything about me.'

She began to wonder why she didn't have female friends in her life, expressing to *Photoplay* that, 'I've never in my life had girls talk – never talked about men, woman to woman ... I want women friends ... If you had even one girl friend with whom you could discuss all your innermost thoughts I do believe it would be very comforting.'

On 15 September 1952, Marilyn moved once again, this time to 2393 Castillian Drive, which she leased from landlord Frank Klein Archer. Joe DiMaggio became an almost permanent feature in the home, and would often invite friends and family to share meals and evenings together. For the first time in many years, Marilyn began to feel fairly settled and took great joy in learning how to cook steak, toss salad and make a mean spaghetti.

Still, all was not perfect, as Natasha Lytess disliked Joe intensely, feeling that the baseball star was threatening her position in Marilyn's life. He was, she said, 'a man with a closed, vapid look', and when she phoned Marilyn shortly after the first meeting, DiMaggio apparently answered the phone and told her that if she wanted to speak to the actress, she would need to contact her agent. According to Lytess, she told Marilyn she never wanted to be treated like that again, but the star didn't have the courage to stand up to Joe about it. Lytess also claimed that Marilyn would phone day and night – sometimes in tears – complaining about the way DiMaggio misused her.

Certainly on 1 October it was reported that Joe was having custody issues with his ex-wife, Dorothy Arnold, and the relationship with Marilyn had cooled. 'It's hard for me to discuss,' she told reporters. 'Perhaps later things can be worked out. Right now we're not seeing each other.' The separation was short-lived, however, and by the time Thanksgiving came round, they were back together and enjoying a meal with their friend Bernie Kamber.

Marilyn was extremely busy towards the end of 1952, and after recording an episode of the Charlie McCarthy radio show on 18 October, she began preparing for her role in *Gentlemen Prefer Blondes*, attending costume tests on 31 October, and then moving into the Beverly Hills Hotel. She also began thinking seriously about her future, and on 24 November, reporter Aline Mosby ran a story that stated Lytess was convinced the actress could one day win an Academy Award: 'I think tragic roles are her forte. There is a strangeness about her . . . an unreal quality,' she said.

To the same reporter, Marilyn had the following, despondent view on how her life was shaping up at the time: 'I'm trying to find myself now, to be a good actress and good person. Sometimes I feel strong inside but I have to reach in and pull it up. You have to be strong inside way deep inside of you. It isn't easy. Nothing's easy, as long as you go on living.'

Part of her plan to become a better person involved a trip to the Goldenberg Galleries on 3 December, in order to bid on a collection of Max Reinhardt notebooks. It had been Lytess who had encouraged her student to take an interest in the German theatrical producer, and after bidding against Jake Zeitlin from the University of Southern California (USC), she managed to win the collection for $1,335, which included 178 manuscript books full of personal notes of dialogue, action and scenery.

In the years since, it has been widely believed that Marilyn bought the notebooks for herself, but was later 'forced' to hand them over after pressure from Max Reinhardt's son and various universities. This is not true. From the beginning Marilyn had every intention of donating the collection to a 'worthy' university, as reported in the *Pottstown Mercury* on 5 December 1952.

As soon as they heard about the donation, several universities contacted her to express their interest; USC was particularly interested, as they already had 3,000 Reinhardt items and the additional notebooks would complete the collection. Librarian Lewis F. Stieg conveyed his desire to newspapers almost immediately, prompting Marilyn to release a statement on 6 December which declared that she intended to stand by her original plan to give the books to the worthiest bidder. 'Certainly Dr Stieg has made a case for USC,' she said, 'but I must study the applications of other schools which want them. I will not consider giving them to any of the museums which also want them because such institutions could not make them of use to drama students.'

Making a decision about the notebooks was a thrill for Marilyn at first, but by 13 December it had become a chore. When asked by reporters, she declared that the collection had become 'a Jonah to me. So many schools want them I hardly know what to do.' The University of Kansas had joined the list by then, and USC tried a new tactic by sending an invitation from Lewis Sticg to Marilyn, asking her to join him in his box at the Rose Bowl football game on New Year's Day. Marilyn was not moved, however, and turned him down flat, before she and Natasha continued to assess the situation.

By 6 January 1953, Marilyn was heavily involved in *Gentlemen Prefer Blondes* and she had had enough of the whole Reinhardt situation. She released a statement saying, 'I feel that placement of the books should be the decision of Mr Reinhardt's son, Mr Gottfried Reinhardt. He insists on reimbursing me for the auction price.'

Chapter 12

'Whatever I am, I am the blonde'

Marilyn spent Christmas with DiMaggio, who unexpectedly showed up at her hotel room on Christmas Eve with a tree and presents. After that she gave her full attention to the making of *Gentlemen Prefer Blondes*, which had begun shooting earlier that month.

Directed by Howard Hawks and co-starring Jane Russell as Dorothy Shaw, Marilyn played the part of Lorelei Lee, a gold-digging blonde who has snared an innocent millionaire played by George Noonan. Dorothy meanwhile, is a romantic at heart, who falls in love with Ernie Malone, a private detective hired to spy on Lee by her future father-in-law. The film is witty and colourful but the greatest part is the on-screen chemistry between the two stars – Marilyn and Jane.

From the start, the media found great joy in trying to set up a rivalry between the two women, with various rumours of which star was demanding what privilege, and even going so far as to ask Russell if she could start a 'fight' and tell the newspapers about it afterwards. The supposed 'feud' actually amazed both women, and Russell was quick to defend Marilyn to the media: 'Marilyn is not a girl you can feud with. She is too busy doing the best job she can before the cameras. Her sincerity is impressive and her willingness to listen to and take advice is one of her outstanding qualities.'

In fact, the two got on so well that Russell actually had a pet name for Marilyn – 'The Round One' – while Marilyn defended her co-star when she had to do an imitation of her towards the end of the film: 'Why should this bother me?' she asked friends, 'I know Jane wouldn't do anything that would hurt me.' This was backed up by make-up artist, Allan 'Whitey' Snyder, who remembered: 'I know the friendship and support of Jane Russell was special to her. She often commented on what fun it was being with Jane. Jane seemed to understand her.'

Jane Russell was earning $150,000 for her part, while Marilyn was restricted to $750 a week, which she assured reporters was not a problem. What was a dilemma, however, was that she couldn't get a dressing room. Every time she asked for one, she was told, 'Remember, you're not a star,' which understandably aggravated her a great deal. In the end, she decided to be firm: 'Look,' she said, 'This is *Gentlemen Prefer Blondes* and I am the blonde. Whatever I am, I am the blonde!' The executives eventually relented, and she was presented with her very own dressing room, which had once belonged to the other star on the lot – Betty Grable.

Gentlemen Prefer Blondes boasted a variety of musical numbers, including 'Little Girls from Little Rock' and 'When Love Goes Wrong', but the biggest of them all was 'Diamonds Are a Girl's Best Friend', which Marilyn performed with a host of male dancers. One of them was future Oscar-winner George Chakiris, who was very impressed by Marilyn's dedication to her role: 'I have the loveliest first impression of Marilyn. She was a darling – sweet, quiet and hardworking, and dedicated above and beyond the call of duty. She cared at a level that went beyond what we usually see.'

Shooting 'Diamonds Are a Girl's Best Friend' was relatively easy, and Marilyn always arrived on time and thoroughly prepared. Wearing no make-up, she rehearsed the scene as though her life depended on it: 'She was concentrated and dedicated to her role,' remembered Chakiris. It took three days to shoot and when they finally reached the end at 9 p.m. on the third day, dance director Jack Cole left almost straightaway in order to travel to New York. 'He left without saying goodbye and when Marilyn found out he'd gone, she ran off the stage to try and find him and thank him,' said Chakiris.

Twenty-seven-year-old Gwen Verdon worked as assistant to Jack Cole, and her son, Jim Henaghan Jr, remembers: 'Marilyn and Jane Russell were the stars but neither one could dance. Both had trouble moving to music and mom was given the job of changing that; in watching the movie one sees that she was more successful with Marilyn. At the time I would go to the studio now and then and always remember mom and Marilyn working very hard to get things just right for every shot.

'The willingness to work that hard – and it was HARD – was my mom's life motivation and the reason that she held Marilyn in such esteem. Marilyn had trouble remembering steps and moves from one day to the next, which was an ability not a substance problem, but never gave up or had tantrums or anything else but [always behaved in] a professional manner. All through her life my mom would not sit still for attacks on Marilyn's lack of will. She was and remained very fond of her. Ms Russell fell into that category also; she worked very hard [but] her problem was she didn't move in a sexy manner.'

Another person anxious to get the best from Marilyn was vocal coach Hal Schaefer, who had been assigned to help Jack Cole with Russell and Monroe's musical numbers. Schaefer had worked with the likes of Betty Grable, and as such had a great reputation for work in his field, and Marilyn took to him and respected him immediately. However, Schaefer soon learnt that her dedication to lessons did not extend to punctuality. On the first day of training she showed up late: 'The first thing I told her,' remembered Schaefer, 'was that she better not be late or I wouldn't teach her, so she showed up on time after that.' The two got straight down to work with the first lesson consisting of Schaefer telling his student to buy the album *Ella Fitzgerald sings George Gershwin*. 'Marilyn had heard of Ella but had never heard her songs. Marilyn had a problem with singing in tune, but everything else she did was wonderful. I told her to listen to this album because never had there been a singer more in tune than Ella.' This first lesson would lead to a life-long love for Ella's music, which would eventually spill over to a love for the artist herself.

Ella later praised Marilyn for personally calling Charlie Morrison, owner of the Mocambo nightclub, to ask if Ella could play there. In return Marilyn promised that she would sit in the front row every night, which she did. Unfortunately, in the years since then it has been presumed that the reason Ella Fitzgerald had never previously been allowed to play Mocambo was because she was black. This is not true, as a variety of black entertainers had been booked there long before Ella, including Dorothy Dandridge in 1951 and Eartha Kitt in 1953. The truth is that while Charlie Morrison encouraged and applauded performers of all races in his club, he didn't see Ella Fitzgerald as being glamorous enough to bring in the crowds. It would take Marilyn to change his mind, and once Ella had her foot in the door she successfully played at the Mocambo on a variety of occasions. '[Marilyn] was an unusual woman,' Ella later remarked. 'A little ahead of her times and she didn't know it.'

Although Marilyn didn't open up to many people on the set of *Gentlemen Prefer Blondes*, she did confide to Hal Schaefer that she believed one day she might be a good actress. Unfortunately, she had no such confidence in her ability to be a good singer, and it was this that Schaefer had to work on above anything else: 'The essence of singing is confidence because you don't have any other instrument – no trumpet, violin, etc. I tried to get her to be more confident, as singing is no rocket science; it isn't such a profound thing. I gave Marilyn help with her confidence and enjoyment of singing – I didn't want her to feel that she had to prove herself.'

While most people on the set were intent on helping Marilyn, one constant presence caused problems with director Howard Hawks and choreographer Jack Cole. Drama coach Natasha Lytess may have wanted to help Marilyn, but in doing so seemed to cause stress to everyone around her: 'One day Lytess was on the set,' remembered George Chakiris. 'Jack Cole was facing

Marilyn, talking to her; but behind him and unknown to him was Lytess. I think Cole must have been giving direction to Marilyn, but there was Lytess, shaking her head to Marilyn, in response to what Cole was saying. Jack had no idea what was going on. I think this showed a real sweetness in Marilyn, as she was being courteous to both Lytess and Cole – she was in the middle of the situation, being polite to both. I thought the way she handled it was very sweet.'

A reporter, on set during a scene where Jane Russell and Marilyn were reading through the ship's passenger list, remembered watching Lytess looking as though she was 'quietly having a stroke', as she reflected every expression and word coming from Marilyn's direction. The scene was shot three times before Hawks called 'Cut' and Lytess hurried over to Marilyn, dragging her away in order to lecture her on her performance.

Elliott Reid played Ernie Malone in the film, and he worked extensively with both Jane Russell and Marilyn. He remembered: 'I thought she was lovely-looking, beautiful and charming. She was quiet and shy but we didn't really get to know each other during the shoot because as soon as the scene was finished Marilyn would go to her dressing room to work with her drama coach.'

Once again her lateness became legendary on the set, but by now the other actors and actresses were becoming used to it, as Reid remembered: 'She was often late – sometimes ten minutes or so, but not extreme; her lateness was well known and it was just how she was. She was charming and everyone understood her lateness and nobody got mad. There were no problems during the making of the film because she was so sweet; she was never aggressive – she just wanted to do her best.'

Jane Russell sympathized with the nerves that caused Marilyn to be late, and made a point of trotting past her dressing room in order to walk her to the set each day. This helped with her punctuality, but not her nerves, and she would visibly shake between scenes, as George Chakiris observed on the first day of shooting the 'Diamonds' number: 'Marilyn was sitting on the round sofa used during the song, and I noticed the muscles in her back quivering from nerves,' he later recalled.

She may have been terrified but she was absolutely determined to do her best, and took to writing little notes to herself on her script such as 'Know the lines, go over it intelligently.' She was anxious to think about what was going on inside, rather than outside, as Chakiris remembered: 'Marilyn would do the take, and if it was not right, the director would shout "Cut". She would not go to her dressing room or a mirror; instead she would go back to her starting position and just wait for it all to start again. I never saw her look in a mirror.'

With the filming eventually finished, everyone went back to their normal lives, but the experience left many happy memories, as recalled by George Chakiris: 'I am so glad that I got to be in the chorus, it was a wonderful thing to be behind Marilyn and Jack Cole. I was there and it was a wonderful, wonderful time. It was a feather in my cap!'

In February 1953 rumours circulated that *Niagara* was not doing as well at the box office as had been hoped. Meanwhile, Marilyn attended the Photoplay Awards dinner, dressed in the gold gown briefly glimpsed in *Gentlemen Prefer Blondes*. When she got up to receive her award, the audience yelled and shouted, and Jerry Lewis stood on a table to whistle. Marilyn, loving the attention she was receiving, gave it her all, and the result was electrifying; but one person not impressed was actress Joan Crawford, who couldn't believe her eyes.

A few days later, according to Crawford, columnist Bob Thomas interviewed her and, afterwards, asked, 'Don't you think that dress Marilyn Monroe wore at the awards dinner was disgusting?'

Crawford presumed that the question was 'off the record' and answered, 'It was like a burlesque show. Someone should make her see the light; she should be told that the public likes provocative feminine personalities; but it also likes to know that underneath it all the actresses are ladies.'

On 24 February, Marilyn appeared on Dean Martin and Jerry Lewis's radio show, performing a short skit entitled 'So Who

Needs Friends', before picking up another award, this time for the *Redbook* award for Best Young Box Office Personality. She should have been happy, but on 3 March, when Bob Thomas published Crawford's comments in his column, Marilyn was devastated. She couldn't understand why Crawford had attacked her in such a way, and was unsure what to do when reporters from around the country kept ringing to ask for her comments.

Louella Parsons spoke to Marilyn and observed that she had been crying all night long, to such an extent that she sounded as though she had a bad cold. 'I don't believe Miss Crawford said those things about me,' Marilyn told Parsons, before deciding that possibly she had been speaking impulsively, without thinking.

Meanwhile, Crawford herself was thoroughly embarrassed by the whole episode. She told Parsons, 'I wish I could say I didn't say those things but I did say them! I was not misquoted! But believe me, in the future I will think twice before I talk so openly.' She started receiving scathing letters from Marilyn's fans, and through Parsons released a statement apologizing to the actress but projecting her opinion that 'for this thing to go on and on, as though someone has been murdered, is ridiculous.'

Marilyn too began receiving letters, albeit of a more positive nature than the ones Crawford was getting. GIs were bombarding her with support, and even Betty Grable, her idol and co-star on her next picture, *How to Marry a Millionaire*, took her to lunch in order to advise her to 'Just keep on plugging'. Finally, Marilyn decided to draw a line under the whole sordid affair, declaring, 'I'm beginning to look at it as a blessing in disguise. If it had never been printed, I might never have realized how many friends I have, even ones I have never met.'

Back in the summer of 1952 Marilyn had been concerned to discover that her mother, Gladys Baker, had unexpectedly turned up at Grace Goddard's home. Unpredictable as usual, Gladys announced that she'd recently married a mysterious man called Colonel John Eley, who had turned out to be a bigamist. She then told Grace that she had started divorce proceedings only for him to die before it was all complete, and then proceeded to move herself and her belongings into the Goddard home.

The entire family were so confused by her half-baked stories that many rumours swirled around for years, with some even believing that the mysterious Mr Eley was actually just a figment of Gladys' overactive imagination. In truth, however, he most certainly did exist.

Born on 13 June 1889, John Stewart Eley was a retired Colonel in the Signal Corps and had lived in Los Angeles for six years before his death on 23 April 1952. Despite Gladys turning up at the Knebelkamp home to declare her intention to live with Eley in a tent, in reality they actually lived together at 10538 Santa Monica Boulevard. Eley had most certainly been married before though no records can be found to support Gladys' claim that he was a bigamist. Indeed, when his obituary was printed in the 26 April edition of the *Los Angeles Times*, there were only two relatives mentioned: his sister Helen and his widow Gladys.

Whilst living with Grace Goddard, Gladys' behaviour became so erratic that Grace started to note down the disturbing things she was saying. According to her notes, Gladys felt that she was now 'confused' because she had once taken an aspirin during her marriage to Eley; felt she was being punished because during prohibition she had taken a drink of liquor; kept a photo of Marilyn in her bedroom, but slept at the foot of her bed so she didn't have to look at it; and had a fear of Catholics, thinking that they were out to harm her.

Grace had suffered from depression for many years, and soon became exhausted with her new lodger, particularly when Gladys started to accuse her of stealing or moving items that she herself had misplaced. Grace suffered a stroke, and Gladys ended up moving in with the Bolender family, who had looked after Norma Jeane all those years before. Mrs Bolender, who had never seen any of Marilyn's movies, later recalled: 'I talked to Norma Jeane on the phone when her mother was staying with me. On the phone I said, "Norma Jeane why don't you come to see me?" She said, "I always thought because I'm in the movies you might not like me anymore." I said, "Because you're in the movies don't make any difference, you come to see me," but she didn't.'

Eventually Gladys took off to Florida in search of her daughter, Berniece, but was soon back in California, banging on the door of Grace and Doc Goddard in such a frenzy that the police were called. Gladys was admitted to the Metropolitan State Hospital and Grace was left with the unenviable task of travelling to 2713 Honolulu Ave, Los Angeles, to make arrangements for her to be placed permanently in Rockhaven Sanitarium.

Rockhaven was established in 1923 by a nurse called Agnes Richards, who wanted to improve the treatment of mentally ill women. Set in 3.5 acres of gardens, the establishment grew to include fourteen different buildings and housed around a hundred patients – or residents as the staff liked to call them.

On 9 February 1953, Gladys became a resident there, and on 1 March Marilyn sent a cheque to Grace for $851.04 to cover her mother's expenses. It was to be the first of many cheques written to pay for her mother's care, though Marilyn herself would have very little to do with Gladys' day-to-day life at the institution.

There has been a great deal of mystery regarding Gladys' time at Rockhaven, with stories becoming wilder and more exaggerated as time goes on. However, in 2010 biographer Lois Banner interviewed Agnes Richards' granddaughter Pat Traviss about life at Rockhaven and found that Gladys' time there was not the horror story one has been led to believe. Pat worked at the institution herself, and became the administrator after her grandmother had retired. According to Banner, Traviss relayed to her that contrary to what previous biographers have reported, Marilyn absolutely never visited her mother. In fact Agnes remembered only one telephone call from the star, in which she asked Gladys if there was anything she could buy for her. The answer? A bar of ivory soap.

Gladys' life at Rockhaven was a relatively solitary one. She was quiet, kept herself to herself and never talked about intimate or private matters with anyone – especially the medical staff. In fact, she especially disliked anyone who was considered a 'nurse' and it was only because Traviss wasn't in the medical profession that she was able to become friendly with Gladys. The two would often go out for ice cream and at one point Gladys even knitted socks for a member of Traviss' family.

Traviss disputed recent stories that Gladys Baker could hear voices in her head. She told Lois Banner that Gladys believed there was nothing wrong with her and would never have said she was hearing voices. 'She didn't really think she was ill,' recalled Traviss. This would tie in with a letter Grace once wrote to a friend back in the 1930s, when Gladys was first admitted to a mental institution. In it she explained that Gladys didn't know she was ill and even thought she would soon return to work. That she believed herself to be absolutely sane is also confirmed in a remark Gladys made to Grace that she believed she had only been sent to the institution because she was working as a nurse there. At no time did Gladys believe herself to be ill and, if there were voices in her head, she would never have dreamed of making them public.

There has been talk of many traumatic events while Gladys was confined, including staff selling their stories, but actually it seems that nobody ever gave any information for money, even when offered a large amount. There was one incident, however, that did stand out in Traviss' mind, as she remembered: 'I left Gladys alone in my office and I came back to find my furniture overturned and there was red ink spilled. I never left her alone again.'

Keeping thoughts of her mother to a minimum, on 18 March 1953 Marilyn moved into a three-roomed apartment at 882 North Doheny Drive, which Jane Russell and interior designer Thomas Lane helped her to decorate. The comfortable home was furnished with thick carpets, white and beige furnishings, and, of course, her book collection. She also collected her black piano from storage, painted it white and installed it in the home, where she was to stay for almost all of 1953.

A new friend came into Marilyn's life at this time, when she met actor and author John Gilmore during a party at neighbour John Hodiak's house. Gilmore and Marilyn had much in common and spoke easily with each other. He remembered: 'Marilyn told me she'd dreamed of waltzing through movies as another Jean Harlow. Even then she didn't know she'd someday eclipse Harlow and emerge from a kind of imposed, personal cocoon as the most beautiful and important movie star in the world.

'Marilyn was shadowed and strange; diffident yet vivacious, determined while fearful. She was intense and funny at the same time, and was very, very far from being "dumb". I remember my conversation with her verbatim; how she looked, what she wore and how she smelled; what her hand felt like and how the aroma of her lingered on my hand after shaking hers. From that time on, Marilyn and I ran separately in and out and backwards and forwards through the Hollywood milieu ad nauseam, her career skyrocketing. We caught up again, encountering the same people, the same spots on the Strip; Mocambo, Ciros, etc.'

Marilyn's next film was a comedy entitled *How to Marry a Millionaire*, in which she played opposite Betty Grable and Lauren Bacall. The filming followed an altogether familiar pattern: the press tried to create a feud between the stars (they failed); Natasha's direction caused friction on the set; and Marilyn was continuously late, leading love interest David Wayne to describe the experience as, 'One of the worst times I've ever had in my life.'

While Lauren Bacall could hardly disguise her impatience and irritation with the fledgling star, idol Betty Grable could not have been more patient and understanding. Knowing that Twentieth Century Fox expected her to resent Marilyn's new popularity, Grable went out of her way to give advice and help her successor. She encouraged her ambitions and the two became firm friends, especially when Grable commented, 'Honey I've had mine; go get yours,' to the excited young star. The two got along famously and Grable always remembered her time on the set with particular fondness.

Another person who was happy to be there was a young man called Jim Gough, whose father worked at the studio, giving him the opportunity to meet Marilyn and Betty: 'Meeting these two fabulous women was a teenager's dream come true and it changed my life. Marilyn and Betty were not only beautiful, but also very kind and down to earth – without an ounce of pretension. One day, they invited me to have lunch in the "Commissary". They were both made up and were in costume with dressing gowns over their costumes to protect them. My entrance into the restaurant, between these two women, was the answer to a young man's prayers! During the meal, we chatted about school matters, friendships, and, most of all, about pets. Marilyn loved dogs especially. After the filming of *How to Marry a Millionaire*, I occasionally met Marilyn, who always seemed to remember me.'

The beginning of April 1953 was a busy time for Marilyn. On 7 April she attended a birthday party with Betty Grable in honour of columnist Walter Winchell, and then she signed a new agency contract, this time with the Famous Artists Agency. But by 14 April she was in hospital being treated for her ongoing endometriosis problem, which unfortunately would never be resolved.

Coming out of hospital, Marilyn rested at home on Doheny Drive, reading her books and talking to friends. Grace Goddard was still a big part of her life, especially now that Gladys had been re-institutionalized, and the two would speak on the telephone every day. 'It used to drive me crazy!' remembered Bebe Goddard. 'It's because she confided every minute of her night and day to Grace. Totally. Everything. And Grace would sympathize and advise, and believe me, Marilyn never took her for granted.'

However, although Grace was more than happy to listen to Marilyn's problems, she had many of her own, including a dependency on alcohol and a heart problem, for which she was taking phenobarbital. In May Marilyn invited her to rest at the Doheny Drive apartment and the two enjoyed many hours in each other's company.

Tragedy soon struck Marilyn's life while she and Joe were away for a short break. He received news that his brother, Mike, had been killed in a fishing accident off the coast of Bodega Bay. A devastated DiMaggio went straight to San Francisco, while Marilyn returned to Los Angeles and spent her birthday quietly with Grace, Bebe and Bebe's brother Fritz. She then travelled up to San Francisco to be with DiMaggio and his family during the mourning period and offering her support to the devastated Joe. She made a good impression on his entire family, and it was during this period that DiMaggio realized how much he was in love with her, while Marilyn confessed to friends that she knew at that time that she really did want to marry him.

On 26 June Marilyn received the recognition she had craved since a child, when she placed her hands and feet into the wet cement outside Grauman's Chinese Theatre. Together with Jane Russell, she stood in the very spot where she had admired the prints as a child. She later remembered: 'I did have a funny feeling when I finally put my foot down into that wet cement. I sure knew what it really meant to me – anything's possible, almost.' Two days later, she walked to the theatre in the middle of the night to see how her footprints really looked. 'It was like hearing all the applause in the world,' friend Sidney Skolsky later observed.

By this time Marilyn was involved in the production of *River of No Return*, a lightweight Western which she was not impressed by, but agreed to do because she liked the songs. In it she was to play the part of a saloon singer, opposite Robert Mitchum, an old workmate of first husband, James Dougherty. She liked Mitchum a lot and the two immediately gelled, as she cheerfully told reporters, 'It's nice when you hit the ball and somebody hits it back.'

From the beginning, Marilyn got along very well with producer Stanley Rubin, whom she had unsuccessfully auditioned for all those years ago, but the two had a common enemy in director Otto Preminger, who was known to be something of a bully. Rubin remembered: 'The problems between Otto and I began when I told him he wasn't my choice for director – he was the studio's choice. Otto didn't take kindly to that. Otto had something in him that made him capable of bullying, and he bullied Marilyn, but never Bob Mitchum because he knew he wouldn't get away with it.'

In fairness to Preminger, while he was a tough director, he did have a reason to be upset with Marilyn, in the shape of none other than Natasha Lytess, who once again accompanied the star on to the set. 'When the take was finished,' remembered Rubin, 'Marilyn looked past Otto to Natasha, who was standing a few feet behind the director. It was not a good arrangement – Otto was a very proud man and didn't like Natasha being on set. The problem went all the way to the Head of the Studio – Darryl F. Zanuck – and for a while Natasha was banned from the set, but then Marilyn went to Zanuck herself and Natasha came back.'

When the cast and crew travelled to Canada for location shots the problems were intensified whilst shooting scenes on a raft. On one occasion both Marilyn and Robert Mitchum almost hit rocks and had to be saved by a rescue boat, and on another Marilyn slipped and fell into the water, as remembered by make-up artist Allan 'Whitey' Snyder: 'We had a raft tied to the shore and Marilyn and Robert Mitchum were supposed to push it off. The river bed had a rocky bottom, and when she took two or three steps, she twisted her ankle and fell down.'

From then on Marilyn was to be seen around the set with a bandaged foot and crutches, but all the same, some people have disputed the sprained ankle story, stating that Marilyn did it in order to take her revenge on 'bully' Preminger. Producer

Stanley Rubin thinks otherwise: 'I believe she did sprain her ankle badly. She had to hobble around and they shot around her for a few days and also shot scenes where she didn't have to move. I find it very hard to believe it was fake. She did trip on the raft – either getting on or getting off – she did fall.'

The sprained ankle did give Marilyn a few perks, one of which was the arrival of Joe DiMaggio, who hurried to the location as soon as he heard the news. The other was some time off, which she spent relaxing beside the hotel pool.

Marilyn spent much of the summer of 1953 taking photographs with New York photographer Milton Greene, and then on 13 September she made her television debut on the *Jack Benny Program*, and was presented with a new car in lieu of payment. She was so proud of her new vehicle that she drove it up to show Uncle Sam and Aunt Enid. The Knebelkamps' son-in-law, Forrest Olmstead remembers Marilyn's relationship with the family, and her ability to leave her movie star image behind: 'A new room had been added to the house and I was putting up button board for plaster on the wall; Marilyn would hand me the board so I could attach it to the wall. Then another time I was working on a new cess pool and she would hand me down bricks . . . She was the only woman there that wanted to help.'

She also went to great lengths in order to spoil her foster family, buying gifts and holding parties during special celebrations: '[Diane and I] bought a house in Long Beach,' recalls Forrest, 'and Cousin Pat and her husband Ben also bought a house. Marilyn gave both of us a house warming in Pat and Ben's back yard. She came down in a limousine with her chauffeur and gave us both a gift; we had a whole tub of beer and got the chauffeur a little drunk.'

Unfortunately her relationship with the Knebelkamp/Goddard family changed when Grace Goddard was rushed to hospital with breathing difficulties, and passed away on 28 September 1953. 'I was horribly sad and devastated,' Grace's stepdaughter Bebe remembered. 'And Marilyn was 50,000 times as much.'

It has been rumoured over the years that Grace was suffering from cancer at the time of her death. This may be so, but the death certificate states that her death was suicide caused by barbiturate poisoning, due to the ingestion of phenobarbital. 'She did have a whole box of pills like nothing you've ever seen before. And in those days they were much easier to get,' remembered Bebe. Whether or not Marilyn knew the exact cause of death is unclear, but if she did it must have been extremely upsetting; for her whole life Marilyn had dealt with her mother's emotional problems, and now to discover that Grace had taken her own life must have been truly disturbing.

'I believe that Marilyn loved Grace more than anybody in the world,' Bebe Goddard recalled. 'Grace had been a second mother from the time she was born, and had been such a fair person, and as much a mother, or more so, than Gladys had been. Grace was the single most constant factor throughout Marilyn's life.'

Many people have said that Marilyn refused to attend Grace's funeral, but this is simply not true: 'She absolutely was at Grace's funeral,' Bebe Goddard later told the 'All About Marilyn' fan club. This is also confirmed by Will Sykes, who was married to Aunt Ana's niece, Sybil Louise Howland. 'Marion said she met you at Grace's funeral. How is Doc getting along?' he asked in a letter to Marilyn in October 1954.

The funeral was a quiet, family affair and afterwards Marilyn travelled to Aunt Enid and Uncle Sam's house, where she sat solemnly with the other family members. Diane Knebelkamp's husband, Forrest, remembers: 'I was sitting in Diane's old room which had been turned into a den, when Marilyn walked in and sat down. She didn't say much because she was so upset.'

After recovering sufficiently from the passing of Aunt Grace, Marilyn attended the premiere of *How to Marry a Millionaire* on 4 November 1953, and shortly after underwent more gynaecological surgery. Having spent a huge amount of time working in 1953, she was quite literally exhausted, as she told reporter Rita Garrison Malloy: 'I'm so tired. I've been working seven days a week at the studio. My doctor Elliot Corday says I'm anaemic.' Doctor Corday prescribed an iron-rich diet that consisted of raw eggs, raw ground liver (which she spiked with lime and Worcestershire sauce to mask the taste), gelatine, orange juice, rare steak and spinach, along with iron and vitamin shots. Unfortunately nothing seemed to help and Marilyn still felt absolutely awful.

When Fox announced that she was to star in *The Girl in Pink Tights*, Marilyn agreed to do it only if she could see the script first. In the twenty-first century, that would be an understandable request, but in the 1950s, when actors were just cogs in the machine, it was unheard of. Zanuck rejected her request and she found herself in the unenviable position of being threatened with suspension from the studio. She dug her heels in further on discovering that while she was going to be paid her by now usual $1,500 a week, her co-star, Frank Sinatra, would be paid $5,000. She stood firm and when an executive told her, 'I've been in this business a long time and I know what's good for you,' she retorted, 'I've been in this business a very short time but I know better what's good for me than you do.'

'They throw me from one picture into another,' she complained in December. 'I don't travel, see things, meet people and know them under normal circumstances . . . Directors think all I have to do is wiggle a little, not act.'

When Marilyn did not show up for filming on 15 December, the studio was incensed and sent various executives and staff members (including Lytess) to her Doheny Drive home; there they were met by a furious DiMaggio, who ordered each one away from the door. Although he did not like to get involved with Marilyn's career matters, he was adamant that she would not be taken advantage of again, noting that as she made millions for the studio, she surely had a right to share some of it.

Finally, after fighting off illness, studio executives, Lytess and countless reporters, Marilyn packed her things and on 23 December she flew to San Francisco for privacy and rest in the DiMaggio family home at 2150 Beach Street.

Chapter 13

Mrs DiMaggio

By the time Marilyn reached San Francisco, she was feeling worse than ever, and was put to bed by DiMaggio's sister Marie, who still lived in and looked after the family home. A relative of Joe's ex-wife Dorothy Arnold recalled: 'She cooked, cleaned, etc. as Joe wouldn't spend money to pay someone. I didn't know her but I was told she was a dear lady, waiting on him hand and foot.'

Once Marilyn moved into the home, Marie also began caring for her too and soon warmed to her new house guest: 'She's just like Joe,' she told reporter Alice Hoffman in 1954. 'They were made for each other. I know it sounds corny but it's true.'

Marilyn settled into DiMaggio's world easily, enjoying the company of his family and taking part in pursuits he enjoyed, such as fishing with his brother, Tom, who later recalled: 'Marilyn was tops. Never a peep or a complaint out of her. When I came home that night my wife Lee said, "What do you think of Joe's girlfriend?" And I say, "Funny thing. She's just like Joe. She's quiet and plain and shy and I like her very much."'

She also integrated herself into the general running of the Beach Street home, and enjoyed simple pleasures such as washing Joe's car and making breakfast for the household, including coffee (although she herself drank tea and milk), freshly squeezed orange juice, and bacon and eggs. 'She's really very handy in the kitchen,' remarked Marie DiMaggio. 'I knew she was a good girl the first time Joe brought her up. Right away she was helping with the dishes.'

On New Year's Eve, the couple dined out at the famed DiMaggio's restaurant, run by family members Tom and Dom, and Joe's closest friend, Reno Barsocchini. When they returned to Beach Street, Joe took the opportunity of asking Marilyn if she would like to marry him, and she agreed.

The couple decided to keep it quiet, apart from telling a few friends and relatives, such as sister Marie, who went to Joseph Magnin's with Marilyn for a wedding outfit. While there she was mobbed by fans and insisted on signing all autographs before she left with a $149.50 suit, complete with ermine collar.

By this time Fox had relented and sent Marilyn the script for *The Girl in Pink Tights*, but were outraged to discover that far from persuading her to do the film, the script only reinforced her feelings that the part of a teacher turned saloon dancer was not for her. 'It is just not in the same league as *Gentlemen Prefer Blondes*,' she later told reporters. 'If I'd done *Pink Tights* there would have been "Yellow Tights", "Blue Tights", and "Green Tights", afterwards.' On 4 January she was suspended without pay, and Fox announced that newcomer Sheree North would act in *Pink Tights* instead.

The rumour mills went into overdrive, firstly wondering where Marilyn was, and then deciding that she and DiMaggio had run away to be married. They were apparently spotted tying the knot in Mexico, Hawaii, the High Sierras and even in New Orleans with Rock Hudson. There was also talk of a wedding being booked at the Hotel El Rancho in Vegas, only to be cancelled at the last minute.

A Fox spokesman denied all stories, however, insisting that Marilyn 'promised to notify us if she decided to get married,' and adding that she was missing from the set because, 'She's mad at the studio and wants a raise.'

Natasha Lytess was also kept out of the loop and was forced to admit on 4 January that she hadn't heard anything from her student. By now Marilyn's relationship with her coach was starting to deteriorate; a result, some say, of the feud between Lytess and DiMaggio. However, things had never been entirely stable between them with Marilyn often complaining that Natasha was just too possessive of her. Lytess was also not opposed to commenting on her student in the press, declaring in 1953, 'She is not a natural actress. She has to learn to have a free voice and a free body to act. Luckily Marilyn has a wonderful instinct for the right timing. I think she will eventually be a good actress.' A private person at heart, comments such as this must surely have added to the irritation being felt by both DiMaggio and his fiancée.

Towards the end of 1953, Marilyn began working on her autobiography with talk-show host, Joe Franklin. They worked for two weeks on the project and Marilyn even chose suitable photos for the book, before her studio discovered what she was up to. 'She was under contract to work on another book and she was stopped from working on [mine],' remembered Franklin, who went on to complete the book himself, which became the first of its kind dedicated to the star.

The book she was under contract to write was a 200-page 'autobiography' ghostwritten by respected author Ben Hecht, on which she began working on 2 January 1954. Hecht had been asked by a studio representative to travel to San Francisco, and together with his secretary, Nanette Herbuveaux, he spent four days asking Marilyn questions on all aspects of her life. She was extremely cooperative and agreed to both magazine and book publication, and promised to ask her lawyer, Loyd Wright, to draw up a contract giving her a 50 per cent share of the book rights and a 15 per cent share of magazine rights.

During the interviews between Marilyn and Hecht, she surprised the writer by declaring that she had twice tried to commit suicide, both times after the failure of a relationship: 'The full reason was that I didn't want to live. There was too much pain in living,' she told him. She also claimed that when she had been revived after the second attempt, she felt angry that someone was forcing her live, even when she didn't want to. 'But now I'm glad it happened the way it did. I'm glad I'm alive. I hope to stay glad for a long time.'

The interviews showed Marilyn to be a somewhat sad and unfulfilled young woman, especially when she confided, 'I've never liked sex. I don't think I ever will. It seems just the opposite of love.' Although she didn't admit it to Hecht, it has been widely rumoured since that she had never been able to achieve orgasm, and if that is true, it was an ironic and tragic twist that the most famous sex symbol of all time never found any fulfilment in sex herself.

When the interviews were done, Hecht travelled back to Los Angeles in order to write up what he had so far. Publisher Doubleday advanced him $5,000 in royalties, and there was even talk of the *Ladies Home Journal* wanting to serialize it. However, after writing almost non-stop for five days, Hecht received word from Marilyn's lawyer Loyd Wright that she had changed her mind – she no longer wanted a book publication, but was still happy for the magazine printing. Hecht was confused and dismayed; he knew that if the book publication did not go ahead, he would be forced to pay back his $5,000, but for now he continued work on the story, and waited to hear from Marilyn once again.

Back in San Francisco, Joe and Marilyn decided that they should get married as soon as possible, so that they would be together when DiMaggio travelled to Japan on a baseball-coaching trip the following month. He took advice from an old friend, Judge Charles Peery, who was happy to help; he arranged for the licence to be typed in his chambers and suggested they marry during the lunch hour, since the building would be quieter at that time. Meanwhile, Natasha Lytess finally managed to get Marilyn on the telephone and blasted the star with her grievances towards DiMaggio, declaring that she saw the man as a punishment in her life. Marilyn ignored her advice, however, and three days later she became Mrs DiMaggio.

At 12.30 p.m. on 14 January 1954, Marilyn telephoned Fox to tell them she would be married 'in some courtroom' in a few minutes. It had originally been decided that the couple wouldn't tell anyone until after the ceremony itself, but Marilyn – loyal despite being suspended – knew that she owed it to Fox to let them know. Unfortunately, the loyalty did not extend far within the studio, and an enterprising executive phoned everyone he could think of to let them know what was going on.

By the time Marilyn, Joe and their witnesses arrived at the San Francisco City Hall, at least 500 people were present: 'We were amazed when we walked into the City Hall and saw that mob of people,' DiMaggio later said.

Due to a slight mix-up with the licence, the reporters had the opportunity to interview the couple waiting outside the chambers, asking such futile questions as, 'How many children will you have?' 'Are you excited?' and 'Will you give up your career?' to which Marilyn retorted 'What difference does it make? The studio has suspended me.' Finally deputy county clerk David Dunn appeared with some blank licenses, which he proceeded to fill out, before Judge Peery threw everyone out of his chambers to begin the ceremony at precisely 1.46 p.m.

Within two minutes the couple were pronounced man and wife, and they came bounding out of the court room, only to find themselves wedged in by hundreds of reporters and fans. The entire building was crammed with people, forcing them to ride the elevator to the basement instead of the first floor, a trip which was made all the more bothersome when a spectator forced himself in and lambasted the couple: 'This is a fine thing – dodging your loyal fans like this.' DiMaggio is reported to have angrily replied, 'Don't tell me what to do.'

Finally, the couple reached outside and, watched by hundreds of people, climbed into Joe's blue Cadillac and sped away. On her departure from the building, one reporter asked Marilyn when they had decided to get married, to which she mysteriously replied, 'We've been thinking about it for a long time, but we were not too sure until we walked into the door here now.'

In order to put reporters off their scent, the couple headed to Monterey and registered at the Mission Inn Hotel, before secretly travelling on to Paso Robles, where they ate quietly at the Hot Springs Hotel, and checked into the Clifton Motel. There, the surprised manager, Ernest Sharp, promised not to tell the media of their whereabouts until after they had left the premises the following morning. He was true to his word, and when they did leave, he refused to even look in which direction they were headed, lest he give away any information to the eager paparazzi. Meanwhile, one of the staff at the Hot Springs Hotel told reporters that Marilyn said she was going back to Los Angeles in order to work.

This must have been good news for Fox, but it was a red herring, as instead of returning to Hollywood, the couple headed to a mountain hideaway in Idyllwild, close to Palm Springs. Marilyn's attorney, Loyd Wright, loaned the honeymoon house to them and they were assured complete privacy, with only the tight-lipped Wright and his caretaker Harry Gibbons knowing anything of their whereabouts.

On 16 January, Fox reinstated Marilyn and instructed her to report to work on 20 January. When that day came and went, another letter was written, this time demanding she report to the office of producer Sol Siegel at 12 noon on 25 January, for the purpose of rendering her services in connection with the much hyped (and much loathed) *Pink Tights*. They also reminded their rebellious star that her portrayal of Jenny in the aforementioned film was all in accordance with the terms and provisions of her contract, which she had signed on 11 April 1951. Marilyn may now be Mrs Joe DiMaggio, but for the studio, she was still just the girl who couldn't get a dressing room.

It is highly unlikely that Marilyn made it to the office of Mr Siegel on 25 January, but after her honeymoon she did slip quietly into Los Angeles for a meeting with her business manager, before heading back to San Francisco. By this time many presents had been delivered from friends, family and fans: vases, linens and silverware all arrived, but notably absent was anything from Twentieth Century Fox. Marilyn was very upset at the snub and later told Sidney Skolsky, 'I didn't get a present from anybody at the studio or from any player.'

On 28 January Marilyn was vaccinated by Dr Clifton Bennett, in order that she could travel with DiMaggio to Japan for his coaching trip. That evening she somehow broke her thumb, the cause of which has never been fully known. When the couple left San Francisco International Airport the following day, they were almost late as Marilyn was having the thumb bandaged and splinted. When reporters caught sight of it as she tried to hide it in her coat, they immediately asked what happened. 'I just bumped it against the door,' she said. 'Joe was there. He heard it crack.' This could be the truth, but over the years many writers have blamed DiMaggio for it, claiming that he had become violent towards his wife from early in their marriage. Certainly, a relative of Joe's first wife, Dorothy Arnold, believed this story: 'Joe was extremely possessive of Dorothy; also Marilyn. He once broke Marilyn's finger [*sic*] on their trip to Japan – it is very clear in some of the Korean tour pictures.'

After a quick stopover in Honolulu, the couple were flown to Tokyo, where they were greeted by literally thousands of fans and reporters, so much so that they were unable to leave the plane by the main exit. Instead, they had to leave via the baggage door on the side of the plane, although even that didn't stop a stampede, with some enterprising fans climbing on top of their car for a better look.

Although Marilyn had been surrounded by fans in the past, this was the first time she had ever been mobbed in such a way and she was terrified. 'These people, they're mad!' she was heard to cry, as she was hustled into the car, en route to the Imperial Hotel, along with Joe's friend and fellow baseball expert Frank 'Lefty' O'Doul and his wife. When they reached the hotel there were even more riots, with people falling into the hotel pond, trying to break down the doors and even scaling the walls. Finally, the police dragged fans away and the honeymooning couple were able to enter the hotel, where they held a press conference in the Treasure Room.

Once the fans and media had calmed down somewhat, the couple were able to spend some of their time visiting quiet areas such as Kawana, a fishing village where they were photographed meeting the locals. Shortly after, DiMaggio headed south to fulfil his coaching job, along with Lefty O'Doul. Meanwhile, Mrs O'Doul stayed in Japan to keep Marilyn company, and on 7 February they both visited the US Army Hospital in Tokyo.

During the visit Marilyn met countless injured GIs, signed autographs and posed for photographs. One of the soldiers, Corporal Donald Wakehouse, had his cast signed by the star, but later insisted that his wife back home looked better to him than Marilyn did. However, another GI, Corporate Allison Ittel was thrilled to meet the visiting film star, as he remembered fifty-seven years later: 'I found out what time she was to be on the sunroof and went up. We all lined up and she was late as usual, but when Marilyn came in through the doorway she was just beautiful. She did a little skip – kind of a dance – with quick motions and a little song and came down the line to greet us.

'When she got to me I congratulated her on her marriage to Joe DiMaggio and then I went through the doors back into the hospital. Someone grabbed me and told me to go with them, and then suddenly Marilyn was there and linked arms with me. There were photographers everywhere, and Marilyn asked me what my name was and where I was from. I told her I was from Minnesota, twenty-five miles away from Indianapolis and she said, "Oh I went to visit my best friend Jane Russell up there and it was beautiful." We talked for a while and I asked where Joe was. She told me he was playing baseball and seemed disgusted by that. I got the feeling she felt he should have been up there with her.'

Later that day, having cheered up the patients at the hospital, Marilyn was sent to bed with a stomach bug. However, that didn't stop her making plans to travel to Korea to entertain the thousands of US troops that were stationed there, a surprising decision that had been made on the way to Japan: 'I hadn't expected this. I didn't bring the right clothes,' she was heard to say.

On 16 February, Marilyn began her Korea tour, which involved singing a set of songs, accompanied by a band called

Anything Goes, who had already been touring the Far East for three months. One member, Don Obermeyer, remembered the experience well: 'Since I was the show manager, I was introduced to Marilyn Monroe and Joe, and was told that our group was going back to Korea, after a week's rehearsal in Osaka, Japan. My first impression of Marilyn and Joe was very pleasant. They were both very friendly. At the rehearsal, Marilyn was so very cooperative. She had never seen an upright mike, as she was used to "boom" mikes in Hollywood. It was pretty funny, but we got her trained on the PA system. She was so easy to get along with!! Marilyn never really mentioned her private life but on the way from Osaka to Korea, she excused herself from the "brass" in the front of the plane, and sat down with each one in the show group and asked about where we lived before going into service and about our lives growing up! She was very personable and [it was] a surprising move on her part. We all appreciated her interest in "us".'

By the time Marilyn began the first show in Korea, it was snowing, but even so she appeared in a purple evening gown, and later claimed that she didn't even notice the snow falling around her. 'In fact,' she said, 'it melted away almost before it touched my skin. That was the happiest time – when the thousands of soldiers all yelled my name over and over.'

Marilyn performed several songs, including 'Diamonds Are a Girl's Best Friend' and 'Kiss Me Again', and joked and talked with the GIs in the crowd. One of them, Don Loraine, remembered: 'I was a young Marine in Korea. Marilyn came out dressed in a heavy parka. She started to sing; suddenly stopped and said, "This is not what you came to see," and took off the parka. She was dressed in a low-cut purple cocktail dress. She was so beautiful, we all went wild, and I might add it was colder than hell that day. She brought a lot of joy to a group of combat-weary Marines and I for one will never forget her.'

The shows were a huge success, and on at least one occasion Marilyn created such a stir that the troops caused a near riot. She gave it her all, as Don Obermeyer remembered: 'Marilyn did not appear to be nervous before or after each performance, except a few times she messed up some of the lyrics, but recovered! She was always greeted by a wildly energetic bunch of GIs, and time permitting she would stand in front of the stage, talk to them and let them take snapshots. At the end of each day of performances, she was swept off to the Officers Club. From the very first day on tour, she insisted that her "bunch of guys" would go with her!'

Despite being exhausted from appearing before 100,000 servicemen in just four days, Marilyn found time on the last day to give a heartfelt speech, declaring that she had never felt like a movie star before, until her trip to Korea. She added, 'Now I'm flying back to the most important thing in my life – Joe. And I want to start a family. A family comes before a career.'

On her return to Japan, Marilyn excitedly told DiMaggio, 'Joe, you never heard such cheering,' to which he replied, 'Yes I have.' This cutting put-down was made worse by the fact that the freezing conditions had given her not just a bronchial condition but pneumonia too. By the time they arrived in the United States, Marilyn wearily told reporters, 'I'm ill and just want to go to bed.' The tour had ended; she was back to reality.

Almost as soon as the couple arrived in San Francisco, DiMaggio went to work in New York, and at 11.38 p.m. on 28 February 1954, Marilyn sat down to write him a letter. In it she poured out her feelings, telling her husband how much she missed his love and cuddles; how she felt so sad and wanted to be near him. She also apologized for her continual lateness; promised to try a million times harder; and shared her hopes that he would one day be proud of her as a wife and mother of his children. The letter shows that even in the early stages of the marriage, there were troubles, and in an effort to find answers to her problems, Marilyn continued seeing therapists and was also said to have consulted psychic, Kenny Kingston. He remembered: 'I had my large house high atop Pacific Heights in San Francisco when film great Clifton Webb telephoned me and made an appointment for a "Mrs DiMaggio" to come for a private psychic reading. The DiMaggio name is fairly common in San Francisco, so I thought nothing out of the ordinary about it. We set a time for the appointment – which I recall vividly as being 9 p.m. Clients are rarely late for appointments, thus when "Mrs DiMaggio" had not arrived by 9.15 p.m., my Philippine houseboy Modesto asked if he should extinguish the lights outdoors. (The fog was rolling in heavily). I instructed him to leave the lights on, though I told him he could retire for the evening and I would take care of it. Shortly thereafter, the doorbell chimed. When I opened the door, there she stood – in a black coat with a white ermine collar, and a kerchief on her head. Instantly I recognized the "Goddess of Love". She was breathless.

'I invited her into the library and asked if she'd like a glass of water. I also asked why she was breathless, and with a smile I was to remember forever, she replied, "I got out of the cab five blocks from your home." I asked her why and she said, "The story broke in this morning's paper that I was seeking psychiatric help and I didn't want your reputation spoiled." So you see, this was the loving type of a girl that Marilyn Monroe was ... It was a friendship that began that night and would last until Marilyn's final days.'

On 8 March Marilyn won a Photoplay Award for her performance in *Gentlemen Prefer Blondes*, and officially signed with the Famous Artists Agency, although in reality, associates Charles Feldman and Hugh French had been looking after her for some time. They agreed that *The Girl in Pink Tights* was an unsuitable project for their client and became involved with negotiations at Fox. They did a good job and it was decided that Fox would drop the film and, instead, Marilyn would appear in the musical, *There's No Business Like Show Business*.

She was not thrilled with the prospect of a supporting role in this movie but was overjoyed when Fox offered her the role of 'The Girl' in Billy Wilder's movie, *The Seven Year Itch*, and promised that a new contract would be drawn up in August 1954, with a $100,000 bonus for *The Seven Year Itch*.

On arriving in Los Angeles, Marilyn and DiMaggio checked into the Beverly Hills Hotel, before moving into 508 North Palm Drive in Beverly Hills, which Marilyn described as, 'A simple house. Not too big, or new, or wonderful – but it's comfortable.' It also happened to be just doors away from the last home of Jean Harlow, a fact Marilyn declared was just 'too eerie for words'.

On 9 April Marilyn met again with author Ben Hecht, who by this time had completed around seventy pages of the manuscript. He read the pages out to Marilyn and according to Hecht, she laughed and cried and was thrilled with the results, promising to go through the pages and come back to him with her amendments. When they met again several weeks later, she had edited a dozen pages of the manuscript, and promised to do more, but by 19 May he had heard nothing and was forced to write to Loyd Wright to ask what on earth was going on.

By this time the story had been provisionally sold to *Collier's* magazine, with the proviso that Marilyn had to approve the article first. It was a futile request, as shortly after, the manuscript appeared in London newspaper the *Empire News*, which was a shock to everyone involved. Louella Parsons contacted Hecht to ask if he was the author of the piece, which he denied, then Marilyn was quoted in the press as saying she had never seen the manuscript, which was, of course, untrue. Sadly for Hecht, he was unfairly believed to be the person who had sold the story without permission but, as it turned out, Hecht's agent Jacques Chambrun had sold it for £1,000 without his permission, humiliating Hecht and forcing everyone to wash their hands of the whole, sorry affair. (*My Story*, an edited version of the book, was finally published in 1974.)

The book fiasco wasn't the only upset suffered by Marilyn in spring 1954: on 21 May she accidentally crashed into the car of physical education instructor Bart Antinora, who responded by suing her, but later settled out of court for the sum of $500. Then on 29 May, *There's No Business Like Show Business* began shooting, with Marilyn soon realizing that it wasn't going to provide her greatest role. The film was a long and tedious story of a show-business family, dealing with the ups and downs of life in the business, and staring Ethel Merman as mother of the clan. Marilyn played Vicky, a supporting character who dates Tim Donahue, played by Donald O'Connor. She said, 'I was miscast. I had to be continually taking off my shoes because of the difference in statures between Donald O'Connor and me.'

George Chakiris, who was a dancer in *Gentleman Prefer Blondes*, also became involved in *There's No Business Like Show Business*, and found himself working on a version of 'Heat Wave': 'The choreographer for all dance numbers was Robert Alton, but Marilyn had worked with Jack Cole previously and wanted him for "Heat Wave". Alton created the number for Marilyn, using a girl in her place, along with dancers – one of which was me. We worked on it and when it was finished Marilyn came in quietly and sweetly on her own and sat down and watched. At the end she thanked Alton and left, but she still wanted Cole, so he came in and choreographed the number. She was absolutely right to want Cole; he was right for the number and had a totally different style to Alton. Cole was brilliant with musically gifted women and Marilyn was gifted in those areas. She wasn't a professional dancer but she knew how to move.'

Marilyn spent a great deal of time in rehearsals for the musical numbers, and Chakiris remembered one particular day when the cast were having a small party to celebrate the end of a busy day: 'No one was dressed up, everyone – including Marilyn – was in casual clothes and no make-up. My dance partner, Druscilla, wanted to ask Marilyn to kiss me but I absolutely didn't want her to do it. Druscilla went over though, and Marilyn turned round, looked in my direction and said, "But I don't know him." I thought this was very sweet and meaningful because she knew it was inappropriate to kiss me. I wasn't disappointed because I was shy and didn't want Druscilla to do it in the first place!'

More rehearsals centred on the film's songs, and Marilyn found herself in the company of Hal Schaefer, who was once again acting as her vocal coach. Hal was a sensitive, quiet man and the two had much in common, not least of which was their desire to get the best out of her performance. For now the relationship was platonic, but it was not long before Hal had become extremely fond of his student, and when things started unravelling at home, Marilyn began to see him as someone more than a vocal coach.

For now, filming continued in earnest, but as with all her film appearances, Marilyn began turning up late on a regular basis, and she was still suffering with anaemia and bronchial problems. George Chakiris was witness to her punctuality problems: 'She was a wonderfully talented artist, but during the filming of "Lazy", she kept Mitzi [Gaynor] and Donald [O'Connor] waiting until 3 p.m. Her lateness was never malicious – she was a truly kind human being. But nobody likes to be kept waiting, which is why certain actors have said things about her.'

Disturbingly, she also began turning up with bruises on her arms. 'I bite myself in my sleep,' she joked, but no one thought it was funny. Rumours began to surface of problems at home, which were not helped when DiMaggio told Fox he would not tolerate any invasion of their privacy. Also notable was his absence from the set, but he eventually decided to visit during the filming of the 'Heat Wave' number, which – with Marilyn's revealing costume and sexy performance – wasn't the best time to arrive. DiMaggio was not pleased and refused to be photographed with his wife, which caused even more problems at home.

Things were not helped when fans began turning up at North Palm Drive and ringing the doorbell, which Marilyn admitted bothered Joe no end. 'Joe wanted a wife, not a star,' his friend Mark Scott later told reporters. 'Marilyn would come home at night too tired for anything but sleep. That would leave Joe looking at the television.'

In a rather telling interview during the making of *There's No Business Like Show Business*, Marilyn told a reporter that she'd like to make Joe proud of her. 'He's not proud of you?' asked the bemused reporter. 'I mean more so,' she corrected. 'Proud of me as a performer. It makes no difference to him whether I work or not. Joe knows he comes first, before everything.'

What went on inside 508 North Palm Drive will forever remain a mystery, but several clues are provided by a letter written to DiMaggio by Marilyn herself, after an argument between the couple. In the note she admitted she was wrong to say the things she did; that she said them because she was hurt; and urged him never to be angry with 'his baby'. Marilyn then went on to apologize to her husband, and signed it 'your wife, (for life), Mrs J.P. DiMaggio'.

Later she explained her philosophy on how to treat her husband: 'When I sense there's something wrong, I ask "What's the matter? Sorry if I did something." If Joe doesn't answer I don't push it. There are some men who when they have trouble, become silent. You have to respect that.'

In public, both DiMaggio and Marilyn tried to squelch the rumours of discord, with various comments in the media. DiMaggio declared that while he didn't interfere in her work, he was definitely interested in it: 'I think it's entirely possible for two people to have careers and live a happily married life. It's going on around us every day,' he said.

Meanwhile Marilyn told reporters that, 'Marriage has given me roots. Joe is so strong and vital, so stable and understanding. With him beside me I have nothing to fear.'

Friends also got in on the act, with hairdresser Gladys Whitten declaring that Marilyn had never been more bubbly and effervescent, and Sidney Skolsky writing a long article about Marilyn's life as a housewife, and saying that DiMaggio had invited him to drop in any time to watch the TV and have dinner. 'Make this your home away from Schwabs [Drug Store],' he was quoted as saying.

Skolsky became quite a confidant during the disturbances within the marriage, and Marilyn would often visit him at Schwabs or Googies, the restaurant next door. The manager of Googies, Steve Hayes, wrote in his book, *Googies: Coffeeshop to the Stars*, that she became an occasional 'night owl' at his restaurant, often wearing a disguise and sitting with Skolsky in a booth in the hope of no one recognizing her. Hayes knew Marilyn when they were both struggling actors and remembers one evening in 1954 when she telephoned him out of the blue: 'She had called me from a public phone outside Googies, saying she couldn't reach Sidney [Skolsky] and could I drive her home? I started to say no, that I couldn't just leave the coffee shop, but when I went out and saw how desperate and bedraggled and dazed she looked, I changed my mind. Telling one of the waitresses to take over for me at the cash register, I put Marilyn in my car and drove off.'

During the journey Marilyn began talking about how miserable she felt and that she didn't know how much longer she could go on living 'like this'. She became so emotional that Hayes genuinely became concerned that she might be planning to do something to herself; he asked her but she remained silent. 'When she didn't answer, I pressed her on the subject and finally she began sobbing and said that she could never kill herself; it was against her religious beliefs. I gently reminded her that reportedly she had already tried to commit suicide on more than one occasion. I must have hit a sore spot because she suddenly lost her temper and said shrilly that she had matured since those mistakes and was trying to be a better person . . . It was the first time I felt that Marilyn was a human being and my heart went out to her.'

In spite of everything that was going on in private, Marilyn still wanted things to work out between Joe DiMaggio and herself. She cooled her friendship with Schaefer, and shockingly he responded by trying to commit suicide. 'I did it because I didn't see any way out,' he remembered, 'I thought my career was finished and my relationship with Marilyn was over. I thought there was no solution.'

On hearing of Schaefer's suicide attempt, Marilyn raced to the hospital to lend her support. This did not help matters at home, especially when Schaefer's hospitalization hit the headlines and it was reported that Marilyn had never been far from his hospital bed.

On 30 August, Marilyn and her co-star Ethel Merman filled in on Drew Pearsons' syndicated column while he was away. In it she gave a glimpse into her private life, by admitting, 'I work hard and study hard and have little time even for my husband. But I do divorce my private life from my career as an actress and that is why you never see Joe and me posing together around Hollywood.'

Finally, *There's No Business Like Show Business* was over, and she immediately went into production on *The Seven Year Itch*, flying to New York on 9 September with an entourage that included Natasha Lytess. On her arrival at Idlewild Airport, a reporter asked, 'No Joe?' to which she replied, 'Isn't that a shame?' and nervously giggled. When asked about a rumour that Joe was spending a large amount of time away from home, playing poker with his friends, she denied it completely, adding that it was hard enough to get him out of the house – he much preferred pottering around, taking a swim in the pool and lounging in the armchair.

The cracks in the marriage were very definitely beginning to reveal themselves to the media. Columnist Hedda Hopper recalled that on her way to the airport en route to New York, Marilyn had called into her house for a quick interview. Joe had sat outside in the limousine until finally he knocked on the door to hurry Marilyn along. Hedda commented to the baseball star that his wife looked wonderful, while Joe barely gave his wife a glance before retorting, 'She looks nice.' Hopper asked Joe why he was not accompanying his wife to New York, only to be told by DiMaggio that he had hives that were bound to flare up on the plane. On 11 September she wrote in her column, 'I could be wrong but I got the feeling they're fooling,' and years later recalled, 'I knew then that the marriage was over.'

Marilyn's role as 'The Girl' in *The Seven Year Itch* was to be a landmark in her career. Her co-star was Tom Ewell, who had originated the role of Richard on Broadway and had beaten

Walter Matthau to the film role. The story itself centred on Richard, a happily married man whose wife and son have gone to the country for the summer. He is alone with his fantasies until the girl upstairs (Monroe) drops a tomato plant from her balcony, and a sordid affair develops within the confines of Richard's fertile imagination. The play revolved around Richard actually having a real-life affair with the girl upstairs, but because of worries over censorship, this part of the script was taken out of the film, which makes his advances all the more humorous.

After a bout of stomach illness, an exterior scene involving Marilyn waving out of an apartment window was shot outside a real-life apartment. One person lucky enough to witness the shoot was Joe Coudert, who was assigned to take photos of the star: 'I was taking photos of Marilyn in her brownstone with the rest of the photographers and had to take a break to reload my camera. When I returned, I was all alone with Ms Monroe! I asked her if I could continue photographing her, she said "Yes" and I shot several rolls of film. She was very friendly and talkative. The "girl next door", though a little overused, is an appropriate description and she was a real professional with the camera. She was highly relaxed posing and she knew exactly how to make my camera fall in love with her, over and over.

'She asked me a lot of questions about my wife and my photography – she seemed genuinely interested in learning more about my family. She also talked a lot about the events surrounding the filming and her concerns about the New York crowds that followed her every move . . . she was nervous about the fans and the press stationed outside her windows. She was very anxious; her fans would go to great lengths to touch her as she passed. It was impossible for her to accommodate them all, and she was concerned about being mobbed.'

One scene in the film featured The Girl and Richard walking down the street after an innocent trip to the cinema. As she walks over a subway grating, her skirt flies into the air; 'Isn't it delicious?!' she exclaims, as the wind bellows around her thighs. The scene was shot in the early hours of 15 September, in front of a crowd of thousands. Unfortunately, Joe DiMaggio had arrived just in time to witness the spectacle and was not pleased, especially when he saw the fans ogling his wife in her white panties.

As it turned out, the scene was unusable due to sound problems, and had to be re-shot on a soundstage in Hollywood, but the damage was done. When the couple returned to their hotel, they had a huge argument and other guests later claimed to hear a fearsome row coming from the DiMaggio room. Friend Amy Greene also later claimed that when she and her husband Milton met the couple for dinner shortly after, she saw bruises on Marilyn's back. Whatever happened that night will forever be shrouded in mystery, but it certainly caused irretrievable damage and by the time they left New York on 16 September 1954, the marriage was over.

The day after her arrival in Los Angeles, Marilyn called in sick at the studio, and her doctor confined her to bed with flu. DiMaggio returned to San Francisco, where he met up with friend Reno Barsocchini. He confided that he would be travelling back to Los Angeles to see Marilyn, before heading back East for the World Series, but showed no sign of any marriage troubles. 'I'm sure everything was OK,' Barsocchini later commented, when asked by reporters.

But things were obviously not OK, and Marilyn spent some time crying on the shoulder of Fred Karger's mother, Anne, and her close friend Hal Schaefer. She decided that while she still loved DiMaggio, divorce was the only option, and when she phoned lawyer Jerry Giesler, she struck him as a confused woman who was still in love with the person she wanted to leave. Giesler spent time speaking with the actress, trying to determine what was best, but Marilyn was adamant – she wanted a divorce, with no request for alimony or property.

Hal Schaefer was privy to Marilyn's very personal thoughts at this time, and to him she confided much: 'DiMaggio had got physical with her and although she didn't have a great deal of self-esteem, she did finally have enough and picked up and left. She was very serious about divorcing him, which is why she hired Jerry Giesler – she wanted to get away from Joe. Marilyn was a super-sensitive woman and had a real artistic thirst to grow; she loved the arts, but Joe was into none of these things. Marilyn didn't want any part of him – she was hurt and emotionally fragile and turned to me.'

By this time, DiMaggio was back in Los Angeles and living on the ground floor of North Palm Drive, while Marilyn spent her time upstairs. When Jerry Giesler arrived at the property on 4 October, he found DiMaggio sitting in the living room where, after talking to him for some time, he served the divorce papers.

At 2.45 p.m., Giesler and Fox publicity chief Harry Brand left the DiMaggio home, and gave a statement to the press (who were rumoured to have been tipped off by the Fox publicity department), informing them that the charges would be mental cruelty and that neither Joe or Marilyn would make any comment. He also said that both parties were still friendly and that the separation had nothing to do with the skirt-blowing scene. To quash any rumours before they began, he added, 'She is not pregnant.'

The next day DiMaggio left the home, announcing that he would never be back, while Marilyn departed shortly after, leaning on the arm of her lawyer, with friend Sidney Skolsky close by. Although she tried to speak to the press, she was too upset to do so, and was quickly shuttled to a waiting car, which took her away from the North Palm Drive home forever.

Moving into an apartment at 8338 Delongpre Avenue, she continued her friendship with Schaefer, visiting him at Apartment 203, at 1327 North Vista. It quickly developed into a physical relationship: 'We became lovers and were going to get married,' said Schaefer. 'She wanted to convert to Judaism because I was a Jew. She was still legally married to DiMaggio but had already moved out and had started divorce proceedings.'

Whether or not Marilyn was fully truthful about her feelings to Schaefer is not known, but DiMaggio was concerned enough by the relationship to hire private detectives from the City Detectives and Guard Service to follow the couple. The company began surveillance on 20 October, and trailed both Marilyn and Schaefer between various Los Angeles neighbourhoods, witnessing her picking up friends, visiting her attorney and calling on Natasha Lytess. On 24 October they followed the actress to the apartment of ex-boyfriend Fred Karger, who was now married to the actress Jane Wyman. However, if they were hoping to uncover some scandal there, they were disappointed as a quick check on the car parked outside revealed that Jane was at the apartment too.

They hoped for more success when they followed Schaefer to a nightclub, where they reported that he looked 'very dopey', though he was not drinking. Bizarrely, the detectives claimed to witness him 'doing something to his arm', and wondered if he was 'shooting up', but if they believed they were being inconspicuous, they were mistaken. Marilyn and Hal were very much aware they were being followed. 'It was a sick and hostile situation because of DiMaggio,' remembered Schaefer. 'He hired private detectives and bugged Marilyn's car, my car, and my apartment. We were followed everywhere and it was very scary. Marilyn was terrified.'

When she appeared at Santa Monica Court House on 27 October, Marilyn did not mention the surveillance, even though it was still going on. Instead, she leant on the arm of her business manager, Inez Melson, and told how her dream of marital bliss had turned into a nightmare of 'coldness' and 'indifference'. She added, 'My husband would get into moods where he wouldn't speak to me for days at a time – a week, sometimes longer, maybe ten days. If I tried to coax him to talk to me, he wouldn't answer at all, or he would say, "Leave me alone, stop nagging me!"'

As she dabbed her eyes, Marilyn explained that she had even offered to give up her film career to make the marriage work, 'But his treatment of me made me ill and I was under the care of a physician quite a bit of the time.' Despite Skolksy's earlier claims of being invited to dinner by DiMaggio, Marilyn explained that Joe refused to permit visitors to North Palm Drive, and when a friend came to visit her during an illness, 'it was a terrible strain'.

Inez Melson also took to the stand and explained that she had witnessed DiMaggio pushing his wife away, and that he had admitted to Melson that he was indeed cold and that he now regretted his actions. Finally, after much tears and testimony, Marilyn was awarded a divorce and she left the court, noting that while she was glad it was all over, she and Joe would continue to be friends, adding, 'I still don't know anything about baseball.'

But Joe's 'friendship' with Marilyn was verging on the obsessive, and on 5 November it came to a head when the private detective tailed her to 754 Kilkea Drive, the apartment block of Sheila Stewart, a friend of Marilyn and an ex-student of Schaefer. Bizarrely Joe DiMaggio was tailing the detectives (a fact that was recorded in their report). He was determined to catch Marilyn 'in the act' with Schaefer and stormed the apartment, along with the detectives and his friend, Frank Sinatra.

Aside from the fact that this was a ludicrous and highly illegal act, it was made even more absurd when it was discovered that the foursome had broken into the wrong apartment – that of Florence Kotz, who later described it as a 'night of terror,' adding, 'I was terrified. The place was full of men. They were making a lot of noises and lights flashed on. They broke a lot of glasses in the kitchen getting out of there.'

Frank Sinatra later claimed that he had stayed in the car and smoked a cigarette, and when the case went to court in March 1957, Joe DiMaggio backed him up (though he wasn't in court himself), while Private Detective Phil Irwin insisted that Sinatra was an active participant in the raid.

Active or not, the 'Wrong Door Raid' shook the entire apartment block, including Marilyn and Hal Schaefer, who were together in the apartment upstairs. At the time, both parties denied they were in the building, but some fifty years later,

Schaefer came clean: 'The apartment belonged to an ex-student of mine who had become a friend. She knew about Marilyn and I, and when she went out of town, she gave me the key to the apartment so that we could use it. It was just Marilyn and me in the apartment when the raid took place and Marilyn was terrified. I don't believe I'd be around today if they'd found me in the apartment. They almost wrecked the building – rammed the door down of the wrong apartment and the woman ended up suing. Marilyn and I managed to get out the back door.'

The very next day, on 6 November, Marilyn was honoured at a party held at the famed Romanoff's restaurant. The stars invited that night included Marilyn's childhood idol, Clark Gable, and she fulfilled a fantasy by dancing in his arms. 'I turned the colour of my red chiffon dress,' she later exclaimed. A couple of weeks later, on 21 November, it was reported that Monroe and Gable were 'Hollywood's Newest Romance'; it was not true, of course, but it was an interesting story nevertheless.

The rest of the year was busy and Marilyn was full of plans for the future. However, having been presented with the script for *How to be Very, Very Popular*, she knew that there was no way she wanted the part, and decided to move to New York to set up her own production company with photographer Milton Greene. Unfortunately, before she could put any of her plans into action, she first had to contend with another gynaecological operation, which took place on 8 November.

In spite of everything, Joe and Marilyn somehow remained friends and he sat beside her hospital bed for many hours, prompting the press to wonder if there was any chance of reconciliation. Some friends stated that DiMaggio was being successful at winning his wife back, while others said there was no chance at all and he should move on. Finally, after they had been seen dining at the Villa Capri on 13 November, Marilyn released a statement which read, 'Joe and I are just friendly, that's all. There's nothing to it.'

After that, Marilyn sought privacy at the home of old friend Anne Karger, Fred's mother, while making plans for the move to New York to begin her new life. Before she left, however, she had a few loose ends to tie up, including breaking the news of her departure to Hal Schaefer. He remembered: 'Shortly after the Wrong Door Raid she went to New York to begin her new life, and that was the last time I ever saw her. She phoned me and said she didn't know how long she'd be there, but I never saw her again.'

But it wasn't all bad news for the respected vocal coach, as not long after he met the woman who was to become the love of his life: 'I was extremely happy with my wife, Brenda – who shared the same birthday as Marilyn. Brenda was the best thing that ever happened to me. She was a remarkable woman.'

Chapter 14

New York, New Marilyn

When Marilyn arrived in New York she was met by Milton and Amy Greene and taken immediately to their large sixteen-room farmhouse in Weston, Connecticut. She was rundown, suffering from anaemia and in desperate need of a rest, which she received during the festive season with the Greenes, their baby son, Joshua, and their maid, Kitty Owens.

For Marilyn, this must surely have been a strange time: unwell; living with a family she did not know particularly well; and in an environment very different from the one she'd known in California. But despite that, she busied herself with everyday life; babysitting Joshua, talking to Kitty in the kitchen and sharing housework with Amy. She also talked excitedly with Milton about their future venture, Marilyn Monroe Productions, for which she planned to produce films and television, along with a book to showcase Milton's photos of her. In her spare time she would read, speak to Joe DiMaggio on the telephone and take walks in the woods near the Greenes' home, content to be by herself for the first time in many months.

Meanwhile, virtually no one knew where Marilyn was living; Fox insisted that she was still living in California, while reporters wondered where she was and continued to run stories of affairs with Frank Sinatra and Clark Gable. Marilyn had no intention of giving herself up just yet, and instead transferred all her business affairs to New York. She dropped Inez Melson as her business manager (although she continued to handle all affairs related to Gladys Baker); fired Charles Feldman as her agent; and neglected to contact Natasha Lytess, who was at a loss as to what was going on with her star pupil.

On 3 January 1955 Marilyn attended a meeting with the new board of directors for Marilyn Monroe Productions, including Milton Greene, Joe Carr and Frank Delaney. Delaney had found several 'holes' in her contract with Fox and, much to her joy, declared Marilyn a free agent. With that in mind, on 7 January the 'new Marilyn Monroe' appeared at the home of Delaney, where she announced her intention to take the female lead in *The Brothers Karamazov* by Dostoevsky, and also raised eyebrows by claiming she no longer had a contract with Fox.

This news came as quite a shock to the studio, and by the time Marilyn arrived at Fox on 9 January for retakes on *The Seven Year Itch*, the executives were in no mood to discuss it. While they declared they would use 'very legal means' to enforce the agreement, Marilyn was forced to admit she was still under contract but hoped that they could reach an understanding. Delaney was not so accepting, however, and reaffirmed that her contract had been terminated and abandoned.

All this resulted in media frenzy, with newspapers predicting that if she were kept off-screen until her contract expired, she might end up a has-been. So-called friends also came out of the woodwork to pronounce Marilyn 'stubborn and impatient', while even Natasha Lytess got in on the act by commenting, 'nobody's indispensable'. Marilyn herself saw it in quite a different way: 'I never tried to be independent just to show my independence. It wasn't so much that I objected to doing one kind of role. I merely wanted the freedom to do other kinds of roles too.'

She tried to forget her business problems and instead busied herself with improving not only her talents, but her social life too. She moved into New York's Gladstone Hotel on 19 January, and began going to museums and attending the theatre on a regular basis. 'People often recognize me in museums,' she said, 'but they seem to leave me alone there. They don't come up to me unless they're children.' She began mixing with theatre actors such as Dame Edith Sitwell, and authors like Elsa Maxwell, who described Marilyn as, 'The most exciting girl in all the world,' whilst also observing that she seemed like a child, 'who was trying to appear sophisticated and grown-up'.

Marilyn began acting lessons with Constance Collier in early 1955, and shortly after, Broadway producer Cheryl Crawford encouraged her to take lessons with Lee and Paula Strasberg, who ran the Actors Studio, which Crawford had helped found. The studio taught the 'Method', a technique derived from the teachings of Constantin Stanislavski, which was considered controversial due to its requirement that the actors completely immerse themselves in the characters they played. 'I feel that I can learn many things about acting in New York,' she said. 'What I want is to apply in Hollywood what I learn in New York. I think it will bring the best result.'

When Marilyn first began studying with the Strasbergs, she attended lessons with Lee, and later became an observer at the Actors Studio itself. She enjoyed the experience, although worried that she felt so much older than the other students there: 'I guess I'm not a lot older than they are, but I feel like it,' she said.

Meanwhile, her arrival at both the Actors Studio and the private lessons was treated with curiosity by many of the students there, although reports of a hostile reception were perhaps exaggerated. Fellow student Stefan Gierasch was witness to Marilyn's early days at the school and remembered: 'I was surprised to see someone like Marilyn in the Studio. We were like a club, but we tried to welcome her; I don't believe we were unkind to her at all. Strasberg was her mentor and he and Paula were always around her. After class the students would sometimes dine together for lunch; Lee and Paula would escort Marilyn and she would be quite giggly. She was quite retiring and quiet, but that depended on circumstances. She sat at the back, blended into the crowd, and didn't draw any attention to herself. She came to be more relaxed in the restaurant as time went on, and she was always tended to by Paula.'

Another student, Mark Weston, remembered Marilyn being known as 'The Golden Girl': 'Before Marilyn arrived in Lee's private class, he asked us all to treat her like just another student. My introduction to Marilyn was abrupt and painful; she would attend class and just take up space. She'd wear mink coats in the summer and different coloured shoes on each foot. Well, I had arrived late to class while a scene was in progress. My usual seat was on the middle aisle three rows behind where Lee sat. I groped myself across the aisle and accidentally stepped on the Golden Girl's open-toed high-heeled shoes. I sat and watched the scene being performed. I eyed the Golden Girl then turned away ... on my third viewing of her I realized it was Marilyn! Ms Monroe never again wore make-up, dresses, furs, and heels!

'My first impression and sympathy towards Marilyn, who sat next to me, was when something humorous happened on the stage all would laugh, including Marilyn. However, instead of an instantaneous laugh she would look at someone then laugh, stop, and repeat the action again and again. My feelings were that the studio had created a robot. She was aware of her every response.'

While she seemed quite unapproachable at first, Marilyn longed to make friends and later said that the greatest thrill of her life came one morning when she arrived late to class. 'Most of the other students were already there,' she said. 'A couple of them looked up, waved and said casually, "Hi Marilyn." It was a simple thing, but it meant they had accepted me. I was one of them.'

Away from the lessons, she was happy to take part in charity and publicity functions such as acting as an usherette at the premiere of the James Dean movie, *East of Eden*, and riding on a pink elephant at Madison Square Garden. Despite being away from Hollywood, for the first time ever her fan mail at Fox hit 8,000 – the highest of any star in the entire history of Fox studios. She had finally arrived, but despite being one of the world's most famous women, she never stopped caring about the man on the street, as witnessed by Richard Shepherd, who handled her PR for a short time during 1955. His friend and client Steve Hayes later remembered: 'My agent Richard Shepherd [who would later co-produce *Breakfast at Tiffany's*] was in his New York hotel waiting to escort Marilyn to an awards dinner, when after being two hours late she showed up with a sailor who was battered and bleeding. He'd had an accident of some kind and Marilyn, on seeing his condition, picked him up and insisted Dick help her get the unfortunate man to an emergency hospital.'

On 8 April Marilyn appeared on Edward R. Murrow's television show, *Person to Person*, during which she answered questions with the help of Milton and Amy Greene. Shortly after she was interviewed by Dave Garroway for his radio show, and then by Peer J. Oppenheimer, who was working at the time as editor-in-chief of *Family Weekly*, a Sunday supplement which is now *USA Weekend*. He met Marilyn on several occasions, but the first was in 1955, while she was living at the Waldorf Towers. He remembered: 'I took her out to dinner for a story in "Family Weekly". I found her totally helpless in the presence of a man. I was willing to do anything for her although I had a slight suspicion that maybe it was partly an act. Nevertheless, she gave a great interview. While there were hundreds of people I interviewed for "Family Weekly", and later for a television series I created and produced for NBC, the two hours with her were the most memorable I spent with a star.'

But one thing Marilyn wouldn't have discussed was her decision to begin taking therapy with Milton Greene's ex-therapist, Margaret Hohenberg, which led her further down the road of psychoanalysis. She declared Freud her hero, but due to the technique of continually going back to childhood problems and situations, the therapy sessions were not easy for her. 'It is the biggest waste of anyone's time to keep looking back,' she said in 1953, but by 1955 she was willing to give it a try, though time would tell if it was doing her any good at all.

One friend who disliked both the journey into psychoanalysis and the Strasbergs was Arthur Miller, to whom Marilyn had been reintroduced in 1955. Although he was still married to his wife, Mary, he began to fall in love with the actress, and the two spent many stolen hours together in her apartment at the Waldorf Towers.

Obviously Marilyn was keen to play down any talk of a romance between Miller and herself, and probably didn't worry when rumours began circulating that she was secretly dating Actors Studio actor, Eli Wallach. Stefan Gierasch once witnessed the two actors together: 'I followed her up Broadway, while she was walking with Eli Wallach. She had grease on her face and was dressed down, but everyone still recognized her. Everyone always wondered if she was dating Eli, but they never knew for sure.'

The rumours reached the newspapers and also Eli's wife, Anne Jackson, but after persuading her that he was merely a stand-in for real-life boyfriend, Arthur Miller, Anne laughed at the stories and the four became friends.

Another friend at this time was Norman Rosten, who knew Arthur Miller and was introduced to Marilyn through her friend, photographer Sam Shaw. They first met on a rainy afternoon when Shaw took her to dry out at the home Rosten shared with his wife, Hedda, and his daughter, Patricia. Wearing no make-up and wet through, Marilyn was completely unrecognizable and by the time the Rostens finally realized they had Marilyn Monroe sitting in their living room, they had accepted her as a person, not a superstar, and a lifelong friendship soon developed.

However, her relationship with the Rostens was not always an easy one: she would call in the middle of the night, giving bulletins on the health of her pregnant cat; or ask if anyone wanted to meet up for coffee. Then during one visit to the beach, she almost got herself and Norman drowned when fans clambered around them, forcing the couple to go deeper and deeper into the sea, until a passing boat was able to save them from a grizzly end.

Another trip to the beach – this time with Milton Greene – was slightly more light-hearted, as described by John Thorndike, son of Joe Thorndike, the managing editor of *Life* magazine: 'My father had long been friends with Milton Greene . . . Marilyn was spending the weekend in Connecticut with Milton and his wife, and mentioned to them that she wanted to try out the new sport of waterskiing, so Milton called my dad. We lived on Long Island and had a little boat, though the motor was barely strong enough to pull a skinny twelve-year-old out of the water. I was twelve and, disastrously, had gone off with a friend for the day, but Dad knew someone with a bigger boat. Charlie Goit leapt at the chance, and Milton, Marilyn and a small retinue drove over to our place . . . All I really know is that someone had to get into the chest-deep water with Marilyn and help with her skis and keep her from tipping over until the line drew taut. And that was my father.

'Up she surged, then crashed. Charlie circled around, Dad held Marilyn, and off she went again. On the third try she skied for a hundred yards, and Charlie got to haul her into the boat. But when I came home that evening the detail I heard from friends, neighbours and family, over and over, was how Charlie had to drive while my father stood in the water with his arms around Marilyn Monroe. I think everyone liked the irony of that, because Charlie was kind of lascivious, and my father more of a gentleman.'

Long Island was also where Norman Rosten had a home, and Marilyn would often visit at weekends, helping to cook, playing badminton and walking in the woods with the cat. The friendship was also extended to the Rostens' daughter, Patricia, who was thrilled when she found herself amidst Marilyn's make-up, several years later: 'She plunked me down at her vanity mirror and said that since I was so intrigued by the art of make-up, she would show me how to do the job right.'

Twenty minutes later the job was finished, and Marilyn then showed Patricia off to the Rostens, proud of her handiwork on their daughter. Patricia wasn't the only one to experience Marilyn's affinity with young people; Lee Strasberg's daughter, Susan, became close to her, and Sam Shaw's daughters, Meta and Edith, were friends too. For Edith, who shared a birthday with the actress, Marilyn was just a friend of her parents, not a celebrity, and on one occasion, she even accompanied her to the circus as a celebration of their joint birthday.

Halfway through their big-top excursion, somebody in the crowd recognized Marilyn, but she was adamant that nothing was going to interfere with the birthday trip. She denied her identity, pretended to be someone else, then took Edith to get some cotton candy. 'As we went down the escalator,' remembered Edith, 'Marilyn turned to me and said in quite a soft voice, "When you talk to me, don't call me by my name. Say: Hey you, Hey there, or Haystack." She laughed. I thought she was so funny and I will always remember these words to me.'

Meanwhile, Marilyn continued her acting lessons, attending private sessions with Strasberg and observing studio classes five times a week. She worked hard but found the lessons challenging, as often her mind was elsewhere, and that made it difficult to concentrate. She also found the regular Marilyn Monroe Productions meetings taxing, as witnessed by a friend who saw her getting 'pretty bored after a while. It's hard to keep her attention after an hour, even on matters that concern her vitally. She sort of stops listening and stops absorbing.'

Despite having moved across country to begin a new life, Marilyn still kept in touch with Joe DiMaggio, who was even now hoping to win his ex-wife back. He kept a journal during 1955, in which he wrote notes to himself to stop being jealous and try to be patient. He knew his behaviour in the past had made Marilyn unhappy, and was determined to make it up to her; he spoke to her on the telephone, sent her letters and telegrams, and they met occasionally when he was in New York.

Marilyn even found time to travel to Boston with Joe in late January 1955, and he accompanied her to the premiere of *The Seven Year Itch* in June. His hopes were definitely raised but he was confused by her signals; when asked if they had reconciled, he answered, 'I couldn't answer that question if I wanted to, or even if I had the answer. Marilyn is the only person who can do that.' But his hopes were dashed when Marilyn was asked the same question in front of him, 'No,' she answered, 'Let's just call it a visit.'

In early August 1955, Arthur Miller went to Cape Cod with his family and the cast and crew of *A View from the Bridge*, while Marilyn travelled to Bement, where she was to take part in the town's centennial celebrations. Although feeling the effects of a kidney complaint and limping as a result, Marilyn travelled with photographer Eve Arnold, who was to record the event for posterity. It has been said that Marilyn was tricked into thinking the event would purely be about Abraham Lincoln and had no idea she would have to perform duties such as judging a beard contest, but this is not true. Before she left New York, she told reporters that she was 'going to Bement to see the lovely men with the beards; they are so powerful and masterful.'

As well as giving a speech on her idol Abraham Lincoln, Marilyn also travelled to a local nursing home where she met the eldest resident, 100-year-old Clara. Albert Wincr's mother was proprietor of the residence, and he took great pleasure in meeting Marilyn. He remembered: 'I thought Marilyn was a very beautiful lady. She had an injured ankle and was hobbling around – walking with a noticeable limp – but seemed happy to be there; enjoyed being there.'

Back in New York, Marilyn was becoming an avid fan of Arthur Miller's work, and attended three performances of *A View from the Bridge*. The press picked up on her new-found interest, but to try and quash any unwanted attention, after a performance on 29 September she went to the El Morocco with composer Harold Arlen. She was also rumoured to be dating Marlon Brando, but in reality she was very much involved with Miller, and by October, his marriage had finally imploded. He moved into a hotel just as Marilyn received her final divorce from Joe DiMaggio and moved into an apartment at 2 Sutton Place. There both Marilyn and Arthur spent many evenings together, looking out over the city and planning their future.

But Miller wasn't the only one who had developed a relationship with Marilyn in 1955. During the course of the year she built up a unique friendship with her fans, particularly seven eager teenagers who would wait each day outside her hotel. Six of the fans were nicknamed 'The Monroe Six', while the seventh fan may never have been an official member of the group, but did enjoy a close friendship with Marilyn that lasted until her death in 1962. James Haspiel was so close to Marilyn that the two would share taxis, drink coffee and otherwise 'hang out'. He took photos of her that were later compiled into a book, *The Ultimate Marilyn*, and took delight in documenting her going about her normal life. But he was not the only fan to be allowed to do this: Peter Mangone spent much of winter 1955 outside Marilyn's hotel, and she even agreed to let him film her while she went shopping. She welcomed the attention, although from time to time she was known to wear disguises in order to maintain some kind of anonymity.

During her days off, Marilyn was unconcerned with her physical appearance and would go round town with no make-up and sloppy clothes, and never be recognized. 'A pretty girl like you doesn't have to wear a lot of make-up like Marilyn Monroe,' she was amused to hear from an unsuspecting taxi-driver.

Meanwhile her hairdresser at the time, Julius Caruso, complained that after hours spent fixing her hair, she would mess it up the moment he'd finished. But when Norma Jeane felt like 'being Marilyn', it was all hands on deck, as stylist George Masters found out when he was assigned to work on her face and hair, later in her life.

Describing her as 'the biggest egomaniac I ever worked with,' Masters complained that it took her up to eight hours to get ready for a night out, and he would spend the first couple of hours trying to get her out of bed or away from sipping champagne and listening to Sinatra. If she was in a bad mood, she would splash water on her face so that he would be forced to start again, or would jump into the bath, completely ruining his work. Masters also claimed that she became upset when someone mistook the fair-haired Masters for her brother and asked him to dye his hair black. Masters resisted her wishes, eventually dying her hair a lighter shade than his to try and keep the peace.

On 31 December 1955, the year-long feud between actress and studio was resolved when Fox executives announced that they had given Marilyn a new contract. It called for her to make four movies for them over the next seven years, but gave her both director approval and the opportunity of appearing in outside movies, television programmes and plays. At a time when the studio system was still very much in force, the contract was remarkable and paved the way for other actors and actresses to gain more independence too.

Of her new contract, Marilyn admitted that it was a compromise on both sides; 'I do not have story approval, but I do have director approval. That's important. I have certain directors I'll work for and I trust in them and will do about anything they say. I know they won't let me do a bad story.'

On 9 February, Marilyn and Laurence Olivier held a press conference at the Plaza hotel to announce their joint project, *The Sleeping Prince* (which was later retitled *The Prince and the Showgirl*), the first film to be made by Marilyn Monroe Productions. The relationship began on a positive note, with Marilyn impressing Olivier so much that he feared he would fall in love with her, but his opinion soon changed. He had played opposite his wife Vivien Leigh in the stage version of the play, and Marilyn became concerned when it was announced that he intended to direct the film as well as star. She feared that their techniques would clash and she was proved right when production began in July 1956.

But back in February 1956 Marilyn had other things on her mind when she invested money into *Mr Johnson*, a play written by her friend Norman Rosten and starring Earle Hyman, who later went on to star opposite Bill Cosby in *The Cosby Show*. 'She probably lost the money,' remembered Hyman, 'because the play was not a success financially – it only ran six weeks.

But it was a success for me because I was able to join the Actors Studio because of my performance.'

The first time Marilyn saw Hyman in class, she greeted him warmly, and he found her, 'Extraordinarily beautiful in a way that was never fully captured on screen. She was an extraordinary actress. She sat at the back, wearing black slacks and a mink coat, and exuded an incredible light. Even if it wasn't Marilyn, people would have still wondered who she was.'

When Hyman performed his first scene at the studio he was very nervous, and when he'd finished Lee Strasberg asked everyone for their comments. Hyman recalled, 'People were quite nice about it but then Eli Wallach said, "I don't think Earle's work was clear." There was a silence and a pause and everyone turned to Marilyn who had raised her hand for the first time ever. She said, "Well I don't know, Lee, but it seems to me that life is sometimes unclear." I thought she was extremely brave to stand up and say that and I never forgot it.'

By mid-February 1956, Marilyn had built up enough confidence to perform a serious scene at the Actors Studio. 'I don't want to do just light roles always,' she later said. 'Some people say I should, maybe because they've never seen me do more serious things. But I can – I did *Anna Christie* at the Actors Studio and other plays like that.' Her partner for the performance was Maureen Stapleton and together they worked on a scene from the Noel Coward play, *Fallen Angels*, before eventually settling on *Anna Christie*. Although it was initially kept quiet, word soon spread around school and when the day eventually came, everyone was very excited, except Marilyn. 'I was terrified,' she remembered. Fellow student Stefan Gierasch was witness to the spectacle. He remembered: 'Everybody piled in to see the event; the studio was full and everyone enjoyed it. After she had done the scene, the students realized she was talented and were in awe of her in a way.' Indeed, after she had finished the scene, the whole room broke into applause, which was to be the first time in the studio's history.

Another student who witnessed her performance was Mark Weston, who recalled: 'At the end of the scene Lee asked as always for comments. I said "Lee, I couldn't hear a single word from Marilyn." Lee responded, "But you felt her sensitivity!" That was so true. Once while watching acting exercises in the darkened theatre I noticed Marilyn doing a "sunshine" exercise next to me. Oh my, it was so sensual.'

Shortly after the scene at the Actors Studio, Marilyn visited friend Elsa Maxwell who found her in a happy, excited mood as she had just discovered that famed photographer Cecil Beaton was going to take her portrait. But even at this point she was still denying a serious relationship with Miller, telling Maxwell that although she was happy to have Miller as a friend, she had no plans to marry him – yet.

On 25 February 1956, Marilyn departed New York to return to Los Angeles and star in *Bus Stop*, a Fox film about a saloon singer called Cherie, who dreams of fame in Hollywood, but finds love in the form of unsophisticated cowboy, Bo, played by Don Murray. As she departed, she was given a great send off by fans and reporters. 'I'll be back by June,' she said. 'My real home now is in New York.'

The welcome she received in her former home town was frostier than expected. Although reporters were thrilled to see her return, Judge Charles J. Griffith was not so enthralled. On 21 November 1954, Marilyn had been driving in Hollywood when she was stopped and charged with three traffic violations: driving without a licence, driving too slowly and driving after her licence had expired. She took such a long time to settle the matter that by the time she appeared in court on 29 February, the charge of failing to appear had been added to the list.

Marilyn pleaded guilty to all charges, but Judge Griffin was not amused. He fined her a total of $56 – $5 for traffic costs; $50 for failure to appear; and $1 for court costs – and told the actress, 'If you had settled the citations by appearing, or having a rep appear, I would have dismissed the charges. Laws are made for all of us ... whether our name happens to be Miss Monroe or not.' He went on, 'You may have the idea that this is good publicity. For your information I've received many letters and it would seem that your so-called public doesn't think it's such good publicity.'

Marilyn replied, 'I'm very sorry for the trouble I have caused, but I was out of California, studying acting in New York.' To which Judge Griffin retorted, 'Well this kind of acting won't bring you an Oscar. I would suggest, Miss Monroe, that in the future I would much rather pay to go and see you perform than have you pay to come and see me.'

Court case over, Marilyn concentrated on the business at hand, and held a press party at the Beverly Glen home she was sharing with the Greenes. She happily answered reporters' questions but, when asked about Natasha Lytess, was quick to change the subject. 'She was a great help to me,' she said adding, 'whatever road leads to growth you take.' A short time later Lytess made her way to Marilyn's rented home, in the hope of reconciling with her famous student. Her trip was in vain, however, as she was refused an audience with Marilyn, the only glimpse of her being from an upstairs window, as she walked away from the house.

Several months later Lytess poured scorn over her former student's new life: 'She's surrounded by these people who don't let her do anything by herself. They're afraid to lose her. She never goes anywhere alone, they're stuck to her like glue.'

Bus Stop was the first movie Marilyn had appeared in since her training at the Actors Studio, and the difference in her role and acting was unprecedented. She immersed herself in the role of Cherie, and together with Greene devised several character traits such as 'pasty' make-up, torn stockings and a thick, hillbilly accent.

Unfortunately, her intense acting lessons had not made any difference at all to her conduct on set, and both cast and crew became quite irritated by her behaviour. A friend offered a reason for it, whilst talking to reporters: 'When she is late, she feels guilty, and since she has always felt guilty she feels comfortable that way. It is easier for Marilyn to take guilt than responsibility.'

Natasha Lytess had been replaced by the ever-present Paula Strasberg, which irritated the director, Joshua Logan, who would have to wait until they'd finished talking before he could step in and direct the scene. Meanwhile, Marilyn's temperament was also causing problems and when a young press rep called Pat Newcomb was assigned to her during the shoot, Marilyn began to see her as a threat and had her replaced.

Logan felt the brunt of her anger when she disapproved of him cutting a scene, while on another occasion tempers flared when Don Murray was required to pull the tail of Marilyn's costume during an argument. After several attempts at the scene, Marilyn slapped Murray across the face with the tail, causing him to be cut by one of the sequins sewn on to the fabric. Needless to say, he was furious with his co-star and had to be calmed down by the director.

But at the same time she could be quite charming off set, playing catch with co-star Eileen Heckart's sons and signing autographs for fans. It was a confusing situation, made more so when she came down with a bronchial infection and had to be hospitalized for several days.

Whilst on location in Phoenix and Idaho, it was the fans and security who caused the disruption. When police escorted her from the airport, they turned on their sirens and ran red lights, much to the chagrin of the Chief of Police. Then when filming took place at the local parade, fans were asked to behave normally, stand back and refrain from taking photos, but even so, one spectator saw fit to set up his campstool in the middle of the street to get a better view. There were problems with the press, too, who complained that they had been unable to interview Marilyn or take any good photos of her. When one enterprising photographer took a shot of her putting on make-up, she hid her face and screamed, 'Don't shoot pictures while I'm making up! Are you crazy or something?'

After reporters blamed Milton Greene for the lack of access to Marilyn, several photo opportunities were arranged, although the media intrusion never died down, and by the end of May 1956, Marilyn was miserable. On weekends she had been visiting Miller in Reno, where he was residing during his divorce, and had also stayed with him at the Chateau Marmont hotel in Los Angeles, but it was not enough. On 24 May she had a fight with Milton Greene about money, and shortly before that became involved in a heated discussion about Paula Strasberg. She confided all this to Miller, who felt that Greene was becoming threatened and worried that she could be led out of 'the circle of glamour', and into the 'circle of art'. This was slightly dramatic, but nevertheless it had a grain of truth; as Marilyn was now relying on Miller more than her film partner, and it was apparent to all corners that Miller did not think particularly highly of either the Greenes or the Strasbergs.

But Miller had more on his mind than his dislike of Marilyn's friends. In 1947 he had attended several meetings with a communist-tainted organization, but had never actually been a member. However, this did not stop Congress' House Committee on Un-American Activities from calling him before them on 21 June 1956 after he had applied for a passport to travel overseas. Standing before the Committee, they demanded he name the other people who attended the meetings, and when Miller refused point-blank to do it, he was declared in contempt of Congress.

After his appearance, reporters asked why he had applied for a passport. He answered, 'I have a production which is in the talking stage in England, and I will be there with the woman who will then be my wife.' When asked if the woman was Marilyn Monroe, he admitted it was. Back in New York after completing *Bus Stop*, Marilyn heard his declaration on the radio and was pleasantly surprised.

They had never formally discussed their marriage, but she was thrilled enough to phone the Rostens and tell them all about it. Of course, the announcement sent the press into a frenzy and she was unable to leave her home without being cornered in the lobby of Sutton Place to answer their questions. Finally, publicist Arthur P. Jacobs recommended a small press conference outside the apartment block, and scheduled a bigger one at Miller's Roxbury home on 29 June.

Now that their secret was finally out in the open, Marilyn and Arthur could show their joy to friends and family, who had been semi-aware of the relationship for some time. She tried hard to befriend Miller's children, but while seven-year-old Bobby warmed to her, she had a harder time with eleven-year-old Jane, who was upset that her parent's marriage had broken up and found the relationship with Marilyn unacceptable. Still, she persevered, and even when her marriage to Miller broke down, she did not hide her desire to stay friends with his children.

The next introduction came when Miller drove Marilyn to Brooklyn, where she was formerly introduced to his parents, Augusta and Isidore. She adored both her in-laws but particularly Miller's father, with whom she developed a close relationship that lasted until the end of her life. She also met various friends, including Mr and Mrs Louis Untermeyer, enjoying a home-cooked Sunday meal with them in early summer 1956. Wearing a simple black shirt, black and white trousers and no make-up, Marilyn cooked borscht, and ham with cloves and apricot. Untermeyer later wrote that the couple had acted as though it was their first date and seemed very much in love.

As rumours spread that Marilyn and Miller were to tie the knot sooner rather than later, a mass of reporters gathered at his home on Old Tophet Road in Roxbury for the scheduled press conference. The couple had been lunching at the home of Miller's cousin, Morton, and on leaving were followed by Princess Mara Scherbatoff, from *Paris Match* magazine, photographer Paul Slade and his brother, Ira. Driving through the winding roads leading to Arthur's house, the driver lost control of the car and ploughed into a tree, severely injuring Scherbatoff and Ira Slade.

On hearing the crash behind them, Marilyn and Arthur were mortified and ran back to help, but there was nothing they could do; although an ambulance was called, Scherbatoff lost her battle for life just four hours later.

The press conference went on regardless, and the couple somehow battled their way through; Marilyn hanging on to her fiancé for support, and stuttering over some of her answers. It had been a traumatic and tragic day but when the reporters finally left, Marilyn and Miller headed to White Plains, New York, and at 7.30 p.m. were married in a courthouse ceremony by Judge Seymour Rabinowitz. Shortly afterwards, Miller released a statement saying, 'We're just spending a few quiet minutes now. Marilyn is very happy and very tired; it's been a hectic day. We plan to have some kind of party in the next few days, but we hope for that to be kind of quiet too.'

Two days later, on 1 July, the couple had a Jewish ceremony at the home of Miller's agent, Kay Brown, before which Marilyn received a short instruction to enable her to convert to Judaism. Then on 6 July, Miller was issued with a temporary passport in order to accompany his new wife to England, where they hoped to enjoy a quiet, working honeymoon.

How wrong they were.

Chapter 15

Great Hopes

In the spring of 1956, months before the wedding, preparations were underway for Marilyn's arrival in England, with Laurence Olivier working with Terence Rattigan on his script of *The Prince and the Showgirl*, and auditioning the supporting cast.

When actress Vera Day walked into the office of Laurence Olivier Productions she was twenty years old, and had been in show business for about a year. Olivier looked at the blonde-haired actress and exclaimed, "Oh dear, she's so like Marilyn." While Vera Day was naturally flattered by such a comparison, Olivier feared the worst, knowing that Marilyn would not take kindly to another blonde on set. And so it was that before Day was allowed anywhere near the film, she found herself sporting a brunette wig to play Betty, one of Marilyn's friends.

In recent years it has been said that a house called Tibbs Farm in Ascot was rented for Marilyn and Arthur Miller, purely as a red herring, on 13 June 1956; a way of putting the press off the scent of the real home, Parkside House. However, this cannot be correct, as on 25 April newspaper reports first surfaced to say that the owners of Tibbs Farm, Mr and Mrs Cotes-Preedy, had been asked to rent the home to Marilyn during her stay in England. More reports surfaced on 26 April and 14 May, and even included interior shots and interviews with Mrs Cotes-Preedy herself. This media intrusion was simply unacceptable and another home was sought, this time in the form of a Park Lane apartment. Unfortunately, on 16 June, the owner Michael

Ferszt leaked the news to the press and those plans were immediately shelved.

While Milton and Amy Greene would still stay at Tibbs Farm,
an ideal alternative was found for the Millers in the shape of
Parkside House, a large mansion situated in Englefield Green,
Surrey. The owners, Lord Moore and his wife, Joan Carr, were
happy to move to London during Marilyn's stay in their house,
and it was agreed that the housekeeper, Elizabeth 'Dolly' Stiles,
the gardener, Bernard Stiles, the butler, Franz Gettliner, and the
cook (Gettliner's wife) would stay on during the four months of
Marilyn's visit. Other members of staff would include a chauffeur and a detective to oversee Marilyn's security.

Despite these arrangements, no one told Mrs Cotes-Preedy
that the plans for Tibbs Farm had changed, and she continued her public-relations campaign, being interviewed and even
appearing on television. It eventually came down to the cook to
inform her of the change of plans, having seen the news on the
television just hours before Marilyn's arrival.

Meanwhile, preparations at Parkside began with the instal-
lation of new locks on the gates and the painting of Marilyn's
future bedroom. The Parkside staff were expected to work
long hours during this period and discretion was of the utmost
importance. Even the exterior of the home was revamped, when
a gentleman called Gordon Bolton (who later claimed that he'd
never heard of Marilyn Monroe) placed new tiles on the roof.

Next came a security meeting between London airport officials, the Ministry of Civil Aviation and Marilyn's publicity men.
It was originally decided that there would be no extra security
at the airport but the officials changed their mind at the last
minute, after hearing about the fiasco that took place at Idlewild
Airport on 13 July, during the Millers' departure for London,
with the plane being delayed due to a stampede of excited fans
and reporters.

On the morning of 14 July 1956, around 150 British reporters gathered behind the newly erected security barriers,
complained about the rain, and waited for Marilyn Monroe to

arrive in England. Finally, at around 10.40 a.m., one hour after the expected arrival, the plane touched down and the reporters waited with baited breath.

The other passengers on board started to make their way down the steps, but Marilyn was nowhere to be seen. Several minutes later, a bouquet of flowers was carried into the plane and, later still, someone representing a knitwear company delivered a sweater. When she eventually appeared, Marilyn glided down the steps dressed in the same outfit she had worn at Idlewild Airport – a jersey dress, dark glasses and a raincoat thrown casually over her shoulders – she had flowers in her arms and Arthur Miller close by.

Airport staff were balanced on the wings of the plane to take personal snaps and get a better view, and although security was tight, there were a few fans who were able to say a few words. One of them, Frank Williams, remembered: "My job [at the airport] was to dig holes, tunnels and whatever was needed. We were told that Marilyn would be arriving one day with her new husband, Arthur Miller and in no uncertain terms [our boss] wanted no nonsense when she arrived – no whistles, no catcalls etc. Marilyn and her husband arrived right next to the foundations we were digging – probably only fifty yards away from where the aircraft came to rest. She walked straight up to the foundations trench and she said "Hello boys," and we said "Welcome to England, Marilyn." She was quite stunning and from four feet down in the trench, we had a very, very good view of her.'

Once inside the terminal building, Mr and Mrs Miller were met by Laurence Olivier and Vivien Leigh. Photographs were taken and Marilyn chatted about Vivien's recently announced pregnancy, before collecting her twenty-seven pieces of luggage and making her way officially to meet the world's media.

The press conference at London Airport would go down in history as being one of the most bizarre ever. After walking into the room with Miller and the Oliviers, Marilyn surprised everyone by refusing to speak into a microphone; her reason being that she found it too impersonal, adding that she much preferred talking directly to reporters. This, of course, resulted in many of those present not hearing a word Marilyn was saying, and a mini-stampede began, with reporters clambering to get the best view, knocking over chairs and tables in the process.

Finally, in order to gain some kind of order, she was asked to stand on a raised platform behind a snack counter. Once there, the reporters were instructed, rather absurdly, to give their questions to Olivier, who in turn would pass them on to Marilyn. She then gave her answers back to Olivier, who passed them on to the rather impatient reporters.

The questions ranged from the serious ('What are your plans whilst in England?') to the tongue-in-cheek ('What do you think of Diana Dors?') to the plain silly ('Can I have a lemonade please, Marilyn?' referring to her position behind the snack counter). After declaring that the thing she most wanted to see was, 'the little fellow with the bow and arrow in Piccadilly Circus,' the press conference was over and it was finally time to leave.

Of course, when the Millers and Oliviers arrived at Parkside House, they were not alone. The dozens of reporters who had greeted her at the airport were now at the house and, after posing for numerous photos, Marilyn entered the drawing room in time for press conference number two. Again, the questions came thick and fast but when asked what she thought of her new home, Marilyn revealed that she had rather expected to find a cottage. Unfortunately, Parkside House would never live up to her fantasy and, by the end of her trip, she was rather glad to leave it.

When one reporter asked what she planned to do for relaxation, she replied, 'Go for bicycle rides.' However, on realizing that she did not have a bicycle, she added, '. . . if I can borrow a bike.' This seemingly innocent comment would later cause considerable bad press for her, but for now the reporters were charmed.

Once the reporters had gone, Lord Moore took the Millers on a tour of their new home, although much to Marilyn's bewilderment he missed out one long hallway, claiming that the walk was so boring that he didn't go down there any more.

Tour over, the Millers were then formally introduced to their staff before retiring to their newly painted, white bedroom. Exhausted from the plane trip and the two chaotic press conferences, they rested for a number of hours, before having dinner served by the butler, Franz Gettliner. Later that evening when the sun had finally gone down, the Millers went for a stroll around the grounds of their new home, before finally retiring to bed.

The next morning, Marilyn dozed until 12.30 p.m. before Olivier visited to show her photographs of the *Prince and the Showgirl* set, along with the costume she would wear in the film. Afterwards she left for a scheduled press conference at the Savoy Hotel in London, stopping to chat first to the local people waiting outside her new home. Along with various items of small talk, the star was intrigued to know if any fans came from Scotland, declaring with pride, 'I've got a Scottish name. Monroe is pure Scots you know.'

Eventually she was able to leave, but by the time the car arrived at the back door of the Savoy, she was extremely late and surrounded by fans once again, with only a human chain of policemen to protect her. Finally though, both Marilyn and Miller made their way into the hotel, and to the great relief of just about everyone, joined Laurence Olivier on a raised platform, in order to begin the press conference.

The questions asked that day were very much on the same level as those asked at the airport and Parkside House. If there were many questions related to *The Prince and the Showgirl*, they certainly didn't make the press coverage the next day, the reporters being much more interested in comments of a personal nature and, in particular, anything related to the Miller marriage and Marilyn's personal aspirations.

One item that caused a lot of interest was her outfit. The black dress was tightly fitted and included a window of net to show off her midriff. Photographs of the revealing outfit were beamed nationwide and caused such a stir that a copy went on sale just weeks later. When asked to describe what she was wearing, Marilyn hesitated, then answered that it was 'a simple black dress'. She then showed her famous quick wit to reporter Donald Zec, by declaring that although the dress wasn't her idea, it was her midriff, referring to the bare skin displayed under the net.

Marilyn answered most of the reporters' questions in good spirit. However, she was understandably a little curt when one journalist asked what her definition of an intellectual was: 'I guess you could look it up in a dictionary,' she said. Another asked if she believed in the idea of *The Seven Year Itch*, to which she exclaimed, 'Do you know, I never understood the point of that film?'

Olivier played his part in the proceedings by once again repeating questions to Marilyn, before she answered them; while the press reported that the only time Arthur Miller seemed to smile was when the couple left the room. However, he did have his chance to speak, too, when one of the reporters asked him how he saw his wife; Miller replied, 'With two eyes.'

The questions continued for the next hour, and just before they ended the *Daily Sketch* presented a surprised Marilyn with her very own bike, to enable her to ride through the English countryside. She was thrilled with her gift, which sported a huge gift-tag bearing the words, 'To Marilyn Love From The Daily Sketch.' While Miller looked on in amusement, his wife exclaimed, 'There are so many things I must do first. It'll be two or three days before you see me riding round the lanes.'

There was indeed a lot for her to do, and one of those things was meeting a young man called Alan who was chosen to work at Parkside House as Marilyn's rehearsal pianist: 'I was a music student and used to work during vacations. My agent provided temps for the theatre and I had done a couple of jobs for him, but one day he rang me up to tell me about an interesting job, that I'd be a nitwit to turn down. Apparently Marilyn wanted a pianist for singing practice and as she was limited on the amount of non-British people she could use, she had asked her New York agent, who rang someone in London to find a personal pianist for her.

'I was summoned to Parkside and told, "Mrs Monroe-Miller will see you now." It was like being sent to see the Headmaster and I was rather apprehensive and more than a bit nervous. I had met actresses before and knew they could be fearsome, so what on earth would such a great Hollywood star be like? I need not have worried. Marilyn was sitting on the sofa with her legs tucked up under her. As I went in she gave me that wonderful smile, uncoiled gracefully and came towards me. She put out her hand, took mine and said softly, "Hi, I'm Marilyn!" Her manner was so sweetly shy and modest that I felt instantly at ease. She was such a pleasant and thoroughly nice lady.'

Marilyn would spend a great deal of time with Alan over the coming months, but for now it was time for another press conference on 16 July, and then afterwards a trip to Claridges to meet her husband for lunch. Eating salmon, turkey and fruit, Mr and Mrs Miller looked every inch the newlywed couple, and restaurant staff spotted them kissing between courses. However, it was Miller's outfit that caused the most concern, when staff commented on his grey sports coat, dark trousers and white shoes. Indeed, his casual dress caused such a scandal that it even gained its fair share of column inches the next day.

After lunch, Marilyn and Arthur departed from London and headed back to Surrey, for what they no doubt hoped would be a restful evening in the privacy of their new home . . .

Shoreditch Training College was located approximately two miles from Parkside House, and like most of the local people, the students who studied there had long anticipated the arrival of Marilyn Monroe. For two days before Marilyn's arrival, gossip swirled around the college, and there was a great deal of lobbying to form a group that would be willing to go to Marilyn's house and entice her out.

At around 8 p.m., on the night of 16 July, a group of eighty students met in front of the college to make the hike to Marilyn's house. The plan was to sing under her bedroom window, and some of the students even took along trumpets and other musical instruments to add further excitement to the proceedings.

However, everything did not go to plan, when the College Principal, Ted Marshall, turned up to try to persuade the revellers to go home. Unfortunately for him, most of them had just finished their exams, so they felt that there was nothing the college could do to stop them and Mr Marshall's attempts at discipline went unheard. The trip to Marilyn's house further exasperated Mr Marshall when he discovered that one of the young men had borrowed his car to catch up with friends. The vehicle was even stopped by police during the short journey, and the driver cheekily gave his name as that of the Principal before abandoning it near Parkside House.

Once the group reached the vicinity of Marilyn's home, they immediately started chanting, 'We want Marilyn, we want Marilyn,' before lifting the gates clean out of their hinges and marching up the driveway and singing the twenty-third psalm outside Marilyn's bedroom window. However, it soon became clear to most of them that she had no intention of coming out to meet them.

Nevertheless, although they didn't get Marilyn's attention, they did receive a great deal of notice from the police, who had been tipped off and were making their way to Parkside House. As they approached, most of the fans scattered, as one former student, Allan R. Pemberton remembered: 'It was dark and I had fled into long, wet grass. I got soaking wet and I recall clearly seeing the searching lights being scanned over the area where I was hiding. I'm not sure how long I remained in hiding, but when I thought it safe, I returned to the college, where quite a few of the group had already returned. Quite a few hadn't, I remember [and] there were many stories of "escapes", but no one saw Marilyn and we never knew whether she was aware of our escapade.'

Marilyn was, indeed, very aware of what went on outside her bedroom window that night. In his autobiography, *Timebends:A Life*, Arthur Miller described waking up to the sound of singing outside. Once awake, he and Marilyn both watched out of the window in amazement at the spectacle below, but because of security concerns, neither of them talked to or met any of the students. Housekeeper Dolly Stiles remembered the students' obsession continued and they were often at Parkside, shouting for Marilyn.

On 17 July the Millers accompanied Laurence Olivier to the Lyric Theatre where Vivien Leigh was performing in *South Sea Bubble* by Noel Coward. The play opened at the theatre on 25 April and had received its fair share of newspaper coverage, but on this particular night, it was Marilyn who stole the show.

Shortly before the performance was due to start, the Millers and Olivier took their seats in row J. Marilyn, wearing a flesh-coloured, skin-tight dress and a raincoat almost identical to the one she wore on her arrival in England, immediately drew attention from the other theatregoers, and although the visit was supposed to be secret, word soon got round that Marilyn was in attendance.

By the time the performance had finished, a huge crowd had gathered around the theatre, but with Marilyn's chauffeur parked at the stage door, and Olivier's parked at the front, fans had no idea where to wait. This resulted in them crowding around both entrances in a bid to catch even the smallest glimpse of the star and her playwright husband.

Finally, at 10.50 p.m., and after several van-loads of police had been called, Marilyn and her companions made their exit from the front door of the theatre and were taken to Olivier's London home at Lowndes Place, where they spent a few hours before leaving at 2 a.m. to return to Parkside.

Before Marilyn arrived in England, *Bus Stop* director Joshua Logan wrote a letter to Olivier, advising him on how best to work with her. Unfortunately, although Olivier wrote to Logan on 26 June to say that his comments had been 'carefully noted', it would seem that Marilyn's way of working still came as a shock, since from the very first day of rehearsals on 18 July, the two stars did not get on at all well.

Olivier's first and probably greatest mistake was to introduce Marilyn in what she took to be a patronizing manner. Whilst generally polite, Olivier made a large speech to the cast, explaining that they would have to be patient with Marilyn, as her methods were perhaps different to theirs. Enormously insecure, this comment made her suspicious of Olivier and she was on her guard from that moment on.

Marilyn's pianist, Alan, remembers visiting the set on several occasions and being told to 'stand over there and don't breathe ...' From his corner, however, he was able to see firsthand what Marilyn went through during her time on set: 'Olivier ran a very strict ship, as though he was working in the theatre, with rehearsals etc. Everyone was curious to see what Marilyn was like, but some were "sniffy" and thought Marilyn was wrong and amateur because she wasn't from the West End. They had all worked with Olivier before and felt that it was like putting on slippers, but Marilyn just wasn't used to working like that. Dame Sybil Thorndike was an angel though. She had put in a good word about me with Marilyn and told her that she'd known me since I was in short trousers.

'Marilyn kept to herself on the set. She would have liked to have mixed with the others but there was a barrier there. She went into it wide-eyed, looking at Olivier as "my hero" but she got very upset by him and felt a lot of contempt for him and the other cast members who never went out of their way to be nice to her.'

Meanwhile, Marilyn's personal life was becoming a constant source of speculation in the newspapers, and rumours appeared that she would be holidaying in Paris and Scotland, visiting the local cricket green and attending at least one wedding. All of these stories were false, but it didn't stop people wishing them to be true, and just four days after her arrival, major excitement was caused when 'Marilyn' showed up in Shakespeare Country.

During one of the several press conferences that took place after the Millers' arrival in London, Arthur had expressed his desire to visit Stratford-upon-Avon. This intrigued fans living in the town, who waited with baited breath to see whether or not they would make the trip. Imagine the excitement then, when on 18 July, a chauffeur-driven car pulled up outside Shakespeare's birthplace, and a woman, looking remarkably like Marilyn, stepped out of the vehicle.

Brenda Porter, who was standing in the crowd of people who swarmed round the woman that day, remembered: 'There were quite a few people in the crowd [and] we all stood and waited for quite a while when a chauffeur-driven car drew up outside Shakespeare's house. A lady got out of the car and the crowd tried to cross the road to see her. There was no one with her, [and] she took video pictures of Shakespeare's birthplace, but very quickly got back into the car. People in the crowd said it was not Marilyn. I can't honestly say if it was either.'

Indeed, when questioned by people in the crowd, the chauffeur claimed that the woman was a Mrs Horace Dodge of Windsor, but refused to say anything else on the matter. However, with no security and no husband, the chance of 'Mrs Dodge' turning out to be Marilyn was pretty remote.

This may have been the first time a 'fake Marilyn' would make news during the England trip, but it certainly wasn't the last. In October, another impersonator made headlines, this time by booking false appointments with five of London's top dressmakers and booking singer Tommy Steele for a fake party. She gained a lot of column inches but this fake Marilyn was never found.

The first week in England had been a busy one, for both Marilyn and the press who were reporting anything remotely Monroe-related, however weird or wonderful it seemed. Coverage included a report which stated that Dame Edith Sitwell wished to visit the star sometime soon; and on 20 July *The Times* ran the story of a German communist magazine called *Junge Welt* which gave Marilyn the thumbs-up for daring to become a serious actress and for marrying Arthur Miller. Certainly for the first week of Marilyn's visit she could do no wrong, but it quickly became apparent that the mood of reporters was beginning to change from one of excitement to one of impatience.

The reason for this sudden downturn seems to be related to Marilyn and Arthur's desire to have privacy during their stay in England. Whereas she had made herself freely available to reporters during the first few days, once the press conferences were over, she almost completely dropped from public view, preferring instead to spend time at home, learning her lines for *The Prince and the Showgirl.* The British reporters did not like this sudden bid for privacy and were quick to comment on it in the newspapers.

Marilyn and Arthur had decided to spend the next weekend quietly at Parkside House, but quite bizarrely some members of the press took this stance to assume that Marilyn was now playing hard to get. They complained that not only had she stayed in her house whilst fans waited outside to see her, but had also changed her phone number to discourage unwanted calls. Added to this, when one reporter had his request for an interview turned down, it prompted some members of the press to compare Marilyn's apparent aloofness with the friendliness of the English star, Diana Dors, who was in the United States at the time and giving many interviews, a lot of which had more than their share of questions about her 'rival'. When asked about Marilyn, the blonde star stated quite plainly that she did not like to be compared to her. Talking to Art Buchwald she quipped: 'The only similarity between us is that she's a sex symbol of her country and I'm a sex symbol of mine.'

Meanwhile, back in England, there were some extremely personal comments being leaked to the newspapers, such as allegations that the honeymooning Millers actually slept in separate bedrooms (housekeeper Dolly Stiles confirms that this rumour was untrue), and there was even an article published in the *News Chronicle* that described Marilyn as dowdy, with a spare tyre and crumpled clothes.

During the weekend of 21–2 July, Oscar-winning cinematographer Jack Cardiff visited Marilyn in order to talk about his involvement with *The Prince and the Showgirl*. She knew all about his work and was very excited to meet him, and Cardiff later wrote that on meeting her, he was convinced he had just met an angel. While Marilyn couldn't be described as an angel to work with, Cardiff always thought of her as a warm and lovely person, and was one of the only members of cast and crew to socialize with her off set. He gave her books to read, visited an art gallery with her and even accompanied her to a private screening of *Bus Stop* at the Fox offices in Soho Square.

Despite members of the Weybridge Division of the Surrey Constabulary working shifts around the clock, and a personal bodyguard in the shape of PC Hunt, there was a major security issue one afternoon, when journalists somehow managed to gain access to the roof of Parkside House. Once there, one of the enterprising men held on to the feet of his friend and dangled him upside down outside Marilyn's bedroom. The aim was to take a photograph of Marilyn in her bedroom, but they were out of luck; the pair were spotted and escorted off the premises before any disaster could occur.

But it wasn't just journalists causing concern. Fans continued to hide in the bushes and dozens of admirers crowded around the gates, hoping to catch a glimpse of Marilyn coming and going. One of these was Mr G. Pearson, who was fourteen years old in 1956 and spent most of his school holidays at Parkside House. He was thrilled when Marilyn waved to him on two occasions, but was later involved in a more dramatic incident that showed security at Parkside perhaps wasn't as tight as it should have been. Mr Pearson remembered: 'I was outside the gates with my friend, when a couple of reporters approached us, and asked if we would like to earn a large, silver coin. We stated the obvious "Yes", but what did we have to do for such a sum of money? One of the reporters handed me an envelope and said, "Go in and give this letter to Marilyn."'

'The envelope just had "Miss M. Monroe" written on it. I remember we had to jump over the gates (about four to five foot high), as they were locked, and walked up to the house. Upon reaching the house we rang the bell, the door was opened by a maid and I said, "Would you give this letter to Marilyn please?" She then shut the door, and we waited.

'Shortly after the door opened again, and we were confronted by Arthur Miller. He enquired as to how we got in, and who the letter was from. I answered that we had jumped over the gates and that a man had given us the letter. He then told us to go back the way we had come. His actual wording I cannot remember, but it was loud, abrasive and in words that I had heard adults use before.

'We hastily retreated down the drive, and I do recall being photographed as we hurdled the white gates. The reporters then took details of what had happened and gave us half a crown each. As far as I am aware, a short report of the incident appeared in a national paper.'

Another fan with a delivery for Marilyn was fifteen-year-old Michael Thornton, who went on to become a highly successful author and critic. Michael was staying with friends during the summer holidays when he heard that Marilyn had arrived. After some initial research he discovered her address and set off on his bike, complete with some hand-picked roses strapped to the handlebars: 'On arrival in the tiny village of Englefield Green, my breathless enquiries to highly suspicious locals – already alienated by the descent of countless Fleet Street reporters – elicited the information that Parkside House was in Wick Lane, which I eventually found. The house was white, with tall white windows and white chimneys, extremely attractive and very secluded, with a long drive through trees and hedges. I parked my bike opposite the main entrance, undid the rapidly wilting roses, and waited . . . and waited . . . and waited.

'In all, I think I must have been there for several hours, until finally a large black car drove up and turned into the drive. Inside I saw two men in the front (one the driver), and another man and two ladies in the back, one wearing a headscarf and large dark glasses. I later learned that next to the driver was a plain-clothes detective, that the man in the back was Arthur Miller, and the second woman – rather plain, round-faced and dumpy – was Paula Strasberg. The figure in the headscarf and dark glasses was Marilyn.

'I moved up the drive, into a position where they could all see me standing with my bunch of wilting roses. The policeman/detective came towards me, waving his hands, and said, "This is private property. You cannot come into the drive." At that moment, the lady in the headscarf and dark glasses divested herself of both and became instantly recognizable as the devastating siren I had only lately seen in *The Seven Year Itch*. In her unmistakably breathy voice, she called: "Hey, don't send him away."

'She came trotting forward in a rather tight dress and white high heels, moved around the police officer and said: "Hello, honey, are you waiting to see *me?*" (in a tone that suggested that was the most unlikely thing in the world). I was conscious of blushing, and stammered nervously: "Miss Monroe, I just wanted to say, 'Welcome to England', and to give you these," and I handed her the wilting roses.

'The expression on her face and in her eyes was as if I had handed her something priceless from Cartier. "Oh sweetheart, that is *so* lovely of you." I noticed that her blonde hair was rather dishevelled – possibly the result of wearing a wig – and that her face and eyes had traces of screen make-up that had not been entirely removed. There was nothing grand or standoffish about her. One might have thought she had never been given flowers before in her life, and her simplicity of manner certainly did not suggest that this was the most famous woman in the world.

'Behind her I saw her stern-faced husband, in heavy horn-rimmed glasses, glowering and frowning at this encounter. He then called out to her in a very autocratic voice: "Will you come into the house now please?" "How old are you honey?" she asked. "I'm fifteen," I said. "Fifteen? And you went to all this trouble to bring me these? I'm going to go and put them in water right away. Thank you, my darling."

'She turned towards the detective, then turned back, and to my amazement, she planted a very gentle kiss full on my lips – the sort of innocent kiss a child might give. "Bye bye honey," she called as she walked away, leaving me in a state of surreal disbelief.

'The detective said: "Don't go telling your schoolfriends where the house is, will you?" I promised I wouldn't.'

On 9 July, shortly before the Millers arrived in England, Vivien and Laurence Olivier sent a letter to ask if the couple would like to attend a party given in their honour. The get-together eventually took place on Tuesday, 24 July, and was hosted by Terence Rattigan at Little Court, his home in Sunningdale, Berkshire. It was a lavish affair that included a hundred guests, twenty chauffeurs, waiters, a porter, a chef and a huge candelabra hired specifically for the occasion. The garden was adorned by fairy lights and the whole atmosphere was one of romance and enchantment. The drinks bill, which came to £103, included forty-two bottles of champagne, seven bottles of Gordon's gin, two bottles of sherry and various other items.

The guest list for the party consisted of such luminaries as Alec Guinness, Dame Margot Fonteyn, John Gielgud, Richard Wattis and Douglas Fairbanks Jr, but the person everyone had come to see was, of course, Marilyn Monroe. Everyone that is, except a policeman by the name of PC Packham, who had been asked to stand at the gate of Rattigan's house to check invitations and prevent gatecrashers.

Unfortunately for PC Packham, the young constable hadn't been told Marilyn was on the guest list, so when her car pulled up, he treated it like any other and asked to see the invitation. Newspapers took great delight the next day in describing how the policeman had never heard of Marilyn Monroe and hadn't recognized her in the back of the car. However, PC Packham's version of events differs greatly from the exaggerations of the newspapers: 'The peace was shattered when what was clearly a VIP limo travelling from the Sunningdale direction, swung into the drive to stop abruptly at my feet. Some lunatic immediately leapt from the nearside front passenger seat and, actually brandishing an empty wine glass in my face, told me aggressively to get out of the way. It was, to say the least, an unusual greeting; neither did his arrival inspire confidence regarding the other occupants of the car. I relieved him of the wine glass and was desirous of knowing what precisely he was up to. "It's Marilyn, you fool," he hissed, "Get out of the way."

'Of course! In a blinding flash of the absolute obvious the penny dropped. Everyone in England must surely have known that Marilyn was in town. The tabloids were full of it.

'I looked in at the open door of the limo. It was, of course, Marilyn and, had any further proof been necessary, she was accompanied by her then husband, Arthur Miller. I told the driver to carry on, closed the door, and they sped away without the little dogsbody, or whatever he was. He was last seen hoofing it up the long drive to the house, muttering as he went dire imprecations on all coppers.

'Press cars which had tailed the limo down the A30 had by then been bumped up on to the grass verges at the side of the main road, their occupants coming hot-foot to join the fray. They were a trifle late, for their real quarry had by then sped off, but they were not too late to weave their usual fairy tales. The tabloids' following day's accounts were founded principally on the story of one of "yer ole tyme rural bobbies" who spoke with a rich West Country accent, called men "Zur", and didn't know Marilyn. Any semblance of accuracy in their reports was purely coincidental.'

An exaggerated version of the night's events soon reached PC Packham's boss, Sergeant Gray, who was told, incorrectly, that his constable had been threatened with a broken wine glass. This led Terence Rattigan to send a letter to Sergeant Gray, thanking him for the handling of the difficult situation, and enclosing a £10 cheque to be donated to a charity of his choice.

Thankfully for everyone who had come to see her, Marilyn finally entered the party, wearing a dress very similar to the one she was to wear in *The Prince and the Showgirl*. Looking happy and relaxed, Mr and Mrs Miller made a big impact on the other party guests and danced cheek-to-cheek during George and Ira Gershwin's 'Embraceable you'. Sir John Gielgud remembered: 'Marilyn wore an Edwardian dress – she had, I think, worn it in the tests for the film – and she held court in a tent in the garden, where everyone queued up to shake her hand. As I was speaking to her, a rather formidable-looking lady in black suddenly appeared at Marilyn's side and introduced herself as Louella Parsons. Arthur Miller kept at a discreet distance. I had no opportunity of talking further with Marilyn, but remember how graceful she looked, dancing with Terry Rattigan as I took my departure.'

Marilyn made an impression on everyone who attended the party, and Terence Rattigan received a great many letters after the event, thanking him for his hospitality and commenting on the famous guest. Marilyn herself was thrilled to have the party thrown for her, and wrote a very poetic letter on Parkside House stationery, thanking her host for the party, and commenting on the memorable Charleston, which she danced with him.

Chapter 16

Sir Laurence and the Showgirl

Rehearsals for *The Prince and the Showgirl* finished on 3 August, and filming began on the 7th. Marilyn later described her role as 'an actress from six in the morning until noon, and a producer during lunch. Then I was an actress the rest of the afternoon – and a producer from 6.30 until 9 p.m. when we looked over the day's rushes.'

For the first two-and-a-half weeks, Marilyn reported for work every day but her punctuality left something to be desired. At no time during those first weeks was she on time, and she repeatedly kept her co-stars waiting, so that by the time the film finally wrapped in mid-November, she had been on time on just three occasions, out of a total of fifty-three days on set.

That said, although she was continually late throughout the shoot, she doesn't deserve many of the stories that have been written about her lateness over the years. Various tales have been woven about Marilyn keeping cast and crew waiting until late afternoon while she went cycling with her husband. However, on 9 January 1957, a document was written that detailed what time Marilyn arrived each day. Yes, she was continually late, but on most occasions it was less than an hour. Furthermore, according to the document, the latest Marilyn ever showed was on 30 October, when she arrived at 12.35 for a 10.30 call-time.

From the beginning, Marilyn's 'Method' approach to acting clashed with Olivier's classically trained ideas. When he apparently told her to 'Be sexy', it put her on edge; she had no idea what Olivier meant by this comment, and despite reassurances from her friends, her confidence never recovered. From that moment on, she referred to him as 'Mister Sir'.

Marilyn did, however, get one-up on Olivier when she discovered that someone in the crew – she suspected it was Olivier himself – was running a book on how many takes she would need for a fairly tricky scene. Pianist Alan remembers: 'Marilyn got wind of this and was not amused at the overt insult to her capabilities . . .'

She went home and studied hard so that on the day of shooting she was more than prepared. She delivered the line and then left the room, closing the door behind her as directed. However, within seconds the door flew open again and Marilyn stuck her head through the gap. 'Pretty good huh?' she exclaimed, before shutting the door for a final time. This line was not in the script and was an obvious dig at those who doubted her ability to do the scene. However, it fitted in so well that it wasn't reshot and can now be seen in the final cut.

Marilyn's continued distrust of her director made her reliance on acting coach Paula Strasberg even more apparent, and completely alienated her from other actors on the set. Whenever Olivier cried 'Cut', Marilyn was ushered away to discuss the scene and to rest, and on one occasion, when the director was in mid-sentence, Marilyn turned to her drama coach to ask what he was talking about. At one point Olivier became so enraged by Strasberg that he had her removed from the set, but his satisfaction was short-lived when an enraged Marilyn stormed to her dressing room, refusing to return until Strasberg was reinstalled.

Writer Wolf Mankowitz remembered that he visited the set during a hiatus in shooting, which had been caused, 'because the relationship between Olivier and Marilyn was very, very bad. He couldn't stand her at all and found her acting – her way of setting about acting – and Mrs Strasberg's presence, absolutely unbearable.'

Many of the actors who worked on *The Prince and the Showgirl* have passed away, but the few who remain remember the influence Paula Strasberg had on the set of the film. Strasberg was witnessed telling Marilyn she was the greatest woman living, and that she was more popular than Jesus. Marilyn endured this kind of flattery, but the crew found it amusing if not a bit irritating, and as a result most of them didn't attempt to befriend Marilyn, finding her inaccessible and remote.

Daphne Anderson, who played Fanny, remembered that she was often unable to speak to Marilyn because she was reserved and spent so much time with Strasberg; while Vera Day recalled there weren't many amusing incidents on the set, as Marilyn was always surrounded by her group and kept strictly to herself. This sort of behaviour led many of the actors and crew to think of her as aloof, and it won her no points when it came to popularity.

But Paula Strasberg wasn't the only person invading the set of *The Prince and the Showgirl*: Marilyn constantly telephoned Lee Strasberg (running up a bill that was still being discussed months after she'd gone home); Vivien Leigh popped in occasionally and even watched the rushes; and Arthur Miller visited on a regular basis, giving Marilyn a perfect excuse to stop everything and walk off set.

As happened on most film sets, Marilyn had difficulty remembering her lines, and her scenes often required many takes as it was discovered she never said a line the same way twice. One cast member commented that Laurence Olivier aged about fifteen years during the making of the film, and Marilyn's continuing reliance on Paula Strasberg caused considerable irritation. All this soon gained Marilyn bad press among many of her colleagues: Jean Kent, who played Maisie Springfield, remembered that she was more concerned with the bust line of her dress than anything else, while Esmond Knight, who played Colonel Hoffman, described Marilyn as 'an absolute cretin', such was the level of his discord.

For the sake of everyone working on the film, Laurence Olivier ordered a closed set and banned all members of the press. Despite this, however, one eager fan dressed as a window cleaner and climbed on to the roof to try and catch a glimpse of Marilyn in her dressing room. He failed, but several others succeeded, such as the *Daily Mail* reporter who bumped into her in the corridor. His colleague, Edwin Sampson, took the opportunity to snap the star and although his camera was quickly confiscated, it did lead Laurence Olivier to release two photographs in a bid to calm the reporters. It wasn't enough though, and several months later, reporter Marcus Milne gatecrashed the studio and spent several hours pretending to be an extra before being removed by one of the third assistant directors.

The banning of the press both at home and at work just succeeded in making them even more determined to 'dig the dirt' and write whatever they could about Marilyn. When the Oliviers sent her a large bouquet of flowers, the press chastised her for not sending a thank you letter, but this particular rumour was unfair and untrue, as she certainly did write a note of thanks, which Olivier kept in his personal files until his death in 1989.

Still, few journalists were concerned with reporting on Marilyn's grace and kindness and in August 1956 they were more concerned that the butler was the only person seen riding the bicycle presented to Marilyn at the Savoy press conference. When she was eventually spotted cycling, on 12 August, journalists were so pleased to see 'that girl' on 'that bike' that they failed to notice she was riding a completely different cycle to the one she'd been given by the press.

One person who spotted Marilyn on her bike was Gerald Searle, as he cycled home towards Egham one evening. As he arrived at the junction with Wick Lane, he was surprised to see the Millers turning on to the A30 road on their bicycles. Searle noticed that they were not accompanied by bodyguards or entourage, and both looked extremely happy together.

However, not everyone recalled Marilyn's cycling outings with such warmth. Joyce Jackson was walking through Windsor Park with her husband, their three-year-old toddler and twelve-year-old nephew, when Marilyn and Arthur cycled up behind them. According to Mrs Jackson, her nephew was trailing a long stick behind him, and this made Arthur Miller angry that his wife could somehow be knocked off her bicycle. Unconvinced, Mrs Jackson aired her concerns that the couple shouldn't be riding in the park, to which Miller allegedly said, 'But this is Marilyn Monroe, and I am her husband.' The couple then went on their way, leaving Mrs Jackson very unimpressed with her 'Marilyn encounter'.

Shooting continued until 22 August, when Marilyn was suddenly struck down with a mystery illness and was unable to work. Newspapers reported that she was suffering from a stomach illness and this led to rumours that she could be pregnant. The pregnancy rumour would not die down for the remainder of her stay, and indeed there is still discussion now as to whether or not she lost a baby whilst in England.

The idea of Marilyn miscarrying during the making of *The Prince and the Showgirl* seems unlikely. The actress was very open about subsequent miscarriages, and the official announcement of a lost baby would have won her a great deal of sympathy both on and off the set. But no official announcement ever came, and both Amy Greene and the daughter of the Strasbergs, Susan, denied any knowledge of her being pregnant. Arthur Miller rubbished all reports of a pregnancy at the time, made no mention of it in his autobiography and declined to comment when asked about it some fifty years later.

Furthermore, aside from the third assistant director, Colin Clark, no one on the set seems to have heard about any such pregnancy. There is no record or mention of a miscarriage in any of Olivier's production files and the first Dolly Stiles, Marilyn's housekeeper, heard of it was when she read Colin Clark's book. It seems surprising that household staff wouldn't have had at least some inkling of such an intense situation.

What seems more likely is that Marilyn was suffering once again from endometriosis, since many of her absences occurred around the same time each month. Susan Strasberg remembered Marilyn requiring special pills to get her through a bad menstrual attack, while Esmond Knight later wrote that Marilyn didn't come to the set one day because of menstrual problems. This seems to have been the case on several occasions.

Adding to the pressure surrounding this bout of poor health was the discovery that the Millers' cook and butler had been trying to sell their stories to the press. This came as a huge shock to everyone involved, and on 24 August it was announced that the couple had been relieved of their duties. What is surprising about this incident is that before the Millers moved into the house, there were no meetings to discuss confidentiality; it was just expected that the staff would not talk. Added to that, although PC Hunt was in charge of Marilyn's safekeeping, he had very little to do with the staff, which lead to there being gaping holes in her security. Thankfully for Marilyn, Dolly Stiles fiercely guarded her confidentiality, and when she too was approached to sell her story, she adamantly refused.

As if all this wasn't enough, Marilyn's world fell apart when two weeks into the production she apparently found a notebook that Miller had left open on a table at Parkside. In the notebook, Miller had poured out his thoughts of what was happening during the making of *The Prince and the Showgirl*, detailing problems between Olivier and Marilyn, and saying how disappointed he felt with his wife and how he was ashamed of her.

Marilyn read the notebook in disbelief, and later broke down to the Strasbergs, who were concerned as to how Miller could write such things about his new wife. Although they tried to console her, Marilyn was convinced the notebook had been left open on purpose and took it to mean that her husband was now siding with Olivier. The incident could not have come at a worse time and no amount of comfort could convince her that perhaps what he wrote was just in the heat of the moment. Things were made worse when Marilyn's staff – as well as the film's crew – somehow found out about the incident, and although they were unsure of the exact details, they were fully aware that Marilyn was completely distraught by what she saw as her husband's betrayal.

Alan, Marilyn's pianist, remembers how the couple behaved around each other during this time: 'I didn't like [Miller] and found him very arrogant. He would look at me in a way that seemed like he wanted me to apologize for breathing. That wasn't Marilyn's way. She saw how he reacted to other people and this could have been the start of the rot. Marilyn was lovely with kids and old folk; in fact she was nice to everybody but had times when she could be "off" and then people just remember that. Arthur sized you up – you didn't count if you weren't in his group.

'At Parkside I stayed in a corner and tried to blend in with the wallpaper; my mum said it was very vulgar to be seen. Marilyn was certainly ill, I could tell. She was miserable and puffy and her temper was short. She had a temper towards Arthur mainly – it was hot and strong [and] I couldn't help overhearing stuff. There were rows but there were equally nice times too. I can't remember the specific diary incident but tensions would blow due to something on the set.'

Marilyn felt betrayed by all sides: in her eyes her husband had been disloyal; Olivier was becoming more and more condescending; the press was turning against her; and even peace-keeping Milton Greene felt Marilyn's wrath when he was accused of being on Olivier's side. For Marilyn, her only allies were the Strasbergs and Hedda Rosten, but even that didn't last long, since Lee only visited briefly and Hedda returned to New York just weeks into production, deciding she didn't want to risk her friendship by staying in a situation that was quickly reaching boiling point.

Marilyn's temper was witnessed by pianist Alan during a particularly stressful time at Parkside: 'One day I wasn't there when I was supposed to be, and Marilyn exploded at me. I was very careful after that. She seemed very lonely – like she was on her own in a little bubble. Marilyn was often full of fun but at times it was like talking to a black hole.'

Marilyn decided to take her mind off her problems by going on a shopping trip. Alan remembers: 'The first time she went shopping in London, Marilyn asked Colin Clark where would be a good place to go. He said Bond Street and of course she was mobbed.' Indeed, by the time she reached Regent Street she was surrounded by hundreds of fans and the police had to be called.

But while the first trip to London was something of a disaster, it didn't put her off and soon Alan found himself executing various escapes into the city. 'We used to get out of Parkside through the service route at the back,' recalled Alan. 'We'd go under trees and through the property to next door – the Gardener's Lodge. Marilyn would wear various disguises – hats, overcoat and floppy hat with a shoulder bag. She always had a book or a poetry volume in the bag. Her bottom didn't wiggle – she used nothing to associate herself with being Marilyn. Sometimes people would look to see who she was but they didn't recognize her.'

Once in London, Marilyn would behave just like any other tourist. She squealed with delight when she heard Big Ben chime, declaring it 'Just like the movies,' and also made a point of visiting the National Gallery, Piccadilly Circus and Charing Cross. She also took the chance to extend her book collection, as confirmed by pianist Alan: 'Marilyn would make a beeline for Foyle's bookshop and once you got her in there, you would have to drag her out.'

One day Marilyn took a 'sicky' and she escaped into the city with Alan. Once there they did some sightseeing in Trafalgar Square, where she got much more than she bargained for, as Alan recalls: 'A pigeon went "splat" on the brim of her hat and she didn't want to take it off because it was part of her disguise. We had to use a hanky and nail brush to scrub most of it off using water from the fountain. Many years later that same hat came up at auction and it still had the stains on the brim!'

But pigeons weren't the only ones to give Marilyn unwanted attention, as witnessed by Alan. 'We were in Trafalgar Square and an old lady came up to her. She was about five foot tall, all in black, wearing a hat with fruit and carrying a shopping bag.

She stood right in front of Marilyn, poked her between her ribs and said, "Ere, you're that Marilyn Monroe tart ain't ya?" She actually winded Marilyn with the poke. Marilyn looked down and in her "Queen" voice said, "Oh thank you, you're so kind. I'm often being compared to her." "Snotty cow," said the old woman and stormed off. Marilyn was in hysterics laughing.'

Another escape came one evening when she wanted to get away from the stifling security at Parkside House. 'I asked where she would like to go,' recalls Alan, 'and she said she'd seen a print of Salisbury Cathedral and had always wanted to see it. Off we went and we toured the cathedral and sat for quite a while. When we left she told me she was hungry and I panicked because I hadn't thought about what we'd have to eat. We walked past a "chippy" and she said, "That smells good," so she kept her head down, and we bought some chips and sat on a bench to eat them. She had never had fish and chips before but she wasn't proud.'

But while these adventures were fun, working in a strange country was still daunting, and made worse on 26 August when Arthur Miller returned to the United States in order to see his children. Still feeling betrayed after finding his notebook, Marilyn went with him to the airport, and the couple sat quietly together in the back of their car, saying their goodbyes. The following day, on 27 August, she was back on the set, but it didn't last long; on 31 August, she was once again unavailable for work, and shooting had to be rearranged to make allowances for her absence.

Reports surfaced that she was suffering from gastritis, and various doctors were called to her bedside. 'While she often went out when she was supposed to be ill, there were times when she was actually ill, there was no mistake about that,' remembered pianist Alan. For the next week Marilyn remained at home, and housekeeper Dolly Stiles recalled that she spent all her time either alone in her bedroom, or pottering around the garden. Finally, on 4 September, Arthur Miller cut short his trip to the United States and returned to England.

Although Olivier had problems of his own when Vivien Leigh miscarried his baby, on the surface at least he appeared calm during Marilyn's absence. In a letter to his friend Radie Harris, he said they had been able to fill the time perfectly well with scenes Marilyn was not involved with. However, the full extent of her absence was later revealed when it was estimated she had cost the film approximately £38,305 and it could have been finished three weeks earlier if she had been on set, and on time.

The stress of the England trip was certainly taking its toll on Marilyn: she was drinking and her reliance on sleeping pills was growing; she became hysterical when the pills didn't work or wore off. Her New York analyst was flown in to help and finally she received treatment from Anna Freud, the daughter of her hero, Sigmund Freud.

Added to her misery was the increased security at Parkside House, overseen by PC Hunt, or Plod as he was known. According to pianist Alan, 'Security was beyond all reason and she resented it. Curtains were drawn in the car; no waving allowed; police at the gate, on the drive and the porch . . . it was far too much and far in excess of reason.'

Disturbingly for Marilyn, she found out that PC Hunt was keeping a diary of her comings and goings at Parkside and then reporting them back to Olivier. 'She reacted badly,' remembered Alan. 'There was no more politeness with Plod. He would go hopping mad – he was in cahoots with [Colin] Clark and Marilyn would like baiting them. One day Plod caught me coming back into the house with Marilyn and it was very unpleasant. "Where have you been?" he shouted at me. "Sorry, what do you mean?" I asked. "I've been out." "Don't be cheeky young man," Plod said. I told him that I worked for Marilyn – to Plod she was always Mrs Miller – and that if he wanted to know, he should ask her. Plod got very worked up and Marilyn overheard. She came out and told him that he was very much out of order and what I did was none of his business. She told me to go with her into the drawing room, and closed the door. "Never mind him," she said and gave me a kiss on the cheak. He had started out being an old uncle but there was more to him than that.'

But PC Hunt wasn't the only one on Marilyn's blacklist. She now considered peacekeeper Milton Greene as untrustworthy, and Miller found himself drawn into the business side of Marilyn Monroe Productions. Marilyn accepted Miller's help until he tried to get her on set, which she considered as him once again taking sides, and subsequently began to resent his involvement. Additionally, she believed that Greene was buying English antique furniture and charging it to Marilyn Monroe Productions, which caused more mistrust between the business partners, and in turn resulted in her relationship with Miller becoming even tenser.

Still, during quieter moments Marilyn continued to share her dreams with her husband, detailing her plans to study history and literature; and her determination to have a quieter, calmer life in New York. They spent time travelling around the countryside, visited Brighton beach and ate at the Shelleys Hotel in Lewes, as remembered by receptionist Peggy Heriot: 'One afternoon I was in reception at the Shelleys Hotel and in walked Marilyn with her husband Arthur Miller. She wore no make-up but looked really beautiful; they were both very casually dressed. They asked to look around the hotel then came back to reception saying they were hungry and wondered if I could give them something to eat. I telephoned our then chef who was resting in his room, saying that Marilyn Monroe would like some food. He thought I was joking but, once convinced, came down and talked to the couple. They ate in the drawing room and when they left they thanked the chef and me profusely and went on their way.'

On 7 September, although she was unavailable for work, Marilyn attended a production of *The Caucasian Chalk Circle* at the Palace Theatre on Shaftesbury Avenue. Once again the event made it into the newspapers, and rumours abounded that Marilyn visited the theatre manager, Harry W. Briden, during the interval in order to discuss acting. However, if this was the case, he certainly didn't write about it in his desk diary. Instead, he revealed that the Millers arrived late and members of the press crashed their way into the theatre during the excitement.

Another theatre trip came on 9 September, when the Millers visited the Comedy Theatre in order to publicize the upcoming production of Arthur's *A View from the Bridge*. The play had been refused a public performance licence by the Lord Chamberlain because it included references to homosexuality, but the New Watergate Theatre Club – a membership based organization dedicated to presenting banned plays – had agreed to put on the drama at the Comedy Theatre.

Marilyn sat on the stage with actor Anthony Quayle, while Arthur Miller introduced his play to the audience. However, the press seemed to forget that the event was really nothing to do with Marilyn, and some newspapers severely chastised her the next morning for not making a speech herself. The *Daily Sketch*, who had presented Marilyn with her own bicycle just a few months before, gave her a thoroughly bad review, calling her appearance a 'strictly dumb blonde role,' and criticizing the fact that she had giggled in Arthur Miller's ear and even sucked her thumb.

Come Monday morning, she was back on the set and seemed ready for work. However, the difficulties surrounding the shoot never really eased, and Marilyn caused her fair share of conflict, especially when she had a row with a member of the crew who accidentally walked in on her whilst she was changing. Some of the cast complained that she didn't bother to say good morning or goodnight, and there was trouble too when *Bus Stop* director Joshua Logan visited the set and Marilyn refused to let him in her dressing room. Still angry that a scene had been cut from the film, no amount of apologies would calm the agitated star, and Logan eventually left.

Vera Day recalled another episode when Olivier was setting up camera angles, and politely told Marilyn that he couldn't see her in the position she was standing in. She immediately retorted, 'Oh well, if you can't see me I will go home,' and swept off the set, leaving cast and crew completely dumbfounded.

In spite of that, and possibly even unknown to her, Marilyn still had her allies on the set. Dame Sybil Thorndyke, who was cast as Olivier's mother-in-law, never gave up praising her, often telling Olivier off if she thought he'd been too hard on her. She once told him that Marilyn was the only one of them who really knew how to act in front of a camera, and later when interviewed she denied that Marilyn was ever hard to work with: 'She's the most charming person; I don't think she takes direction very well, but then I don't see why she should. [Olivier] wanted her to do certain things and I said why don't you leave her alone? She is married to the camera; she is a darling girl and I never found any difficulties with her.'

Vera Day also cared about her co-star, saying that she was, 'Difficult yes. But there was only one Marilyn and she jolly well deserved to be difficult . . . She was sensationally beautiful, [and] I know she irritated nearly everyone but she was surrounded by a lot of "po-faced actors" who gave her a hard time.'

One day on the way home from Pinewood Studios, Marilyn's car broke down, much to the annoyance of the chauffeur, who had no idea how to fix it. As he stood gazing vaguely under the bonnet, Tommy Hand, a long-distance lorry driver, got out of his cab to help. His son, Tony, remembered: 'The driver was happy to let him have a go and my dad soon had the car going again. As he was about to walk away the driver said that the lady he was driving wanted to say thanks, and the back window of the car rolled down and a blonde head popped out. My dad leaned down to say hello and noticed that the lady was with a sour-faced man wearing glasses. The man never so much as looked in his direction but the lady was nice and really grateful. She said she was always being accused of being late but this time it wasn't actually her fault and laughed at her own remark.

'My dad was no movie fan and rarely went to the cinema unless there was a James Cagney or John Wayne movie showing but he thought the woman was familiar. He asked if she was an actress and she said yes and he asked her if she was Diana Dors. The lady laughed at this but didn't say yes or no so he thought she must be Diana Dors and she was laughing at him for not being sure. Dad told her that my mum was a really big film fan and she would never believe that he had met her, so the lady offered to give him an autograph to prove it. She asked if he had any paper but he said no, he only had a pencil, so she reached around and came up with a copy of a theatre magazine that someone at the studio had given her. The magazine showed Laurence Olivier and Vivien Leigh together as they appeared in the play *The Sleeping Prince* and the lady said she thought it was meant as a mean joke but dad had no idea what she was talking about and just nodded. She signed the magazine and gave it to him and he said goodbye and thanked her.'

Tommy returned home still thinking he had met Diana Dors, until some weeks later when his wife spotted the magazine and put him straight. However, this wasn't the end of the story, as some years later son Tony was on a train to London when he spotted a familiar face: 'I saw a guy in first-class reading a script of *Brideshead Revisited*. It was Laurence Olivier. I couldn't believe it at first but he was alone and I summoned up the courage to say hello to him. He smiled in a very cold way and I told him that my dad had met one of his co-stars once. Olivier raised an eyebrow and said "Really?", so I said yes and told him about the time my dad had met the woman he thought was Diana Dors but who was really Marilyn. Olivier didn't laugh as I thought he might; he just said, "How disappointing for your father," and went back to reading his script as if I had become invisible. I thought he was rude and left him alone after that. I didn't ask for his autograph but wondered at the double entendre of his remark.'

This comment speaks volumes on what Olivier thought of his co-star, and the feeling was pretty mutual. But thankfully, during this difficult time, Marilyn was able to take a great deal of comfort from her fans and the local people at Englefield Green, and several admirers reported being invited into her home for tea. Margaret Gibbon, who lived in Englefield Green, recalled a touching story, as told by her daughter, Susan Elliott:

'On working in the front garden of her home on Tite Hill, my mother would sometimes see a limousine drive by with a body-guard in the front and a lady in the back seat and she realized it was Marilyn Monroe going home from filming.'

Mrs Gibbon got into the habit of waving to Marilyn as she passed, and later, whilst having a Sunday drink at the Fox and Hounds pub, she was surprised to be recognized at the bar by the same bodyguard she had seen in the car. Recalls Susan Elliott: 'As she waited for drinks they struck up a conversation, as he recognized her as "the lady who waves". He told her that Marilyn was feeling lonely and not enjoying being alone. She cheekily asked if she could get Marilyn's autograph and he said he would be on duty at the entrance gate the next day and would see what he could do. We drove down to the house, and sure enough, we now have a small signed photo of Marilyn Monroe Miller and I have a signature in my autograph book.'

Another signed photo was given to Beryl Belmont, the daughter of housekeeper Dolly Stiles, who recalled meeting Marilyn during a visit with her mother, in which the star jokingly asked if she could take the ten-year-old back home to America. In September she was also happy to participate in a local charity event, by donating a self-portrait entitled *Myself Exercising*. The yellow watercolour was signed Marilyn Monroe Miller and later purchased by Terence Rattigan at auction.

Marilyn's pianist, Alan, remembers some happy moments at Parkside House, when she helped him with his study of poet and essayist Walt Whitman: 'Marilyn came in and asked what I was doing. She chose a passage for me and we discussed it. One day I couldn't find my manuscript and went into the drawing room. There was Marilyn propped up on cushions on the sofa with tatty robe and curlers and slippers, holding the paper. One passage had been causing me trouble and Marilyn told me how I should treat it. She wrote, "This has to be read loving, doesn't it?" on the paper.

'One day I was listening to Gracie Fields and Marilyn asked who it was. She listened and giggled, and got the drift of what it was about. She wanted to learn how to talk like her and did a pretty good job of it. She wouldn't say "damn" though because she thought it was rude. She also liked George Formby and was fascinated by the fun and the banjo playing. Marilyn laughed like a drain at the rude bits. She would sing Gracie Fields around the house which was surreal. She was very quick to pick things up and didn't do a bad job of it.'

Meanwhile, back on the set of *The Prince and the Showgirl*, Marilyn's morale was helped along by comedy actor Norman Wisdom, who was working at Pinewood at the time. He recalled: 'I was delighted to meet Marilyn Monroe at Pinewood Studios when she was making *The Prince and the Showgirl* with Laurence Olivier. At that time I was making my film *A Stitch in Time*, and on several occasions she came in to watch my work. In fact, she quite unintentionally ruined a couple of takes. Obviously, of course, once the Director has said "Action", everyone must remain silent, no matter how funny the situation might be, but Marilyn just could not help laughing and on two occasions she was politely escorted off the set. The nicest thing that happened was that we passed each other in the long hallway one lunchtime. It was crowded but she still caught hold of me, kissed and hugged me, and walked away laughing. Everybody in the hall could not believe it, and I remember my Director, Bob Asher, shouting out "you lucky little swine" – I agreed with him.'

On 28 September Marilyn was once again unavailable for work, but her mood must have been lifted when she received a letter from TV channel ABC, offering her a part in *The Brothers Karamazov*. At any other time this would have been her dream job, but it was not to be; with personal and professional strains reaching boiling point, the last thing Marilyn needed was yet another project to complete, and the offer was turned down.

During Marilyn's time in England, she was presented with various opportunities by the BBC to further her dreams of becoming a serious artist: her participation was invited for a production of Aristophanes' comedy *Lysistrata*; her input was requested for a tribute to NBC in which she was asked to talk about how radio and television should be used for the education of children; and both Arthur and Marilyn were asked to take part in a serious interview for a series entitled *At Home and Abroad*, as well as a discussion on 'Man's Role in Society' for the *London Forum* series. Unfortunately, none of these projects came to anything, and the only reply the BBC received was from agency MCA, stating that Marilyn would be unavailable for any engagements during the making of *The Prince and the Showgirl*.

On 11 October, after being off set all day, Marilyn and Arthur attended the opening of Miller's play, *A View from the Bridge*, at the Comedy Theatre. To show a united front, the Millers left for the theatre from the home of the Oliviers, and caused a near riot when they arrived at the venue, with Marilyn wearing a scarlet satin gown and wrap from designer De Rachelle. The gown was extremely low-cut and photographers wasted no time in climbing to the balcony of the theatre to take photos that looked directly down the front of her dress.

Sitting on seat 16, three rows from the front of the stage, Marilyn appeared relaxed and happy, with her husband on one side and Lord and Lady Olivier on the other. Any tensions from the set of *The Prince and the Showgirl* were well hidden, and during the evening Marilyn even found time to converse with members of the audience seated behind her.

After the production had ended, the Millers took a bow on stage, and then met with members of the cast and crew backstage. Author Colin Wilson remembered driving past the Comedy Theatre and seeing a huge crowd gathered around the stage door. Realizing what was going on, he and his companion gatecrashed the after-show party and met Marilyn in Anthony Quayle's dressing room. Wilson found her to be very attractive and charming, while his companion was amused to see her quite shamelessly standing in front of the mirror, desperately trying to heave up her low-cut gown.

The next day, filming continued but tensions were still tight, particularly behind the scenes. Marilyn's expenses were now causing a great deal of concern, and on 17 October a letter was sent to Milton Greene, requesting a complete breakdown of expenditure. However, there was no response to this and subsequent letters, until a final demand had to be written on 12 August 1957.

On the other hand, it wasn't all doom and gloom on the set and lighter moments were had when Elizabeth Arden's assistant made a visit to Pinewood in order to pamper Marilyn, Olivier and Greene with manicures and pedicures. Marilyn was also thrilled when hairdresser Gordon Bond taught her rhyming slang in her dressing room. 'She was a great mimic,' said pianist Alan. 'It was a hidden talent and living in Surrey, Marilyn would put on her English accent.'

Thankfully for everyone, the bulk of the work had been completed by this time, and Paula Strasberg returned to the United States for a holiday, much to the joy of Olivier. Marilyn shocked everyone by becoming more cooperative but this soon changed when it was claimed that Strasberg was unable to return to England due to a visa problem. Marilyn hit the roof, and Paula soon returned, much to the dismay of almost everyone – especially when her costs later showed up on Marilyn's expense report.

The week beginning 22 October was an eventful one for Marilyn. On Monday she arrived some eighty-five minutes late, then kept cast and crew waiting for a further two hours and fifty-five minutes. On Tuesday and Wednesday she called in sick, whilst also taking delivery of clothes and shoes from Paris House, Anello & Davide and De Rachelle, and on Thursday and Friday Marilyn was on set, filming an exhausting ballroom scene. Finally, on Saturday she met with Dame Edith Sitwell, after turning down an invitation from Dame Margot Fonteyn to attend the Bolshoi Ballet. The meeting with Dame Edith was a very big deal, but it was nothing compared to the one that was to take place on Monday evening, when the Queen of Hollywood met the Queen of England.

On 29 October 1956, hairdresser Gordon Bond was sent to Parkside House in order to ready Marilyn for her trip to the

Empire cinema, Leicester Square. It was to be a glittering night, full of celebrities and royalty, and she wanted to look her best. Bond created a very regal looking hairstyle, complete with a 'bun', and although at least one reporter complained that it was the untidiest he had ever seen Marilyn's hair, she looked stunning and very confident.

She arrived at the Empire with her husband, wearing a gold lamé gown, with topaz straps and a gold cape. Her outfit included white gloves worn past her elbows and she carried a gold handbag, whilst expertly teetering on clogs with two-inch platform heels. The film shown that evening was *The Battle of the River Plate*, and afterwards Marilyn was presented to both Queen Elizabeth II and Princess Margaret.

Although she was anxious about where she should stand and what she should say, everything went well on the night, and Marilyn performed an expert curtsy. In footage of the event, Her Majesty can be seen looking at Marilyn's revealing outfit, before the pair talked for a minute or two about being neighbours (the Queen lived in Windsor which was just minutes away from Englefield Green), while Marilyn claimed that although she was leaving England in a matter of weeks, she was doing so reluctantly.

The Queen then moved on to other stars in the line-up, while Marilyn talked to Princess Margaret about the possibility of her attending a performance of *A View from the Bridge*. Much was made of this in the newspapers the next day, as it was considered highly controversial that a royal should see a banned play, but Princess Margaret did indeed take Marilyn's recommendation and attended a performance shortly afterwards.

As she emerged from the cinema, Marilyn declared that the evening had been one of the nicest things that had ever happened to her, adding that she wasn't at all nervous and found the Queen to be warm-hearted and sweet. She even joked with reporters about her curtsy, giving them an impromptu replay in order to prove she could do it correctly.

Unfortunately, by the time the next day arrived, Marilyn had forgotten all about the success of the night before, and instead was highly agitated and angry on set. Complaining to Gordon Bond, she revealed the basis for her anger was another blonde star – Brigitte Bardot – who had been at the Royal Command Performance too. Upset that the French starlet had upstaged her, Marilyn was heard to call her 'that silly little girl' and ask, 'Who does she think she is?' The star's anger was completely unfounded, however, and a look at the morning's newspapers would have shown her that although Brigitte was mentioned in the stories, the bulk of articles were dedicated to Marilyn.

By this point the production of *The Prince and the Showgirl* was almost at an end. Marilyn was given four official days off in early November, and her last days on set were the 15–16 November. Eager to end filming as soon as possible, she managed to get to the set for her 6.45 a.m. call-time on both days, although she did keep everyone waiting for two hours and twenty minutes on the 15th.

Still, despite the hold-ups and lateness, the film finally wrapped for Marilyn on 16 November 1956, eleven days after it was scheduled to end. Before leaving the set, she found herself apologizing to the cast and crew for her behaviour, claiming poor health as the reason for the delays and begging them to forgive her. This proved to be a worthwhile thing to do, and although some members of cast and crew would never hold Marilyn in high regard, others proved very forgiving and would always speak of her in a respectful and honourable way.

Although Marilyn's part in the film may have been complete, she did not leave England immediately. Miller had recently spent several days away from his wife, meeting Simone Signoret and Yves Montand in Paris, but now that he was back the couple spent a quiet few days together at Parkside House.

On 18 November, during a last public appearance in England, the Millers attended an intellectual discussion at the Royal Court Theatre. The event was supposed to be dedicated to the state of British drama, but was quickly transformed into a war of

An early 1950 publicity still, showing a relaxed, happy Marilyn. Her career was blossoming and despite emotional upheavals, for the most part she was enjoying her rise to stardom. *(unknown photographer)*

(above) Marilyn arrives in Jasper by train, prior to filming 'River of No Return'. She posed happily with some soldiers, and fan Sandy Robinson was there to record the event for posterity. *(Sandy Robinson)*

(right) Amid the paraphernalia of location shooting, Marilyn looks elegant whilst filming 'Niagara'. When shooting was over and Marilyn left town, she also left behind two pairs of her new shoes plus a generous gratuity for her chambermaid, Blanch Maj. "We were all so excited and most impressed with the fact that we had Marilyn's very own shoes in our family," remembered Blanche's niece Pat Brennan. *(George Bailey)*

Marilyn and Joe DiMaggio arrive in Japan for a working honeymoon. Marilyn was full of hope for a happy marriage, but it would be tumultuous from the start.
(from the collection of Tina Garland)

On tour in Korea. Although the photo shows a sunny day, it snowed for much of the time. Even so, Marilyn abandoned her thick coat for a low-cut beaded evening gown.
(Don Obermeyer)

Marilyn and Joe DiMaggio tried to settle into a normal life together, but the balance between a private and public life caused strain in the marriage. Marilyn was always happy to be photographed, while Joe found it intrusive and unnecessary. *(unknown photographer)*

(left) Marilyn gets ready to depart England, seen here with her husband Arthur Miller, following behind. The experience had not been a particularly positive one. "It was raining all the time," she later said, "Or maybe that was just me." *(Horace Ward)*

(below) Marilyn and the Oliviers – Vivien Leigh in fur coat, gloves and pearls, Laurence Olivier next to her, talking to Marilyn. They smiled on, but the press showed scant regard, aside from a young Alan Whicker, in trademark glasses with a cigarette dangling from his mouth, seen busy taking notes. *(Horace Ward)*

Marilyn with Dean Martin and Frank Sinatra. In 1961 Marilyn became
something of a mascot for the infamous 'Rat Pack', visiting them in
Las Vegas and hanging out at their homes. The friendship between
Marilyn and Sinatra had cooled by 1962, but she remained close to
Dean Martin. After she was fired from 'Something's Got to Give',
co-star Martin refused to work with any other actress and immediately
walked off set. *(unknown photographer)*

Marilyn 'off duty'; she would often go out wearing old clothes, no make-up and with her hair un-styled. It was a disguise that often worked, although the evidence of these photographs indicates that she was occasionally still recognized. *(unknown photographer)*

12305 Fifth Helena Drive. This was Marilyn Monroe's last home, and also where she passed away on the night of the 4/5 August 1962. The tile beside her front door read 'Cursum Perficio', which translated means 'I've finished my journey'. *(Eric Woodard)*

The wall crypt where Marilyn Monroe now lies. Every year thousands of fans visit the site, and often leave mementos, flowers and notes. *(Eric Woodard)*

words between authors Colin Wilson and Wolf Mankowitz. The two writers had opposing views on most subjects, leaving the other members of the discussion panel, Arthur Miller, Kenneth Tynan and Benn Levy, lost for words. Sitting on the fourth row and dressed demurely in a black suit, Mrs Miller looked tired but calm as the discussion took place on stage. Wolf Mankowitz remembered there being a great deal of excitement when Marilyn entered the building, as once again there were rumours abounding that the star was pregnant. He recalled that there was a lot of fuss in order to find her a seat, and many people were 'running around as if she were about to have a baby on the spot'.

Having been brought in to discuss great British drama, Mankowitz was disappointed to discover that Marilyn's presence destroyed the point of the occasion, as the audience was far more interested in trying to see her, and Arthur Miller seemed so preoccupied that he could hardly concentrate on the discussion at all. Still, Mankowitz managed to say a few words to Marilyn at the end of the discussion, although he remembered she wasn't too communicative – something he put down to the rumoured pregnancy.

Colin Wilson also remembered meeting Marilyn in the backstage of the theatre, after the discussion had ended. By this time the crowds had become huge outside, so Wilson found himself helping the Millers make their escape by the back door, and recalled Marilyn grabbing his hand during the ensuing escape.

A few days before Marilyn was due to leave England, she bid farewell to her pianist Alan, and presented him with a pen and pencil set and a card. But while Alan would forever hold his brief friendship with Marilyn in his heart, it wasn't all a positive experience for him. 'Working for Marilyn caused so much spite for my home life, with people asking "why him?" so my family clammed up about it. I went to see *The Prince and the Showgirl* but nothing else – we just didn't talk about it; it was a non-subject.'

On 20 November 1956, the events of the previous four months finally came to an end for Marilyn, too. She said goodbye to her staff, bid farewell to the baby fish she'd befriended in the Parkside fish tank and climbed into her car for the last time.

She surprised everyone by arriving at the airport on time, and a scheduled press conference was held at 6.15 p.m., but contrary to the huge excitement that erupted when Marilyn arrived, her departure was treated in very unflattering terms. There were comments about her untidy hair; snide observations about the lack of autograph hunters at the airport; and absurd remarks about her intellect, with one newspaper commenting that she mentioned Charles Dickens 'as if she read books every day'.

Photographer Horace Ward, who snapped two pictures of Marilyn that day, recalls: 'I remember a crowded press conference in the old tin-hut terminal with dreadful drab green curtains they had up as a backcloth, which everyone moaned about. There were hardly any fans around; it was mostly airport staff and a few police.'

Before Marilyn climbed the steps, she told reporters how reluctant she was to leave the country, that she had enjoyed meeting the Queen, and took pleasure in attending the opening of Arthur's play. She even tried to dampen the rumours of a rift between herself and Olivier, by stating that there had been difficulties on the set, but no more than usual.

Olivier returned the compliment by declaring that Marilyn was a wonderful girl; he was delighted with the film, and he'd do it all over again if he had to. Whether or not this was true is another matter, since when he later travelled to New York to show the film to Jack Warner, he made it very clear that the event was to be completely private, and Marilyn herself did not receive an invitation.

Perhaps it is best left to Marilyn to sum up her experiences of the England trip. When asked about it some years later, she exclaimed, 'It seemed to be raining the whole time. Or maybe it was me.'

Chapter 17

Mrs Miller

1957 was to be a year of new beginnings for Marilyn and Arthur. After a brief honeymoon in Jamaica, they decided to modernize a home in Roxbury, just down the road from Miller's old house, and also leased an apartment at 444 East 57th Street, New York, where they settled down to a 'normal' life. In fact so 'normal' was their time in New York, that Marilyn later commented to columnist Elsa Maxwell that, 'No one ever notices us, no one pays any attention to us any more. Arthur and I can walk in the streets and no one bothers us.'

The new apartment was located just yards from her old home at Sutton Place, and Marilyn began redecorating: painting almost every room white; taking out the wall between the living and dining rooms; hanging a portrait of Abraham Lincoln on the wall; and making sure her childhood piano had pride of place.

She threw herself into the role of housewife: 'I get up every morning and fix his breakfast. It's a wonderful thing to know you're looking after somebody. There's this wonderful cook-book I'm reading called 'The Joy of Cooking'. I read it every day. Oh, I'm learning!'

The result of all this was that her husband gained eighteen pounds during the first six months of their marriage, leading his doctor to request he cut down on his intake of fatty foods. When asked why he had gained so much, Miller declared, 'Her cooking and general contentment.'

'I'm mad about this man,' Marilyn told reporters in 1957. 'I never felt before that I had roots; that I had a home life. Fine discovery to make at my age! Arthur has caused me to change. Playwrights are interested in everything about life, and all people. Since I've been married to Art, life's a lot bigger for me.'

As well as playing housewife, Marilyn also spent time writing poetry, riding her bicycle along the East River, playing tennis and pottering around the household department at Bloomingdale's. 'I have no sales resistance when it comes to anything for the house – especially when there's a sale,' she later said. 'I'll go absolutely berserk buying furniture, garden implements, seed for birds and clothes for Arthur.' She also enjoyed seeking out his favourite foods, and was excited one day in Bloomingdale's when she overheard two old ladies discussing the merits of a sausage shop they had once frequented on Third Avenue. Rushing from the store, she jumped in a taxi and headed to the shop, only to find that it had been demolished and replaced with a parking lot. Disappointed she returned home empty-handed.

But there were also more serious issues to attend to, such as continuing her acting classes with the Strasbergs; getting to know her secretary, May Reis; and taking therapy sessions with a new psychiatrist. Marianne Kris had been born in Vienna fifty-seven years earlier, and had lost her husband on 27 February 1957, just weeks before Marilyn's first therapy session. Anna Freud had recommended her to Marilyn, but the relationship would be a volatile one, with devastating consequences just a few years later.

Despite continuing to pose for Milton Greene's still-camera, the gaps began to widen in their relationship and Marilyn decided she wanted him out of Marilyn Monroe Productions. The last straw came when she decided she disliked the idea of Greene being credited as executive producer of *The Prince and the Showgirl*. She held an emergency meeting with the directors of the company, then on 11 April she released a statement which said she was never informed that Milton had elected himself to the position of executive producer of *The Prince and the Showgirl*. She went on to say that the company was formed to make better pictures and improve her work, but instead she had had to defend her aims and interests against the demands of Greene himself.

Quite unnecessarily, Greene had lost his job, but he refused to believe that Marilyn could have had anything to do with his departure, blaming Miller instead for her change of attitude. When they sat down to discuss the matter, Greene surprised everyone by only asking for the return of his original investment of $100,000, and when the contract was finally dissolved, he was devastated.

Speaking about a failed business relationship a little later, Marilyn said: 'I went along with it as far as I could, but you get to a point where – well enough is enough! At that moment I couldn't believe it was happening, but for the first time in my life I really yelled my head off!' She had not been specific but everyone knew to what she was referring.

While all this was going on, rumours abounded that Marilyn was expecting Miller's child, with both newspapers and magazines providing 'exclusive' details. On 22 March, after it had been rumoured that Marilyn turned down a part in the MGM film, *The Brothers Karamazov*, because she was pregnant, she released a statement: 'I have nothing to say at this time. I am sure that everyone will agree that some things are private matters.'

Two months later, President of Twentieth Century Fox, Spyros Skouras, flew to New York to try and convince Miller to name communist sympathizers during his forthcoming court appearance. He was unsuccessful, and just days later the Millers travelled to Washington, DC, in order to fight the contempt of Congress charge, staying at the home of Arthur's friend and lawyer, Joe Rauh, and his wife Olie. While Miller and Joe went to court, Marilyn's days were simple and quiet: she would read; ride a bicycle; and occasionally iron Arthur's shirts; but mainly she would potter around and wait for Arthur to come home.

By the time the trial was over, Miller had been found guilty on two counts of contempt and immediately launched an appeal. Federal Judge Charles F. McLaughlin withheld sentencing, but reporters were quick to declare that he could face up to a year in prison and a $1,000 fine for each count. Marilyn faced report-ers wearing gloves to hide her unmanicured nails, and told them she was, 'pretty confident that in the end my husband will win this case.' She refused to comment on the persistent rumour that she was pregnant, and instead left Washington with Miller, bound for their 57th Street, New York apartment.

In early June, Marilyn welcomed several reporters into her home, including Herbert Kamm and Hal Boyle, who both inter-viewed her on the subject of *The Prince and the Showgirl* and her life in New York. Marilyn instructed them that there were three subjects off-limits: religion, politics and pregnancy, but opened up about other aspects of her life. 'The thing I'm scared of most is myself,' she said, 'But I do feel I've grown both as an actress and a person, and I hope I'll keep growing.'

On 13 June Marilyn and Arthur attended the premiere of *The Prince and the Showgirl* at Radio City Music Hall, then shortly after left for a summer vacation to the town of Amagansett on Long Island. 'We have a little house, right on the ocean,' Marilyn described. 'It's just big enough for us and the children.'

The arrival of Marilyn, Arthur Miller and their basset hound, Hugo, sent the town's people into a frenzy: three teenagers who met the Millers at the local gas station asked for autographs, although twelve-year-old Dicky Gosman made the couple laugh when he declared that he preferred Jayne Mansfield; Bob O'Brien, the delivery boy from Toppings grocery store, had his photograph taken with her; while Roger Mattei, owner of the Corsican restaurant, phoned numerous New York eateries to enquire after Marilyn's favourite food.

Most townspeople were pleased to admire from a distance, but two enterprising youngsters, Stephanie Baloghy, and her cousin Maureen McArdle, had bigger plans, which they took pleasure in reminiscing about together, almost fifty years later.

Stephanie: 'We set off on an adventure to see Miss Monroe. We waited outside the house for some signs of life and, finally, Marilyn appeared. My recollection of her at that moment was of a beam of sunshine. She was so gorgeous, that she looked illuminated. She looked so fresh and delicate. Her whole being just said "star".'

Maureen: 'We jumped out from behind the hedges and asked for her autograph. She said she would have to check with her husband. She then said something to Arthur Miller and very sweetly told us that her husband said she could not do this or everyone would be at their house trying to get an autograph.'

Stephanie: 'I know we asked – pleaded – for her autograph; told her we had walked so very far; but to no avail. I do recall her saying in that breathy voice of hers that we were "so sweet". I do remember the long walk back – empty handed – but elated. Considering that we had barged in on her I think Miss Monroe was exceedingly kind to us!'

Eventually, Marilyn and Arthur settled into a normal and happy existence in their summer home: in the morning they would both take a walk with Hugo, then Marilyn would often run errands in town, visiting Toppings to do her shopping, and occasionally talking to the locals. In the afternoon, Arthur would sit in the garden and write, while his wife would water the plants or tend to the flowers: 'I planted some seeds that grew, and to my amazement I had flowers,' she later said.

For the first time in her adult life, Marilyn was able to lead a quiet existence away from career problems and business affairs, and she relished the simplicity of it all. She occasionally went horse-riding, wrote poetry and even took delight in trying her hand at watercolour paintings, some of which she gave to the Strasbergs. Sometimes Miller's children would visit with his parents, or the Rostens would drop by; while at other times they'd spend hours at the beach, walking, holding hands and paddling in the surf. It was during one of these excursions that Marilyn discovered some fish washed up on the shore, and refusing to let them die, scooped each one up and popped it back into the sea.

The time in Amagansett was joyful for Marilyn; taking things easy, enjoying her privacy and most of all relishing a secret – she was expecting a baby. Although the couple were ecstatic, they decided not to make an announcement right away, but two old ladies apparently noticed 'a look' about her whilst she was doing chores in the Post Office and even went so far as to congratulate her. Marilyn, obviously embarrassed, mumbled something before making a hasty retreat, but her reaction was enough to confirm their thoughts and the rumour spread around town within days.

1957 was a year of very few public appearances: Marilyn had attended the premiere of *Baby Doll* early in the year, kicked out the first football during a soccer match on 12 May and attended the premiere of *The Prince and the Showgirl*, but apart from that she had laid low. Even the doormen in New York commented that for the most part, the only time they ever saw the Millers was when they walked their dog, Hugo. However, another appearance was scheduled on 2 July, when Marilyn was to meet Laurence S. Rockefeller in New York for an inauguration ceremony at the construction site of the Time-Life Building.

Scheduled to appear at 11 a.m., Marilyn failed to show up until 1.20 p.m., by which time Rockefeller had had enough. 'I've never waited that long for anyone,' he was heard to mutter, as he stormed from the site. When she finally appeared wearing a pink and white dress, Marilyn blamed her lateness on her anniversary celebration the night before: 'Oh was I sick,' she complained. 'We celebrated with champagne, but instead of it going to my head it went to my stomach.'

During this short trip, Marilyn was given a tour of the *New York Times*, where author Carl Schlesinger worked at the time as a Linotype machine operator in the composing room: 'When tourists came through our department the foreman had designated me as the official "explainer" as to how the complicated but fascinating Linotype typesetting machine worked. I gave Marilyn the "gold-plated" demonstration of the machine, ending in my giving her a warm Linotype bar of type, freshly cast with her name on the surface. Marilyn seemed interested so I explained and at the end of my demonstration she thanked me and leaned over me (I was seated and she was standing), and kissed me on top of my balding head. Several of my co-workers, who had been watching "the show", broke out into applause. I didn't wash my head for a week!'

When Marilyn moved on to another department, Schlesinger started to regret not being able to give Marilyn something other than a simple cast of her name. A few days later he went to a coin store and bought an uncirculated 1926 penny, which he cast into the side of another lead bar bearing her name, then sent it off to her. 'Months passed and I forgot all about the incident, then one day the *Times* mailroom sent a letter addressed to me from Miss Monroe. She apologized for the long delay in answering my note and gift, and thanked me for thinking of her.'

After the success of the short New York trip, Marilyn returned to Amagansett to enjoy the rest of the summer and rest. Unfortunately, her joy at being pregnant was short-lived, when on the morning of 1 August 1957, she collapsed in the garden whilst tending to her plants. Miller was in the house at the time and an ambulance was called.

Amagansett local Edward Damiecki was with the ambulance crew when they arrived at the Miller home, and afterwards he told his brother John that when they tried to put Marilyn on the stretcher, she spat in the driver's face. This act was one of anguish and despair; having been bombarded with stories of 'women's problems' by her foster family for many years, Marilyn was acutely aware that something was very wrong.

By the time the Millers and her doctor arrived at the hospital, Marilyn was covered from head to toe in a blanket, and in great pain. The townspeople of Amagansett gathered in the grocery store, and it was not long before they heard the news they dreaded: Marilyn had lost the baby.

It had been discovered that the foetus was growing in the fallopian tube, rather than the uterus, and in order to save the life of the mother, it was removed by an emergency operation. Marilyn's doctor, Hilliard Dubrow, announced that she had been five or six weeks pregnant but it was too early to detect if the lost baby was a boy or girl. He could see no further difficulties should she decide to try again.

In the hospital, Marilyn was devastated and in great pain, after needing a blood transfusion during the operation. On 2 August Miller released a statement that read in part, 'Marilyn wants as many [children] as she can get. I feel the same way,' and then on 10 August she finally left the hospital, walking slowly and wearing the same pink dress she had worn during her appearance at the Time-Life Building. It was a distressing experience; footage is gut-wrenching to watch, and shows Marilyn in full make-up, smiling and making comments such as 'I'm feeling wonderful' to waiting reporters. When asked what her future plans were, she answered, 'I definitely still plan to have a large family. I'm going to rest, rest and more rest.' God only knows how quickly the smile fell from her face as the ambulance door finally closed.

Marilyn was reluctant to return to the summerhouse in Amagansett, and when she did go back, something was very different. Gone was the happy girl who greeted the locals, and in her place was a nervous young woman who would not speak to other customers in the Post Office, and was rumoured to drink a lot. Even her relationship with Miller's family became strained when his mother came to visit the couple, only to find Marilyn distant and suspicious of her; she cut short her visit and returned to New York.

Local farmer John Damiecki remembered one episode that occurred after the Millers' return to Amagansett: 'I would be in my potato fields when Marilyn would ride her horse through the field. She was never in any hurry and I would have to stop work in order to let her through. One time Marilyn was riding through the field and she was drunk and fell off the horse. My brother and I had to catch the horse and Arthur Miller walked it back to the house. He came back and invited us up to the house and when we got there he said, "Marilyn, John is here," but she paid no attention – she was out of it by then.'

There were reports too that Marilyn had tried to overdose either in the Amagansett home or at her 57th Street apartment; luckily Miller was there to prevent the incident becoming fatal, but the emotional scars were everywhere apparent.

After spending the rest of the summer in Amagansett, the Millers returned to their 57th Street apartment and tried hard to pick up the pieces after the miscarriage and overdose. 'I'm almost well again,' Marilyn told reporter Bob Thomas. 'I don't have all my energy back but it's returning bit by bit.' The couple also met architect Frank Lloyd Wright who was known for his 'organic architecture', and commissioned him to design a huge family home on the land connected to their Roxbury house: 'He'll go with us the next time he's in town. We'll need a house with plenty of room. We have two children [Jane and Bobby Miller] and there'll be plenty more.'

The plans drawn up by ninety-year-old Wright are a wonder to behold. Drawing inspiration from a home he had designed in 1949, he drew up blueprints for a huge house which included a large domed living room, library, luggage room, storeroom, gallery, dining room, kitchen, breakfast room, conservatory, card room, dressing room, outdoor swimming pool, servants quarters, guest rooms, costume room, children's room, sewing room, dressing room and much more. The unique feature was the domed living room that had three tiers, each slightly lower than the other, with a large crystal chandelier, glass walls and a movie screen. Showing that babies were still very much on the agenda, the home also came with ramps instead of stairs, and a large nursery.

When she told reporter Radie Harris about the house, she seemed bright and happy, but in the end the plans were dropped and the Millers instead continued to remodel the existing farmhouse, adding a garage and studio for Miller, and also building a nursery. 'We do long so much for a child, but that will come I'm sure,' she later said. 'I look at our house, and I know that it has been home for other families, back through all those years. And it's as if some of their happiness has stayed there even after they went away, and I can feel it around me.' The history of the home and its previous owners was something Marilyn was intrigued by, and when she found an autograph book in the attic with the signature of General Grant in it, she was intrigued and enjoyed the thrill of wondering if it was authentic.

Meanwhile, she was buoyed to hear that her mother, Gladys Baker Eley, was showing relatively good progress at Rockhaven Sanitarium. News came that not only did she take part in a Christmas bazaar at the home, but had also presided over the refreshments stand, arranging cookies and sandwiches on a tray and showing off a candy wreath that she had made herself. Inez Melson, Marilyn's former business manager and Gladys' guardian, also sent Marilyn a Christmas gift of four table mats, which were made by her mother on the Rockhaven loom, and reported that not only was she the only resident to use it, but she was now working on a rug for her room.

Marilyn was glad hear that her mother was showing improvement, though she knew their relationship could never be a close one, no matter how well she became. Marilyn would continue to pay for her mother's treatment (although on several occasions the payments were extremely late in coming), but would never see her again. 'Marilyn purposely stayed away because her mother would become very upset,' Melson later said.

1958 started in much the same vein as 1957: weekdays in New York and most weekends and holidays in the country. It was around this time that a young artist by the name of Tom Tierney (who would later go on to write the successful *Marilyn Monroe Paper Dolls* book) met Marilyn and Arthur whilst living in a loft on First Avenue, New York: 'My neighbors on the top floor were Jack Hamilton and Charles Schneider. One was the movie editor for *Look* magazine and the other the movie editor for *Life*. They had made their loft into a very elegant apartment with a wonderful view. After a few weeks I noticed that on each Saturday they seemed to be throwing a party and I asked [my friend] Shirley about it. She told me that actually they were holding interviews for actors and movie stars who wanted to be featured in their particular magazines.'

Eventually Tom was asked if he'd like to help out at the interview parties and as such he occasionally worked as a greeter, making sure everyone coming into the apartment was comfortable and had drinks. One day there was a knock at the door, which Tom went to answer. He remembered: 'There stood Marilyn Monroe and Arthur Miller! Marilyn was a very quiet girl and Miller did all the talking, holding court for all and sundry. They came on several occasions so that I finally felt comfortable chatting with them, especially Marilyn.

'One day, in the middle of the week, I had cleaned up my studio and was carrying a couple of large paper bags full of crumpled paper, pencil shavings, and other debris down the stairs to put in the garbage cans in front of the building, when I was suddenly face to face with Marilyn coming up. Because my arms were full she couldn't get past me and she sweetly said, "Here Honey, let me help carry your packages down for you." I am probably the only fellow in the world who ever let Marilyn Monroe carry out his garbage! She was definitely a sweetheart . . . and I'll never forget our brief acquaintance.'

But while Marilyn was happy to potter around New York, she was also beginning to think about work too. 'My Marilyn Monroe Productions company is all set to start things going in a big way,' she later said, and she wondered whether she should do a remake of the Marlene Dietrich movie, *Blue Angel*. In the end though the decision was made for her when she read a brief outline of a movie entitled *Some Like it Hot*, which Billy Wilder was in the process of writing. He was writing the screenplay with Marilyn in mind, and told her that if she liked it, he would finish it for her. 'So I read it, and I loved it,' she later said, and agreed to do the film without even reading the rest of the script.

Her instincts were right. *Some Like It Hot* was to be a box-office smash and all-time great. Jack Lemmon and Tony Curtis shone in the parts of Daphne and Josephine, male musicians disguised as women in order to escape the unwanted attentions of the Mafia, while Marilyn had never been funnier, her innocence of character gelling with the roughness of Josephine and Daphne perfectly. (However, Marilyn herself was slightly disappointed in the outcome of the movie. In an unidentified interview in 1960, she declared that she thought the film was 'all right' but would have cut it differently, insisting that, 'I thought I did some of the scenes better than the ones that were kept in.')

While Marilyn made plans to fly to Los Angeles to make *Some Like It Hot*, Miller stayed at home to hear if his 1957 guilty verdict would be overturned. When Marilyn left for California, he wrote her a loving letter to say how 'entirely alive' and at home he felt with her, and expressed the joy she gave him, describing her as his dear baby girl and comrade. Without her he felt lonely, he said, and wrote that if they ever had children together, he would know what to do and how to be with them. Many people have declared that the Miller marriage was over as soon as Marilyn discovered his notebook during *The Prince and the Showgirl*, but in actual fact, all evidence (including Miller's letter) seems to show that the two were very much in love during this time period, and trying hard to make their marriage a success.

In early August, whilst staying at Roxbury, Miller received news that his name had been cleared on the grounds that he had not been adequately informed of the reasons why he was answering questions before the House Committee on Un-American Activities. He celebrated with workmen at the Roxbury home, who had been keeping a case of beer and bottle of whisky for just that occasion; then jetted off to reunite with Marilyn in California. She was thrilled by the result and called for Miller's lawyer, Joe Rauh, to run for President, while even Fox's Spyros Skouras (or 'The Spiral Staircase' as Miller called him) sent a letter of congratulations and admitted he had been wrong to try and convince him to name names.

Meanwhile, shooting on *Some Like It Hot* had begun on a positive note at the Goldwyn Studios in Hollywood. Curtis and Lemmon had fun being coached by a German drag-queen and rehearsals were littered with jokes and laughter. The cast would often go to the Formosa restaurant for lunch, while Marilyn and 'Josephine' took trips to the ladies room together to see if Curtis would be recognized. The whole set had a light-hearted approach and discovering that Goldwyn Studios had banned smoking after the set of *Porgy and Bess* burned down, Wilder pinned a sign on the door that read, 'Come on the Billy Wilder set and smoke your little hearts out. Some Like it Hot!'

But before long, the problems began, as Marilyn was recovering from an ear infection, found it hard to adjust to working after a long absence, and missed her homes and her dog on the East Coast. 'Will you return to New York after the picture?' asked a reporter, to which she replied, 'Just as fast as the airlines can take me. This is nice but it isn't home.' As an antidote to the loneliness for her dog, hairdresser Sydney Guilaroff presented her with two parakeets, from which she chose one – a male called Butch. Inez Melson described the bird as 'peachy and frothy,' and trained it for Marilyn while she worked.

The problems on set followed a familiar pattern: lateness; drama coach interference; absences; and forgotten lines. 'The whole thing is kukie,' said Jack Lemmon. 'We were called for the first shoot this morning, so we arrived at 7 a.m. Here it is noon and we still haven't been in front of the cameras. They've been retaking Marilyn's scene.'

'Marilyn is frequently late, it's true,' said Billy Wilder. 'But she does beautifully once she gets under way.' It got to the point where Marilyn's non-appearance on the set led her to be nicknamed 'MM: Missing Monroe' by the press, and once again reports started to circulate that she was pregnant. This time the rumours were right; she had became pregnant during the production, which led Miller to request Wilder to excuse her from early starts. However, the demand left Wilder completely bewildered since Marilyn never arrived until at least 11.30 a.m., long after everyone else had got there.

The lateness was something that caused a great deal of tension between Marilyn and the cast and crew. 'She doesn't know we're alive,' commented one disgruntled crew member, while Lemmon later remembered that she would drive everyone crazy with her lateness, and would lock herself in the dressing room, refusing to come out until she was psychologically ready.

Anyone knocking on her door before that moment was told to 'Fuck off' in no uncertain terms.

But not everyone was annoyed by Marilyn's lateness; for some it was also an advantage. Peggy McGuiggan was hired to portray a trumpet player in the 'All Girls' Band', and thought Marilyn was 'adorable; very, very charismatic. The first time I saw her, she was walking down the street, just coming from the hairdressers. She had rollers in her hair and was wearing slacks, but still all the attention was riveted on her; she looked spectacular. Marilyn was always late on the set, but that was an advantage to me because I was originally contracted for two weeks, but that went up to four months.'

Perhaps the absences would not have been such a problem if Marilyn was able to work once she was on set, but often she found it impossible. During one famous incident, she had to walk into the room and ask, 'Where's that bourbon?' but she stumbled on the lines so much that it required approximately seventy takes and, in the end, the lines had to be pasted into a drawer so she could read them. Added to that, Marilyn was so cut off from others on the set that rumours began to circulate that attempting friendship with her was a guaranteed way of losing your job. Despite that, Marilyn claimed she had never been happier and declared herself to be more thoughtful than ever.

Reporter Peer J. Oppenheimer visited the set on one occasion, and discovered a rule in place that demanded female co-stars had to have their hair darker than Marilyn's. When some of the girls rebelled against this rule and had their hair bleached, they were immediately sent back to the hairdresser. Remembered Oppenheimer: "I interviewed her several times [over the years], and gradually noticed a pronounced change in her. On the set of *Some Like It Hot*, I witnessed Billy Wilder and her co-stars becoming very agitated because Marilyn could never remember her lines. Billy always had to use her best take. But in the long run, no one held it against her.'

Off the set Marilyn took some time to visit Aunt Enid and Uncle Sam Knebelkamp, whom she hadn't seen for many years.

As James Glaeg, friend of neighbour Catherine Larson, later recalled: 'When Marilyn first became an international celebrity, she began very deliberately to ignore the Knebelkamps. This hurt their feelings and they confided to Catherine their misgivings that perhaps Marilyn had not completely forgiven them for not having provided her with a home at some certain time [when the Goddard family were moving to West Virginia in 1942]. Marilyn didn't call for a long time, and Enid was very sad about it.'

This was sad and completely misguided, of course, since she had been very close to the family for many years after 1942. The truth is that since Aunt Grace's death, Marilyn had cut ties with most if not all of her foster family, although she was always unwilling to discuss her reasons why.

Shortly after she had renewed her friendship with Aunt Enid, James Glaeg and his friend Robert Larson visited the Knebelkamp family and heard first-hand about the feelings they still held for their foster-niece: 'Bob [Larson] asked if she had been hearing from Marilyn lately. Enid answered that she had called recently. "She's pregnant now, you know," Enid said. I mentioned then that I was a fan of Marilyn, and Sam, who had so far said little, now said, "She's a good girl," almost painfully. As though conscious of falling away from that male pose which isn't supposed to think of Marilyn Monroe in terms of goodness. They said nothing more about her, but later Sam remarked that show business was a good business to stay out of. No doubt Marilyn's experiences had given him this conviction.'

'They were glad [she had visited],' recalled Sam and Enid's granddaughter, Jo Olmstead. 'They really did care about her and the main reason they never wanted to talk to anyone in the media about her was that they did not want Norma Jeane to feel hurt or betrayed.'

After her family ties were renewed, the *Some Like It Hot* production moved to the Hotel Del Coronado in San Diego, where Marilyn seemed happier than she had in Los Angeles: her husband was on set; she believed the sea air would be good for the baby; and her fans cheered her on whilst she was filming on the beach. But her continued happiness was not to be; she became frustrated with the number of photographers, and once screamed, 'No pictures, no pictures,' at a bemused onlooker.

Frequently scenes were disturbed by the sound of jets from a nearby Navy base and fans were disturbed to see Marilyn being carried from the set in the arms of her husband on several occasions. More drama occurred when, after filming a love scene on 14 September, she was driven by Miller to the Cedars of Lebanon hospital, where she was treated for exhaustion, although some believe the episode was the result of another drug overdose.

The film had originally been slated to shoot in three months, but at this point in time it was clear to everyone that this would not be the case: on 18 October it was reported that once again Marilyn was absent from the set, and although she persistently claimed to be 'just tired', everyone knew she was pregnant.

Finally, *Some Like It Hot* wrapped towards the middle of November, but Marilyn's problems were far from over. On 10 November she had collapsed on set, and cast members remembered her expressing concern that she was losing her baby. She was taken to her hotel room and there she remained for several days before finally being allowed to fly back to New York for medical tests. On doctors' orders she was forced to rest and cancel any publicity appearances, but it was all in vain; on 17 December it was confirmed that Marilyn had lost the baby and was truly devastated. (It has been widely reported since that Marilyn miscarried on 17 December, but actually this was the date it was confirmed, not when it happened. Indeed, Marilyn's press representative told reporters that doctors determined earlier that week that she had miscarried, but they did not say exactly when.)

During this time, one of the gynaecologists responsible for Marilyn was Dr Oscar Steinberg, who adored her on sight and did everything he could to comfort her. His daughter, Vanessa Steinberg, remembered him talking about Marilyn with great respect, but the same cannot be said of his feelings for Arthur Miller, who he felt was rude and dismissive of Marilyn's problems. 'He treated her like an inferior,' he was later to tell his daughter.

On 22 December *Life* magazine published an article with text by Arthur Miller and photos by Richard Avedon, which depicted Marilyn in the guise of various film stars including Jean Harlow, Theda Bara, Clara Bow, Marlene Dietrich and Lillian Russell. Marilyn and Avedon took a great deal of care and attention to recreate the sets and make-up, and the result was that she became completely absorbed in the roles she was playing. Perhaps inspired by this project, Marilyn later made plans to play Jean Harlow in a movie, but as with many of her proposed projects, it unfortunately did not come to fruition.

After what must surely have been one of the most depressing Christmas periods of her life, Marilyn lay low for most of 1959, confining her public appearances to publicity for *Some Like It Hot*, receiving several awards and meeting Nikita Khrushchev at the Twentieth Century Fox studios. The rest of the year was, for the most part, spent trying to recover from her recent tragedy, which had sent her into a spiral of depression and prescription drug use.

Norman Rosten remembered several disturbing events during this time. In the first of his memories, he recalled a party in which Marilyn stared moodily down to the street, complaining that she had been having trouble sleeping and wondering if anyone would notice if she fell from the window. On another occasion, Rosten and his wife received a 3 a.m. phone call from Marilyn's maid, begging them to come over to the apartment where Marilyn was recovering from an overdose of pills. When he asked Marilyn how she was, she replied, 'Alive. Bad luck.'

And yet, although the walls seemed to be caving in, Marilyn still had her moments of optimism and during 1959 she had several gynaecological operations designed to help her have children. On 23 June 1959 it was publicly announced that Dr Mortimer Rodgers had performed an operation of a corrective nature at Lenox Hill Hospital. Then on another occasion, Dr Steinberg discreetly performed an operation which was one of the first of its kind, attempting to unblock her fallopian tubes and remove scar tissue to enable her to have children. He later told his secretary, Kae Turner, that Marilyn had a uterus ten years older than her years; 'She'll never have a child because her uterus is such a mess,' he said, adding that he believed her uterus was in such disarray because of a past history of septic abortions. 'She had also had numerous pelvic infections that had gone untreated, which had contributed to the scar tissue and infertility problems,' remembered his daughter, Vanessa.

Arthur Miller was present at the hospital during the operation performed by Dr Steinberg; 'It was a dismal failure,' said Vanessa Steinberg. 'My father had the unfortunate task of telling her that she would never be able to have children. Apparently he walked into her room, she looked up at him and said, "Thank you doctor, I already know." He told her that if he ever had a daughter he would name her after her, which he did.'

Chapter 18

Catastrophe

Coming to terms with the hand she had been dealt, Marilyn tried to continue her everyday life in New York: shopping for cakes and bread at the 400 Cake Shop; grocery shopping in the Gristede Brothers Superior Market, browsing for antiques on Third Avenue and picking up books from the Sutton Place Stationers. She also continued attending sessions with psychiatrist Dr Kris, taking classes with the Strasbergs and conducting the occasional interview. 'I'm sorry to report that I'm not pregnant again,' she told one reporter, adding, 'I feel fine now, but it takes time to get over the feeling of loss.'

She also spoke of the strength of her relationship with Miller, insisting that her marriage was in a wonderful state and adding – perhaps to convince herself – that she didn't mind if her husband didn't send her flowers or remember anniversaries: 'I can buy my own flowers,' she said.

One thing that did keep her spirits up during 1959 was her relationship with the Miller children, Bobby and Jane. 'It's such fun for all of us to plan different things to do together. I really look forward to each visit,' she said. She had a particularly friendly relationship with Bobby, who on at least one occasion wrote her a touching note thanking her for her 'hostessing and hospitality', and urging that if she needed to reach him, she could do so through the bedroom phone. Together with Jane, he bought Marilyn a subscription to *Horticulture Magazine* for her birthday, and when the children travelled to Europe in the summer of 1959, Bobby filmed his adventures and sent them back to New York. Marilyn was excited to receive the films: 'I have only been to England and Korea and Japan, and through Bobby I am now seeing Paris and the rest of Europe,' she said.

Although Marilyn was eager to return to work, she was not sure what to work on next. She wondered whether to play Holly Golightly in *Breakfast at Tiffany's*; she was interested in playing opposite Marlon Brando in *Paris Blues*; and she also hoped to act in a film written by Miller, entitled *The Misfits*. It was with this in mind that Arthur invited producer Frank Taylor, his wife Nan and their three boys to visit the Miller home in Roxbury. Son Curtice remembered the meeting with great affection: 'I was fairly young – maybe 9 or 11, when I first met Marilyn. The whole family were taken to the Roxbury farm for a reading of Arthur Miller's play, *The Misfits*, which he was hoping my father would produce. Marilyn didn't come down right away – she was upstairs vacuuming, which is what she did when she was nervous. She eventually came down and she was very sweet. She liked children and she was very drawn to my brother Mark, who had had the most problems out of all the children. She immediately recognized that and made an extra effort to reach out to him – she recognized people in trouble and would reach out to them in some way.

'My mother helped her make lunch; unfortunately the script reading went on forever and the lunch was burnt and had to be made again. There were no seats left after all the family had sat down, and Marilyn told me to come and swing on the hammock with her. I lay down on the hammock with Marilyn and all my brothers were jealous, although they all eventually got a turn.'

On another occasion, Curtice saw the soft side of Marilyn's personality, during a trip to the 57th Street apartment: 'Marilyn decided she had to go out to get some shopping, so she took me with her. She wore a crazy disguise – dark wig and dark glasses, and people were looking because of it. She walked like Marilyn but didn't look like her. There was a homeless man and Marilyn walked right up to him, not at all afraid. "Things are not going well at the moment, are they?" she said. "No they're not," he said. She opened her purse and gave him $5 before walking on.'

In an interview in 1959, Marilyn spoke freely about the Roxbury home and explained that there was a working farm on the land. She admitted not knowing much about what went on there, but she did know that the farmer kept cows. Unfortunately, it became apparent exactly what happened to the animals, during an incident witnessed by Curtice Taylor: 'We [Curtice and his brother] were out in the field which belonged to Arthur but was managed by a farmer. While we were walking we saw a cow that had just given birth, and said, "Wow look at that"; we knew we had to go and get Marilyn because she would be thrilled. We got her and she was thrilled and amazed. The farmer came, checked the sex and discovered it was male. This was not good because he bred milking cows and wasn't interested in males. He went to the van and came back with a bag to put the calf in. Marilyn went completely hysterical and shouted, "You can't do that! You can't take it away from its mother!" She went absolutely crazy. She rushed back to the house and brought back money to try and buy the cow from the farmer. He wouldn't take the money and instead told her that he was the farmer, he had to do his job and the calf was going to be veal. She just didn't understand.'

Adding to Marilyn's distress that day was the discovery of a hawk trying to get some swallow chicks, which were nesting above her front porch. Upset by recent events, she spent a long time throwing rocks up at the hawk to chase it away, and spent the rest of the day feeling low and upset.

Towards the end of 1959, the events of recent years were beginning to take their toll, and although rumours still persisted that Marilyn was pregnant, her marriage was beginning to unravel and she was miserable. One friend described the East 57th Street apartment as the home of an industry, not a love-nest, while Susan Strasberg remembered that Marilyn would sometimes stay at their family home, just to get away from her husband.

Whilst still working on the script of Marilyn's next film, *The Misfits*, Miller accompanied his wife to Los Angeles, where she was to star in the Fox movie, *Let's Make Love*, with Gregory Peck. The script revolved around the relationship between an incognito billionaire and an actress employed in a musical show that ridiculed him. It was a lightweight role and even before shooting started, the problems began, with Miller rewriting the script, and Peck deciding in the middle of dance rehearsals that he no longer wanted the part.

With Marilyn ready and willing to shoot, the departure of Peck was a hindrance they did not need, and a replacement was immediately sought. Charlton Heston, Rock Hudson and newcomer Steve Boyd were all named but in the end, the male lead went to French actor, Yves Montand, with whom Marilyn was hoping to make a television play in autumn 1960. (The play was going to be produced by Litchfield Productions, a company set up by Marilyn, Arthur Miller and Frank Taylor. The company was designed to produce Miller's plays, Marilyn's films and the occasional television show, although in the end, personal events would prevent anything being produced by the company at all.) Montand had appeared with his wife, Simone Signoret, in Miller's play *The Crucible*, and Marilyn had attended a performance of his one-man show in September 1959. Although his English was limited (so much so that he had a French version of the script), he saw the part as his big break, and eagerly accepted.

A press party was arranged, during which Marilyn was photographed with Miller, Montand and Simone Signoret, and declared happily that, next to her husband, Yves was the most handsome man she had ever met. It was a bad sign; with the Miller marriage crumbling, his wife's attraction to another man was probably the last thing Arthur needed to think about. But despite any personal problems she had, Marilyn threw herself into arranging Christmas treats for her stepchildren, organizing a variety of events, including a trip to the MGM studio to see a Western being made.

When the holidays were over, the delayed shooting of *Let's Make Love* finally began, and Marilyn proved to be popular with other members of the cast and crew. Bob Banas was a dancer in the film, and he remembered her fondly: 'She was very nice and comfortable but very childlike. She was not like some other big stars, with closed doors etc. She was very happy to talk and when I brought people on to the set to get autographs, Marilyn was very nice about it and spent time with them. All the dancers asked her for an autographed picture at the end of the shoot and they all got one.'

There were also some relaxed moments on the set, particularly during the filming of 'My Heart Belongs to Daddy' when she had to pull two dancers (including Bob Banas) by the hair, before swinging round a pole. 'I had so much grease on my hair,' remembered Banas, 'that when Marilyn went round the pole, she really flew round fast and was very alarmed. She went up to the director and jokingly said, "I don't want to say but someone has too much grease on their hair!" after which I was sent to have my hair shampooed. Later, when we filmed the part of the song where Marilyn had to kiss me, she had lots of lip gloss on, and I slid off her face! I went to the director and jokingly told him that she had too much grease on, and Marilyn laughed.'

But it wasn't all light-hearted. Marilyn was late once again, leading Yves Montand to leave a note under her door, chastising her for keeping him waiting. Tony Randall, who played Montand's sidekick, remembered, 'Marilyn would report to work around 5 in the evening. You've been in make-up since 8.30 in the morning waiting for her. That ceases to be amusing after about a week.'

Another problem was caused by the requirement of countless rewrites, undertaken by Arthur Miller. This didn't do anything to lighten relations between Marilyn and her husband, and on 8 March, when she received a Golden Globe award for her performance in *Some Like It Hot*, her publicist acted as her escort, while Arthur Miller stayed behind at the Beverly Hills Hotel.

After the rewrites came an actors' strike, which, coupled with Marilyn's illnesses and lateness, led to extreme time delays on set. Yves Montand was scheduled to leave the United States for a thirty-day tour of Japan on 15 May 1960, but with all the disruption this was deemed impossible. As a result, Fox sent representatives to Tokyo to try and stall the tour, but despite the promise of a cash remuneration, the tour's producers refused to postpone. When the Japanese producers threatened legal and even government action, the *Let's Make Love* set went on a twenty-four-hour grind to complete the movie by mid-May, but it was a losing battle. Marilyn's habit of phoning in sick pushed them even further behind, and, finally admitting defeat, Montand ended up paying the Japanese producers $120,000 to be released from his contract, a sum that was reimbursed by Fox.

Another person feeling the stress of day-to-day life on set was costume designer Dorothy Jeakins, who was not only working on costumes for *Let's Make Love* but for *The Misfits* too. Initially, the relationship between the two women had run smoothly, and everything had begun with a fair amount of hope. By early February they had had meetings on the kind of clothes Marilyn would wear in *The Misfits*, and Jeakins was very pleased with the way it was working out. But even at this early stage, Jeakins noticed that Marilyn had a marked personality change whenever Paula Strasberg was in the room.

This was a sign of things to come and before long Marilyn was refusing to wear Jeakins' costumes in *Let's Make Love*, substituting them for items of her own. Added to that, there were problems with *The Misfits* costumes too when Marilyn refused to attend a ten-minute meeting to see the designs Jeakins had drawn. Strangely, Marilyn then began to insult Jeakins not only in private, but also in front of other cast and crew members, which the costume designer felt quite astonishing. Not knowing how to react to these outbursts, Jeakins would stare into space without saying a word, but the failure she felt soon mounted up.

By 3 May the situation was hopeless and Jeakins wrote a heartfelt letter to Marilyn, apologizing if she had displeased her, declaring that she felt defeated and should be replaced. She then wrote to C.O. Erickson, production manager on *The Misfits*, asking to be omitted from the credits and proclaiming that she would expect no remuneration for work already done. Then, on 4 May, she wrote to Frank Taylor, giving her side of the entire story. There remains no trace of Marilyn's response (if any) to all of this, but Jeakins was not credited on *The Misfits*, and Jean Louis was later hired as Marilyn's official costume designer.

She may not have made a friend out of Dorothy Jeakins, but Marilyn found several other confidants during the making of *Let's Make Love*. The first was psychiatrist Dr Ralph Greenson, whom she met at the Beverly Hills Hotel on the recommendation of her New York analyst, Marianne Kris; the second was Ralph Roberts, a massage therapist and actor who became her masseur and friend; and the third was Evelyn Moriarty, a young woman hired to be Marilyn's stand-in on *Let's Make Love*.

Moriarty worked with Marilyn for six weeks, without a single word being said between them: 'I didn't talk to her and she didn't talk to me,' she told the 'Marilyn: Then and Now' club; 'I had heard that she was difficult and I wasn't going to go up to someone that I didn't know.' This was a big problem for Marilyn on the *Let's Make Love* set, and Jack 'Waukeen' Cochran, who was hired to play an Elvis impersonator in the film, remembered that everyone was frightened to talk to her, which just added to her frustration and insecurity. He took matters into his own hands one day when she appeared on set, and he greeted her with a huge hug. She was surprised but delighted, and so he continued this practice for the remainder of his time on the film.

Moriarty was less sure how to approach her, and was pleased when Marilyn eventually took the initiative and came up to introduce the stunned stand-in to her pet cat, Serafina. 'It was a sweet, funny sort of thing to do,' remembered Moriarty, and after that the two became good friends. In later years she would always describe Marilyn in the most positive of ways, as demonstrated in the 'Marilyn Then and Now' interview: 'She was the most wonderful person that lived. I think that when she got up in the morning she used to wonder who she could help. You couldn't tell her that she had something nice on, because you got it the next day. She was very giving. She was fantastic.'

When Marilyn appeared on set looking slightly heavier than normal, her wardrobe lady could be seen leaning in before takes, telling her to hold her tummy in. This led to whispers of a pregnancy, but these stories were quickly forgotten when yet another, more explosive rumour began.

Before leaving for a trip to Europe, Simone Signoret had declared, 'I love Marilyn very much. She's clever. She loves her husband, which is a quality I like in women.' It was a heartfelt but ironic comment as, shortly after her departure, an affair began between Yves Montand and Marilyn.

Miller was out of town, working on *The Misfits*, and although the affair was conducted in private, it did not take long to filter not only on to the set, but into the media too. Adding fuel to the fire were Marilyn's comments that as well as being a brilliant actor, singer and dancer, Yves Montand was 'very, very romantic'. How she intended this comment to be interpreted was not clear, but Yves added his own fuel when he later made the mistake of declaring that he'd have no objection to marrying her if they were not already married to other people. For his part, Miller kept quiet about the subject, while Simone Signoret kept a stiff upper lip. When later questioned she declared, 'If Marilyn is in love with my husband, it proves she has good taste, for I am in love with him too,' before adding poignantly, 'She is a warm, delightful person . . . but this business could spoil our friendship.'

Marilyn felt an intense attraction to Montand but the affair had run its course by the end of filming, and although she made a much ballyhooed trip to the airport to say goodbye, she never publicly announced any romantic tendencies towards her co-star. In fact, when Louella Parsons later asked if her marriage was breaking up because of Yves Montand, Marilyn retorted: 'Of course not! Just because Yves is a gentleman and treated me like a lady is no reason to say we are in love.' To Hedda Hopper she declared, 'I think anyone would find he's an attractive man. Didn't you find him so?'

But in spite of playing down any adoration, in private Marilyn was hurt tremendously when she read that Yves had accused her of having a schoolgirl crush. The quote was false, as Montand declared to columnist James Bacon: 'Even if it were true, which it isn't, no Frenchman would ever make such an ungallant statement,' but the damage was done. Marilyn never heard from her lover again, although she forever retained what she described as, 'such a strong, tender, wonderful memory'.

Although physically exhausted towards the end of filming *Let's Make Love*, Marilyn went straight into work on pre-production of *The Misfits*, and also gave interviews with the *Sunday Times*, *Marie Claire*, *Daily Mirror*, *Look*, *Life* and *Paris Match*. For any person the tireless workload would be extreme, but for someone who was anaemic and frequently unwell, it was lethal. By 20 July, when she travelled to Reno for location shooting on *The Misfits*, Marilyn was absolutely exhausted.

The people of Reno and Dayton were extremely excited about the arrival of *The Misfits*' cast and crew, and when Marilyn touched down at the airport, she was met by several Reno VIPs including Councilman Charles Cowen, who presented her with the key to the city. There then followed a cocktail party and reception at the Mapes hotel, where Marilyn mingled with members of the press and city officials. It gave the illusion of a positive start, but it was not to be; the filming of *The Misfits* would be a nightmare for all involved.

There had been many problems with Marilyn's hair on the set of *Let's Make Love*, and one of the things Dorothy Jeakins had done before her departure was to recommend the actress wear a wig to help with the wind, dirt and dryness of the desert. It was a good suggestion and saved time on hairdressing, but it was not enough to prevent major delays on *The Misfits* set, caused mainly by rewrites demanded by Huston. 'I thought the original script was wonderful,' Marilyn later said. 'They didn't use it because Mr Huston wanted changes.'

But rewrites weren't the only problem, as Marilyn's illnesses were becoming more and more apparent: '*The Misfits* should never have happened,' declared Allan Snyder to the 'All About Marilyn' fan club. 'She wasn't feeling well when they insisted on starting shooting and there were so many script changes in her part that Arthur made so often, she became less and less happy with her role and character.'

The problem with the character of Roslyn was that she was based very much on Marilyn herself. It had been written as a valentine to his wife, but Arthur's script became so personal that at times the film is painful to watch. Roslyn is a woman who is in Nevada to obtain a divorce from her husband; she meets three cowboys, played by Clark Gable, Eli Wallach and Montgomery Clift, and accompanies them on a mission to catch horses for use in the dog-food trade. At one point in the story, Roslyn describes how she never wanted children with her ex-husband, which led Marilyn to note in her script that this was just like her feelings towards Joe DiMaggio.

There were other character similarities too, including a heart-wrenching scene where Roslyn screams for the release of the captured horses. This was a reminder of the way she had reacted towards the calf being sold for veal in Roxbury, and also an incident in New York where she bought caged pigeons from some teenagers, in order to release them back into the wild.

Angela Allen was script supervisor on *The Misfits*, and on meeting Marilyn at rehearsal, she discovered what she thought was a charming and delightful actress. Unfortunately, her thoughts quickly changed when shooting started and, according to Allen, Marilyn would sometimes arrive five hours late, and then only work for one-and-a-half hours before leaving. This is reiterated by Curtice Taylor, who remembered that, 'She was late on the set every day – hours late – because she was recovering from the pills. It was like working with a hangover.'

Her growing reliance on prescription pills was evident to everyone and both cast and crew were shocked to see her stagger around the set. Indeed, at one point the cameraman commented, 'I can't focus on her eyes, there's nowhere to focus.'

Adding to Marilyn's misery were the ongoing marital problems between herself and Arthur Miller, made worse by the Yves Montand rumours. There were no specific incidents between them on set but it was apparent to all that the couple were not getting along, with one member of the crew describing Marilyn's treatment of Arthur as 'appalling'. Both had their own resentments of each other – the feeling that they hadn't lived up to expectations – and although Miller told friends that he and Marilyn were planning a trip to Europe, in reality they could hardly bear the sight of each other.

Friends recalled that even in the privacy of their hotel room, neither would speak to each other. 'There seemed to be a barrier come between them, going from professional to cool and eventually hostile,' remarked Allan 'Whitey' Snyder to the 'All About Marilyn' club. As time went on Marilyn started to believe that anyone associated with her husband was against her and producer Frank Taylor was unfairly accused of being on Arthur's 'side'. Script supervisor Angela Allen also found herself under attack when Marilyn began spreading scandalous rumours that she was Miller's new girlfriend. Meanwhile, Howard Sheehan Jr, who had met her briefly while his father was producing the 1947 movie *Dangerous Years*, saw her on the set and went up to say hello: 'I asked her if she remembered me and she just looked at me coldly, said "No" and walked away.'

And yet despite all this, there was still a side to Marilyn that was giving and friendly, particularly to her fans and her 'group': Allan 'Whitey' Snyder; Evelyn Moriarty; Marjorie Pletcher; and Ralph Roberts. 'When *The Misfits* was going bad, it was her employees who rallied round,' remembered Curtice Taylor. She was also well liked by Eli Wallach (who had known her for many years) and Thelma Ritter, who she had worked with twice before. When interviewed on the set, Ritter was asked how Marilyn had changed from when they first met during Marilyn's 'formative' years: 'I think she has grown but I mean what she has now she had then; she's had a chance to develop it. It's been rather fashionable to underrate Marilyn; to say that she's just another blonde but of course there are so many other blondes and Marilyn's not one of them. I have great respect for her and a very deep affection for her.'

Although Marilyn categorically turned down another appearance on the *Person to Person* television show, she did take time to meet certain members of the press, including Harry Brandon, who interviewed both her and Miller for the *Sunday Times*. Marilyn had little to say during that interview, but with reporter Peer J. Oppenheimer she found it hard to hide her misery: 'The last time I saw her was when she was making *The Misfits*,' remembered Oppenheimer. 'I was there to interview both her and Clark Gable, who became extremely upset with Marilyn's inability to get to the set on time and remember her lines. Gable was not the sort of man to become aggravated easily, but he was extremely upset with Marilyn. I think she realized there was a real problem with her career. I felt sorry for her because things were beyond her control.'

Despite that, Marilyn told Oppenheimer that she still intended to be a mother. In the article, which was published on 11 December, she described how she would take her child with her on filming trips, and would hire a tutor so it didn't impair the child's education. 'I realize it takes more thought to raise a child in show business, but it doesn't need to work out badly,' she stated.

Children were very much on her mind during the shoot, and Marilyn spent time with youngsters on set, and the ones she met in town. Whilst filming a rodeo scene, she took a real delight in walking some dogs with thirteen-year-old Bob Plummer Jr; while eight-year-old Gene Walmsley took his friends to the set to meet 'the prettiest lady I'd ever seen'. Dayton resident Edna MacDiarmid told *Lyon County Reflections* that Marilyn treated both her son Tom and the other children in town in a very special way, and this was extended to a fan who admired one of her diamond rings: Marilyn went out and bought her one of her own.

Still, despite this generosity and kindness, the residents all noticed an unhappy air about her. Reporter Art Long visited the set and witnessed Marilyn to be 'so sad, so down in the dumps', while a shop assistant at the Joseph Magnin store described her as 'the saddest looking woman, really tormented'. Meanwhile, during a scene filmed in Harrah's Casino, one employee, Mark Curtis, noticed Marilyn looking seemingly oblivious to everything, before finally looking up at Curtis and smiling, 'a smile from a sick bed,' as he later told the *Reno Gazette-Journal*. 'Though she was adored by millions, I could not imagine a more pathetic or lonely creature.'

According to stand-in Evelyn Moriarty, Marilyn was not treated well on the set, and remembered an incident during the rodeo scene, which had her sitting for hours on end in the blazing sun while rewrites were being done. Another episode involved the filming of a long shot that Moriarty was convinced could have been shot without Marilyn, but instead the actress was forced to sit in a car for almost two hours, in the 115°C heat.

By this point in shooting, she was very close friends with massage therapist Ralph Roberts, who also appeared in the film as an ambulance driver. In order to try and relax her, Ralph Roberts got into the habit of massaging her as she fell asleep, talking of his childhood in Salisbury, North Carolina, and making plans to take her there one day. Then one night he was shocked to be called to Marilyn's room, only to find her barely conscious and in very bad shape. He managed to bring her round before letting himself out, only to be called back slightly later to find Marilyn unaware of what had happened just a few hours before.

Because of her painful periods, Marilyn had an agreement that said she did not have to work whilst menstruating and on 26 August, while off set, Marilyn decided to fly to Los Angeles for a rest. She consulted her doctor, Hyman Engelberg, who was shocked to see her in such bad shape, and recommended she enter the Westside Hospital to be treated for extreme exhaustion.

Arthur Miller, Paula Strasberg and May Reis accompanied Marilyn to Los Angeles, while several days later Ralph Roberts drove down with Susan and Lee Strasberg.

Back in Nevada, Clark and Kay Gable were extremely concerned for her welfare, and sent a huge, elaborate bouquet, along with a heartfelt note. The set closed down and the cast and crew left Reno. Unfounded rumours surfaced of Marilyn being taken from the set wrapped in wet towels and that John Huston sent her to Los Angeles so he could regain money lost in local casinos. In reality, the director was so concerned that he felt if she worked much longer in the state she was in, she would surely die. 'Marilyn got very ill up there during filming,' remembered Allan 'Whitey' Snyder. 'She was under too much pressure with the situation with Arthur and all.'

After resting for over a week, Marilyn returned to Nevada on 5 September, declaring 'I'm looking forward to getting back to work. I'm feeling much better. I guess I was just worn out.' The cast and crew also returned to work, and filming carried on as it did before, but it was exhausting for everyone, especially Clark Gable, who at fifty-nine was the oldest member of the cast and insisted on doing his own stunts.

The weekend before location filming ended, Marilyn, Ralph, Paula, May and Agnes Flanagan travelled to San Francisco to see Ella Fitzgerald in concert. For Marilyn this trip was not just a chance to see Ella perform, but also an opportunity to renew ties with her old 'family', the DiMaggios. Joe was not in town, but Marilyn spent time with his brother and sister, along with best friend 'Lefty' O'Doul, and even visited the famous DiMaggio restaurant, where she had spent much of her time in 1954.

That weekend was a turning point for Marilyn, and by the time the production moved to Los Angeles, she had decided her marriage was well and truly over. Ralph Roberts witnessed a huge row between Marilyn and her husband at the Beverly Hills Hotel, and while they kept up appearances on set, both knew that Miller had moved out of the hotel and out of her life.

Snyder later summed it up during an interview with 'All About Marilyn': 'I felt extremely disappointed that Marilyn once again had lost something that she had cherished so much ... The normality of a happy marriage and life of security with the one you love.'

'Arthur is a brilliant man,' she later told Louella Parsons. 'Maybe it wasn't his fault that he was a much better writer than he was a husband. I'm sure that his writing is the most important thing in his life.'

The day before the film wrapped, Clark Gable saw a rough cut of the movie and declared it to be the best thing he had done since *Gone with the Wind*. When they said goodbye the day after, Marilyn told Gable he was her hero, but couldn't get up enough nerve to tell him just how much she idolized him: 'I don't know how he would have reacted if he had known how important he had been to me all those years,' she told *Family Weekly* magazine. Alas, she was never to find out; on 5 November Clark Gable suffered a massive heart attack and, just eleven days later, on 16 November 1960, he passed away after suffering a second attack.

On 7 November, just over a week before Gable's death, Miller went home to Brooklyn in order to break the news of his marriage break-up to his stunned parents. He told them there was no hope of a reconciliation and added that he had left because 'it could not go on this way'.

'It hit us like a bomb,' Augusta Miller later told *Motion Picture* magazine. 'We never interfered. They had their own lives to live. And we've always been very fond of Marilyn. She was just as fond of us too.' Augusta was right. They had been a huge presence in Marilyn's life and she determined to keep in touch not only with them but with her stepchildren too: 'I take a lot of pride in [Joe Jr, Jane and Bobby] because they're from broken homes. I can't explain it, but I think I understand about them. I think I love them more than I love anyone; their lives that are forming are very precious to me and I know that I had a part in forming them.'

Back in New York on the day of Gable's death, Marilyn was woken up at 4 a.m. in order to be told the news by a reporter. She was heartbroken and by the time she rang her friend Ralph Roberts, she was absolutely hysterical. Things were made no better when rumours began to circulate that suggested Marilyn was responsible for Gable's death. She had become extremely close to both Gable and his wife Kay during the making of *The Misfits*, and these stories hit her hard, even though they did not have a kernel of truth in them. She was further disturbed to walk out of her apartment one day, only to be confronted by people shouting 'Murderer' at her on the street.

This event convinced her that she was to blame for Gable's death and she spiralled into a deep depression, spending many days alone in her bedroom, refusing to see any of her old friends, and playing sad songs on her phonograph. In his book, *Marilyn:An Untold Story*, Norman Rosten described how, when his wife Hedda eventually got through to Marilyn, 'her voice was blurred, distant, unhappy'. It was a desperate situation, and no one knew just how to help her. 'I was completely run down,' she later admitted, 'and was more unhappy than I remember being at any time in my life.'

During this period of turmoil, May Reis took charge of the practical aspects of the separation, and packed up Miller's books and papers, sending them on to Roxbury and a nearby hotel. Miller was given custody of the Roxbury house and also Hugo, the basset hound Marilyn had adored so much, while she remained in the 57th Street apartment they had leased at the beginning of their marriage. Meanwhile, on 23 November Miller officially resigned as a director of Marilyn Monroe Productions, and on 28 November, an emergency meeting was held at the offices of Weissberger and Frosch to discuss the resignation not only of Miller, but of Secretary John C. Taylor, and Advisory Committee members John F. Wharton and Robert H. Montgomery.

With the realization that both her company and marriage were in tatters, Marilyn found little to be happy about during the run-up to Christmas, but New York publicist John Springer tried to cheer her by sending various requests for interviews, along with a tape of poet Robert Frost reading his own poetry. She even received a card from her mother, Gladys, addressed to Norma Jeane Miller though quite bizarrely signed, 'Loving good wishes, Gladys Pearl Eley'.

Christmas day was spent quietly with Patricia Newcomb, the publicist who had worked briefly on *Bus Stop* and who had returned to work at the end of 1960. Despite any problems they had had in the past, Marilyn was happy to welcome Newcomb into her group, and gave her a mink coat as a Christmas present. That night, Marilyn was surprised to receive a forest of poinsettias from Joe DiMaggio, sent, he said, because he knew she would call to thank him, and 'besides, who in the hell else do you have in the world?' Despite the fact that the two hadn't seen each other in a long time, Marilyn agreed to see him on Christmas evening, later saying, 'I was glad he was coming though I must say I was bleary and depressed but somehow still glad he was coming over.'

On New Year's Eve, Patricia Newcomb returned to Los Angeles wearing the mink coat Marilyn had presented to her, and during the flight wrote a heartfelt letter, urging her friend to ring any time, day or night; she sympathized with what she was going through and asserted what she hoped would be a lifetime friendship. It was a genuine gesture and one that Marilyn would appreciate during the bleak months ahead.

Chapter 19

'I'm working on the foundation'

January 1961 started in a very positive fashion, with Marilyn announcing that she was to bring W. Somerset Maugham's *Rain* to television for NBC. 'I'm going to play Sadie Thompson,' she told reporter Margaret Parton; 'I'm really excited about doing the part because [the character] was a girl who knew how to be gay, even when she was sad. And that's important – you know?'

Even Somerset Maugham was delighted with her plans and made no secret of letting her know: 'I am so glad to hear that you are going to play Sadie . . . I am sure you will be splendid,' he wrote in January 1961.

Negotiations began in earnest and newspapers were buzzing with the news that Marilyn could be turning her hand to television. On 6 January, executive producer Ann Marlowe told newspapers: 'I started to work on the idea of 'Rain' and Marilyn Monroe a year ago. Although her agents never had been able to get her to do television, I talked to her about it and she said she was interested but would have to wait until she finished a picture and came back to New York. When she returned from the coast, we started working on it and now the lawyers are drawing up contracts.'

Marilyn's press rep got in on the act with a statement declaring, 'It is not firm yet but the deal is pretty sure,' while newspapers reported that Marilyn herself was determined to include Lee Strasberg in the production and was considering giving her fee to the Actors Studio.

But it wasn't all work. During January 1961, Marilyn and Joe DiMaggio began seeing each other on a regular basis,

and although they wished to keep their renewed friendship secret, it took only days for the press to start reporting
reconciliation. The rumours became so persistent that on 11
January John Springer confirmed that they had been seeing
each other again, but played down any romance. Marilyn
herself later denied any romance to columnist Louella
Parsons: 'Believe me, no matter what the gossip columns say,
there is no spark rekindled between Joe and me.' For once
Joe was happy to be just friends, and even admitted that he
didn't blame Marilyn for divorcing him in 1954: 'I'd have
divorced me too,' he said.

Divorce was on Marilyn's mind too, and on 20 January,
she travelled with Pat Newcomb to Juarez, Mexico, in order
to obtain a divorce from Miller. Choosing the day of John F.
Kennedy's presidential inauguration so as to avoid publicity,
Marilyn cited 'incompatibility of character' at a special night
session with Judge Miguel Gomez and her attorney Arturo Sosa
Aguilar, before quietly returning to New York. 'The plane was
delayed and I got upset,' she told reporters; 'I don't feel like
being bothered with publicity right now, but I would love to
have a plate of tacos and enchiladas.'

Back in New York, the weather was getting Marilyn down
considerably. 'New York was terrible last winter with so much
rain and snow. It was depressing,' she told Hedda Hopper in
July 1961. But regardless of her depression, she continued
her studies at the Actors Studio and one day was surprised to
see W.J. Weatherby, a reporter she had met on the set of *The
Misfits*. Being a fan of Miller, he wasn't particularly impressed
by Marilyn at first, but after seeing her again at the studio, he
asked her to have a drink with him at a little bar on the corner
of 8th Avenue. She agreed and, over the next few weeks, they
met around four times to discuss all manner of subjects, including books, civil rights, actors and personal issues. They even
touched upon politics when Marilyn declared that John F.
Kennedy spoke a lot of sense, and that she admired his family's
zest for life.

But despite the interesting conversation, Weatherby noticed sadness in the actress, and was disturbed on one occasion to see that her hair needed washing and she had a faint body odour. There were times, too, when she would not respond when he spoke to her, something she attributed to the pills that made her feel 'dopey sometimes'. She was certainly in a retrospective mood, confessing that she had put Miller through a lot, and even discussing her feelings when Gable had died, admitting that she had not attended the funeral because she was frightened of breaking down.

Marilyn also told Weatherby that although she had felt guilty when Gable died, she had now accepted he had a bad heart and it wasn't her fault. However, she then read in a newspaper that Kay Gable had implied Clark's death was her fault. There was not a grain of truth in the story, but it was enough to unlock the deep-rooted blame she felt, and sent her once more into a deep depression.

In just two months, Marilyn had reportedly visited psychiatrist Marianne Kris a staggering forty-seven times. None of the sessions was surely as disturbing as one held towards the beginning of February, when she confessed that after hearing Kay Gable's quote, she opened her living room window as far as she could, and seriously thought about throwing herself out. The only thing that stopped her was the realization that a lady whom she knew was at that moment walking past the building.

Kris was obviously alarmed to hear this latest development, and that, coupled with her continuing drug problem, was enough to persuade the doctor that Marilyn needed complete hospital rest. On 6 February the actress telephoned Joe DiMaggio, then on the 7th, just as her lawyers were negotiating for her to have complete control over the *Rain* production, she checked into the Payne Whitney hospital as Mrs Faye Miller for what was described as, 'study and treatment of an illness of undisclosed origin'. Unfortunately, and unknown to Marilyn, Payne Whitney was an establishment for disturbed patients, and this became quite apparent within hours of her admittance there.

Quite alarmingly, on her arrival at the hospital, Marilyn claimed a psychiatrist conducted a physical examination which included a breast inspection. This was something to which Marilyn quite rightly took great exception. Once that was completed, she was taken to her room: a depressing cell-like space complete with cement blocks, bars on the windows and the markings of former patients. Everything was under lock and key, including the bathroom, closets and electric lights, while the main door into the room came complete with a window through which she could be 'observed'. There was no way of buzzing for assistance.

In a letter dated 1–2 March 1961, Marilyn told Dr Greenson that she had been encouraged to 'mingle' with other patients, and take up such occupational therapies as sewing, knitting and playing checkers. As a person continually reminded of the mental illness that plagued her family, Marilyn was appalled to be placed in such an establishment, and made no hesitation in saying so. 'Why aren't you happy in here?' they asked, to which she replied, 'I'd have to be nuts if I liked it in here.'

Deciding to telephone the Strasbergs for help, she stood in line with other patients waiting to use the phone, only to find herself forbidden to make any calls on the orders of a security man. Dismayed, she returned to her room and began thinking of the part she played in *Don't Bother to Knock*, in which she had to threaten to hurt herself with a razor blade. This inspired her to do to her own version of this story, and before she knew it, Marilyn was banging on the door with a chair: 'It took a lot of banging to get even a small piece of glass,' she later wrote to Dr Greenson, but once she had achieved it, she sat with glass in hand, waiting for the doctors to appear.

Threatening to harm herself, the arrival of the doctors did nothing to calm Marilyn's nerves, and quite disturbingly, the four medical staff picked her up by all fours and carried her, face down and sobbing, to the seventh floor – the ward for extremely disturbed patients.

Told she was a 'very, very sick girl', Marilyn was forced to stay at the hospital for four nights, during which time she was able to write a letter to Lee Strasberg, begging for help. Unfortunately, the Strasberg family had no power to secure her release, but thankfully for Marilyn, Joe DiMaggio did. He arrived at the hospital and threatened to take it apart 'brick by brick' if they did not release her into his care. Later Marilyn took great pride in telling friends of DiMaggio's rescue, and consulted her lawyer Aaron Frosch in order to draw up a document that ensured DiMaggio, Frosch and Reis would all have to be notified before she could ever be locked up again. Before she left the hospital she turned to the doctors who had 'cared' for her: 'You should all have your heads examined,' she told them, before leaving in the care of DiMaggio.

She was driven back to her apartment to confront Dr Kris, 'like a hurricane unleashed', according to friend, Ralph Roberts. Kris was shocked, frightened and deeply apologetic, but the damage was done. Marilyn never forgave her psychiatrist and in future turned to Californian therapist Dr Greenson for support.

Still emotionally disturbed and exhausted, Marilyn was persuaded to enter Columbia-Presbyterian hospital on 11 February, where she was admitted for 'a rest and check-up', according to a hospital spokesman. Her publicist, John Springer, elaborated by telling reporters, 'She is here for a complete physical check-up. She's had a hell of a year. She had been exhausted, really beat down.' Trying to quash rumours of her treatment at Payne Whitney, he added, 'More than anything else, this was just meant for her to go in and have a chance to rest and recuperate a little. It has been blown up all out of proportion.'

Meanwhile, NBC executives were becoming increasingly alarmed with the situation, declaring to her representatives that they wanted 'concrete evidence' that she could physically perform in *Rain*. This request left her lawyer in the unenviable and impossible task of trying to compile a detailed report of her condition, including whether or not she would be capable of showing up on set at all. On 15 February, a letter was sent from NBC to Marilyn's reps at MCA, declaring that 'in view of Miss

Monroe's recent illness, it is perfectly clear that we do not have an agreement with respect to [her] services'.

But while negotiations were going on behind the scenes, Marilyn was still in hospital, where Joe DiMaggio was a frequent visitor: 'She went to the hospital for what amounted to exhaustion and nothing more,' he told reporters. 'The girl has been working very hard with pictures she has done, and Clark Gable's death did not help matters.'

Journalist and author Peter Evans, who had met Marilyn several times during the making of *The Prince and the Showgirl*, was also staying at the same hospital, suffering from dehydration. As he later recalled: 'All outside calls to her room had been blocked by the switchboard on the orders of Joe DiMaggio, but I discovered it was possible to dial her room directly from my room. I got the number of her room from a friendly nurse, and tried my luck. Marilyn Monroe answered in her unmistakable voice. "Oh," she said when I told her who I was and how I got through to her. But she didn't seem to mind. She sounded frail, but was absolutely friendly.'

She told him, 'They won't let me listen to the radio. The news is always so disturbing. Tell me, what's happening in the outside world?'

Evans told Marilyn that he had met Arthur Miller several days before, and she asked how he was. She was concerned with his living arrangements, observing that she'd been told he wasn't comfortable living in a hotel. Evans told her that Arthur was thinking of moving out, though felt the Connecticut house was too large just for him. 'He said he didn't like being alone,' Evans remarked.

'Oh my God,' Marilyn replied. 'He should get another wife.'

Later in the conversation Evans told Marilyn that Arthur was bemoaning the loss of a button on his overcoat. 'I must get somebody to sew a button on this coat. It's been off for weeks,' he had said.

According to Evans there was then a silence on the line before Marilyn eventually spoke. 'That is so poignant,' she said. 'That is beautiful. It says so much about the end of a marriage. I want to cry. I will write a poem about that missing button.'

'I wondered whether she ever wrote that poem,' Peter Evans later recalled.

On Tuesday, 7 March, having been out of hospital for just two days, Marilyn attended the funeral of her former mother-in-law, Augusta Miller, who had suffered a fatal heart attack the day before. Arriving unexpectedly, Marilyn put her own problems to one side and comforted Arthur and Isidore Miller, before leaving quietly to return to her apartment. Then on 10 March she attended a fundraiser for the Actors Studio and appeared to be feeling much better.

However, just days later, publicist Rupert Allan sent some newspaper clippings to John Springer, which implied that once again Kay Gable was blaming Marilyn for Clark's death. The story was once again untrue, but knowing Marilyn's fragile state of mind, Allan instructed Springer not to bring the clippings to her attention. On 17 March, Springer forwarded the comments to lawyer Aaron Frosch, where Marilyn accidentally saw them, sending her into a furious rage. She immediately wrote a note to May Reis, demanding she get Frosch on the telephone so that she could discuss the issue with him, and expressing her anger at Allan for trying to keep 'this kind of thing away from me'.

'I must know my own business, so I can protect myself. Keeping things from me is no protection,' she told May Reis.

By this time, a production schedule for *Rain* had been compiled, and Marilyn had been due to start pre-production on 13 March, with one week of shooting beginning 27 March. However, because of her illness, NBC took any definite dates off the table. In order to take her mind off this, Joe DiMaggio asked Marilyn if she would like to travel to Florida with him instead. She agreed, and checked into the Tides Hotel at St Petersburg Beach. On her arrival, Marilyn declared, 'I came down here for some rest, some sun and to visit Joe,' though it was also an opportunity to regain her strength and recover from the trauma of the past months.

Always a fan of 'the man or woman on the street', whilst staying in St Petersburg Marilyn began a friendship with Lynn Pupello, a teenage reporter who in 1961 won an award for best writer for the American Newspaper Association. 'I sat near her [on the beach] and struck up a conversation as if she wasn't famous,' she remembered. 'At first she was shy but my enthusiasm won her over.'

For Marilyn, talking to the young woman was a welcome diversion, though Joe DiMaggio at times seemed to resent her presence, as remembered by Pupello: 'I wasn't nervous being with Marilyn. She had a loving nature and ability to put you at ease. Joe DiMaggio was aloof with me; he said "Hello" but wanted to be alone with her, quietly talking. She smiled occasionally but told me she would not reconcile with him because of his bad temper during the night of the skirt-blowing scene in New York City.'

According to Pupello, during their long conversations Marilyn admitted to having met John F. Kennedy: 'She said she had been in South Florida before, visiting the President. She lit up speaking of him and said, "he has always been very kind to me."' Marilyn had shown an interest in Kennedy during her conversations with W.J. Weatherby, but had not mentioned a meeting, so her comment is an interesting one. She did not make any suggestion to Pupello or Weatherby (at that particular time) that she thought of him in a romantic way, but made no secret of the fact that she was a huge supporter of Kennedy both as a person and a politician.

Almost immediately on her return to New York, rumours began to circulate that Frank Sinatra had been in Florida at the same time as Marilyn, and that she was in love with him. This is intriguing since on 2 March 1961, whilst staying at Columbia-Presbyterian Hospital, she wrote a letter to Dr Greenson, admitting to a 'fling on a wing' affair with an unnamed man, possibly Sinatra. Marilyn described the lover as being very unselfish in bed, but also admitted that she knew Greenson would not approve of him.

Marilyn had encountered Sinatra several times over the years, and actress Annabelle Stanford remembers her as being a little less than enamoured with him during a trip to Palm Springs in the late 1940s. 'A group of us were doing a photo shoot with Bernard of Hollywood, and afterwards we were all having dinner. Frank Sinatra was there and having something of an argument with a male friend. I remember Marilyn looking over, shaking her head and throwing her arms in the air. She was not happy and when the argument continued she left.'

As a result of a possible romance with Sinatra, any plans DiMaggio may have had to reconcile with Marilyn were put on hold. He was not at all happy that his old friend was being seen around with his ex-wife, but he continued to see Marilyn on a social basis and even attended a baseball game with her at Yankee Stadium on 11 April.

Ten days before that, on 1 April, Kay Gable wrote a letter to Marilyn, asking when she planned to go to Los Angeles to meet her baby son, John Clark. She told her that she still missed her husband each day but planned to spend the summer at their ranch, where she hoped Marilyn and Joe would visit. The letter was friendly and informal; and as a result any thoughts Marilyn may have had that Kay blamed her for Gable's death were finally dispelled.

In need of a break, Marilyn travelled to Los Angeles in April where she enjoyed going on dates and lying on her private patio at the Beverly Hills Hotel. She even took time to speak with Hedda Hopper about the *Rain* project, explaining, 'I've been looking forward to doing 'Rain' on TV for a long time. We expect to have Fredric March and Florence Eldredge playing the Rev Davidson and his wife.' However, it didn't all go to plan. Firstly, Marilyn began to learn that the stalled negotiations for *Rain* were forcing co-stars to pull out of the project, and then she was admitted to hospital for a minor gynaecological operation on 24 May. Marilyn later told her half-sister, Berniece, that during her time in the facility her father, Stanley Gifford, arrived to visit her. They sat for some time talking, though she felt the meeting lacked the affection she had always craved and found the whole episode extremely hard to process.

If this meeting took place, Gifford never publicly talked about it, not even to his son, Charles Stanley Gifford Jr, who always had a very hard time believing that Gifford Sr could be the father of Marilyn Monroe. During a 2001 conversation between Gifford Jr and Mary Sims, president of the 'Immortal Marilyn' fan club, Mary expressed how proud he must be that his father was believed to be Marilyn Monroe's father too. 'Proud of what?' Gifford Jr asked, 'That he walked out on Norma Jeane and never acknowledged her or admitted he was her father?'

'I got the distinct feeling that his concern was the perception that his father didn't do right by Norma Jeane, and the disgrace that comes down on the family name because of it,' remembered Sims. 'I said he wouldn't be the first man to have done that in history; he agreed, and then we both said at the same time "That's life."'

Declaring to Earl Wilson, 'I like my freedom; I like to play the field,' Marilyn lost weight, cut her hair short and bought a wardrobe full of new clothes. 'I'm very glad to be free again; this is the happiest I've been in a long time,' she told Hedda Hopper. She also upped her social life, too: meeting poet and idol, Carl Sandburg; travelling to Palm Springs (where she spent time with Sinatra); then dashing to Las Vegas to see him perform with Dean Martin, Peter Lawford and Sammy Davis Jr at the Sands Hotel.

Marilyn became something of a mascot for the 'Rat Pack', as Sinatra's posse were labelled. She spent time with Dean Martin and his wife in Newport Harbor; discussed making a film with Sinatra; and surprised herself by quite happily settling into life in Los Angeles. 'I've never had such a good time ever – in Hollywood,' she confided to Louella Parsons. 'For the first time in many years I am completely free to do exactly as I please. And this new freedom has made me happier. I want to look for a home to buy here; I think I'll settle in Beverly Hills.'

This was backed up by make-up artist 'Whitey' Snyder, who commented, 'Since her divorce from Arthur Miller she's been in her best condition for a long time. She's happy! I'm amazed at how well she is.'

In June 1961, Marilyn was thrilled to visit Kay Gable and meet her son, John Clark. Talking into the night with Kay, she later described the meeting as 'Wonderful . . . kind of sad too,' and declared John Clark as 'My real love; he's the big man in my life, even if he is a little young for me.' Shortly after she was honoured to attend the baby's christening, where she gleefully posed for the cameras and later mingled with guests at the Gable family home.

Marilyn seemed perfectly happy with her life in Los Angeles, but she was still desperate to get the *Rain* project off the ground. Letters had been going back and forth between parties for the past six months, and finally on 13 June a tentative production schedule was again drawn up, with Marilyn due on set from 27 July to 19 August. She returned to New York and once there held various meetings with her lawyer Aaron Frosch and NBC. She also met writer Rod Serling at her East 57th Street apartment, where they spoke about the script until the early hours. The meeting went well but Serling was furious to discover later that Marilyn was privately rehearsing a 1923 version of the play, and not the one he had written himself.

As a result of a meeting with Lee Strasberg on 21 June, Marilyn decided that he should get more control of the project and on 26 June told NBC of her plan. It was rejected immediately. However, on 27 June it was decided that Marilyn would only sign for *Rain* if she could have Richard Burton as a co-star and George Hill as director. Once again NBC refused and wrote to Marilyn to inform her of its decision to cancel the project completely.

Marilyn was disappointed but executive producer Ann Marlowe was even more so. She immediately wired the actress, declaring: 'I would like to again offer you 'Rain' for television . . . Lee Strasberg told me you were a superb Sadie Thompson.'

The telegram didn't work, however, as Marilyn replied saying she would only consider the project if Lee Strasberg was hired as the director, a request that nobody wanted to fulfil.

On 28 June the entire correspondence was filed away, with Marilyn's representatives noting that unless something new was to occur, 'this is the kiss-off'. A statement was prepared which said that Marilyn had been advised not to take part in the programme and later that day she was rushed to Polyclinic hospital suffering from what her spokesman described as 'a mild intestinal disorder'. However, it was quickly determined that there was much more to her pain than that, and a two-hour operation was performed on the evening of 29 June to remove the entire gall bladder.

The operation was a success, though Marilyn was in some considerable discomfort, especially after her departure from the hospital: 'Right after I had my gall bladder operation the crowds in the street pushed at me so hard that it opened up the incision again,' she said. She required a great deal of convalescence on her return to 57th Street, but Joe DiMaggio was on hand and Marilyn's sister, Berniece, travelled from Florida to look after her, sleeping in what was once Arthur Miller's study, helping around the house and walking Marilyn's new dog, Maf, a present from Frank Sinatra. But something was troubling Marilyn, and Berniece became worried not only about her intake of prescription pills, but also by the problems she continually seemed to encounter.

There were worries about money; anxiety over the will she had signed in January (but apparently disapproved of); concern for her career; and stress over the letters of complaint she was receiving from her mother, Gladys, who continued to live at Rockhaven Sanitarium.

Perhaps with her mind on family connections and relationships, Marilyn invited her friend from Florida, Lynn Pupello, to stay with her during the summer. To the young woman Marilyn told something she would never forget: 'She said that if she could pick out someone to be her daughter that it would be me; she liked the fact that I was a professional writer on an important newspaper; someone interested in and knowledgeable about archaeology, art history, architecture, film, theatre, literature and fine arts. She talked to me for hours about how depressed she was about her divorce [but also] talked about moving back to LA, so she gave me some of her nightgowns and jewellery, which she said I should wear whenever the time came later in life to marry.'

Other erstwhile close relationships came to the fore when, together with Ralph Roberts and Berniece Miracle, Marilyn travelled to Roxbury in order to sort out some personal items which had been overlooked during the separation and divorce. Marilyn seemed in good spirits, introducing her new dog Maf to her old love Hugo. She smiled continually as if the whole meeting had been well rehearsed. She was even cordial to Miller, and while he asked about her health and poured her a cup of tea, she took delight in showing him her gall-bladder scar, as if to prove the point that she really had been ill all those years.

But in spite of her outward confidence, being in the house she had shared with Miller all those years was a painful experience and, at the end of the meeting, she appeared to stall her departure. Getting into the car, she sat back in her seat and waved silently goodbye not only to Miller but to the place she had once thought would make her happy. She had dreamed of raising children there, of living a quiet life in the country, but it was not to be; and as she was driven past the trees and flowers she had once helped to grow, she knew she would never return to Roxbury again. It was time to move on.

By the time Marilyn had fully recovered from the gall-bladder operation, it was time for Berniece to return to Florida and Marilyn's thoughts returned once again to work. She refused Twentieth Century Fox's requests for her to do *Loss of Roses* (which later became *The Stripper* with Joanne Woodward) but they did insist she star in *Something's Got to Give*, a George Cukor-directed film, which was a remake of the 1940 movie, *My Favourite Wife*. This, along with a desire to see therapist Ralph

Greenson, prompted a return to Los Angeles in September where she settled into 882 North Doheny Drive, the apartment she had lived in before her marriage to DiMaggio in 1954.

On 22 September Marilyn returned briefly to New York, only to encounter problems during take-off, which forced the plane to return to Los Angeles. The episode disturbed her and, as soon as she touched down, she sent a telegram to Joe DiMaggio, informing him that she would be leaving again at 5 p.m., and confiding that when the plane was in trouble, the two things she thought about was, 'you, and changing my will,' before adding, 'Love you, I think, more than ever.'

On 5 October, Patricia Newcomb sent an internal memo to her own boss, the publicist Arthur P. Jacobs, informing him of Marilyn's new Los Angeles address, and urging that all mail should be addressed to Marge Stengel (a woman who had acted briefly as Marilyn's assistant). To Jacobs she urged that Marilyn's name not be put on any envelopes, and that even the street must remain secret; Marilyn was back in Los Angeles, but this time her main concern was most certainly her privacy.

But one person who did know her address was friend Ralph Roberts, whom Marilyn asked to drive cross-country to join her in California, in order to give her massages and act as something of an unofficial chauffeur. Together they enjoyed eating steaks on the barbecue, and talking quietly into the night, until it all came to a sudden halt when Marilyn told him something quite disturbing: Dr Greenson was urging her to drop old friends and, as a result, Roberts found himself travelling back to New York.

This has also been confirmed by Whitey Snyder, who told the 'All About Marilyn' club: 'Marilyn mentioned several times that Greenson often suggested there were many of her so-called friends that were only using her and she should only trust him. She laughed and said that she often trusted her so-called friends more than him. I am sure Dr Greenson did everything to keep Marilyn under his thumb.'

Much has been made of Greenson's treatment of Marilyn during her last few months, and the relationship is still shrouded in mystery today. Marilyn became Greenson's most famous client but his family now refuse to talk about her. We may never know the full extent of his control over her life, but what we do know is he did something very few doctors have done before or since – welcomed her into his home and into the bosom of his family.

The children of former therapist Marianne Kris were not involved with Marilyn in any way, but Greenson's children, Joan and Daniel, became friends with their father's patient, walking with her and sharing friendly chit-chat. It was a strange way of doing things, but he was hopeful of a successful outcome, confiding to friends that she was showing some improvement though admitting to Anna Freud that he had improvised in her treatment, often wondering where he was going yet knowing he had nowhere else to turn.

Dr Greenson discovered that Marilyn took a variety of pills including: Demerol – a narcotic analgesic; the barbiturate Phenobarbital HMC; and Amytal. She also had a unique knack of being able to get large doses of drugs from a variety of different doctors, never informing them of each other, or of other pills and prescriptions. He was concerned, especially about her use of Demerol, which was believed to be dangerous if used on a regular basis.

To Freud he described Marilyn as a sick, borderline paranoid addict and expressed how hard it was to treat someone who had such severe problems but who was also incredibly famous yet totally alone. To this end he hired a housekeeper for Marilyn: a middle-aged woman called Eunice Murray, whom he had known since he purchased her former home in Santa Monica.

Eunice seems to have been a jack of all trades, turning her hand to many different skills: dressmaking, cooking, landscaping, interior design, bookbinding and even psychology. She had worked with several psychiatrists and their patients, helping in their homes to give support of whatever nature was required. Greenson believed Murray to be an ideal choice as companion for Marilyn and so it was that in November 1961, she began work at Doheny Drive, chauffeuring Marilyn around town, helping with the groceries and performing simple housekeeping errands such as washing and cleaning. 'I was everything Marilyn needed,' Murray later said, as she recalled the vast number of tasks she undertook for the actress.

But even though Murray believed herself a trustworthy companion, this thought was not reciprocated by Marilyn's friends, with many of them wondering why she was there and what were her real motives. 'My impression of Eunice Murray was that she couldn't be trusted and that every move Marilyn made was reported immediately to Dr Greenson,' commented Whitey Snyder to the 'All About Marilyn' club. 'She was extremely quiet, secretive, and always hovering around Marilyn.' He also wondered if Dr Greenson's treatment was at all beneficial: 'As the months went by it was obvious his influence was becoming stronger and stronger,' he said. Furthermore, he felt that the frequency of visits and his twenty-four hour availability to her was 'unprofessional and greedy'.

During this time Marilyn was still extremely busy, getting ready for her next Fox production, contributing to articles for *Paris Match*, *Tempo* and *Redbook*, and giving interviews to Vernon Scott, Joe Hyams and Henry Gris. But one project was to leave a lasting impression, when photographer Douglas Kirkland was assigned to do a portrait of Marilyn for the twenty-fifth anniversary special edition of *Look* magazine.

Arriving at the small Doheny Drive apartment, his first impressions were positive: 'She was amazingly pleasant and playful like a sister and not at all intimidating as I had imagined her to be,' remembered Kirkland. 'She sat beside me, laughed easily and made small talk, putting me at ease. I was young and did not know how to ask her to pose for the sexy images I hoped to get, but she simplified it all by suggesting she should get into bed with nothing on but white silk. We discussed the details and Marilyn said she wanted Frank Sinatra music and chilled Dom Perignon.'

On the day of the photo shoot, she arrived very late and when she stepped into the room Kirkland was amazed to discover that she was now Marilyn Monroe, the superstar. He remembered: 'It was an extraordinary photo session. She was wonderful; luminous as she floated under that semi-transparent silk sheet. She arrived with her hair and make-up already done and an assistant carrying various changes of clothes although they were not really needed. She told everyone in the room, "I'd like to be alone with this boy. I find it usually works better that way." There was sexual tension in the air and it reflected in the resulting photos.'

However, the next afternoon, when Kirkland took the transparencies to Marilyn's department, there was a distinct difference in her demeanour: 'She seemed depressed. She was wearing dark glasses and might have been crying, but she eventually brightened up and decided she loved the pictures.'

Another photographer who had the opportunity of working with Marilyn in late 1961 was Eric Skipsey, who took photos of her with Maf, her small puppy. He remembered: 'Marilyn was a friend of mine but I only had one occasion to do a portrait sitting which was a success. It was a bit complicated in that the publicist was three-quarters of an hour late in arriving, during which time we talked and joked and even had a small taste of champagne to pass the time away. When the female publicist finally arrived she turned to me and said, "You have ten minutes Mr Skipsey," and Marilyn immediately said, "You have as long as you wish Eric, they are my pictures, not hers." We worked together for another hour and in fact Marilyn said I could have more time if I wished. This attitude was typical of her: she did not behave like a superstar; she was a nice and considerate person.'

By December 1961 Marilyn's therapy with Greenson was having its ups and downs, though she was committed to it, despite the pain it was causing. One aspect of the treatment – that of Greenson's desire to get Marilyn working and studying once again – inspired her to write to Lee Strasberg on 19 December. In the letter, she informed her coach that through the absence of his lessons, she felt as though only half of her was functioning. She had big plans for the future and was desperate for Strasberg to move to California to work as part of a new independent production unit she was hoping to form; so determined was she that she even wrote to Marlon Brando asking for his opinion on how best to get Lee to Los Angeles, declaring that 'time is of the essence'.

She once told reporters that, 'I seem to be a whole superstructure without any foundation,' and as 1961 rolled into 1962, she said that she was now 'working on the foundation'. At her side once again was Joe DiMaggio, shopping with her for Christmas presents on Olvera Street, buying her a little Christmas tree for her apartment, and even attending a seasonal dinner with the Greenson family and their friends. But the event wasn't altogether successful, when the men at the house gathered around DiMaggio and bombarded him with baseball questions. Marilyn laughed when it was commented that the men were paying no attention to her at all but, in reality, she did not find it particularly funny.

In January 1962 Marilyn's relationship with the Strasbergs started to cool slightly when she discovered that a television project was being planned about the Actors Studio and that Lee initially did not want her to know about it, changing his mind only at the last moment. She then received a letter from Paula, asking her to sign a statement so that work could begin, which left her 'confused by the entire situation'. Writing to Lee in mid-January, Marilyn demanded to know what her part would be in the television programme; what the idea and purpose was behind the project; and made it clear that there was no way she could possibly become involved when there were so many unanswered questions.

Another difficult friendship was the one she had with Frank Sinatra, which went off the boil one day when Marilyn started telling him about her childhood. 'Oh not that again,' he exclaimed. Marilyn was not pleased by his rebuttal of her woes, and shortly afterwards she surprised friends by refusing to give him copies of photos from a recent boat trip. 'I've already given him enough,' she told them.

Marilyn was a warm-hearted person to people she liked, but she could also be something of a 'monster', as she admitted to reporter W. J. Weatherby in 1961. One person who saw this side of her was Michael Selsman, who worked with her through the Arthur P. Jacobs agency. 'She was Pat Newcomb's client,' said Selsman, 'but Pat was frequently busy with some of her other clients, so I was detailed to cover certain PR functions for her. It was always difficult to work with Marilyn – sometimes unpleasant. I had other "difficult" clients but they were also kind and generous, which Marilyn was not. She made it hard for me (and others around her) to do our jobs – just because she could. It's tempting to say she was a spoiled brat, but it went deeper than that. She could be mean, spiteful, threatening and duplicitous; to the point I dreaded having to see her.'

On one occasion in January 1962, Selsman and his wife Carol Lynley travelled to the Doheny Drive apartment for a meeting with Marilyn: 'Carol was nine months pregnant, due any moment now. I couldn't and didn't want to leave her at home by herself, so I took her along to Monroe's apartment, where Marilyn was to look at negatives from a photo shoot she had just done with the hot new photographer, twenty-one-year-old Doug Kirkland, for *Look* magazine. I knocked on her door, as Carol stood shivering beside me. Marilyn opened the door and looked at Carol, whom she knew, since they had adjacent dressing rooms at the studio, and said, "You come in," motioning to me, "but she can wait in your car." This was unexpected and I was momentarily stunned. Carol and I exchanged glances, and I assured her I'd be out in fifteen minutes. I was frankly scared. Monroe was one of our biggest clients and I did not want to confront her, or lose my job.

'Every other actor I worked with would use a red grease pencil to put an X through the negatives they didn't like, but not Monroe. She took scissors and cut out every one she did not like, then cut those into tiny splinters and threw them in the wastebasket. This laborious process took three hours, during which I repeatedly got up to leave. Marilyn kept ordering me to sit down. To be young is to be stupid, someone said, and if I were ever in a situation like that again, I might be out of a job, but I might have still had a wife. It was my first evidentiary of Marilyn Monroe's capacity for cruelty.'

Despite suffering from flu, Marilyn continued with her own projects, among them getting out of her contract with MCA; and hiring a new lawyer, in the shape of Milton 'Mickey' Rudin – Greenson's brother-in-law. On a creative level she attended a meeting with Alan Levy from *Redbook* on 25 January and then another with Richard Meryman, who wished to do an interview for *Life* magazine. According to memos from the Arthur P. Jacob's agency, Marilyn reacted very well to Meryman, though less so with a reporter who was also in attendance and apparently a little drunk. Constantly interrupting both Marilyn and Meryman, the reporter spoke to the actress as if she were 'underprivileged' and became absolutely hysterical when told that all photos not approved by Marilyn would be destroyed. 'How can you dare such a thing?' she demanded, to which a surprised Marilyn replied, 'You're giving me a fishy-eyed stare but I love you anyway.'

On a personal level, Marilyn decided she wanted her own home, becoming tired of living in hotels and rented apartments. She ideally wanted something near to the coast and with a Mexican style close to that of the Greenson home, which she idolized. Eunice Murray was pleased to help and over the course of several weeks took Marilyn to various locations, looking for the ideal home. Unfortunately, the happy search was marred slightly when she was literally thrown out of one house by the female owner who resented the presence of the movie star in her home. This was not a happy incident by any means, and according to friends it disturbed Marilyn greatly.

However, not long after there was cause for celebration when Murray found the ideal property in the shape of 12305 Fifth Helena Drive, a small house in Brentwood, located at the end of a tiny side street. The bungalow had thick walls, heavy beams and bars on the front windows, which afforded Marilyn a sense of security, along with a tile at the front door which read 'Cursum Perficio' – meaning 'I've finished my journey'. At the back of the house there was a terrace, a kidney-shaped swimming pool and large garden that cascaded down the hillside, giving out to a magnificent view of the streets below; Marilyn loved it.

After asking Joe DiMaggio to look over the house for her, it was decided that the kitchen would be remodelled completely and other rooms would be decorated in both Mexican fixtures and fittings. She had her lawyer, Milton Rudin, draw up the papers and, despite feeling saddened by the fact that she was buying a home on her own, she signed and began making plans for the future. 'The house was important for Marilyn,' recounted Eunice Murray, 'her doctor thought it would take the place of a baby or husband.'

Marilyn herself expressed her love for the house by exclaiming, 'It's the first house I've ever owned and I bought it because it reminded me so much of the orphanages I was brought up in as a child.' This was a strange comment based on her previous statements about orphanage life, but showed a positive shift with regards to the way she viewed her childhood memories.

A variety of people were hired to help restore the Fifth Helena Drive home, including handyman Norman Jeffries and his brother Keith. There was also the Twentieth Century Fox electrician, James A. Gough, whose son Jim went with him to the home one Saturday afternoon. He remembered: 'Marilyn and Mrs Murray were delighted as they had just discovered the original fireplace with Mexican tiles, under a layer of plaster, and they were happily cleaning the tiles when we arrived. Marilyn showed us around the home and the garden and I was surprised to discover that the house wasn't grand. It was a simple, 1930s Spanish renaissance style and Marilyn had found that she loved gardening, although she had never had the opportunity to do it before.'

In early February 1962 Marilyn went briefly to New York and then on 17 February travelled to Miami in order to visit her former father-in-law, Isidore Miller. He had been staying at the Sea Isle Hotel for some time, but feeling lonely had been delighted when Marilyn told him of her plans to visit him. On 19 February, after a poignant few days with 'Dad', Marilyn flew to Mexico along with Pat Newcomb and several other members of staff. There she met up with Eunice Murray, who had travelled down the week before, scouting out places of interest and visiting with her brother-in-law, Churchill Murray.

Despite the fact that the trip was officially to buy furniture for her home, it captured the attention of the FBI, who had been keeping a discreet, watchful eye on Marilyn since the mid-1950s after she expressed a desire to visit Russia, and then began dating Arthur Miller. From Mexico an unnamed informant sent little snippets of information to Washington, DC, declaring that Marilyn had been associating closely with certain members of the American Communist Group in Mexico (ACGM) and that a mutual infatuation had developed between Marilyn and a gentleman called Frederick Vanderbilt Field. Field had served nine months in prison for refusing to name his communist friends, before finally moving to Mexico in 1953. (Although his name is blanked out on most of the FBI documents, there remains one instance where his name has been mistakenly left in, making it almost certain that Fields is the man to whom the reports referred.)

According to the documents, Marilyn spent a great deal of time with the married Field. Whether or not there was any real romance between Field and Marilyn, they certainly spent some time together, such as on 21 February when he was said to have visited her in Suite 1110 of the Hotel Continental Hilton and on 24 February when she travelled with him to a native market in Toluca.

Whoever the informant was for this and other information remains unclear, but it was most definitely somebody who was able to gain access both to Marilyn and her entourage – particularly Eunice Murray (who is falsely identified as Eunice Churchill in the FBI files). The informant seems to have spoken with Murray, quoting her as saying that Marilyn was greatly disturbed by Miller's recent marriage to Inge Morath, a photographer he met on *The Misfits* set, and that she felt like a 'negated sex symbol'.

If the informant is to be believed, the friendship with Field caused 'considerable dismay' both among members of the ACGM and Marilyn's entourage, particularly Eunice Murray, who felt that Marilyn was becoming increasingly dependent on him and was very vulnerable at the present time due to her rejection by Arthur Miller, Joe DiMaggio and Frank Sinatra.

The exact nature of their relationship will probably never be known, but Field was married at the time and his wife Nieves was certainly in attendance during the Mexico trip and later travelled with her husband to New York, staying in Marilyn's apartment for three weeks while she was in Los Angeles. So unless the relationship was carried out in full view of Field's wife and with her approval, it would seem most likely that there was a mutual attraction, rather than a full-blown affair. As well as that, on 25 February Marilyn cancelled a date with a furious Field just five minutes before he was due to collect her, which is hardly the behaviour of a lovestruck woman.

One person who was touted as boyfriend material was José Bolaños, a Mexican fan/scriptwriter who lived with his parents, brothers and a daughter by a previous marriage. How they met remains something of a mystery, but Bolaños showed Marilyn around local nightspots and at the end of the visit gave her every photo he could find of them together. 'She was the most funny person I have ever met,' he later told reporter Glenn Thomas Carter. 'She had one quality that really delighted me – the ability to demolish verbally anyone who proved to be obnoxious to her.'

Apart from an official date at the Golden Globe awards in Los Angeles, the 'romance' between Bolaños and Marilyn does not seem to have been very serious. However, he did agree to help her with something much more important than a relationship – the possible adoption of a child.

*   *   *

According to an intriguing article published in *Motion Picture* magazine, reporter Glenn Thomas Carter accompanied Marilyn during a night out in Acapulco, where she came face to face with an eight-year-old boy who was entertaining customers. The article did not name the child but, according to Carter, Marilyn became intrigued by the youngster and bombarded him with questions about his background. His parents were dead, she discovered, and he had run away from his uncle and then worked on a construction site, where he was allowed to sleep in a hammock on the scaffolding. He no longer worked on the site but his life had not improved, since he was now living in a shack with foster-parents who had taught him how to dance and pickpocket tourists.

Marilyn was dumbfounded and when she broke down in tears, the young boy joined her, crying and asking if he might be able to live with her in California. Impulsively Marilyn said yes, and the next day went to visit his foster-parents, informing them that her friend Jose Bolaños would arrange all the details of the adoption for her.

Shortly afterwards, Marilyn visited a Mexican orphanage where she was given the opportunity of adopting a baby, but turned it down, instead donating $10,000 to further their cause. Then at a farewell party, Marilyn told other guests of her intentions to adopt a Mexican child, and later, her stand-in Evelyn Moriarty recalled, 'It was around this time that I first heard talk of Marilyn trying to adopt a child. I heard that her trip to Mexico was for more than buying furniture.'

Chapter 20

Cursum Perficio

On her return to Los Angeles from Mexico, Marilyn attended the Golden Globe Awards with José Bolaños, where she received an award for the World Film Favourite, then in early March 1962 she enrolled the help of Joe DiMaggio to help move into her new home. The house was still being heavily remodelled and there was virtually no furniture, but Marilyn didn't care. 'I just want to live in my own house,' she told friends, as she busied herself with making the property into a home, ready for the arrival of the child from Mexico.

One or two items were lost in the relocation, among them some questions submitted to Marilyn from *Paris Match*, which were due to run alongside photos by photographer Willy Rizzo. These photos showed a very different side to Marilyn, in that her hair is rumpled, her clothes are plain and she looks thin and exhausted. Still, she loved them and on 9 March Pat Newcomb wrote to Rizzo to express that Marilyn thought the photos were sensational and she looked forward to working with him again.

Meanwhile, costume tests were looming for her next film, *Something's Got to Give*, and she undertook fittings at Fifth Helena with designer Jean Louis, while hosting a champagne and caviar party for the seamstresses and fitters. She seemed happy to begin what was to be her last Fox film, even though the script was still undergoing rewrites. Indeed, from 1960 to 1961 there had been five writers assigned to the project: Edmund Hartman did at least three versions of the script, while Gene Allen, Nunnally Johnson and Arnold Schulman all tried their hands at it. Finally, Walter Bernstein was brought in to do final rewrites to a script that was shaky at best.

One Fox executive said in 1961 that the script was old-fashioned, full of hokum and just not funny, while adding that there was nothing to suggest a successful film could be made from it. He was perhaps right; the story was of a woman who has been stranded on a desert island for five years, only to return home to find herself legally dead and her husband remarried. Her young children do not remember her, so she instals herself in the home as a maid in order to get to know her family once again and win back her husband.

As late as February 1962, the leading man had yet to be cast, while quite disturbingly, Fox Studio Chief Peter Levathes got Greenson involved in production, in order to control Marilyn. This resulted in producer David Brown being 'discreetly' replaced by the psychiatrist's friend Henry Weinstein, much to the dismay of the director, George Cukor.

Already the production was going over budget, which was not a good sign, as Fox was in dire financial straits over the disruption and delays on the set of the Elizabeth Taylor film, *Cleopatra*, being filmed in Rome. Fox employees had been told they had to water their own plants and bring their own lunch to the studio, since the gardeners and cafeteria staff had been laid off. 'The place was like a ghost town,' remembered one Fox employee.

Still, plans continued to ensure *Something's Got to Give* would be ready to begin shooting as soon as possible, and actress Edith Evanson was brought in to help Marilyn with the Swedish accent she would need in order to play 'Miss Tic', the woman 'Ellen' pretends to be when she realizes her husband has remarried. Marilyn was in a philosophical mood during the time they spent together, asking on one occasion, 'Isn't it a terrible thing about life that there always must be something we have to live up to?'

One morning Marilyn came into the house with a magnolia, and when Evanson asked where she got it from, she explained that she picked it while out walking with her boyfriend the night before. Evanson did not ask who her boyfriend was, but assumed that it must have been José Bolaños. When it came time for Evanson to leave, Marilyn pleaded with the actress to accompany her to New York for the weekend, but it was not a possibility: 'She was so pleading,' recalled Evanson, 'but I couldn't leave my husband and my home. She understood.'

In spring Marilyn was happy to hear from an old friend, Norman Rosten, who had travelled to California for six weeks. He visited her often during his trip and she showed him around her new house, urging him to use her pool and laughing at things that had gone wrong in her life. She was optimistic about the future, but still Rosten couldn't help worrying about her, sensing that she was 'tired to her soul'. When it came time for him to travel back to New York, Marilyn seemed frightened to see him go and berated him for not using her pool. To help cheer her up, he took her to an art gallery where she bought a bronze copy of a Rodin statue for over $1,000, before finally bidding her old friend goodbye.

April had the beginnings of a busy month. On 6 April Marilyn heard news of someone who had meant so much to her years before – Milton Greene. She received a telegram from Kathleen Casey, the editor-in-chief of *Glamour* magazine, asking her to join other famous women and the famous hairdresser, Kenneth, for a portrait Greene was taking on 13 April. Although she could probably have gone if she wanted to, she asked Pat Newcomb to send her regrets, and busied herself with other things, such as giving her consent on 9 April to become a Founder Member of the Hollywood Museum, sending her (tax-deductible) fee of $1,000.

On 10 April she attended costume tests at Fox, then on the morning of 11 April Marilyn spoke with photographer Bert Stern about a session he wished to shoot for *Vogue*. She was delighted with his ideas for the shoot. She gave her suggestions as to which designers they should use, and then told him she'd be happy to dedicate an entire weekend to give him 'all the time you need'. There were also plans afoot to film a Christmas Seal charity trailer, which Newcomb thought to be an important public service for Marilyn to take part in, and on 11 April urged Henry Weinstein to film it whenever possible.

Everything appeared to be looking up, but Henry Weinstein remembered a disturbing event on one particular day, when Marilyn was due to attend a production meeting with him. When she didn't show up, he was worried enough to go to Fifth Helena Drive, where he claims to have discovered an unconscious Monroe, almost naked and sprawled across the bed. She had apparently taken an overdose, but Weinstein had arrived just in time, summoning Dr Greenson and Dr Engelberg for help. Both doctors had long-since been concerned with Marilyn's sudden mood swings and her habit of mixing sleeping pills with champagne, to the extent that Engelberg had kept a key to Doheny Drive and both had access to keys at Fifth Helena. When Weinstein returned to Fox that day, he begged executives to postpone the production of *Something's Got to Give*. They refused.

Picking herself up once again, Marilyn headed to New York where she studied with the Strasbergs and saw friends. Unfortunately, she also caught a cold and by 19 April, when she returned to Los Angeles with Paula in tow, she was in the grips of a bad case of sinusitis, which quickly turned into a bronchial infection.

On 23 April, the first official day of shooting, Marilyn did not show up and the schedule was quickly rearranged to shoot scenes between Dean Martin, Cyd Charisse and the child actors. They worked around her for a full week, until finally on 30 April Marilyn arrived on set, where she was greeted by a friendly telegram from Arthur P. Jacobs, wishing her luck for her new movie and signing it with love and kisses, 'The Right Arthur'.

Despite running a 101°C temperature due to her persistent sinusitis, Marilyn worked a full day, shooting a scene in which she reacts to seeing her children for the first time in five years.

The next day, 1 May, she arrived once again with a temperature, only this time the studio physician Lee Seigel examined her, decided it was extremely unwise to expose the children to her contagious virus infection, and sent her home.

Taking to bed on the advice of Dr Seigel, Marilyn was absent for the rest of the week, while shooting continued at Fox, up to the point where executives declared that no more could be done without her cooperation. Adding to her problems was the re-emergence of old teacher Natasha Lytess, who had been found by *France-Dimanche* magazine, and had been paid $10,000 for her cooperation with a tell-all story. Some of the memories she shared with the magazine were so intimate they could not be published, but although the Arthur P. Jacobs agency offered to buy the article from them, the publishers refused, convinced that they could make at least $200,000 if they ever decided to publish.

However, for now Natasha Lytess was the least of Marilyn's worries. At the beginning of production, Marilyn had received permission to travel to New York to perform at President Kennedy's birthday party on the 19 May. She was committed to the appearance, having been specially invited to perform, and in May (while she was absent from the set), newspapers reported that she was 'knocking herself out' to rehearse for her performance.

On 11 May Fox's Peter Levathes spoke to lawyer Milton Rudin to inform him that he would not consent to Marilyn attending the celebration, since they were now so far behind schedule. However, when she returned to the set on 14 May, Marilyn either did not know of this withdrawn consent or did not care. Either way, on 17 May she left Los Angeles for New York, telling reporters, 'I told the studio six weeks ago that I was going. I consider it an honour to appear before the President of the United States.'

Pat Newcomb threw in her two cents' worth by saying, 'It was a democratic fundraising affair and she didn't want to break her promise to such an important organization.' Back on the set, no one could believe she had gone: 'It was like the roof caving in. It was awful,' remembered Evelyn Moriarty.

Rumours of an affair between Marilyn and both Jack and Robert Kennedy have been rife since the 1960s. The general feeling is that she was romanced by Jack, then later passed along to Bobby when the President had become bored. There is no concrete evidence to prove or disprove these rumours, but she certainly met them both on several occasions, including at a party at the home of Peter Lawford and his wife, Patricia Kennedy, in October 1961, when she bombarded Patricia's brother, Bobby, the Attorney General, with questions supplied by Daniel Greenson. Then Whitey Snyder drove Marilyn to the Lawfords' home in February 1962, where there was a party held for President Kennedy, while Ralph Roberts was said to have received a call from her on 24 March 1962 as she was spending time with the President at the home of Bing Crosby.

Meanwhile, Vanessa Steinberg, daughter of Marilyn's gynae-cologist Oscar Steinberg, remembered her father sharing thoughts on the Kennedy relationship with her: 'By the time my father saw Marilyn at Cedars hospital in Los Angeles [*c*.1961] she was well and truly having an affair with Robert Kennedy. According to him it was Bobby Kennedy whom she was madly in love with and she had no intention of returning to a rela-tionship with DiMaggio.' Interestingly, Steinberg also told his daughter that Marilyn had fallen for Kennedy whilst she was still with Miller.

Press representative Michael Selsman firmly believes she was having an affair with both Kennedy brothers at different times: 'Of course she was and everyone knew it, but in those days, the press had a different relationship with celebs, both in showbiz and in politics. I usually gave reporters inside stuff on other clients to assuage their desire to publish something about Marilyn and the Kennedys.'

In the 1980s Eunice Murray affirmed that both brothers were important in Marilyn's life, and certainly we know that she was friends with Patricia Kennedy and Peter Lawford. But as for a romance, some people are doubtful. Certainly a friend of Bobby Kennedy's later told reporters that there was not even the faintest romantic interest on either side, and that the relationship only consisted of Bobby providing a friendly ear for Marilyn's numerous problems. Not everyone in Marilyn's circle trusted the rumours either: 'I never believed 90 per cent of what was written about the involvement with the Kennedys,' remarked Whitey Snyder some thirty years later.

Regardless of that, Marilyn certainly caused a stir at President Kennedy's birthday party, when she arrived with her ex-father-in-law Isidore Miller. Wearing a skin-tight, sparkling dress which was designed to make her look nude, Marilyn shimmered her way on to the stage, after being introduced by Peter Lawford as 'The late Marilyn Monroe', the running joke of the evening being that Marilyn was never on time. She stood for a moment, looking around her, before breathily reciting 'Happy Birthday Mr President', and a reworking of 'Thanks for the Memory'.

In Nevada, old flame Bill Pursel was watching: 'I saw this performance on TV and just shook my head in disgust. I don't think I'm a prude, far from it actually . . . But there's something about this type of public exhibition which lowers the respect for femininity. What in hell was she trying to prove?'

Marilyn was extremely nervous on the evening of the party, and certainly the grainy footage seems to show her a little 'tipsy', but she got through it all okay; prompting John F. Kennedy to announce: 'I can now retire from politics after having had Happy Birthday sung to me in such a sweet, wholesome way.'

When Marilyn returned to Los Angeles, she spoke with reporters about her experience at Madison Square Garden: 'I liked it. I like celebrating birthdays. I enjoy knowing that I'm alive; and you can underline alive.' However, she was sad that she had lost a good luck charm – a pawn from her chess set – and felt extremely fatigued, which once again affected her work on the film, preventing close-ups and forcing filters to be used to hide her exhaustion.

On 22 May Marilyn refused to work with Dean Martin as he had a slight cold and she was afraid of catching it, but on the next day everyone's spirits were raised when she filmed a nude swim scene, which was the first ever by a major American actress. Suffering from earache, Marilyn did not take the scene lightly: she banned most people from the set and demanded that Whitey Snyder look through the lens to make sure it was not too risqué. She was happy with the results, though, and delighted that the photos would 'knock Liz Taylor off the front pages'.

That weekend Henry Weinstein tried to contact her to no avail and on Monday she phoned in sick. When she turned up on Tuesday, 29 May she was unfocused and repeatedly forgot her lines. On the morning of 1 June, Marilyn's thirty-sixth birthday, Evelyn Moriarty went to Farmer's Market to pick up her birthday cake. Arriving back on set, she was shocked to be told that under no circumstances must she bring it on to the set until 5.30 p.m. 'She's got to do a full day's work first,' she was told.

By the end of the day, the sparkle-decorated cake was wheeled out, along with a personalized 'Happy Birthday (suit)' card, which everyone had signed. Marilyn loved the gesture and stayed for a while to enjoy a small celebration, before heading to Dodger Stadium to attend a charity baseball game. For once all seemed to be well, but again it was a misapprehension; on 2 June, the Greenson children were shocked to find Marilyn depressed and inconsolable at her home in Brentwood, so much so that they called Dr Leon Uhley who was standing in for their father while he was holidaying in Europe. Uhley was so shocked to see Marilyn in such a state that he promptly confiscated her pills. Then by Monday she was unable to work once again, reportedly causing everyone on the set to 'tear our hair out'.

By this time it became apparent that Marilyn was in a terrible state, and as a result, Dr Greenson was forced to leave his wife in Rome and return to Los Angeles. He arrived at Marilyn's house to find her heavily drugged but feeling much better, and immediately went into a meeting with Fox executives, assuring them that he could get her back on to the set, and declaring that although he did not want his relationship to be described as a Svengali one, he could persuade her to do 'anything reasonable' that he wanted. But unfortunately for both Marilyn and Greenson, Fox had had enough. Feeling the stresses and strains of delays on the set of Elizabeth Taylor's film, *Cleopatra*, they just could not believe that Marilyn would complete the film without incident, and on 8 June, announced that she had been fired.

Almost straight away Fox took out a $500,000 lawsuit against their star, citing Marilyn's failure and refusal to perform in *Something's Got to Give*, and she even found herself lumbered with an invoice for $5,000 from the production photographer Don Ornitz, a situation that infuriated Pat Newcomb so much that she called in Marilyn's lawyer, Milton Rudin. Meanwhile, people started to blame her for the loss of 104 jobs. 'In my opinion, Marilyn cannot face reality,' commented one crew member, while an extra was quick to tell the press that she took hours to get to the set, stumbled on her lines, then had lunch in her dressing room. Marilyn tried to counteract this backlash with telegrams hand-delivered to cast and crew on 11 June. In each one she explained that what happened was not her fault and that she had so looked forward to working on the picture.

She also confided to staff at the Arthur P. Jacobs Agency that she believed the studio was in a panic, choosing to blame her because it had overextended itself on *Cleopatra*, and pointing out that there were still scenes to be shot that didn't involve her, and which had not even been written yet. In short, Marilyn was angry and for good reason; she had worked at the studio for sixteen years, was by far their biggest player and yet she had still been fired. 'Remember, you're not a star,' they had told her in 1952, a philosophy still adhered to by various executives in the summer of 1962.

Marilyn's representatives were keen to get the film back on track just as soon as possible, with 23 July being put forward as a possible start-date. They informed Fox of their wishes, and the studio replied with a stern letter, stating that if the film were to go back into production on that date, there would have to be a number of strict rules in place: there would be no consultation or approval over co-stars, other players, director, script, number of takes, photos, crew (including make-up, hairdresser or wardrobe); Marilyn would have to arrive at the studio on time and take lunch breaks only at times specified by Fox; Paula Strasberg would not be allowed on set and neither would her PR representatives, agents or associates of her lawyer. In short, Marilyn was to have no control over any aspect of the film but in return, Fox would drop their lawsuit against her.

This letter did nothing for relations between studio and star, but fortunately for Marilyn, she still had her allies on set, with one player declaring that he could not feel bitter towards her: 'I can't forget the sadness I saw in her eyes.' Dean Martin also proved to be a true friend, when Fox told him they were replacing Marilyn with Lee Remick; he shook his head, handed in his resignation, and walked off set, much to Marilyn's delight.

Eager to keep herself in the public eye, Marilyn embarked on a series of PR exercises, one of which was the long-awaited *Vogue* photo spread with photographer Bert Stern, on 23–5 June. Then shortly after she undertook a variety of sessions for *Cosmopolitan*, with friend and photographer George Barris, during which time he took hundreds of photos on the sand behind the Lawford house and in a privately owned home in the Hollywood Hills.

On the surface at least, it appeared that Marilyn was taking control of her life and career: she attended several meetings to get *Something's Got to Give* back into production, she went to a party for Robert Kennedy at the Lawfords' beach house, and enjoyed the numerous photo sessions. But not everything was rosy, as Michael Selsman remembered: 'She was upset about various things – always. It was clear she was unhappy 24/7.' Some of her friends worried about her mental health, too, with the threat of an overdose being high on their list of concerns: 'It was a problem for her friends,' confided one associate. Meanwhile, she was not in the best physical health, still addicted to pills and now receiving liver injections from Dr Engelberg in an effort to strengthen her system.

During interviews she did with George Barris, Marilyn spoke about the subject of adoption, declaring her belief that no single person should ever adopt a child, as 'there's no Ma or Pa there'. Considering her earlier plans to adopt the Mexican boy, these comments are intriguing and lead to questions about whether or not the adoption plans had fallen through.

Shortly after her death, it was reported in the Mexican press that Marilyn had become thoroughly depressed over a sudden coldness from José Bolaños, yet this seems an absurd notion, since the relationship never appeared to be anything but casual. What could be closer to the truth is that her depression was brought on by the realization that Bolaños was unable or unwilling to help with the adoption plans. In 1963, reporter Glenn Thomas Carter asked him why the adoption had fallen through, but he refused to answer, stating that it was between himself and Marilyn. If she had simply changed her mind, or if legal aspects had been the problem, surely there would be no reason to withhold his answer. But if Bolaños had decided not to help with the adoption, perhaps the fear that this had been what finally pushed her 'over the edge' was enough to stop him ever discussing his famous friend.

As for the child himself, reporter Glenn Thomas Carter found him in Mexico City a year after Marilyn's death, where he was living with a couple and going to school. Describing her as a 'beautiful friend', the child told the reporter: 'I was sad for many months because the beautiful blonde senorita did not come for me as she promised.' He has never been found again.

Adding to the complications surrounding Marilyn's life in 1962 is the rumour that, sometime during the summer, she either aborted a baby or suffered a miscarriage. There is no documented evidence to prove or disprove this, but press representative Michael Selsman insists that he heard the story at the time: 'Marilyn didn't directly tell me,' he recalled; 'Arthur [Jacobs] and I were told by Pat [Newcomb], in that we had to know to counter any rumours – since the two major Hollywood columnists, Louella Parsons and Hedda Hopper, had paid spies in the hospitals and labs, so they knew pretty much what was happening.' Selsman believes the pregnancy to be a product 'of either Jack or Bobby, she didn't know which, since the switch had taken place recently'.

Adding to the mystery is a $25 invoice, dated 7 June 1962, from the office of Dr Steinberg and Dr Conti, which states Marilyn underwent an 'X-ray of nasal bones' procedure. This is an intriguing document for a variety of reasons, not least of which is the fact that Dr Steinberg was one of Marilyn's gynae-cologists, not a nasal specialist, while Dr Conti was his anaes-thetist. Daughter Vanessa Steinberg was asked to comment on the invoice and had the following to say: 'The procedure would have been performed at Cedars hospital in Los Angeles. [My father] saw her many times in Los Angeles and I am certain that the procedures did not involve x-raying of nasal bones. My father was not a nasal surgeon and I have no idea what the actual procedures where – I assume follow-on routine dilate and curette procedures for her gynaecological ailments, or else perhaps a termination or dilate and curette after a miscar-riage? Apparently she suffered from severe endometriosis and this may have been a procedure in relation to that, which was written down as x-ray of nasal bones. I can only speculate that the procedure you refer to was something that she wanted to remain a secret and this is not an uncommon practice in medi-cine, particularly if the patient was a celebrity. I know that in New York she was treated and admitted to Mount Sinai under a pseudonym. I can say, with some certainty, that the procedure most likely had nothing to do with x-raying of nasal bones.'

This document not only adds fuel to the abortion/miscar-riage rumour but also to a persistent story of Marilyn visiting plastic surgeon, Dr Gurdin, after what was described by Dr Greenson as a 'fall in the shower'. Dr Gurdin had performed the slight plastic surgery on Marilyn's chin all those years ago, and examined her in the summer of 1962, to determine if she had broken her nose. She hadn't, but the appointment has been tied in with the 'x-ray of nasal bones' procedure over the years, although in reality it is extremely unlikely that they were in any way related.

During the upheavals and obvious health problems, both Marilyn and her representatives continued their quest to get *Something's Got to Give* back into production, with pressure being put on Fox by the White House itself and Robert Kennedy in particular. Meanwhile, Pat Newcomb tried to keep her friend upbeat by sending a letter on 11 July which listed nineteen magazine and newspaper articles that had appeared over the past few weeks, along with a variety of others to look forward to in the future. She also sent a copy of *Redbook* magazine on 19 July, for which Marilyn had done an interview. Both star and representative were disappointed that the article did not contain the human insight they had wanted to see, but Newcomb herself felt it was the first positive story she'd read in quite some time.

Newcomb was trying very hard to cheer her client and friend but it came at a price, as by now unfair and absurd rumours were beginning to spread that their friendship was more than platonic. 'They were very close friends,' remembered Michael Selsman. 'I never saw them do anything of an intimate nature together, but there were rumours.' Disturbingly, Selsman remembered the rumours coming principally from some of the main players in Marilyn's circle – people who she trusted and should have known better than to gossip about their friend and employer.

On 19 July Marilyn hosted a dinner party for Greenson's children at Fifth Helena, then on 21 July, according to some sources, she underwent a gynaecological procedure at Cedars and was picked up afterwards by Joe DiMaggio. She rested for several days afterwards, and then resumed her summer of interviews and photos, while her lawyers continued their negotiations with Fox. One of the interviews Marilyn gave during that time was with *Life*'s Richard Meryman. It was the last one she ever gave, and in it she complained magnificently about the studio and the treatment of their stars, declaring for the first time in her career that fame was a burden. By the time the interview ended, Marilyn was beginning to worry about her comments and asked Meryman not to make her look like a joke. He promised he wouldn't, and kept his word; when the article was published on 3 August 1962 it showed her as a mature, sensible woman, who was obviously learning much from the hand she'd been dealt.

On the weekend of 28–9 July, Marilyn travelled to Cal-Neva Lodge & Casino, in Lake Tahoe, where she visited with Frank Sinatra, Peter Lawford and his wife Patricia. Much has been said about this weekend, from the depressing – Joe DiMaggio followed Marilyn but was not allowed on the premises, leaving her to watch him sadly from afar – to the truly disturbing – she was drugged and photographed in various states of undress in order to ensure her silence regarding her relationship with the Kennedys.

There is virtually no factual information available about the weekend at all, but there are several photos that appear to show Marilyn at the resort, and give us some insight into the mood surrounding her at the time. Much has been said about Frank Sinatra not being happy with his former girlfriend, and the photos show that to be most probably true. Singer Buddy Greco was performing at the resort at the time, and is seen in one photo sharing a friendly embrace with Marilyn, with both smiling broadly. However, Sinatra is also in the photo, sitting on a deck chair, holding a newspaper and looking up at the couple in a disapproving manner. Another photo shows Sinatra still sitting in the chair, continuing to look unhappy, while an unknown gentleman views Marilyn's derrière as she walks away from the camera.

Regardless of the source, the general feeling is that the 'Cal-Neva weekend', as it has come to be called, was not a particularly happy one. Marilyn was said to be depressed and according to some sources almost overdosed in one of the bungalows, saved only by the fact that she had kept a telephone line open to the casino operator. There is also talk of Frank Sinatra being so wound up by her drugged and drunken behaviour that he eventually asked both Marilyn and the Lawfords to leave the premises; Peter and Marilyn flew back to Los Angeles, while Patricia travelled to the Kennedy compound at Hyannis Port.

What is interesting to note, however, is that if the Cal-Neva weekend was as bad as rumoured, Marilyn felt stable enough not to call out either Dr Greenson or Dr Engelberg when she returned home on Sunday. Instead, she was driven to Greenson's office the next day for a routine appointment, and did not see Engelberg again until two days later, on 1 August.

According to some sources, 1 August was a big day for Marilyn – Peter Levathes had visited the actress at home and, as a result, Twentieth Century Fox had renewed her contract, giving her a large pay rise and a promise that *Something's Got to Give* would be resumed. However, there is some question as to whether or not the contract had actually been drawn up by the time Marilyn died. There is no trace of it in either the Fox or Arthur P. Jacobs archives, and no copies have ever been made public.

However, on 1 August she did speak on the telephone to Evelyn Moriarty, who remembered she was happy because negotiations were going well with Fox and she was sure they would be back in production soon: 'that's how close they were to settling their differences,' said Moriarty. George Barris remembers speaking with Marilyn on 3 August and discovered her to be very excited as the studio were going to give her an increase and start the film again in a month. So certainly negotiations did seem to have been progressing, but it must be noted that Twentieth Century Fox never confirmed the contract renewal when she died, and the film continued to be described as 'shelved' in the newspapers.

Meanwhile, Joe DiMaggio was becoming deeply worried about the health and wellbeing of his former wife, and on 1 August he resigned his $100,000 a year job as a representative for military goods supply company V.H. Monette, and travelled back to San Francisco. According to *Where Have You Gone*

Joe DiMaggio? by Maury Allen, DiMaggio told his colleague, Sid Luckman, that he was leaving because he had decided to ask Marilyn to marry him once again. Unfortunately, his decision was in vain, as by the time he arrived in Los Angeles on 5 August, Marilyn was already dead.

Some authors have claimed that the couple were due to be remarried on 8 August – the date of Marilyn's funeral – and that she even had a dress made for the occasion, but this seems highly unlikely, judging by Sid Luckman's comments. It is more likely that DiMaggio planned to propose when he returned to Los Angeles, and the dress she had ordered was for the opening night of the Irving Berlin musical, *Mr President*, in the autumn of 1962.

It is also unlikely that Marilyn would have agreed to such a proposal as she preferred to think of herself and DiMaggio as just good friends. Speaking to Alan Levy during the summer of 1962, she explained, 'Believe me there is no spark to be kindled; I just like being with him.' She also repeated the statement almost word-for-word to reporter Helen Hendricks: 'I've always been able to count on Joe as a friend but there is no spark rekindled. Now I like being with him and we have a better understanding than we've ever had.'

On 3 August Marilyn received an injection from Dr Engelberg and then filled a prescription for twenty-five Nembutal capsules, issued by the doctor. Then in the evening she went to La Scala with Pat Newcomb, who was suffering from bronchitis. Concerned when Newcomb told her she was planning to book into hospital for a rest, Marilyn invited her friend to stay at Fifth Helena to 'bake it out' next to the pool; Pat agreed and the two returned to Marilyn's home.

On 4 August, Pat Newcomb slept late, while Marilyn pottered around her home and lounged in bed in her white towelling robe. 'She wasn't ill,' said Eunice Murray, 'she was just resting.' She drank fruit juice and spoke to Mrs Murray about household matters, such as the three shipments of furnishings expected from Mexico, and a carpet which was being specially woven there. 'The development of the house was so important to her,' said Murray. 'In the past few weeks Marilyn had everything to live for. The plans we made were so wonderful.'

It has been claimed that when Newcomb eventually rose, an argument broke out between the two, a result, it is said, of an insomniac and depressed Marilyn being angry that her friend had been able to sleep for so long. However, peace must surely have been restored, since Newcomb stayed for hours afterwards, leaving around 6 p.m. that evening.

During the course of the day, Marilyn received several phone calls and visitors. One guest, photographer Larry Schiller, came to talk about the possibility of shooting a cover for the December issue of Hugh Hefner's *Playboy* magazine. She had been aware of Hefner's request since July, but had still not decided whether to do it, and told Schiller that she would give him an answer later.

In the afternoon she telephoned her old friend Norman Rosten who found her 'rambling but pleasant'. She talked of the future and was very excited about visiting New York in the autumn, reminding him once again that he had not yet used her pool and urging him to come visit her. 'Let's all start to live before we get old,' she told him; words that stuck with him for the rest of his life.

Several workmen came and went, among them Norman Jeffries and local mechanic Henry D'Antonio, who had been working on Mrs Murray's car and returned it sometime during the day of 4 August. He had been to the Fifth Helena property many times to undertake work for Mrs Murray and Marilyn, and would sometimes take along his eight-year-old son, Tony. On such occasions, remembered Tony, 'they would discuss the work that was done and Marilyn would thank him and of course pay for the repairs. Sometimes Marilyn would ask dad to do some handiwork which he did and would never accept any payment for his time. He liked her and enjoyed doing little things for her. I remember one time she asked him to replace some outdoor light bulbs and while he was doing that, she played catch with me in the backyard, asking all sorts of questions. As

I recall she was a very unassuming person, always had a smile; generous, athletic, and would slip some loose change into my pocket, holding her finger to her lips as this was our secret. Dad would not have approved.' These were happy memories, but on 4 August when Tony's father returned to Fifth Helena, he found Marilyn 'looking tired, not well groomed and as though she might have been crying'.

Dr Greenson was called to the house at 4.30 p.m., arriving at 5.15 p.m. to find Marilyn in a 'somewhat drugged' and depressed state. He telephoned Dr Engelberg to ask him to come over, but he refused; he was in the midst of separating from his wife and understandably had other things on his mind. Concerned for her welfare, Greenson suggested to Marilyn that Mrs Murray should drive her to the beach then stay at the house that night. Mrs Murray later told reporters that she had stayed at the house several times in the past week, because Greenson did not want Marilyn to be on her own.

At around 7 p.m., Peter Lawford telephoned to ask if she'd like to attend a dinner party with several friends; this wasn't the first time they had spoken that day – Marilyn had earlier phoned to ask him for Pat Lawford's telephone number in Hyannis Port. 'She picked up the phone herself on the second ring,' he remembered, 'which leads me to believe that she was fine. She did sound sleepy, but I've talked to her a hundred times and she sounded no different.'

While Marilyn was in session with Greenson, her old friend Ralph Roberts tried to call but had been unable to speak with her; then shortly after the doctor's departure, her stepson Joe DiMaggio Jr telephoned to say he had called off his engagement to a girl she did not approve of. 'If anything was amiss, I wasn't aware of it,' he later recalled. Mrs Murray later told reporters that Marilyn was in bed at the time of the phone call, and she had woken her up to ask if she wanted to talk with him. She then listened in to the conversation, remembering that Marilyn was so pleased by DiMaggio's news that she called Greenson to tell him.

For the rest of the evening, Marilyn stayed in her bedroom while Mrs Murray settled herself in front of the television. According to her, during this time Marilyn received another phone call that seemed to disturb her, although Murray was unable to say who the call was from or what it was about. Marilyn then spoke with Peter Lawford once again, who became concerned when her voice started to 'fade out', and when he called back the phone was busy. At 8.30 p.m. a call was placed to Milton Rudin's exchange from showbiz manager Milton Ebbins, who was concerned by what Peter Lawford had just told him. Rudin later rang Marilyn's home but was assured by Eunice Murray that Marilyn was fine.

According to Murray, at approximately 9 p.m. Marilyn appeared at her bedroom door and called out: 'I think we'll not go to the beach Mrs Murray. I think I'll turn in now,' and she closed the door for the very last time.

Chapter 21

'Say a prayer for Norma Jeane'

At 4.25 a.m. the emergency services received the following call from 12305 Fifth Helena Drive: 'Marilyn Monroe has died. She's committed suicide. I'm Dr Engelberg, Marilyn Monroe's physician. I'm at her residence. She's committed suicide.'

When Sergeant Jack Clemmons arrived at the scene, he discovered Eunice Murray operating the washing machine, and Dr Greenson and Dr Engelberg in the bedroom with Marilyn's body, along with a bed-stand covered in pill bottles. Some were empty, but it would appear not all of them were, however, as Marilyn's former business manager Inez Melson bizarrely told interviewer Barry Norman that she flushed some pills down the toilet so that paparazzi wouldn't find out about them. Since the bottles had already been photographed, however, this was a pointless exercise and also interfered with what was supposed to be a secured area.

From the start, the story of Marilyn's discovery was patchy to say the least. Mrs Murray told police officers that she had awakened at around 3 a.m. and noticed a light and the telephone cord under Marilyn's locked door. (Bizarrely, years later she was to change her mind and claim that the door was not locked after all.) Murray phoned Dr Greenson, who instructed her to pound on the door and look through the window. She did as she was asked and discovered Marilyn lying on the bed with the phone in her hand, and she 'looked strange'. Greenson dressed and readied himself for the journey to Fifth Helena, and Mrs Murray telephoned Dr Engelberg, who did the same. When

Greenson arrived at 3.40 a.m., he broke the window, entered the room and removed the phone from her hand, discovering that rigor mortis had already set in. Engelberg arrived at 3.50 a.m. and declared his patient dead.

By 4.30 a.m., employees at the Arthur P. Jacobs Agency had been told of her death and summoned to an emergency meeting at Marilyn's home. Michael Selsman remembered: 'It was panic of course. Events were already out of control, and now she was dead the press didn't feel constrained to hide what they knew – except of course, for the Kennedy stuff – which came later. I fended off the media by saying we didn't know what the cause of death was, because we didn't.'

By the time Marilyn's body had been picked up by the coroner, the news was flying around the world with tragic results: in Britain, twenty-eight-year-old actress Patricia Marlowe told friends that she understood why Marilyn had died and promptly took her own life with a concoction of sleeping pills; thirty-eight-year-old dancer Gerdi Marie Havious repeatedly asked her husband, 'Why did she do it? Why did she do it?,' then leapt to her death from their third-floor window. In Mexico three teenage girls gathered together their photos of Marilyn, then tried to take their own lives, thankfully being saved just in time.

Closer to home, Marilyn's three husbands were told of the news: Jim Dougherty received a message from his colleague Jack Clemmons and turned to his wife: 'Say a prayer for Norma Jeane,' he said. 'She's dead.' Arthur Miller refused to comment to reporters, but later revealed his feelings in a letter to friend Joe Rauh, confessing that he was stunned at the news; had always worried she'd step over the edge; but didn't believe she meant to do it. His father, Isidore Miller, was heartbroken and told reporters, 'She was like my own. She was a kind, good girl. I'm so sorry I was not out there to be with her. She must have been very lonely and afraid.'

Meanwhile, Joe DiMaggio flew into Los Angeles from San Francisco and, together with Berniece Baker Miracle and former business manager Inez Melson, proceeded to arrange Marilyn's funeral for 8 August. They were all very concerned that they should avoid a Hollywood spectacle and released a statement which said that the funeral would be a private affair, 'so that she can go to her final resting place in the quiet she has always sought'. It went on to explain that they could not invite one personality without offending many others, and urged everyone to 'remember the gay, sweet Marilyn and say a prayer of farewell within the confines of your home or church'.

But not everyone was pleased with the reasons for exclusion and several show-business friends tried to trick guards at the Westwood Village Memorial Park Cemetery gates by replacing them with their own 'security'. The plan backfired however, and Frank Sinatra was just one of the friends turned away from the cemetery. Peter Lawford told reporters, 'I am shocked. Pat flew in Monday night from Hyannis Port, where she had been vacationing with the kids, to just attend Marilyn's funeral. But we were not invited. I don't know who's responsible but the whole thing was badly handled.' Even Arthur P. Jacobs got in on the act when he declared that if Marilyn had been in charge of the invitations, half the people on the guest list would not have been invited, and more of her friends would have been included.

But it wasn't just celebrities that were faced with a ban. Foster family Enid, Sam and Diane Knebelkamp were excluded until Berniece Miracle insisted to DiMaggio that they be allowed to attend. Friend Catherine Larson telephoned Enid after Marilyn passed away. 'Enid felt terrible about the death,' remembered Carson's friend James Glaeg. 'But it made her feel better to be able to attend the funeral and provided immeasurable help in their process of mourning. Afterwards Enid said that Marilyn looked as beautiful in her coffin as she had in life. "Like a beautiful doll of a child," she said.'

Almost immediately, the Abbott and Hast company were brought in to provide help with the arrangements, including hearses, flowers and other services. Both owners, Allan Abbott and Ron Hast, were used as pallbearers and Abbott assisted the embalmer to dress Marilyn in a green Pucci dress and blonde wig before carefully placing her in the velvet-lined coffin.

According to Hast, Joe DiMaggio was 'noticeably heart-broken,' during arrangements, while Abbott remembered that on the night before the funeral, DiMaggio spent four or five hours with Marilyn's body, although what he said will forever remain private.

On the day itself, fans and the curious queued at the gates of Westwood Memorial Park to try and gain access. Inside, around thirty friends and associates said goodbye to Marilyn's open casket, while Lee Strasberg read a heartfelt eulogy. Joe DiMaggio bent down to kiss the forehead of the woman he had never stopped loving, and whispered, 'I love you, I love you, I love you,' before finally the coffin was sealed.

Marilyn's body was entombed in the 'Corridor of Memories' section of Westwood Memorial Park, where Joe DiMaggio sat for several moments, after other mourners had left. Disturbingly, after he had said his final goodbye, hundreds of curious onlook-ers stormed in, knocking bouquets to the floor, crushing flow-ers, taking ribbons and stealing roses from the giant heart DiMaggio had bought himself. Two guards had to prevent the mob from attacking the tomb itself, and by the time they had left, they had taken most of the blooms with them.

Quite bizarrely, the spectators said they did it because of their love for the movie star, completely oblivious to the fact that it was not Marilyn Monroe buried in the crypt that day, but Norma Jeane Baker, the little girl who's only desire in life was to be loved, respected and cared for, and who in the words of close friend Bill Pursel, 'really blossomed into a legend, and along the way she met many men who could have – would have – given her the lasting fulfilment of womanhood. But, like the beautiful flower she was, she bloomed and died . . . and so the cycle of life goes on. The Lord giveth and the Lord taketh away.'

Postscript

Given the innumerable theories over the years about how and why Marilyn Monroe died, it's quite possible that among them the truth of her death has already been told. But the manner of her passing still attracts myriad questions and answers, though some people, including her many fans, would rather an open ending to her life than yet another theory presented as fact about her death.

The official verdict on Marilyn's death was probable suicide, although many people dispute this: why would someone take their own life when they had so many plans for the future?

Ralph Greenson never believed Marilyn purposely took her own life, while Milton Wexler, a psychoanalyst who looked in on Marilyn when Greenson was out of town, never believed it either. His daughter Alice recalls: 'My father admired and respected Marilyn Monroe. He thought she was very intelligent and that she had a great sense of humour. He also firmly believed that her death resulted from an accidental overdose of sleeping pills and that she did not intend to commit suicide.'

The future looked bright for Marilyn: Eunice Murray was about to leave on a six-week vacation and she was looking forward to the arrival of a former housekeeper. The Arthur P. Jacobs agency had advised her that Billy Wilder wanted her for his next movie, and Arthur Jacobs had himself bought the rights to the movie *I Love Louisa* and scheduled a meeting about it for 6 August with Marilyn and director J. Lee Thompson. Added to that, there was also a Jean Harlow biopic with Sidney Skolsky in the offing, an appearance in a hour-long TV special and she was still keen to bring *Rain* to the small screen. She also had meetings to attend, including one on 9 August to discuss a musical version of *A Tree Grows in Brooklyn* with Jules Styne, and renewed negotiations over *Something's Got to Give*.

Summer 1962 had been busy, and it looked as if autumn was going to be, too, certainly when it came to Marilyn's career: it all looked hopeful. On a personal level, however, there are pointers to the possibility that Marilyn may have been struggling emotionally and was possibly unhappy enough to consider suicide. Friendship was always an issue, and Marilyn had few people in whom to confide: she had virtually no friends who were not employed by her in some way.

For reasons known only to herself, she refused to rely on the Knebelkamps, despite her former foster family's desire to love and protect her. She certainly couldn't turn to her parents, with whom she was never going to enjoy a close and supportive relationship. There were various bumps in the road that year, including the cooling of her allegedly close friendship with the Kennedy brothers and her dismissal by Fox being spun to depict her as a has-been, with her career in free fall. To cap it all, Arthur Miller had recently remarried, and his wife was expecting a baby – news of which might have served bleakly to highlight Marilyn's own childlessness. Furthermore there was the apparent collapse of any plans Marilyn may have had to adopt. Was this somehow linked to the mysterious phone call Marilyn had received shortly before she died?

José Bolaños told the press that he had called Marilyn on the night she died and that she had told him something that 'would one day shock the whole world'. While this might seem a tad dramatic on Bolaños' part, was there something he said in the course of their telephone conversation that might have tipped Marilyn over the edge? She had planned a trip to Mexico on 15 September – perhaps a last-ditch attempt to fulfil her plans for adoption. Had Bolaños' phone call put paid even to that? It all remains speculative.

But if Marilyn didn't kill herself, was she murdered? And if so, by whom and for what reason? The possibility that she was killed is awash with conspiracy theories that range widely. There's talk that she may have been killed to stop her publicly discussing her relationship with the Kennedys, rumours of Mafia involvement and CIA plots, and even the absurd notion that she had to be silenced because she'd found out that aliens had landed in the United States. Speculation is incessant; the parade of so-called expert witnesses never-ending; the stories ever more outlandish. Without exception, they each raise questions of credibility.

If Marilyn didn't take her own life, if she wasn't murdered, then was her death accidental, either a deliberate overdose with the hope of rescue or a genuine mistake? Perhaps Marilyn wanted people to know how desperate she felt, possibly by taking an overdose then calling for help? Or did she just lose track of how many pills she'd taken and take too many? Apparently, Marilyn used enemas, even for prescription pills, and might have over-medicated. Could this account for Eunice Murray operating the washing machine in the middle of the night?

Each question invites further answers, on and on, like an endless hall of mirrors.

Over the past fifty years, much has been written about how Marilyn Monroe died. David Marshall and a panel of Monroe experts tackled the subject most thoroughly in 2003, in a painstaking examination of the months leading up to her death. Marshall and his team looked at every theory, story and aspect of Marilyn's demise, her medical and mental health, creating a vast database of files, photographs and emails. The result of their year-long labour is available in the 500-page book, *The DD Group: An Online Investigation into the Death of Marilyn Monroe*. It is the best exploration of Marilyn's death to date and comes closest to establishing exactly what happened that night of 4 August 1962.

But regardless of how or why Marilyn died, it is important to remember that beneath all the rumour and gossip – talk of suicide, murder and conspiracy – Marilyn Monroe was Norma Jeane Baker, a little girl who once dreamt of becoming an actress. The appeal of her life – its fire and magic – is overwhelmingly more captivating than raking over the embers of her death. With this in mind, this book has determined to do justice to her, to the pleasures and the pains of the life of an extraordinary woman who not only brought joy to millions but also succeeded beyond a little girl's wildest dreams. This book is for her.

Remembrance:
Lamenting Marilyn Monroe

*If my life could be lived again I would make every decision –
except about being an actress – differently. But the result would
probably be the same, so it has all been worth it.*

Marilyn Monroe

Paul 'Wes' Kanteman: 'I do remember when she died, as
Uncle Jim had been given the word by an old partner of his who
was investigating the case. It was early in the morning when he
called and told my mother what had happened. I was sad and
wished more than ever that I had tried a little harder to get in
touch with her. I do believe that she and Uncle Jim would still
be together if she hadn't become famous. They were very much
in love and were really meant for each other. She never did
achieve the happiness with the others that they had together –
at least from what I have read she was a pretty unhappy lady.
A lot of years have now passed and I guess all I can do is keep
the thought that she was my Aunt Norma and I really thought
a great deal of her.'

Bill Pursel: 'She didn't find the little cottage and white picket
fence; the three children and loving dog she sought. She loved
the publicity and attention she attracted, but she was not
happy. She sank into the quicksand of Hollywood like many
others have done, but placing blame for the inevitable is folly.
I was surprised at her death. What a tragedy. Norma Jeane

had a pure soul, and an immense love of life. She was kind and generous; loved children and animals and had a strong backbone – she almost single-handed made herself a world-renowned star and was so profound I was almost afraid of her. To me she was like a dream and that is what she really was. Raising this past has brought melancholy to a very private part of my life and if Norma Jeane is looking down on all this, I hope she is smiling.'

Jeanne Chretien: 'I was very shocked when Marilyn died, and very disturbed. We were driving back from Utah and heard it on the radio. My first reaction was, "Oh My God, I just can't believe it was suicide." I was very shocked and very sad. Gee, she was nice, and my mom liked her too.'

Bob Cornthwaite: 'I always felt nothing good could happen to her. She had an aura about her that nothing good could happen. Of course, good things happened to her career, but she was so vulnerable. There were so many things she didn't know and she knew that, but she always said, "I'm going to do it." Her stubbornness was her strength and also her weakness. Perhaps she couldn't help her behaviour, she was so disturbed emotionally and psychologically and just couldn't help it.'

A. C. Lyles: 'I join all her friends in Hollywood who had the privilege of knowing her; we remember her with devotion and love. Each of us felt a personal loss and the industry was deprived of a great talent at an early age. As time goes on she becomes more legend. One has only to say "Marilyn" and everyone knows that means Marilyn Monroe. Her first name is all the identification needed.'

Alan Young: 'When Norma Jeane died I was very annoyed. I was saddened, of course, but very annoyed at how she was used – or misused – by people. She was so sincere and wanted more than anything to have a nice home with a nice family.'

George Chakiris: 'When Marilyn died, I was in Japan making a movie and I remember being so sad because it seemed to be our loss. But she lives forever on film; she gave so much, she had a deep caring for her work and cared a great deal. Actors care about the parts they play, but Marilyn cared even deeper. She was glorious, something else. She stands alone and is incredibly unique. When I need cheering up, I watch "Diamonds" or the opening number of *Gentlemen Prefer Blondes* and it lifts my spirits. Marilyn was a lovely, kind person who wouldn't hurt a fly; she was adorable but that isn't even a good enough word. She was so gifted.'

Elliott Reid: 'I was very sad when she died – surprised, but more than anything I was shocked.'

Peer J. Oppenheimer: 'I have always believed her death was a mistake. I am convinced she simply picked up the wrong bottle or took too many pills. It didn't occur to me then and doesn't now that there was any foul play.'

Jim Gough: 'The memories I have of Marilyn are of a friendly person, full of attention for everyone, from bricklayers to painters and artists. She was far from being a snob, an eccentric, or a manic-depressive during the times I spent with her. Marilyn was slender and full of energy, at peace with herself, and concerned about other people's wellbeing. She was eagerly facing the future and anxious to see what might happen next. She was in full control of her life and seemed to be looking forward to her career as a mature actress. She was excited to harvest the fruits of her labour; her two most precious possessions were her house and her little white dog, Maf, whom she adored so much.'

Joe Coudert: 'It was a surprise when she passed away, since she was so young. That made it even more tragic for us, and we were greatly saddened. I often wonder what Ms Monroe would have been like if she was alive today ... Clearly, she would be the Queen of Hollywood.'

References

Sources

In addition to the books, newspaper reports, magazine articles and archives listed below, the following items/interviews have been referred to throughout this book, but particularly in the following chapters:

Chapter 1:
Census reports and records related to the Monroe, Bolender, Gifford, Guthrie, Flugel and Cohen families;
Travel records for Della Monroe and Charles Grainger;
Birth certificates for Berniece Baker and Norma Jeane Mortenson;
Death certificate for Della Monroe;
Divorce papers for Gladys Baker v Jasper Baker, Gladys Mortensen v Martin Mortensen and Lillian M. Gifford v C. Stanley Gifford;
Marriage certificate for Gladys Baker and Martin Mortensen;
Interviews/Memories: Bonnie Roth, Nancy Bolender Jeffrey.

Chapter 2:
Census reports and records related to the Monroe, Atkinson, McKee, Martin, Gifford, Goddard, Knebelkamp, Wilson and Lower families;
Census and travel reports for the Atkinson family;
Death certificates for Tilford M. Hogan and Robert Jasper Baker;

Guardianship records for Norma Jeane Baker;

Letter from Grace Goddard to Los Angeles Orphans Home, undated;

Letter from Grace Goddard to Mrs Myrtle Van Hyning, 15 August 1935;

Letter from Mrs Dewey to Grace Goddard, 6 December 1935;

Letter from Harry C. Wilson to Berniece Baker Miracle, 1962;

Elyda Nelson manuscript courtesy of Paul Kanteman;

Interviews/Memories: Nancy Bolender Jeffrey, Bill Fredenhall, James Glaeg.

Chapter 3:

Emerson High School year book;

Inscribed photograph of Norma Jeane and friends, 25 February 1940;

Report cards for Norma Jeane Baker, 1942;

Petition to establish the presumption of death of Marion Otis Monroe;

Interviews/Memories: Bob Stotts, Doris Drennen, James Dougherty, Jo Olmstead, Bill Pursel, Roy Turner.

Chapter 4:

Elyda Nelson manuscript courtesy of Paul Kanteman;

Jane Wilkie notes on James Dougherty;

Letter from Bebe Goddard to Norma Jeane Dougherty, 26 October 1942;

Letter from Gladys Baker to Berniece Baker Miracle, 7 October 1944;

Letter from Norma Jeane Dougherty to Berniece Baker Miracle, 2 February 1944;

Letter from Norma Jeane Dougherty to Cathy Staub, undated;

Letter from Norma Jeane Dougherty to Grace Goddard, 14 September 1942;

Letter from Norma Jeane Dougherty to Grace Goddard, 16 February 1943;

Letter from Norma Jeane Dougherty to Grace Goddard, 15 June 1944;

Letter from Norma Jeane Dougherty to Grace Goddard, June 1943;

Letter from Norma Jeane Dougherty to Grace Goddard, 3 December 1944;

Postcard from Norma Jeane Dougherty to Catherine Staub, 28 October 1944;

Wedding announcement for Norma Jeane Baker and James Dougherty;

Interviews/Memories: Bob Stotts, Doris Drennen, James Dougherty, Nelson Cohen, Paul 'Wes' Kanteman, James Glaeg, Jo Olmstead.

Chapter 5:

Divorce papers for Norma Jeane Dougherty and James Dougherty;

Elyda Nelson manuscript courtesy of Paul Kanteman;

Jane Wilkie notes on James Dougherty;

Letter from Norma Jeane Dougherty to Bill Pursel, July 1946;

Letter from Norma Jeane Dougherty to Grace Goddard, 1945;

Letter from Norma Jeane Dougherty to unknown friend, 27 October 1946;

Model release form signed by Norma Jeane Dougherty for M. O. Schwartz;

Postcard from Norma Jeane Dougherty to James Dougherty, 15 December 1945;

Transcript of interview with Harry Lipton, from *The Legend of Marilyn Monroe*;

Interviews/Memories: Bill Pursel, Bob Stotts, Jeanne Chretien, James Dougherty, Paul 'Wes' Kanteman, William Carroll.

Chapter 6:

Agreement between Norma Jeane Dougherty/Marilyn Monroe and Twentieth Century Fox, 11 June 1947;

Contract between Marilyn Monroe and Twentieth Century Fox, 24 August 1946;

Letter from John Carroll to Marilyn Monroe, 4 December 1947;

Letter from Norma Jeane Dougherty to Berniece Baker Miracle, circa 1947;

Letter from Twentieth Century Fox to Marilyn Monroe, 10 February 1947;

Interviews/Memories: Alan Young, Bill Pursel, Annabelle Stanford, Berniece Baker Miracle, Christine Krogull, James Glaeg, Jeanne Chretien, Mayor Johnny Grant, Mona Rae Miracle, Steve Hayes, Kathleen Hughes Rubin.

Chapter 7:

Letter from Columbia Pictures Corporation to Maurice Zolotow, 19 October 1959;

Letter from the Hollywood Studio Club to Maurice Zolotow, 18 September 1959;

Letter from Twentieth Century Fox to Maurice Zolotow, 29 September 1959;

Letters from Johnny Hyde to Marilyn Monroe, various dates;

Natasha Lytess manuscript, 'My Years with Marilyn', as told to Jane Wilkie;

Interviews/Memories: Bill Pursel, James Glaeg, Paul 'Wes' Kanteman, Stanley Rubin, Annabelle Stanford, Mayor Johnny Grant.

Chapter 8:

Letter from Elia Kazan to Marilyn Monroe (transcript), *c.*1951;

Letter from Twentieth Century Fox to Marilyn Monroe, 11 May 1950;

Model release signed by Norma Monroe for Tom Kelley Studio, 27 May 1949;

Natasha Lytess manuscript, 'My Years with Marilyn', as told to Jane Wilkie;

Interviews/Memories: A. C. Lyles, Bill Pursel, Kathleen Hughes Rubin, Annabelle Stanford, Jeanne Chretien, Michael Thornton.

Chapter 9:

Letter from Marilyn Monroe to William Morris Agency, 8 May 1951;

Letter from Natasha Lytess to Marilyn Monroe, 5 May 1951;

Marilyn Monroe's Twentieth Century Fox contract, 11 April 1951;

Marilyn Monroe's UCLA Student record card;

Marilyn Monroe's bank statement, 27 September 1951 to 25 October 1951;

Natasha Lytess manuscript, 'My Years with Marilyn', as told to Jane Wilkie;

Interviews/Memories: Charles H. Page, Dale Robertson, Forrest Olmstead, John Gilmore, Richard Baer, Nanciele Finnegan, Annabelle Stanford.

Chapters 10 and 11:

Documents related to the Red Rock Dairy and Gifford family;

Letter from Mr F. L. Metzler to Mr A. W. Deweese, 26 May 1952;

Transcript of letter from Marilyn Monroe to Dr Rabwin;

Letter from Tom Pryor to Mr A. W. Deweese, 11 June 1952;

Letter from Twentieth Century Fox giving Marilyn Monroe permission to appear on the *Edgar Bergen* radio programme, 13 October 1952;

Natasha Lytess manuscript, 'My Years with Marilyn', as told to Jane Wilkie;

Interviews/Memories: Bill Pursel, Bob Cornthwaite, Darrell Von Driska, Gus Zernial, Jim Henaghan Jr, Lisa Truax, Joseph L. Jacob, Pat Brennan, Timothy Henderson, Friends of Dorothy Arnold, Mayor Johnny Grant, Forrest Olmstead.

Chapter 12:

Death certificate for Grace Goddard;

Documents related to John Eley;

Letter from Will Sykes to Marilyn Monroe, October 1954;

Letter from Twentieth Century Fox to Marilyn Monroe, 8 April 1953;

Marilyn Monroe, pages of script from *Gentlemen Prefer Blondes*;

Marilyn Monroe, pages of script from *How to Marry a Millionaire*;

Natasha Lytess manuscript, 'My Years with Marilyn', as told to Jane Wilkie;

Notes made by Grace Goddard on the behaviour of Gladys Baker Eley;

Transcript of *The Jack Benny Program*;

Interviews/Memories: Forrest Olmstead, George Chakiris, Hal Schaefer, Jim Gough, Jim Henaghan Jr, John Gilmore, Pat Traviss courtesy of Lois Banner, Nancy Thome, Stanley Rubin, Win Rosette, Elliott Reid.

Chapter 13:

Baggage declaration and entry form for Marilyn Monroe and Joe DiMaggio;

Bill from the Beverly Hills Hotel, 13–15 March 1954;

Letter from Ben Hecht to Ben Orlin, 5 June 1954;

Letter from Ben Hecht to Loyd Wright, 19 May 1954;

Letter from Berniece Baker Miracle to Marilyn Monroe and Joe DiMaggio;

Letter from Gregson Bautzer to Ben Hecht, 11 August 1954;

Letter from Marilyn Monroe to Joe DiMaggio, 28 February 1954;

Letter from Marilyn Monroe to Joe DiMaggio, 1954;

Letter from Mrs Ben Hecht to Greg Bautzer, 23 September 1962;

Letter from Mrs Ben Hecht to Ken McCormick and Doubleday, 7 June 1954;

Letter from Mrs Ben Hecht to Loyd Wright, 2 June 1954;

Letter from Twentieth Century Fox to Marilyn Monroe, 20 January 1954;

Marriage certificate for Marilyn Monroe and Joe DiMaggio;

Natasha Lytess manuscript, 'My Years with Marilyn', as told to Jane Wilkie;

Twentieth Century Fox biography of Marilyn Monroe, 1954;

Notes made by Marilyn Monroe in connection with the Twentieth Century Fox Dispute, 1954;

Passport of Norma Jeane DiMaggio/Marilyn Monroe;

Surveillance report from City Detectives and Guard Service, employed by Joe DiMaggio, 20 October–5 November 1954;

Vaccination records for Marilyn Monroe;

Interviews/Memories: Allison Ittel, Bob Vannucci, Don Loraine, Don Obermeyer, Hal Schaefer, Joe Franklin, Kenny Kingston, Steve Hayes, Joe Coudert, Friends of Dorothy Arnold, George Chakiris.

Chapter 14:

Certificate of conversion to Judaism for Marilyn Monroe, 1 July 1956;

Joe DiMaggio notes related to his friendship with Marilyn Monroe, 1955;

Letter from Arthur Miller to Marilyn Monroe, 25 May 1956;

Memo from Darryl F. Zanuck to Spyros Skouras, 29 January 1955;

Person to Person transcript, 1955;

Telegram from Spyros Skouras to Darryl F. Zanuck, 17 March 1955;

Interviews/Memories: Albert Winer, Earle Hyman, Edith Shaw Marcus, George Chakiris, James Haspiel, John Thorndike, Karla Jones, Mark Weston, Patricia Rosten, Peer J. Oppenheimer, Stefan Gierasch, Steve Hayes.

Chapters 15 and 16:

Desk diary entry of Harry W. Briden, manager of the Palace Theatre, 1956;

Letter from Arthur Miller to Kermit Bloomgarden, 20 September 1956;

Letter from Gordon Mosley to Marilyn Monroe, 22 October 1956;

Letter from Gordon Mosley to Marilyn Monroe, 29 October 1956;

Letter from John Morris to Marilyn Monroe, 7 August 1956;

Letter from John Morris to Marilyn Monroe, 15 August 1956;

Letter from Kermit Bloomgarden to Arthur Miller, 11 September 1956;

Letter from Kermit Bloomgarden to Arthur Miller, 1 October 1956;

Letter from Louis Untermeyer to John and Harriett Weaver, 11 July 1956;

Letter from Michael Gill to Marilyn Monroe, 27 August 1956;

Letter from Stephen W. Bonarjee to Marilyn Monroe, 19 October 1956;

Letters and documents related to the Terence Rattigan party, 1956;

Production records and letters related to *The Prince and the Showgirl* from the Laurence Olivier Archive;

Programme from *A View from the Bridge*, October 1956;

Questions and answers between Maurice Zolotow and Milton Greene, 1956;

Telegram from Arthur Miller to Maurice Zolotow, 24 October 1956;

Telegram from Maurice Zolotow to Arthur Miller, 23 October 1956;

Interviews/Memories: Alan A., Allan R. Pemberton, Annabel Whitehead on behalf of Princess Margaret, Beryl Belmont, Dolly Stiles, Brenda Porter, Bryan Godfree, Colin Clark, Colin Wilson, Daphne Anderson, Donald W. J. Foot, Frank Williams, Gerald Searle, Horace Ward, Jack Cardiff, Jean Kent, John Casson, Joyce Jackson, Margaret Gibbon, Michael Thornton, Mr G. Pearson, Norman Wisdom, P. C. Packham, Peggy Heriot, Samantha Corner, Sir John Gielgud, Susan Elliott, Tony Hand, Vera Day, Wolf Mankowitz.

Chapter 17:

Agreement between Marilyn Monroe and Milton H. Greene, 26 February 1958;

Insurance document for Marilyn Monroe and Arthur Miller, *c.*1958;

Letter from Arthur Miller to Joe Rauh, 9 August 1958;

Letter from Arthur Miller to Marilyn Monroe, c.1958;

Letter from Arthur Miller to Mr and Mrs Louis Untermeyer, 9 August 1957;

Letter from Inez Melson to Marilyn Monroe, 5 December 1957;

Letter from Joe Rauh to Arthur Miller, 20 November 1957;

Letter from Marilyn Monroe to well-wishers after miscarriage, c.1957–8;

Letter from Robert Miller to Arthur Miller, 24 July 1959;

Letters from the Miller children to Marilyn and Arthur Miller, c.1958–9;

Memo to stockholders of Marilyn Monroe Productions, 2 April 1957;

Transcript of Marilyn Monroe's arrival at the premiere of *Some Like It Hot*, 1959;

Interviews/Memories: Carl Schlesinger, James Glaeg, Jo Olmstead, John Damiecki, Kae Turner, Peer J. Oppenheimer, Maureen McArdle, Peggy McGuiggan, Vanessa Steinberg, Stephanie Baloghy, Tom Tierney.

Chapter 18:

Telegram from Frank Taylor to John Huston, 9 October 1959;

Initial notes on Marilyn Monroe from Rupert Allen, 11 March 1960;

Letter from Arthur Miller to Joe Rauh, 5 August 1960;

Letter from Arthur Miller to Marilyn Monroe Productions, 23 November 1960;

Letter from Buddy (unknown surname) to Spyros Skouras, 6 April 1960;

Letter from Dorothy Jeakins to Marilyn Monroe, 3 May 1960;

Letter from Dorothy Jeakins to C. O. Erickson, 3 May 1960;

Letter from Dorothy Jeakins to Frank Taylor, 12 April 1960;

Letter from Dorothy Jeakins to Frank Taylor, 4 May 1960;

Letter from Dorothy Jeakins to Frank Taylor, undated;

Letter from Frank Taylor to his mother, 13 October 1959;

Letter from Frank Taylor to his mother, 10 November 1959;

Letter from Frank Taylor to John Huston, 3 February 1960;

Letter from Frank Taylor to John Huston, 25 March 1960;

Letter from Frank Taylor to Leslie A. Fiedler, 12 April 1960;

Letter from John Springer to Marilyn Monroe, 19 December 1960;

Letter from Pat Newcomb to Marilyn Monroe, postmarked 31 December 1960;

Letter from Twentieth Century Fox to Marilyn Monroe, 2 June 1960;

Memo from Arthur Jacobs to Rupert Allen, 16 June 1960;

Memo from Buddy (unknown surname) to Spyros Skouras, 27 April 1960;

Memo from Buddy (unknown surname) to Spyros Skouras, undated;

Memo from Frank Taylor to Eliot Ryman and John Huston, 29 September 1959;

Memo from Glenn Norris to Spyros Skouras, 19 August 1960;

Memo from John Springer to Arthur P. Jacobs staff, 8 December 1960;

Memo from Marilyn Monroe to Marilyn Monroe Productions board of directors, undated;

Memo from Rupert Allen to Arthur P. Jacobs, 17 May 1960;

Memo from Rupert Allen to Arthur P. Jacobs, 8 August 1960;

Recorded interview with Thelma Ritter on the set of *The Misfits*, 1960, provided by Lou Cella;

Telegram from Dorothy Jeakins to Frank Taylor, 8 October 1959;

Telegram from Karl Kunst to Spyros Skouras, 20 April 1960;

Telegram from Spyros Skouras to Buddy (unknown surname), 28 April 1960;

Telegram from Spyros Skouras to Karl Kunst, 21 April 1960;

Interviews/Memories: Angela Allen, Bob Banas, Curtice Taylor, Howard Sheehan Jr, Peer J. Oppenheimer.

Chapter 19:

Documents, telegrams, memos related to the *Rain* project from the Eric Woodard Archive;

FBI documents related to Marilyn Monroe's trip to Mexico;

Letter from Dr Greenson to Anna Freud, 4 December 1961;

Letter from Isidore Miller to Marilyn Monroe, 8 February 1962;

Letter from Joe DiMaggio to Marilyn Monroe, *c*.1961;

Letter from John Springer to Aaron Frosch, 17 March 1961;

Letter from Kay Gable to Marilyn Monroe, 11 April 1961;

Letter from Marilyn Monroe to Dr Greenson, 2 March 1961;

Letter from Marilyn Monroe to Joseph Papp, 17 February 1962;

Letter from Marilyn Monroe to Lee and Paula Strasberg, 1961;

Letter from Marilyn Monroe to Lee Strasberg, 19 December 1961;

Letter from Paula Strasberg to Marilyn Monroe, 16 January 1962;

Letter from W. Somerset Maugham to Marilyn Monroe, 31 January 1961;

Memo from Aaron Frosch to Marilyn Monroe, 14 April 1961;

Receipt for after-hours treatment at Elizabeth Arden, Beverly Hills, 27 April 1961;

Telegram from Marilyn Monroe to Joe DiMaggio, 22 September 1961;

Telegram from Marlon Brando to Marilyn Monroe, 27 February 1961;

Transcript of interview between Marilyn Monroe and *Look* magazine, 1961;

Interviews/Memories: Douglas Kirkland, Eric Skipskey, Jim Gough, Lynn Pupello, Mary Sims, Michael Selsman, Peter Evans, Annabelle Stanford.

Chapter 20:

Autopsy report for Marilyn Monroe;

Death certificate for Marilyn Monroe;

Eunice Murray transcript from *The Legend of Marilyn Monroe*;

FBI records;

Letter from Dr Greenson to Anna Freud, 13 January 1963;

Letter from Dr Greenson to Anna Freud, 22 June 1962;

Letter from Dr Greenson to Anna Freud, 20 August 1962;

Letter from Marilyn Monroe to Twentieth Century Fox, 29 March 1962;

Letter from Twentieth Century Fox to Marilyn Monroe Productions, 15 June 1961;

Letter from Twentieth Century Fox to Marilyn Monroe, 15 June 1962;

Letters to and from the Hollywood Museum Associates, 1962;

Memos and letters related to *Something's Got to Give* from Spyros Skouras, 1962;

Police reports into Marilyn Monroe's death;

Receipt from Saks Fifth Avenue, 20 March 1962;

Pages of Marilyn Monroe's script from *Something's Got to Give*;

Twentieth Century Fox legal records relating to *Something's Got to Give*, 1962;

Interviews/Memories: Michael Selsman, Michael Finn, Vanessa Steinberg, Tony D'Antonio, Bill Pursel.

Chapter 21, Postscript and Remembrance: Lamenting Marilyn Monroe:

Autopsy report for Marilyn Monroe;

FBI records;

Last Will and Testament of Marilyn Monroe;

Lee Strasberg transcript from *The Legend of Marilyn Monroe*;

Letter from Arthur Miller to Joe Rauh, 13 August 1962;

Police reports into Marilyn Monroe's death;

Probate records;

Interviews/Memories: A. C. Lyles, Alice Wexler, Alan Young, Allan Abbott, Bill Pursel, Bob Cornthwaite, Elliott Reid, George Chakiris, Ron Hast, James Glaeg, Forrest Olmstead, Jeanne Chretien, Jim Gough, Joe Coudert, Michael Selsman, Paul 'Wes' Kanteman, Peer J. Oppenheimer, Elliott Reid.

Miscellaneous Documents:

Excerpt from a draft copy of 'Memories of a Famous Composer, Nobody Ever Heard Of' (the autobiography of Earle Hagen);

Legal documents related to Inez Melson;

Letter from L. A. C. Wooster to Marilyn Monroe, undated;

Letter from Marilyn Monroe to Marlon Brando, undated;

Letter from Marilyn Monroe to Sidney Skolsky, undated;

Letter from Milton Spitz to Marilyn Monroe, undated;

Maurice Zolotow notes on Marilyn Monroe, Inez Melson, Marilyn's fan mail and Marilyn Monroe Productions;

Memos and letters between employees of the Arthur P. Jacobs Agency, various dates;

Press releases from the Arthur P. Jacobs Agency, undated;

Telephone messages from Marilyn Monroe to Joe DiMaggio, various dates;

Notes by Joe DiMaggio concerning Marilyn Monroe's disagreement with Twentieth Century Fox, undated.

NOTE: Some of the above items, along with various other documents, are available in Banner, Lois and Anderson, Mark, *MM Personal: From the Private Archive of Marilyn Monroe* (Abrams, 2011). Other letters and documents were found in catalogues from the following auction houses: Bonhams, Butterfields, Christie's, Hunt Auctions, Julien's Auctions, Sotheby's, Swann Galleries.

Archives/Websites

Ancestry.com

Anna Freud Archive – Library of Congress

Arthur P. Jacobs Agency Archive – Charles Von der Abe Library, Loyola Marymount University

BBC Written Archives Centre

Ben Hecht Archives – Newberry Library, Chicago

David Marshall Archive

DD Group Archive

Eric Woodard Archive

FamilySearch.org

FBI Freedom of Information section

Foursquare Church Heritage and Archives Department

Frank Taylor Archive – Lilly Library, Indiana University

Hollywood Bowl Museum
Internet Movie Database (imdb.com)
Joe Rauh Archive – Library of Congress
Kent State University Special Collections and Archives
Kermit Bloomgarden Archive – Wisconsin Historical Society
Kris Peterson – San Juan County Historical Society Archives
Laurence Olivier Archives – British Library
Los Angeles Times Archives
Maurice Zolotow Archives – Harry Ransom Humanities Research Center, University of Texas at Austin
Merja Pohjola Archive
Michael Chekhov Studio, London
MPTV image vault
Natasha Lytess Archives – Harry Ransom Humanities Research Center, University of Texas at Austin
Nevada State Library and Archives
NewspaperArchive.com
New York Times Archive
Roy Turner Archives
Savoy Hotel Archive
Spyros Skouras Archives – Special Collections, Stanford University Libraries
Strickertfamily.com
Terence Rattigan Archives – British Library
Twentieth Century Fox Archive – UCLA
UCLA – Student records section
University of Delaware Library
Whyte Museum of the Canadian Rockies
www.marilynmonroe.ca
www.marilynmonroecollection.com

Documentaries/Television/Radio

Interview with Marilyn Monroe, c.1960
The Legend of Marilyn Monroe, 1966
Marilyn Monroe: Beyond the Legend, 1987

Marilyn Monroe Talks to Dave Garroway, 1955
Marilyn Monroe Talks to Sidney Skolsky, c.1954
Marilyn Monroe: The Final Days, 2001
Marilyn on Marilyn, 2001
The Martin and Lewis Show, 1953
Remembering Marilyn, 1987

Books

Allen, Maury, *Where Have You Gone Joe DiMaggio* (Dutton, 1975).

Arnold, Eve, *Marilyn Monroe: An Appreciation* (Hamish Hamilton, 1987).

Badman, Keith, *The Final Years of Marilyn Monroe: The Shocking True Story* (JR Books, 2010).

Bailey, George, *Marilyn Monroe and the Making of Niagara* (George Bailey and Company, 1998).

Banner, Lois and Anderson, Mark, *MM Personal: From the Private Archive of Marilyn Monroe* (Abrams, 2011).

Barris, George and Steinem, Gloria, *Marilyn: Norma Jeane* (Victor Gollancz, 1987).

Barris, George, *Marilyn: Her Life in Her Own Words* (Headline, 1995).

Beauchamp, Anthony, *Focus on Fame* (Odhams Press, 1958).

Belmont, Georges, *Marilyn Monroe and the Camera* (Bloomsbury, 1989).

Black, Lendley, *Michael Chekhov as Actor, Director and Teacher* (Umi Research, 1987).

Buchthal, Stanley and Comment, Bernard, *Fragments: Poems, Intimate Notes, Letters by Marilyn Monroe* (HarperCollins, 2010).

Buskin, Richard, *Blonde Heat: The Sizzling Screen Career of Marilyn Monroe* (Billboard, 2001).

Cardiff, Jack, *Magic Hour* (Faber and Faber, 1996).

Carpozi Jr, George, *Marilyn Monroe: Her Own Story* (Belmont, 1961).

Carroll, Jock, *Falling for Marilyn: The Lost Niagara Collection* (Virgin, 1996).

Carroll, William, *Marilyn Monroe 1945: Norma Jeane Dougherty* (Coda, 2004).

Christie's, *The Personal Property of Marilyn Monroe* (Christies, 1999).

Clark, Colin, *The Prince, the Showgirl and Me* (HarperCollins, 1995).

Conover, David, *Finding Marilyn: A Romance* (Grosset and Dunlap, 1981).

Cunningham, Ernest, *Marilyn People* (Ernest Cunningham, 2003).

de Dienes, Andre, *Marilyn Mon Amour* (Sidgwick and Jackson, 1986).

Dougherty, James, *The Secret Happiness of Marilyn Monroe* (Playboy, 1976).

Dougherty, James, *To Norma Jeane with Love Jimmie* (Beach House, 2001).

Feingersh, Ed and LaBrasca, Bob, *Marilyn: Fifty-Five* (Bloomsbury, 1990).

Ferber, Edna and Kaufman, George S, *Stage Door* (Dramatists Play Service, n.d.).

Finn, Michelle, *Marilyn's Addresses: A Fan's Guide to the Places She Knew* (Smith Gryphon, 1995).

Freeman, Lucy, *Why Norma Jeane Killed Marilyn Monroe* (Global Rights, 1992).

Goode, James, *The Making of The Misfits* (Limelight, 1986).

Gottfried, Martin, *Arthur Miller: A Life* (Faber and Faber, 2003).

Greene, Joshua, *Milton's Marilyn* (Schirmer/Mosel, 1998).

Guiles, Fred Lawrence, *Legend: The Life and Death of Marilyn* (Scarborough House, 1992).

Haspiel, James, *Marilyn: The Ultimate Look at the Legend* (Smith Gryphon, 1991).

Haspiel, James, *The Unpublished Marilyn* (Mainstream Publishing, 2000).

Haspiel, James, *Young Marilyn* (Smith Gryphon, 1994).

Hayes, Steve, *Googies – Coffeeshop to the Stars*, 2 vols (Bear Manor Media, 2008).

Hutchinson, Tom, *Marilyn Monroe* (Galley Press, 1982).

Jasgur, Joseph and Sakol, Jeannie, *The Birth of Marilyn* (Sidgwick and Jackson, 1991).

Kazan, Elia, *Elia Kazan: A Life* (Knopf, 1988).

Leaming, Barbara, *Marilyn Monroe* (Weidenfeld and Nicolson, 1998).

Marilyn Monroe: The Life, The Myth (Rizzoli, 1996).

Marshall, David, *The DD Group: An Online Investigation into the Death of Marilyn Monroe* (IUniverse, 2005).

Miller, Arthur and Toubiana, Serge, *The Misfits* (Phaidon, 2000).

Miller, Arthur, *Time Bends: A Life* (Minerva, 1990).

Miracle, Berniece Baker and Miracle, Mona Rae, *My Sister Marilyn: A Memoir of Marilyn Monroe* (Weidenfeld and Nicolson, 1994).

Monroe, Marilyn with Hecht, Ben, *My Story* (Taylor, 2007).

Morgan, Michelle, *Marilyn Monroe: Private and Undisclosed* (Constable, 2007).

Murray, Eunice with Shade, Rose, *Marilyn: The Last Months* (Pyramid, 1975).

Peary, Danny, *Close-ups (Patricia Rosten on Marilyn)* (Workman, 1978).

Riese, Randall and Hitchins, Neal, *The Unabridged Marilyn* (Corgi, 1988).

Rosten, Norman, *Marilyn: An Untold Story* (Signet, 1973).

Ryerson, Florence and Clements, Colin, *Glamour Preferred* (Samuel French, 1940).

Shaw, Sam, *Marilyn: The New York Years* (Lardon, 2004).

Shaw, Sam and Rosten, Norman: *Marilyn among Friends* (Bloomsbury, 1987).

Spoto, Donald, *Marilyn Monroe: The Biography* (Chatto and Windus, 1993).

Stern, Bert, *The Last Sitting* (Schirmer, 1993).

Strasberg, Susan, *Marilyn and Me: Sisters, Rivals, Friends* (Doubleday, 1992).

Summers, Anthony, *Goddess:The Secret Lives of Marilyn Monroe* (Victor Gollancz, 1985).

Victor, Adam, *The Complete Marilyn Monroe* (Thames and Hudson, 1999).

Vieten, Bob, *Bob Vieten's Historic Homes of Hemet Prior to 1950 & the People who Lived in Them* (B. Vieten, 2006).

Vitacco-Robles, Gary, *Cursum Perficio: Marilyn Monroe's Brentwood Hacienda* (IUniverse, 2000).

Wagenknecht, Edward, *Marilyn Monroe: A Composite View* (Chilton, 1969).

Weatherby,W.J., *Conversations with Marilyn* (Sphere, 1987).

Wolfe, Donald, *The Assassination of Marilyn Monroe* (Little, Brown, 1998).

Woodard, Eric, *Hometown Girl* (HG Press, 2004).

Zolotow, Maurice, *Marilyn Monroe* (Revised ed., Perennial Library, 1990).

Newspaper/Magazine Articles

'A friend remembers Marilyn in brighter days', *Reno Evening Gazette* (9 August 1962).

'A ghost materialized: Ben Hecht finally credited on Marilyn Monroe's memoir', *Ben Hecht Story and News*, vol. 3, no. 1 (2001).

'A revealing last interview with Marilyn Monroe by Margaret Parton', Unknown publication (n.d.).

'Above all else Marilyn Monroe wanted to act', *Daily News* (17 August 1962).

'Actress Marilyn Monroe attends Miller funeral', *Brainerd Daily Dispatch* (8 March 1961).

'Actress wanted baby by Maurice Zolotow', *Lima News* (12 September 1973).

Adams, Jill, 'Interview with Roy Turner', *Book Club* (2001).

'Aid for orphans' home', *Los Angeles Times* (16 March 1935).

'All about Yves', *Idols Magazine* (n.d.).

Alpert, Hollis, 'An afternoon with Marilyn Monroe', *Woman's Day* (November 1959).

'An intelligent man's guide to Marilyn Monroe', *Sunday Express* (8 November 1953).

'Another Lana?', *Long Beach Press-Telegram* (13 August 1950).

Archerd, Armand, 'Hollywood happenings', *Van Wert Times Bulletin* (9 March 1953).

'Are budgets necessary?', *Movieland* (July 1951).

Arsenault, Lisa, 'Jim Dougherty interview', *Portland Monthly Magazine* (November 1999).

'Arthur Miller likes a movie at last', *Nevada State Journal* (8 February 1962).

Ashley, Anthony, 'Marilyn's fight against insanity', *Inside Story* (October 1956)

Barbour, William, 'The very private life of Marilyn Monroe', *Modern Screen* (October 1955).

'Beauty, brains marriage busted', *Lima News* (12 November 1960).

'Bebe Goddard interview', *All About Marilyn Magazine* (January 1994)

Benedict, Lee, 'What Joe did for Marilyn', *Movie Stars Parade* (October 1954).

'Ben Ross interview', www.asmp.org.

Berg, Louis, 'Marilyn meets Brando', *This Week* (n.d.).

Bolstad, Helen, 'Marilyn in the house', *Photoplay* (September 1955).

Borie, Marcia, 'Marilyn Monroe's twin', unknown magazine (n.d.).

Boyle, Hal, 'The symbol of success', *Lowell Sun* (10 June 1957).

'Brides-to-be feted in Santa Barbara', *Los Angeles Times* (23 November 1942).

Bruce, Jon, 'The inside story of the Marilyn-Jane feud', *Screenland Plus TV Land* (April 1953).

Buckley, Michael, 'Darlin' Eileen, an appreciation of the life and career of Eileen Heckart', www.theatermania.com (7 January 2002).

'California bungalow of 1940s is not just another house for sale, devotees of Marilyn Monroe discover', *Los Angeles Times* (21 April 1983).

Campi, Ray, 'Jack "Waukeen" Cochran', www.electricearl.com.

'Carl Sandburg talks about Marilyn Monroe', *Cavalier* (n.d.).

Carpozi, George, 'Interview with Eunice Murray', *Ladies Home Journal* (n.d.).

Carroll, Harrison, 'Behind the scenes in Hollywood', *Monessen Daily Independent* (21 October 1952)

'Cast/crew list for The Misfits', *Reno Evening Gazette* (20 July 1960).

'Circus will aid orphans', *Los Angeles Times* (15 March 1935).

'Classifieds', *Los Angeles Times* (21 October 1934).

'Classifieds', *Los Angeles Times* (2 July 1950).

'Conflict of careers', *Jerry Giesler's Hollywood* (1962)

Connolly, Mike, column, *Independent* (6 March 1956).

Constantine, Leon, 'What's wrong with sex appeal', *Movieland* (January 1952).

Copeland, Joan 'They really liked me', *Modern Screen* (January 1957).

'Court dates up "Calendar girl" LA Judge calls Marilyn Monroe', Unknown newspaper (26 June 1952).

Cowles, Fleur, 'How Marilyn Monroe took London', *Glamour* (December 1956).

Cronin, Steve, 'Love and learn', *Modern Screen* (May 1953).

Cronin, Steve, 'The secret life of Marilyn Monroe', *Modern Screen* (September 1952).

'Crowds trample Marilyn's flowers', *San Francisco Chronicle* (10 August 1962).

'Data sought on phone call just before actress died', *Chicago Tribune* (8 August 1962).

Day, Vera, 'I won't be catty about Marilyn', *Picturegoer* (12 January 1957).

'Dead from his own hands', Unknown newspaper (1933).

'Death of Mr R. Atkinson JP', *Grimsby News* (18 February 1935).

'Did she try to call DiMaggio?', *Oakland Tribune* (6 August 1962).

Dietzel, Jane, 'It seems to me', *Progress* (29 October 1960).

'DiMaggio's courtship cools off', *Lima News* (7 November 1952).

'DiMaggio visits Marilyn in new hospital', *Oakland Tribune* (11 February 1961).

'DiMaggio weeps over Marilyn at funeral', *San Francisco Chronicle* (9 August 1962).

'Don Murray interview', www.americanlegends.com.

Dougherty, Jim, 'Marilyn Monroe was my wife', *Photoplay* (March 1953).

'Dozens drown as floods sweep California', *Lima News* (3 March 1938).

'Drew Pearson footlight reflections', *Portsmouth Herald* (30 August 1954).

'Earthquake ruins give up 130 dead; 5000 injured', *Syracuse Herald*)12 March 1933).

'Eighty-nine at orphans' home excited over gifts', *Los Angeles Times* (25 December 1936).

Emerson, Shirley, 'Because of Joe', *Motion Picture and Television Magazine* (July 1954).

Evans, Harry, 'What caused Marilyn Monroe', *Family Circle* (1952).

Evans, Peter, 'I knew Marilyn and she really wasn't such a dumb blonde', *Daily Mail* (4 May 2010).

'Evelyn Moriarty interview', *Marilyn Then and Now* newsletter, July 1997.

'Failure was my spur by Marilyn Monroe', *Filmland* (January 1953).

Fardell, Hank, 'Marilyn Monroe: that soul doesn't belong in that body', *Movie Fan* (April 1953).

'Few relatives, friends to attend Marilyn rites', *Los Angeles Times* (7 August 1962).

'Film beauty, Joe DiMaggio romance cools', *Oakland Tribune* (5 November 1952).

'Film star happy but tired after eluding newsmen', *Coshocton Tribune* (30 June 1956).

Finletter, Alice, 'Don't call me a dumb blonde', *Modern Screen* (April 1955).

'Former guardian of Marilyn Monroe dies', *Evening Journal* (1 October 1953).

'Friendship in Mexico may be a clue to Marilyn's death', *Chicago Tribune* (8 August 1962).

'Future plans told by Marilyn Monroe', *Herald Press* (10 November 1955).

'Gable christening is howling success', *Oakland Tribune* (12 June 1961).

'Gable discloses wife expecting', *Nevada State Journal* (1 October 1960).

'Gala event slated at Grauman's', *Los Angeles Times* (28 March 1934).

Gardner, Hy, 'Marilyn gets last laugh in attempted blackmail scheme', *Oakland Tribune Daily Magazine* (11 November 1954).

Garrison Malloy, Rita, 'Marilyn on Marilyn', *Motion Picture* (November 1954).

Gifford, Mary, 'Red Rock Dairy', unknown publication (n.d.).

Goodman, Ezra, 'The girl with three blue eyes', *Cavalier* (August 1961).

Graham, Sheila, column, *Monessen Daily Independent* (12 October 1950).

Graham, Sheila, 'Marilyn talks about Joe and babies', *Modern Screen* (September 1954).

'Grand opening, Frank and Joseph', *Los Angeles Times* (19 November 1945).

Halsman, Philippe, 'Shooting Marilyn', *Photography* (June 1953).

Handsaker, Gene, 'Jane, Marilyn get along well on set', *Austin Daily Herald* (20 January 1953).

Harris, Radie, 'The empty crib in the nursery', *Photoplay* (December 1958).

Harrison, Ward, 'Hello Norma Jeane: Would you believe Marilyn Monroe was named after a Louisvillian?', *Leo Weekly* (15 January 2003).

Hecht, Ben, 'The myth about Marilyn Monroe's death', *Salisbury Times* (29 September 1962).

Hecht, Ben, 'The truth about Marilyn Monroe's death', *Family Weekly* (30 September 1962).

Henaghan, Jim, 'My love affair with Marilyn Monroe', *Motion Picture* (January 1955).

Hendricks, Helen, 'Why Marilyn can't hold on to love', *Screenland Plus TV Land* (July 1962).

'Here there and Hollywood', *Winnipeg Free Press* (6 December 1950).

'Her taste of fame in Korea doomed Marilyn's marriage', *Cedar Rapids Gazette* (7 October 1954).

Hoffman, Alice, 'Marilyn Monroe's honeymoon', *Modern Screen* (April 1954).

Holland, Jack, 'If you were Marilyn Monroe's friend', *Movies* (June 1955)

'Hollywood diary', *Family Circle* (n.d.).

'Hollywood Greats', interview between Barry Norman and Inez Melson, transcript (n.d.).

'Hollywood has haven for girls seeking fame', *Los Angeles Times* (25 January 1948).

'Hollywood's most famous rear view', *Photoplay UK* (September 1961).

'Home life of a bachelor girl', *TV and Screen Guide* (August 1951).

'Hometown flavor from the press', *Los Angeles Times* (12 December 1954).

'Hometown flavor from the press', *Los Angeles Times* (2 October 1955).

Hoppe, Art, 'Joe DiMaggio weds Marilyn Monroe at City Hall', *San Francisco Chronicle* (15 January 1954).

Hopper, Hedda, 'Don't drink – it won't bring back the baby', *Motion Picture* (July 1960).

Hopper, Hedda, *Los Angeles Times* (9 September 1953).

Hopper, Hedda, *Los Angeles Times* (11 September 1954).

Hopper, Hedda, *Los Angeles Times* (1 January 1956).

Hopper, Hedda, *Los Angeles Times* (24 February 1961).

Hopper, Hedda, *Los Angeles Times* (16 July 1961).

Hover, Helen, 'Marilyn Monroe interview', *Motion Picture* (January 1954)

'Hot not to cool down', *Movieland* (December 1954).

Houseman, Gene, 'The strange new life of Marilyn Monroe', *Movie Life* (March 1956).

'How I stay in shape', *Pageant* (September 1954).

'How Marilyn Monroe sees herself', *Parade* (12 October 1952).

Hyams, Joe, 'Marilyn Monroe's beauty biography', *This Week* (11 December 1960).

Hyde, Theresa, 'Tony Randall interview', www.houstontheatre.com (11 March 2000).

'I loved Marilyn, started career, mourns Hollywood photographer', *Los Angeles Times* (8 August 1962).

'I love you, I love you', *Newsweek* (20 August 1962).

'I want to be myself', *Bombay Screen* (n.d.).

'I'll always be alone', *TV and Movie Screen* (March 1955).

'Inquest may be held in Marilyn case', *Los Angeles Times* (10 August 1962).

'Interests obvious says film star when she dates', *Humboldt Standard* (6 September 1952).

'Interview with Evelyn Moriarty', *Marilyn and Then International*, vol. 1, no. 3 (July 1997).

'Interview with Paul Kanteman', *Immortal Marilyn* magazine (May 2003).

'Is Marilyn having heart trouble too?', Unknown publication (1961).

'Is Marilyn Monroe ruining her life?', *Movie Mirror* (August 1960).

'I've nothing against women but I prefer men says Marilyn', *Evening Standard* (3 March 1956).

'Jack Cole made Marilyn Monroe movie', *Los Angeles Times* (9 August 2009).

'James has never said good bye to Norma Jeane', *Sunday Post* (4 August 2002).

Jenkins, Logan, 'That kiss from Marilyn Monroe's lips', *San Diego Union-Tribune* (4 October 1999).

'Joe DiMaggio and Marilyn Monroe stir talk of a second marriage', *Lowell Sun* (23 March 1961).

'Joe DiMaggio visits Marilyn', *Odessa American* (13 February 1961).

'Joe, Marilyn off to Tokyo', *San Mateo Times* (29 January 1954).

'Joe quit $100,000 year job to be near Marilyn', *Salisbury Times* (14 August 1962).

Johnson, Erskine, column, *Frederick Post* (6 April 1956).

Johnson, Erskine, column, *Hollywood Today* (29 October 1953).

Johnson, Erskine, column, *Lima News* (13 October 1958).

Johnson, Erskine, column, *Lima News* (15 October 1958).

Johnson, Erskine, 'Hollywood's Marilyn Monroe: blond, saucy, the new Harlow', *Lima News* (5 August 1952).

Johnson, Erskine, 'Jane Russell knows answer to Marilyn Monroe's problem', *Sunday Tribune* (29 March 1953).

Johnson, Erskine, 'Magazine gets bum steer and apology from Marilyn Monroe', *Daily Register* (12 June 1952).

Johnson, Grady, 'The story behind Marilyn Monroe', *Coronet* (October 1952).

Jordan, Frank, 'Wolf-whistling Japanese mob Marilyn Monroe, DiMaggio', *Nevada State Journal* (2 February 1954).

'Journey into paradise', *Photoplay* (April 1954).

'June bride party guest', *Los Angeles Times* (9 February 1936).

Kamm, Herbert, 'I dressed Marilyn Monroe', Unknown magazine (n.d.).

Kilgallen, Dorothy, 'The voice of Broadway', *Pottstown Mercury* (29 August 1952).

Kilgallen, Dorothy, 'The voice of Broadway', *Pottstown Mercury* (18 September 1952).

Kilgallen, Dorothy, 'The voice of Broadway', *Pottstown Mercury* (12 September 1953).

'La Monroe eager to act again', *Oakland Tribune* (9 November 1957).

'Lawford tells of call to Marilyn', *San Francisco Chronicle* (1962).

'Lessons I've learned in Hollywood', *Movieland* (May 1951).

Levin, Robert J., 'Marilyn Monroe's marriage', *Redbook* (February 1958).

Levitan, Corey, 'Hello Normal Jeane: Marilyn Monroe's unpublicized happy Hawthorne childhood', *Daily Breeze* (June 2003).

Lipton, Harry, 'Marilyn's the most', *Motion Picture* (May 1956).

Louis, Merry, 'How Marilyn spends her nights', *Movie Play* (September 1955).

'Love hungry', *Hollywood Life Stories*, no. 5 (1955).

'Lyons den', *Post Standard* (8 October 1955).

Lytess, Natasha, 'Marilyn owes me everything', *Movie Mirror* (1957).

'The private life of Marilyn Monroe', *Screen World* (November 1953).

Maddox, Ben, 'Peeking in on Marilyn as a housewife', *Screenland and TV Land* (May 1954).

'Mailer's Monroe not the same girl Riverside man knew and dated', *Daily Enterprise* (22 October 1973).

'Marilyn and Arthur plan secret wedding', *Oshkosh Northwestern* (23 June 1956).

'Marilyn and friends hint', *Waukesha Daily Freeman* (5 January 1954)

'Marilyn and The Misfits', *Reno Gazette-Journal* (23 February 1997).

'Marilyn arrives', unknown newspaper (1960).

'Marilyn attempted suicide four times', *Oakland Tribune* (7 August 1962).

'Marilyn back to work after NY sojourn', *Brainerd Daily* (25 May 1962).

'Marilyn changes hospitals seeking rest, checkup', *Lincoln Sunday Journal and Star* (12 February 1961).

'Marilyn denies nude photo notes', unknown newspaper (June 1952).

'Marilyn doesn't impress judge' *Wisconsin Rapid's Daily Tribune* (1 March 1956).

'Marilyn doesn't live here anymore', *All About Marilyn Magazine* (April 1992).

'Marilyn enters a Jewish family', *Modern Screen* (November 1956).

'Marilyn files for divorce but still would like baby', *Coshocton Tribune* (26 October 1954).

'Marilyn finds leading man', *Los Angeles Times* (9 May 1954).

'Marilyn fond of Joe – but she's not ready to marry', *Coshocton Tribune* (26 November 1952).

'Marilyn forms her own film company', *Great Bend Daily Tribune* (10 January 1955).

'Marilyn goes back to work', *Kingsport News* (20 October 1958).

'Marilyn has minor corrective operation', *Oakland Tribune* (8 November 1954).

'Marilyn hospitalized for fourth time in five minutes', *Lowell Sun* (29 June 1961).

'Marilyn hospitalized, The Misfits delayed', *Nevada State Journal* (30 August 1960).

'Marilyn incorporated', *Sunday Express* (30 October 1955)

'Marilyn, Joe leave for Japan', *Albuquerque Journal* (30 January 1954).

'Marilyn keeping her books', *Indiana Evening Gazette* (18 December 1952).

'Marilyn leaves hospital', *Lima News* (11 August 1957).

'Marilyn looked to future to pay debts', *Chronicle-Telegram* (8 August 1962).

'Marilyn may be pregnant', *San Mateo Times* (18 October 1958).

'Marilyn may get divorce decree today', *Odessa American* (23 January 1961).

'Marilyn Monroe', *Life* (22 June 1962).

'Marilyn Monroe', *Sunday Graphic* (29 March 1959).

'Marilyn Monroe: A good, long look at myself', *Redbook* (1962).

'Marilyn Monroe Arthur Miller marriage ends', *Los Angeles Times* (12 November 1960).

'Marilyn Monroe, Arthur Miller now officially engaged, to marry soon', *Kerrville Times* (22 June 1956).

'Marilyn Monroe "art" photo sellers convicted', *Los Angeles Times* (27 June 1952).

'Marilyn Monroe answers 33 intimate questions', *Stag* (August 1953).

'Marilyn Monroe back in town, late for work', *Daily Courier* (29 August 1958).

'Marilyn Monroe collapses on set, fears miscarriage', *Fresno Bee Republican* (14 November 1958).

'Marilyn Monroe comfortable after surgery', *Valley Independent* (30 June 1961).

'Marilyn Monroe confined to bed with influenza', *Sheboygan Press* (18 September 1954).

'Marilyn Monroe given Carl Sandburg praise', *Indiana Evening Gazette* (12 June 1961).

'Marilyn Monroe has gall bladder operation', *Lowell Sun* (30 June 1961).

'Marilyn Monroe in hospital', *Lowell Sun* (15 September 1958).

'Marilyn Monroe insists she did not marry Joe', *Bradford Era* (25 September 1952).

'Marilyn Monroe is buried, 100 guards keep crowd outside chapel', *Fresno Bee Republican* (8 August 1962).

'Marilyn Monroe left a child', *Motion Picture* (n.d.).

'Marilyn Monroe likes men but won't date', *Independent Long Beach* (17 November 1951).

'Marilyn Monroe loses baby after operation', *Hammond Times* (2 August 1957).

'Marilyn Monroe loses her baby', *Ironwood Daily Globe* (2 August 1957).

'Marilyn Monroe loses her baby', *Daily Courier* (2 August 1957)

'Marilyn Monroe may star on TV', *New York Times* (6 January 1961).

'Marilyn Monroe on middle age', unknown publication (1960).

'Marilyn Monroe receives visitors in hospital room', *Florence Morning News* (25 June 1959).

'Marilyn Monroe resting at home', *Oakland Tribune* (25 July 1961).

'Marilyn Monroe rests comfortably', *Nevada State Journal* (4 September 1960).

'Marilyn Monroe rests, seems like old self', *Los Angeles Times* (31 August 1960).

'Marilyn Monroe says husband comes first in "new life"', *Coshocton Tribune* (2 June 1957).

'Marilyn Monroe talks about herself', unknown magazine (n.d.).

'Marilyn Monroe views Clift in unique light', *Reno Evening Gazette* (3 September 1960).

'Marilyn Monroe was a thin, unloved orphan 14 years ago', *Sheboygan Press* (24 November 1952).

'Marilyn Monroe, Joe DiMaggio date again; just friends', *Nevada State Journal* (16 November 1954).

'Marilyn Monroe's figure is tops at book auction too', *Pottstown Mercury* (5 December 1952).

'Marilyn Monroe's Hollywood's honestest', *Newport Daily News* (30 August 1952).

'Marilyn Monroe's pet peeve is getting unwanted advice', *Ironwood Daily Globe* (10 June 1957).

'Marilyn Monroe's secret: she enjoys being a woman', *Oakland Tribune* (5 October 1952).

'Marilyn Monroe's secret tragedy', *Screen Stories* (February 1961).

'Marilyn Monroe's strange interlude', *Screen Mag* (December 1955).

'Marilyn nearly 35, and bouncy as ever', *Press-Telegram* (12 May 1961).

'Marilyn pays price of fame; loses personal identity', *Daily Courier* (16 May 1960).

'Marilyn plans rest before Reno Flicker', unknown newspaper (26 May 1960).

'Marilyn protests as picture jumps from calendar to glassware', *Lima News* (18 December 1952).

'Marilyn really agog over GI reception in Korea', *San Mateo Times* (19 February 1954).

'Marilyn says she is glad to be free', *Odessa American* (18 July 1961).

'Marilyn says she offered to give up film career', *Lincoln Star* (28 October 1954).

'Marilyn says she will still be her old sweet self', *Lima News* (1 April 1956).

'Marilyn seeks divorce from Joe', *Bridgeport Telegram* (5 October 1954).

'Marilyn set for surgery', *Lincoln Star* (6 November 1954).

'Marilyn silent on stork talk', *Charleston Gazette* (22 March 1957).

'Marilyn still hopeful she will become a mother', *Lima News* (3 August 1957).

'Marilyn talks of lost baby, new movie', *Independent Press-Telegram* (15 March 1959).

'Marilyn to let Reinhardt son place manuscripts', *Newport Daily News* (6 January 1953).

'Marilyn upset by phone call', *Independent* (7 August 1962).

'Marilyn will fly to town for Centennial', *Oshkosh Daily Northwestern* (6 August 1955).

'Marilyn's acting seen improved', *Hayward Daily Review* (29 October 1958).

'Marilyn's death was inevitable', unknown newspaper (1962).

'Marilyn's dream is coming true', *Modern Screen* (May 1957).

'Marilyn's first ex sends wishes', *Daily Review* (25 June 1956).

'Marilyn's last coach tells of starlet's unusual philosophy', *Ada Evening News* (18 November 1962).

'Marilyn's life saga of broken dreams', *Los Angeles Times* (7 August 1962).

'Married', *Las Vegas Age* (3 September 1927).

Marshall, David, 'The Anna Christie scene', *Forever Marilyn* (n.d.).

Martin, Pete, 'The new Marilyn Monroe, part one', *Saturday Evening Post* (5 May 1956).

Martin, Pete, 'The new Marilyn Monroe, part two', *Saturday Evening Post* (12 May 1956).

'Maude Atkinson obituary', *Los Angeles Times* (9 March 1944).

Maxwell, Elsa, 'I'll never be the same', *Modern Screen* (July 1956).

'Medical test for Marilyn', *Daily Review* (14 November 1958).

'Memorable meal', *Gourmet* (February 2001).

'Memories of The Misfits in Nevada', *Nevada State Journal* (23 October 1977).

'Men in my life', *Joy* (July 1953).

Meyer, Norma, 'Star turns', *San Diego Union-Tribune* (25 February 2002).

Michaels, Evan, 'What was Marilyn Monroe doing at 685 Third Avenue?', *Photoplay* (August 1959).

'Mike DiMaggio drowning victim', *Oakland Tribune* (30 May 1953).

Miller, Arthur, 'My wife Marilyn, *Life* (22 December 1958).

'Minnie Willett', *Salt Lake City Tribune* (26 May 1950).

'Minnie Willett rites conducted', *Reno Evening Gazette* (29 May 1950).

'Minnie Willett, Vegas pioneer, dies this morn', *Las Vegas Review Journal* (24 May 1950).

'Misfits filmed here with cast in harmony', *Reno Evening Gazette* (2 September 1960).

'MM files in Mexico', *Nevada State Journal* (22 January 1961).

'MM invited to pose for calendar', *Independent Press-Telegram* (23 August 1959).

Monroe, Heather, 'Historical Hemet, California: Movie stars and murders', www.associatedcontent.com.

'Monroe and the wild life', *Modern Screen* (November 1953).

'Monroe gets role in Cold Shoulder', *Charleston Gazette* (18 July 1950).

'Monroe loses second child in 15 months', *Lawton Constitution* (18 December 1958).

Monroe, Marilyn, 'Am I too daring?', *Modern Screen* (July 1952).

Monroe, Marilyn, 'I was an orphan', _Modern Screen_ (September 1951).

Monroe, Marilyn, 'Make it for keeps', _Photoplay_ (July 1951).

'Monroe prepares for long vacation', _Coshocton Tribune_ (13 November 1954).

'Monroe's gotta have that dress', _Picturegoer_ (29 June 1957).

Moore, Isabel, 'If Marilyn has a little girl', _Photoplay_ (October 1954).

Morehouse, Ward, 'How true is Arthur Miller's portrayal of Marilyn Monroe?', _Daily Gleaner_ (5 March 1964).

Mosby, Aline, 'Joe tries to patch up marriage to Marilyn', _Oakland Tribune_ (6 November 1954).

Mosby, Aline, 'Marilyn calls herself one-man-woman', _Ames Daily Tribune_ (15 January 1954).

Mosby, Aline, 'Marilyn may lose her public by holding out, _Great Bend Daily Tribune_ (23 January 1955).

Mosby, Aline, 'Marilyn Monroe has her eye on movie Oscar', _Lowell Sun_ (24 November 1952).

Mosby, Aline, 'Marilyn Monroe's voice secret recalled', _Lowell Sun_ (25 November 1952).

'Most males don't act normal when they meet blonde Marilyn Monroe', _Coshocton Tribune_ (23 November 1953).

'Mr and Mrs R Atkinson's Happy Event', _Grimsby News_ (30 April 1926).

'Mr Hollywood Mike Connolly and Marilyn Monroe', _Independent_ (6 March 1956).

Muir, Florabel, 'Wolves I have known as told to Florabel Muir', _Motion Picture_ (January 1953).

'My greatest portrait', _Screen Album_ (November 1955).

'Never happier in my life says Marilyn', _Bennington Evening Banner_ (14 November 1955).

'Newlywed', _Los Angeles Times_ (2 Apr 1939).

'New Marilyn Monroe has Yen to produce her own movies', _Galveston Daily News_ (8 January 1955).

'New Monroe to come out of two weeks rest', _Chronicle-Telegram_ (6 January 1955).

'New players ring theatre to open', *Los Angeles Times* (12 February 1950).

'New type of Hollywood girl', *Times Recorder* (28 July 1949).

'No leading man for Marilyn Monroe', *Long Beach Press-Telegram* (18 December 1959).

'Now Marilyn can talk as told to Fred Harris', *Screen* (November 1956).

'Norma Jean at 4', *Los Angeles Times* (20 August 1972).

'Now that I'm 35', *Daily Mail* (5 June 1961).

'NY man takes bride', *Los Angeles Times* (19 Mar 1939).

Oppenheimer, Peer J., 'Look who's back: Marilyn', *Family Weekly* (22 February 1959).

Oppenheimer, Peer J., 'The role I most wanted to play', *Family Weekly* (11 December 1960).

'Orphans have haircut party', *Los Angeles Times* (13 Apr 1937).

'Orphans help judge's daughter observe birthday', *Los Angeles Times* (20 Apr 1937).

'Orphans to get shower of jams and goodies', *Los Angeles Times* (14 October 1935).

Palmer, Gitta, 'I know Marilyn's secret', *Movie Secrets* (October 1956).

Parsons, Louella, *Charleston Gazette* (8 February 1951).

Parsons, Louella, *Galveston Daily News* (28 October 1949).

Parsons, Louella, 'Interview with Marilyn Monroe', *Sunday Pictorial Review* (1 April 1951).

Parsons, Louella, 'Joan and Marilyn talk to Louella Parsons', *Modern Screen* (July 1953).

Parsons, Louella, *Lowell Sun* (17 April 1950).

Parsons, Louella, *Lowell Sun* (2 September 1950).

Parsons, Louella, *Lowell Sun* (24 November 1950).

Parsons, Louella, *Modern Screen* (1961).

Parsons, Louella, *Mansfield News Journal* (12 September 1954).

Parsons, Louella, 'Marilyn Monroe's hidden fears', *Modern Screen* (March 1962).

Parsons, Louella, *Modesto Bee and News-Herald* (7 November 1950).

Parsons, Louella, 'Monroe-DiMaggio discord rumours persist', *Mansfield News Journal* (12 September 1954).

Parsons, Louella, *Sunday Pictorial Review* (1 April 1951).

'Party fetes bride-to-be', *Los Angeles Times* (16 August 1936).

Pearl, Una, 'The day I became Marilyn', *You* (24 November 2002).

Peet, Spencer Lloyd, 'The pain of Rain', www.RodSerling.com (n.d.).

Player, Ernie, 'You don't really know Monroe says Clifton Webb in an interview with Ernie Player', *Picturegoer* (11 June 1955).

Pohjola, Merja, 'Interview with George Barris', unpublished (October 2002).

'Pioneer group has benefit for 2 days', *Los Angeles Times* (13 October 1935).

'Plans pushed for carnival to benefit orphans' home', *Los Angeles Times* (10 Mar 1935).

'Police fear mob at Marilyn Monroe's funeral', *Manitowoc Herald-Times* (8 August 1962).

Polsky, N., 'And the Lord taketh away ...', *Modern Screen* (November 1957).

'Popular Beverly deb's betrothal revealed at tea', *Los Angeles Times* (11 Jun 1936).

'Quotes from the news', *Coshocton Ohio Tribune* (4 September 1960).

'Ralph Roberts interview', *All About Marilyn magazine* (April 1993).

Rees, Ed, 'Marilyn', *USA1* (July 1962).

'Remembering The Misfits', *Lyon County Reflections* (1994).

'Remembrances of Marilyn', *Reno Gazette Journal* (23 February 1997).

'Reporters see little difference in "new" Marilyn', *Ames Daily Tribune* (8 January 1955).

'Reports of Marilyn's miscarriage from Fitchburg Sentinel', *Odessa American, New Mexican* and *Lawton Constitution* (18 December 1958).

'Rockefeller walks out on Marilyn', *Lima News* (3 July 1957).

'Rose Post column', *Salisbury Post, Rose Post* (23 October 2006)

Ross, Ben 'Marilyn', unknown magazine (n.d.).

Ross, John M., 'The Joe DiMaggio story by Joe DiMaggio as told to John M. Ross', *True* (1954).

'Rowan Tree holiday farc in Pasadena', *Los Angeles Times* (5 December 1947).

Roxbury Historical Society News (Spring 2005).

'San Diego woman refutes stories about Marilyn Monroe', *San Diego Independent* (1973).

Scott, Vernon, 'Marilyn says she's happy but has not changed', *Middlesboro Daily News* (23 October 1958).

'Screen couple's secret Nevada marriage told', *Los Angeles Times* (19 August 1935).

Seager, Allan, 'The creative agony of Arthur Miller', *Esquire* (October 1959).

Sebastian, Victor, 'Marilyn Monroe tells: I remember Clark Gable', *Family Weekly* (26 February 1961).

'See's Ex Hubby', *Herald Press* (11 January 1961).

'Services slated for Mrs Willett', *Las Vegas Review Journal* (25 May 1950).

Shearer, Lloyd, 'How much time and trouble is Marilyn Monroe worth?', *Independent Press-Telegram* (7 December 1958).

Sherrill, Robert, 'A life devoted to a lost cause', *New York Times* (16 October 1983).

'Simone meets Marilyn Monroe', *Lima News* (20 March 1960).

'Simone Signoret likes Marilyn, but may change', *Newark Advocate* (15 November 1960).

Skolsky, Sidney, '260,000 minutes of marriage', *Photoplay* (August 1954).

'Skyrocket: a star is born', *Screen Fan* (October 1952).

'Small town girl covers The Misfits', *Lyon County Reflections* (1994).

Snively, Emmeline, 'I taught Marilyn how', *People Today* (April 1954).

Snively, Emmeline, 'The Marilyn Monroe story: hamburgers and cheesecake', *Art Photography* (October 1954).

Snively, Emmeline, 'The secret Marilyn's life as a model', *Modern Screen* (July 1954).

'Society aids orphans' ingathering', *Los Angeles Times* (11 October 1936).

'So far to go alone', *Redbook* (June 1952).

'Some Like It Hot at the Hotel Del Coronado', *Hotel Del Coronado* publication (n.d.).

St John, Michael, 'The day I met Arthur Miller', *Michael St John's Confidential File* (27 February 2005).

'Standing in for Monroe', *Picturegoer* (18 August 1956).

'Stars marriage solid despite gossip', *Sunday Gazette-Mail* (8 January 1961).

Stein, Robert, 'Do you want to see her?', *American Heritage* (December 2005).

Stephanos, 'What I saw in Marilyn's palm', *Modern Screen* (July 1959).

'Still together', *Morgantown Post* (3 April 1961).

'Studio suspends Marilyn Monroe for not showing up', *Portsmouth Herald* (5 January 1954).

'Studio workers to stage drama', *Los Angeles Times* (27 September 1935).

Suhosky, Sgt Robert A., 'The Monroe doctrine', unknown magazine (n.d.).

Summers, Anthony, 'How Marilyn Monroe rejected her secret dad in his dying days', *Star* (1 December 1987).

Summers, Anthony, 'Star solves mystery of Marilyn Monroe's missing father', *Star* (24 November 1987).

'Tales of Marilyn Monroe, coronation and dedication', *Lowell Sun* (20 May 1953).

'Tantrums and tiaras', *Times Magazine* (21 July 2001).

'Tea honors bride-elect', *Los Angeles Times* (24 Jul 1938).

'Temptations of a bachelor girl', *Photoplay* (April 1952).

'The confessions of Marilyn Monroe', *News of the World* (12 August 1962).

'The girl's love-happy', *Movieland* (April 1957).

'The house that dreams built', *Photoplay* (November 1949).

'The men who interest me by Mrs Joe DiMaggio', *Pageant* (April 1954).

'The new Marilyn', *Screen Stories* (October 1961).

'The pageant of the film world', *Los Angeles Times* (9 May 1935).

'The patient lover', *Motion Picture* (August 1961).

'The Prince and the Showgirl', *Picturegoer* (29 June 1957).

'The real teen-aged Marilyn Monroe', *National Tattler* (7 October 1973).

'The rebellion of Marilyn Monroe', *New York Post* (28 September 1955).

'The shocking facts behind Marilyn Monroe's crisis', unknown magazine (n.d.).

'The time Marilyn Monroe hid out at our house', unknown magazine (n.d.).

'The woman Arthur Miller went to when he walked out on Marilyn Monroe', *Photoplay* (February 1961).

Thomas, Bob, 'Crawford aims barbs at Monroe', *Syracuse Herald Journal*, 3 March 1953.

Thomas, Bob, column, *Indiana Evening Gazette* (10 November 1955).

Thomas, Bob, column, *Joplin Globe* (11 November 1955).

Thomas, Bob, 'Memories', *Oakland Tribune* (8 August 1962).

Thomas, Bob, 'Prospect of audience scares Grable', *Portsmouth Herald* (12 November 1953).

Thomas, Bob, 'The real Marilyn Monroe', unknown magazine (n.d.).

Thomas, Bob, 'World stunned over death of Marilyn Monroe', *Progress* (6 August 1962).

'Three encounters with a love goddess', *Hollywood Dream Girl* (1955).

'Throngs thrilled at Gilmore Circus', *Los Angeles Times* (17 Mar 1935).

'Tom Ewell feels director of Itch up to scratch', *Chicago Tribune* (1954)

'Too hot to handle', *Modern Screen* (March 1952).

'Top Hollywood make-up artist tells all in book', *Lima News* (31 July 1977).

'Top stars 1955 resolutions', *Oakland Tribune* (2 January 1955).

'To the future and The House of Rothschild', *Los Angeles Times* (26 January 1934).

'Traffic judge fines Marilyn Monroe $56', *Sherboygan Press* (1 March 1956).

'Tragedy of a sex goddess', *San Francisco Chronicle* (6 August 1962).

'Twenty little working girls fete tomorrow', *Los Angeles Times* (5 Jul 1936).

'University appeals to Marilyn Monroe for book generosity', *Pottstown Mercury* (6 December 1952).

'Unmistakable aura of a star', *Oakland Tribune* (8 August 1962).

'Unseen Marilyn Monroe footage unearthed after 50 years in loft', BBC Press Office (n.d.).

Vale, Richard, 'What they don't tell you about Marilyn Monroe', *Inside Story* (May 1959).

'Valentine shower to honor Miss Atkinson', *Los Angeles Times* (14 February 1938).

'Vegas Rebekahs honor assembly president', *Nevada State Journal* (1 November 1936).

'Victim of crash-in aimed at Marilyn Monroe tells story', *Bennington Evening Banner* (20 March 1957).

Wandworth, James, 'One man woman', *Motion Picture and Television Magazine* (September 1953).

Walker, Derek, 'It's your fault Olivier', *Picturegoer* (13 October 1956).

'Warmth, real beauty are noted in the new, different Marilyn', *Appeal Democrat* (24 October 1958).

'Wayback Machine. Starlet wowed Salinas residents by Jim Albanese', www.thecalifornian.com (15 March 2010)

'We knew Marilyn extremely well', *Leader-Courier* (n.d.).

'Wedding announcement between Norma Jeane Baker and James Dougherty', unknown newspaper, (n.d.).

Weller, Helen Hover, 'Why Marilyn and Joe couldn't wait', *Movie Stars Parade* (May 1954).

Wells, Bob, column, *Long Beach Independent* (12 April 1957).

'What's wrong with American men?', *Look* (30 November 1951).

'When childish laughter rang in a garden', *Los Angeles Times* (5 November 1935).

Whitcomb, Jon, 'The new Monroe', *Cosmopolitan* (March 1959).

'Whitey Snyder interview', *All About Marilyn Magazine* (January 1994).

'Who'd marry me? By Marilyn Monroe', *Modern Screen* (September 1951)

'Wife he admits slaying found alive at home', *Los Angeles Times* (8 February 1927).

'Wife of boxer kills self after quarrel', *Independent* (3 Jul 1928).

'Will new love give her a baby?', *Untold Secrets* (October 1961).

Willet, Bob, 'The two faces of Marilyn Monroe by Yves Montand as told to Bob Willet', *Liberty* (October 1960).

Wilson, Earl, column, *Daily Intelligencer* (25 January 1972).

Wilson, Earl, column, *Lima News* (27 December 1953).

Wilson, Earl, column, *Lima News* (4 July 1954).

Wilson, Earl, column, *Lima News* (19 February 1956).

Wilson, Earl, column, *Lima News* (24 June 1956).

Wilson, Earl, column, *Reno Evening Gazette* (24 June 1961).

Wilson, Earl, column, *Times Recorder* (16 September 1954).

Wilson, Earl, 'In defense of Marilyn Monroe', *Modern Screen* (June 1955).

Wilson, Eric, 'Julius Caruso obituary', *New York Times* (14 August 2005).

Wilson, Earl, 'Marilyn Monroe takes Whiteway by storm', *Lima News* (15 March 1955).

Wilson, Earl, 'Memories of Marilyn, *Times Recorder* (15 April 1973).

Wilson, Earl, 'M-m-my M-m-m-m-marilyn', *Silver Screen* (April 1952).

Wilson, Earl, 'On again off again', *Motion Picture* (January 1955).

Wilson, Earl, 'Summit at Las Vegas', *Times Recorder* (14 June 1961).

Wilson, Earl, 'The things she said to me', *Photoplay* (May 1956).

Wilson, Earl, 'Yves Montand's one-man show', *Lima News* (23 September 1959).

Wilson, Liza, 'The truth about me by Marilyn Monroe, as told to Liza Wilson, part 1', *American Weekly* (16 November 1952).

Wilson, Liza, 'The truth about me by Marilyn Monroe, as told to Liza Wilson, part 2', *American Weekly* (23 November 1952).

'Witnesses say Monroe visited the Tri-State', *Herald-Dispatch* (n.d.).

'Wolves howl for "niece" just like Marilyn Monroe', *Los Angeles Times* (27 August 1950).

'Woman escapes guard', *Los Angeles Times* (21 January 1937).

'Woman killed self is jurors' verdict', *Reno Evening Gazette* (3 July 1928).

'Woman suicides', *Woodland Daily Democrat* (3 July 1928).

Woodard, Eric, 'History of the SGTG scripts' (n.d.).

'"Woo Marilyn Monroe", for book collection', *Indiana Evening Gazette* (13 December 1952).

Wrightson, Del, 'I don't owe Hollywood a thing', *Movie Secrets* (August 1956).

Zolotow, Maurice, 'Inez Melson interview', notes (n.d.).

Zolotow, Maurice, 'Mystery of Marilyn Monroe (IV)', notes (n.d.).

Zolotow, Maurice, 'Mystery of Marilyn Monroe (V)', notes (n.d.).

Zolotow, Maurice, 'Mystery of Marilyn Monroe (VI)', notes (n.d.).

Zolotow, Maurice, 'The men in Marilyn Monroe's life', notes (n.d.).

Zolotow, Maurice, 'The riddle of Marilyn Monroe (I)', notes (n.d.).

Zolotow, Maurice, 'The riddle of Marilyn Monroe (II)', notes (n.d.).

Zolotow, Maurice, 'The riddle of Marilyn Monroe (III)', notes (n.d.).

In addition to the above, information was also gained from the following:

Prince and the Showgirl news items from the *Daily Mirror, Daily Mail, Daily Express, Daily Sketch, Sunday Dispatch, Evening News, News Chronicle, Daily Record, Sunday Mail, Evening Standard* (all 1956);

Ticket to Tomahawk news items from the *Silverton Standard & Miner* (1949);

Untitled articles from: *Altoona Mirror* (31 December 1959), *Greeley Daily Tribune* (25 November 1958), *Huntingdon Daily News* (20 August 1935), *Lima News* (15 June 1957), *Los Angeles Mirror* (27 June 1952), *Monessen Daily Independent* (7 June 1952), *Movie Spotlight* (August 1955), *Nevada State Journal* (6 September 1960), *News* (12 Apr 1956), *Oakland Tribune* (6 December 1953), *Picture Week* (2 April 1955), *Portsmouth Herald* (24 June 1959), *Reno Evening Gazette* (5 September 1960), *San Mateo Times* (1 June 1953), *San Rafael Daily Independent Journal* (20 May 1950), *Time* (18 October 1954 and 16 January 1956), *Traverse City Record Eagle* (27 February 1956);

Several other articles on the subject of Stanley Gifford's life in Hemet were given to me with no dates or titles. These items were useful in my research, though I am unfortunately unable to source them due to lack of information.

Index